West Michigan Almanac

West Michigan Almanac

by
Edward Hoogterp

The University of Michigan Press
Ann Arbor
&
The Petoskey Publishing Company
Traverse City

Published in the United States of America by
The University of Michigan Press
&
The Petoskey Publishing Company

Manufactured in the United States of America

2009 2008 2007 2006 4 3 2 1

ISBN-13: 978-0-472-03125-2 (paper : alk. paper)
ISBN-10: 0-472-03125-2 (paper : alk. paper)

Library of Congress Cataloging-in-Publication Data on File

Cover photography
courtesy of Terry W. Phipps

For Millie,
who battled breast cancer
while giving me strength
to finish this Almanac.

And for the medical teams who gave us reason
to hope she'll be here for many more books:
Dr. Bunting, Dr. Gawel, Dr. Gribbin, Dr. Prust
and the staff at Lacks and Biederman cancer centers.

— Edward Hoogterp

ACKNOWLEDGMENTS

The writing and production of this book could not have been accomplished without hundreds of kindnesses, large and small, from friends, family and strangers.

Among the many who gave help or advice are: Roger Rosentreter of *Michigan History* magazine; David Kenyon and Mary Detloff of the Michigan DNR; Chris Meehan of the *Kalamazoo Gazette*; Jennifer Giesey; Michael Chevy Castranova of *Business Review*, West Michigan; Ron Pesch, record-keeper for the Michigan High School Athletic Association; Christine Byron of the Grand Rapids Public Library; Robert Meyers of the Berrien County Historical Society; and Patty Cantrell of the Michigan Land Use Institute.

Millie Hoogterp helped with research and proof-reading. Jim DeWildt designed and laid out the pages. Brian Lewis of Petoskey Publishing Co. and Mary Erwin of the University of Michigan Press handled the gritty details of editing and publishing. Andrea Ford, Malana Hoogterp, Joseph Hoogterp and Adena Roush provided the author with emotional support and occasional lodging during the long research phase of the project.

Any errors or omissions are, of course, the sole responsibility of the author.

CONTENTS

TRANSPORTATION 439-452

(Navigating our region by train, plane or automobile...)

POLITICS 453-467

(Our leaders, past and present)

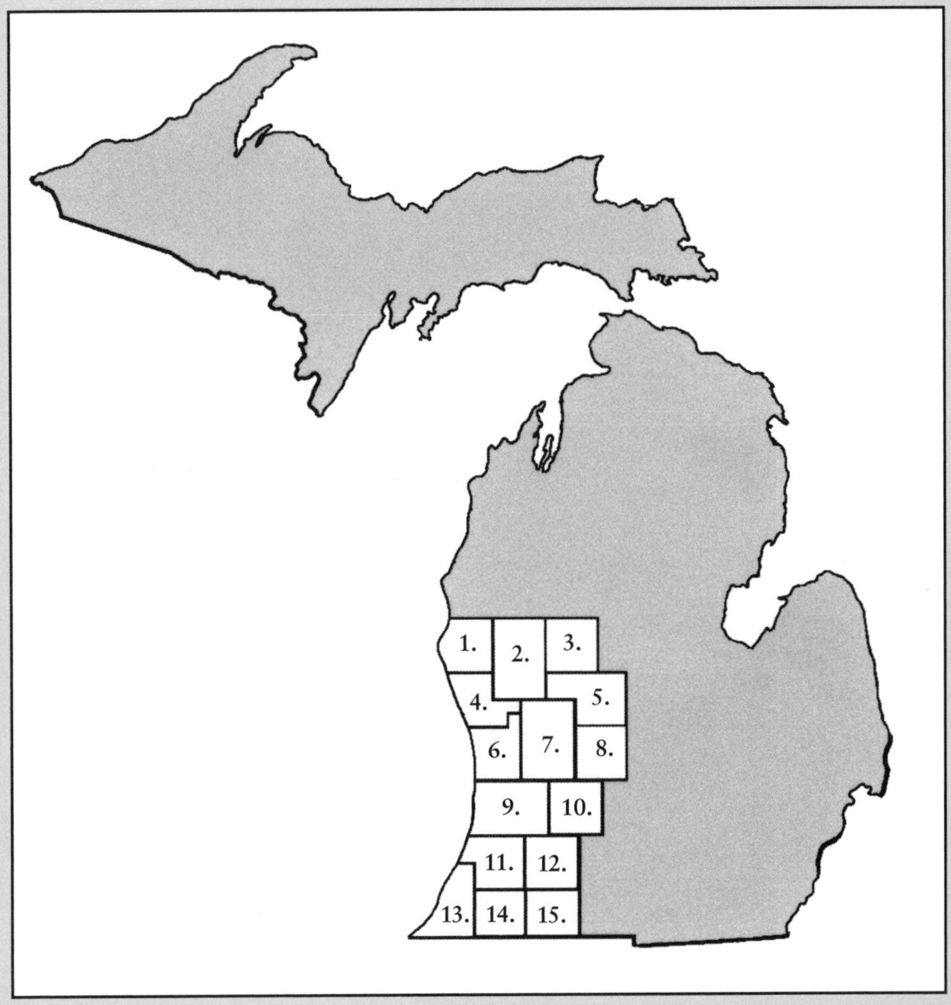

WEST MICHIGAN COUNTIES

1. Oceana
2. Newaygo
3. Mecosta
4. Muskegon
5. Montcalm
6. Ottawa
7. Kent
8. Ionia
9. Allegan
10. Barry
11. Van Buren
12. Kalamazoo
13. Berrien
14. Cass
15. St.Joseph

WELCOME TO WEST MICHIGAN

On a small map of North America, West Michigan appears mostly as empty space between Detroit and Lake Michigan.

But come closer. This land is far from empty. It's filled with factories and farms; cities and sand dunes; small towns and big trees. It has its own history. And its own future.

It's a region that extends from the sandy shores of the Great Lake to the fertile fields of the interior; from solid villages on the Indiana border to the fringe of the North Woods.

It's cut by rivers and punctuated by more than 1,000 inland lakes.

West Michigan covers 9,300 square miles, about the size of Vermont. It's home to two million people, as many as Vermont and New Hampshire combined.

Those 2 million people are black, white, Native American, Asian and Hispanic. They're rich, poor and middle class. They're senior citizens, kids and baby-boomers.

In other words, West Michigan is a piece of America. This book is a snapshot – in text, numbers and photographs – of this place.

Saugatuck is a popular West Michigan destination (photo: Terry Phipps)

Anyone who's lived here recognizes West Michigan as a region, distinct from the Detroit metro area or the part of the state we call "Up North." But it's a region with only two definite borders: Lake Michigan to the west and

A freighter passes the Muskegon South Pier Light (photo: Terry Phipps)

Indiana to the south. The eastern boundary might fall anywhere between Grand Rapids and the state capital city of Lansing. The northern extremity is some indefinite point between Muskegon and Traverse City.

For this *Almanac,* we drew the lines about midway between those cities. We include the following 15 counties, starting at the Indiana border and going north: Berrien, Cass, St. Joseph, Van Buren, Kalamazoo, Allegan, Barry, Ottawa, Kent, Ionia, Muskegon, Newaygo, Montcalm, Oceana, Mecosta.

All of those counties are within 50 miles of Lake Michigan. Together they include more than 150 miles of Lake Michigan shoreline.

FAME AND FORTUNE IN WEST MICHIGAN

OK, we'll admit it right now: West Michigan isn't the grand-prize winner in the celebrity sweepstakes.

It's a long, long way from Hudsonville to Hollywood, or from Benton Harbor to Broadway. And we know S. Westnedge Avenue isn't exactly Rodeo Drive.

To tell the truth, we kind of like it this way. We're the sort of place where you can get noticed for doing something important (or even something outrageous). But around here, you can't be famous just for being famous.

Of course, you could become semi-famous for saving thousands of lives by stopping a deadly childhood disease. Dr. Pearl Kendrick of Grand Rapids did that when she produced a vaccine for pertussis (whooping cough) in the 1930s.

Or, you could get famous by building up one of the nation's most popular Christian television ministries; and then infamous by getting caught cooking the books and, ahem, dallying with the church secretary. Muskegon's Jim Bakker did all that.

Or, you could put your name on a store, (Montgomery Ward), a car (the Dodge brothers), a carpet sweeper (Bissell), a baby-food jar (Gerber), a pill (Upjohn), a world championship belt (Muhammad Ali) or Broadway's Tony Award (Elizabeth Wilson).

Then again, maybe you could spend a quarter-century in Congress and wait for them to make you President. Hey, it worked for Jerry Ford.

Here's a brief rundown of just a few of the famous folks who called West Michigan home over the years. You'll meet more in later chapters.

Gerald R. Ford was a young lawyer and World War II veteran in 1948, when he became

Gerald R. Ford (photo courtesy of Ford Presidential Library)

part of a government-reform movement in Grand Rapids and challenged a fellow Republican for a seat in Congress. He won that election and a dozen more, becoming Republican leader in the House of Representatives.

His world changed in 1973, when President Richard M. Nixon tapped him to become Vice President of the United States, replacing Spiro Agnew who had resigned in disgrace. A year later, in the ripples of the Watergate cover-up, Nixon caught a final helicopter ride from the White House lawn, and Ford became the 38th President of the United States. Though he lost to Jimmy Carter in the 1976 presidential election, Ford is credited with holding the nation together through a difficult period in modern history.

Harry Blackstone (1885-1965), the famed magician, moved to Colon, in St. Joseph County, in the 1920s and made an island in a local lake his base of operations until 1949. His son, **Harry Blackstone Jr,** (1934-97) was born in Michigan and displayed his own unique magic act in a traveling show and such mass media outlets as the Johnny Carson Show.

Carl Sandburg, (1878-1967) the noted historian and poet, lived from 1928 to 1943 in the Berrien County hamlet of Harbert, while he was writing a prize-winning biography of Abraham Lincoln. Sandburg's poems include such classic lines as "The fog comes on little cat feet," and his famous description of Chicago as the "City of the Big Shoulders."

He also wrote a long, introspective poem titled "The Sins of Kalamazoo," which includes the lines: "Listen with your ears on a Saturday night in Kalamazoo, And say to yourself, I hear America, I hear, *what* do I hear?"

Pearl Kendrick, (1890-1980) a microbiologist with a Michigan Health Department lab in Grand Rapids, worked with a colleague, **Grace Eldering,** (1902-1988) through the 1930s to produce a vaccine for pertussis, or whooping cough. At the time, the disease was killing nearly 6,000 American children each year. The state began producing the women's successful vaccine in 1940. It soon was distributed nationally, and whooping cough became a rare disease.

Elizabeth Wilson, born in Grand Rapids in 1921, won a Tony award in 1972 for her performance in "Sticks and Bones" on Broadway. Wilson's long list of screen credits includes the 1967 classic "The Graduate," in which she played Dustin Hoffman's mother.

The rhythm and blues group **DeBarge,** made up of five members of a Grand Rapids family, scored an international hit in 1985 with "Rhythm of the Night." One member of the group, James DeBarge, was briefly married to Janet Jackson. The group broke up in 1986.

Charles Westover (1939-1990) of Coopersville, took the name **Del Shannon** for his singing career, and rocketed to the top of the national charts with his 1961 hit "Runaway." Del Shannon was inducted in the Rock and Roll Hall of Fame, 1999.

Kim Zimmer, born in Grand Rapids in 1955, has taken home three daytime Emmy Awards for her long-running portrayal of Reva Shayne on the CBS soap opera "The Guiding Light." Zimmer first appeared on the show in 1983. She has also appeared on "The Doctors" and "One Life to Live."

Stacy Haiduk of Grand Rapids portrayed Lana Lang in the Super Boy television series in the late 80s. She later played Commander Hitchcock on the undersea action series Seaquest, DSV.

Chris Van Allsburg, an East Grand Rapids native, is among the nation's best-known children's authors and illustrators, with such books as Jumanji and The Polar Express, both of which became major movies.

Jef Mallet of Big Rapids began his career as a newspaper illustrator and became a nationally syndicated cartoonist, with his popular comic strip "Frazz," about a grade-school janitor.

Roger B. Chaffee of Grand Rapids had earned a likely ticket to the moon when he was selected as an astronaut in the Apollo program. His life ended tragically in a 1967 fire during training in the Apollo 1 capsule in Florida. Astronauts Chaffee, Gus Grissom and Edward White died in the fire. Other West Michigan astronauts include **Jack Lousma,** a Grand Rapids native who flew on Skylab in 1973, and **David Leestma,** born in Muskegon in 1949, who was aboard three Space Shuttle flights in the 1980s.

Derek Jeter, a 1992 graduate of Kalamazoo Central High School, made his fame as the MVP shortstop for the New York Yankees. But he went beyond that, showing up in supermarket tabloids when the paparazzi reported he was dating such beauties as singer Mariah Carey, actress Scarlett Johannsen and even a reigning Miss Universe. People Magazine named Jeter one of the "50 most beautiful people" of 1999.

Kalamazoo also was home to **Edna Ferber** (1887-1968), author of the novel "Showboat," which became a popular stage musical that is still produced regularly.

George Latka, born in Kalamazoo in 1914, was a hall-of-fame professional boxer who was hailed as the first pro pugilist to earn a college degree. He appeared as a referee in the film "Raging Bull."

Television news anchor **Mike Wallace** got his first television job at WOOD-TV in Grand Rapids, before he went on to become a news icon at "60 Minutes."

Benton Harbor spawned several well-known actors, including comic **Arte Johnson** of "Laugh-In" fame (born in 1929), and veteran character-actor **Ernie Hudson**, born in 1930, whose list of nearly 100 screen and television credits includes the Ghostbuster movies. Also from Benton Harbor is comedian and actor **Sinbad**, who was born there as David Adkins in 1956.

Screenwriter and director **Paul Schrader**, born in Grand Rapids in 1946, counts the films "Taxi Driver," "Raging Bull" and "American Gigolo" among his screenwriting credits. He also wrote and directed the film "Hardcore", with George C. Scott, which was filmed in Grand Rapids.

Berrien County has been home in recent decades for **Muhammad Ali**, a cultural and religious icon who was perhaps the best-known athlete of the 20th century. Ali, the retired heavyweight champ, has Parkinson's syndrome, which limits his public appearances and his ability to communicate. He was born Cassius Clay in 1942 in Louisville Ky, and changed his name to Muhammad Ali after converting to Islam. His home is on a farm near Berrien Springs.

Anthony Kiedis, leader of the popular rock group "Red Hot Chili Peppers," was born in Grand Rapids in 1962. He spent much of his youth in Los Angeles.

Soul and Gospel singer **Al Green** was born in Arkansas in 1946. His family moved to Grand Rapids when he was a boy. His first song, "Back Up Train" was recorded in 1967 with high school friends. He went on to become one of the top R&B performers of the 1970s. He is an ordained minister, whose work spans multiple genres, from religious music to an acclaimed duet with country crooner Lyle Lovett. Green is a member of the Rock and Roll Hall of Fame and a nine-time Grammy winner.

FROM BEDROCK TO BABY FOOD: A BRIEF HISTORY OF WEST MICHIGAN

Log piles at Slocum's Grove, in Muskegon County (photo courtesy of Grand Rapids Public Library)

This much we know for sure.

For more than a million years in the Pleistocene epoch, glaciers advanced and retreated across the northern half of the continent. The ice sheets, sometimes more than a mile thick, crushed and ground and scraped away at the ancient rocks and sediments laid down by geological and biological forces over the millenia.

About 15,000 years ago, the glaciers finally began melting away for the last time. (Or at least the most recent time – who knows if it was the last?) They left what is now Western Michigan covered with a landscape much like today's arctic tundra.

The land gradually rebounded from the enormous weight of the ice. The Great Lakes formed and shape-shifted as meltwater gouged new riverbeds and the rising landscape opened outlets to the south and east.

Strange beasts followed the changing climate into the land: Giant beavers, musk oxen, mammoths, mastodons, and people.

Michigan's first human residents – anthropologists call them Paleo-Indians; we have no idea what they called themselves – seem to have been hunters who followed the big game into the southern part of the state sometime over 12,000 years ago.

Archeologists have found the remains of their campsites above ancient lakeshores in Berrien County. The Potawatomi, Ojibwe and Ottawa Indians who lived in Michigan when Europeans arrived here in the 17th Century are likely the descendants of those native pioneers.

If humans managed to thrive here, the animals of the ice age didn't fare as well. Every species of large mammals that populated Michigan at that time is gone. Were they unable to adjust to the warming climate? Were they hunted to extinction by hungry humans? The mystery remains, along with the ancient bones that occasionally show up in farm fields or archeological sites.

Over a span of several thousand years, Michigan's climate and vegetation gradually took on the characteristics that European explorers found in the 1600s: Hardwood forests, wetlands, small prairies and oak savannahs in the south; towering pines and hardwoods from about the Muskegon River Valley to the north.

The native people, clustered along the Lake Michigan shore and the inland rivers, lived by hunting, fishing, farming and gathering wild foods. They apparently used fire to maintain the open prairies in what are now Kalamazoo, Cass and St. Joseph counties.

The first Europeans here were Frenchmen who came a century before the American Revolution, either to save the Indians' souls or to trap the wildlife growing in their forests.

Jesuit missionaries including Pere Marquette and Claude Jean Allouez were here in the 1600s, as were such profiteers as Nicolet and LaSalle.

The French built a fort and a mission on the St. Joseph River. Trappers and traders, their names mostly lost to history, deployed up the Muskegon, Grand and other rivers to procure the skins of beaver and other fur-bearing animals. Native people traded for such European goods as muskets, iron axes, metal cooking pots, blankets and other stuff that seemed better than what they could make for themselves.

The lower Great Lakes came under British rule in 1763, following the seven-year conflict known as the French and Indian War. That same year, Indians aligned with Pontiac took over Fort St. Joseph, where the town of Niles now stands. They slaughtered most of the British troops there.

But the Europeans were here to stay.

The region became part of the United States at the conclusion of the American Revolution, 20 years after the British took over from the French.

And still, the economy was based on fur. It stayed that way until the 1820s, when the trappers, spurred on by John Jacob Astor's American Fur Co., finally succeeded in killing and skinning most of the beavers in the state.

In 1821, West Michigan Indians signed the first of several treaties ceding their land to the United States government, in exchange for annual payments and other

The log blockhouse at Muskegon State Park is a 20th century replica of Michigan frontier architecture (photo: Terry Phipps)

Muskegon's Soldiers and Sailors Monument honors the region's Civil War veterans (photo: Terry Phipps)

assistance. A dozen years later, most of the bands that participated in that treaty were shipped off to Kansas.

With the furs gone and the Indians subdued, West Michigan was open for new settlers, new farms and new towns.

Surveyors trudged across the landscape to measure out township, range and section lines that are still the basis for property descriptions. The Erie Canal opened in 1825, creating a water route into the Great Lakes and making it a little bit easier for settlers from the east to reach Michigan.

By the time the first West Michigan land office opened, at White Pigeon in 1831, settlers were already staking out some of the best spots for farms, villages and water-powered mills.

When the Civil War broke out, just 30 years later, about 200,000 people were living in our 15-county West Michigan area. The largest counties – Kent (30,716), Kalamazoo (24,646) and Berrien (22,378) – had as many residents in 1860 as some northern Michigan counties have today. Further north, Mecosta (970 residents) and Oceana counties (1,816) remained largely undeveloped in 1860.

While the region from the Grand River south was mostly settled by farmers and merchants, land along the Muskegon River and points north was timber country. The boom in wood lasted until about 1890, when most of the prime white pine was gone.

Meanwhile, and into the 20th century, West Michigan developed an industrial economy, with many products related to the region's natural resources.

Grand Rapids made furniture from the abundant hardwood, and dug into the earth to mine gypsum. Kalamazoo made paper. Three Oaks made corset stays from turkey feathers. Food processors across the region turned farm produce into everything from pickles to peppermint.

Railroads criss-crossed the state, carrying millions of passengers and employing thousands of workers.

When the automobile industry finally centered itself in Detroit, West Michigan became a prime location for suppliers who made axles, carseats and a hundred other parts.

The primacy of the auto industry – not unlike furs and timber so many years ago – led to a boom-and-bust economy that, unfortunately, has been more bust than boom so far in the 21st century.

High-paid manufacturing jobs have disappeared (or gone overseas to re-emerge as low-paying manufacturing jobs) and so far the region has been unable to replace them with the "knowledge-based" industries that are touted as the employment opportunities of the future.

At least half of the land in West Michigan remains in farm or forest. Economic segments based on those resources are also enduring a wrenching series of changes.

Small dairies and hog farms have pretty much disappeared from the landscape, replaced by agricultural enterprises with thousands of animals. Crops such as apples, Christmas trees and asparagus have seen competition from growers in other states and countries. Tourism, much of it based on the region's forests, lakes and rivers, has lagged behind other states.

It's not all bleak, of course. Some folks are still making good money in the auto industry. West Michigan remains a worldwide center for office furniture. We're still making pills in Kalamazoo, baby food in Fremont, aircraft parts in Whitehall and (for now at least) piston rings in Hastings.

Flowers and nursery plants from West Michigan show up at homes across the nation. And despite slow growth, such prime tourist venues as wineries, art galleries and beaches still get just about all the seasonal business they can handle.

As the *Almanac* goes to press, the economic factors add up to an uncertain future. But the region has recovered before from recession, depression and depleted natural resources.

Maybe we can do it again.

In the meantime, let's remember a few of the great sights of West Michigan: December snow coating the trees along the Little Muskegon River. Spring wildflowers pushing through the dark earth of Dowagiac Woods. Autumn leaves blazing like a black-velvet painting along a gravel road in Lowell Township. August sunshine sparkling off Lake Michigan waves out beyond the St. Joseph Light. In a world of such beauty, everything has to turn out all right. Doesn't it?

ACROSS THE YEARS: A WEST MICHIGAN TIMELINE

Here, from a number of authoritative sources, are a few of the high and low points of our region's history:

West Michigan's orchards are among the state's leaders in apple production (photo: Terry Phipps)

600 million to 4.5 billion years in the past – The Precambrian Period. A thick crust of igneous and metamorphic rock forms across North America. This rock becomes the "floor" that supports later deposits of sedimentary rock and soil in what is now Michigan.

240 Million to 600 million years ago – The Paleozoic Era. The Michigan Basin is covered periodically by shallow seas. Marine deposits and eroded sediments from highlands as distant as the Appalachian Mountains cover the basin with sediments up to two miles thick. Such natural resources as gypsum, salt, oil, natural gas, sandstone and limestone come from the layers of sediment laid down during the Paleozoic.

About 2 million to 240 million years ago – The Cenozoic and Mesozoic eras, including the Triassic, Jurassic and Cretaceous epochs that some have called the age of dinosaurs. Evidence suggests that Michigan was relatively high ground during these millions of years, slowly eroding, rather than building new rocks. No fossils from this time period have been found here. Around the world, the fossil record indicates that dinosaurs thrived and died. The first birds, mammals and grasses appeared.

15,000 to 1.5 million years ago – The Pleistocene Epoch (The Ice Ages). For hundreds of thousands of years, ice sheets as much as a mile thick advanced and retreated across what is now Michigan. They scoured the bedrock and created the outlines of the present Great Lakes. The glaciers deposited hundreds of feet of dirt and gravel (those in the know call it glacial till) on top of the bedrock in what is now West Michigan.

5,000 to 15,000 years ago – The glaciers melt, and the land, freed of the great weight of the ice, begins to rebound. Meltwaters gradually fill the Great Lakes, with runoff going at various times toward the Gulf of Mexico or the Atlantic Ocean. The broad Grand River Valley is created during a period when water from melting glaciers cascades across Western Michigan, through the Chicago area, and down the Mississippi. Archeology indicates that such animals as woodland musk-ox, mammoth and mastodon followed the retreating glaciers into southwest Michigan. Paleo-Indians followed the animals into a land that ranged from arctic tundra to evergreen forests. The earliest evidence of man, dated to about 13,500 years ago, comes from arrowheads or spear points found in Berrien County.

2,500-5,000 years ago – The ground continues to rise and the lakes assume something like their modern dimensions, continually reshaped by water and wind. As climate gradually warms, oak and hardwood forests begin to take over much of the land in southwest Michigan. Further north, where the climate is cooler and the soil more sandy, the forests are made up of conifers such as white pine.

1000 AD – Ancestors of the modern Miami, Ottawa and Potawatomi Indians are growing corn, beans and squash, and participating in a trade network that links the Great Lakes to the Gulf of Mexico.

1618 – French explorer Etienne Brule passes through northern Michigan in search of the Northwest Passage. He may be the first European to set foot in the state.

1634 – Jean Nicolet, apparently on a search for furbearing animals, encounters the Muskegon River, and reports that the river runs through great forests with tall pine trees.

1675 – After ministering to Indians in northern Indiana, a desperately ill Father Jacques Marquette travels by canoe up the shore of West Michigan trying to reach his mission at St. Ignace. He dies along the way, likely at what is now Ludington or Frankfort. Two years later, Indians bring the Jesuit explorer's remains back home for burial at St. Ignace.

1679 – Another French explorer, LaSalle, builds Fort Miami, a temporary outpost at the mouth of the St. Joseph River.

1680 – LaSalle leads a contingent on foot across southern Michigan, dodging bands of Indians and taking notes on the prairies, oak savannahs and swamps as he goes.

1689 – According to tradition, Jesuit Missionary Claude-Jean Allouez dies and is buried at the St. Joseph mission, the present site of Niles. Soon afterward, French troops arrive to build Fort St. Joseph nearby. The fort is garrisoned by French or British troops for almost 100 years before being abandoned during the American Revolution.

1701 – A French party under Cadillac lands in southeast Michigan to establish Fort Ponchertrain at the present site of Detroit. In later years, Detroit will become Michigan's largest city and a gateway into Western Michigan. It will also produce some great cars and some lousy football teams.

The Woolly Mammoth was hunted by Michigan's first residents (photo courtesy of Muskegon County Historical Museum)

1750 – Fort St. Joseph, at Niles, is reported to be home to at least 50 families, including the French soldiers garrisoned there. The rest of West Michigan is pretty much wilderness.

1763 – Britain gains control of Michigan, at the end of the French and Indian War.

1763 – Pontiac's War: Indians, trying to drive out the British, attack forts throughout the Great Lakes region. The small contingent of British soldiers at Fort St. Joseph is killed or captured. The war is named for Pontiac, an Ottawa who built a coalition of tribes to attack the British. Ultimately, the rebellion fails, and Britain retains control of the region.

1776 – The 13 American colonies declare their independence. The American Revolution begins.

1781 – A Spanish raiding party takes over the undefended Fort St. Joseph – for a few days.

1783 – The Treaty of Paris ends the American Revolution. Much of the Great Lakes region, including Michigan, is included as part of what soon will become the United States of America.

1787 – Continental Congress establishes the Northwest Territory, which includes what is now Michigan, Indiana, Illinois, Ohio and Wisconsin. The law certifies that slavery will be banned in the territory.

1805 – Congress establishes the Michigan Territory from part of the Northwest Territory.

1806 – Fur trader Joseph LaFramboise is killed in Grand Haven, apparently by an Indian upset over the trader's refusal to provide whiskey. LaFramboise's wife, Magdelaine, continues the family's trading business at Lowell, on the Grand River. Madame LaFramboise, whose father was French and mother was Ottawa, spends winters in West Michigan and summers at Mackinac Island until her retirement. She is reported to be one of the state's most successful traders.

1808 – John Jacob Astor organizes the American Fur Co. and takes over the fur-trading business in Michigan. His company's representatives trade with Indians and trappers at Lake Michigan rivermouths, and several inland locations.

1821 – In the Treaty of Chicago, Indians give up a large part of West Michigan, south of the Grand River.

1821 – Rix Robinson purchases the Grand River trading operation from Madame LaFramboise. He sets his headquarters at Ada, where the Thornapple and Grand Rivers meet.

1822 – Baptist missionary Isaac McCoy signs a government contract to open missions and schools on the St. Joseph and Grand rivers, under provisions of the Treaty of Chicago. McCoy opens the Carey Mission at Niles and begins work to establish another among the Indians living at what is now Grand Rapids.

1825 – Erie Canal opens, easing travel and leading to a surge of settlement in Michigan and surrounding states. Uzziel Putnam moves his family from New York to the Pokagon Prairie, becoming Cass County's first permanent settler.

1826 – Louis Campau arrives at the Grand River. He spends the winter with local Indians, and opens his trading post the following year.

1828 – William Meek builds a sawmill and grist mill at what is now Constantine. Bazel Harrison settles on Kalamazoo County's Prairie Ronde.

1829 – The Territorial Legislature designates a dozen new counties in outstate areas, including Barry, Berrien and Van Buren in West Michigan. Titus Bronson founds the settlement now known as Kalamazoo. Dolphin and Nancy Morris move to Decatur, the first recorded settlers in Van Buren County.

1830 – Enoch and Deborah Harris begin farming in Oshtemo Township, near Kalamazoo. They are among the first African-American settlers in West Michigan.

1831 – United States Land Office opens in White Pigeon. The going rate for government land is $1.25 an acre. Amasa Parker is first settler in Barry County.

1832 – Samuel Dexter buys land along the Grand River at the present site of Ionia. The next spring, he leads 63 pioneers on a 16-day trip from Detroit to the new settlement.

1833 – Most Potawatomi Indians from southern Michigan are forced to move to Kansas, under a federal policy that calls for relocating eastern Indians to reservations west of the Mississippi. Isaac McCoy accompanies them, and the Carey Mission is closed. Leopold Pokagon's band of Potawatomi is allowed to stay on land they own in Cass County's Silver Creek Township.

Isaac McCoy

1834 – Land Office moves from White Pigeon to Kalamazoo. Two years later, it sells 1.6 million acres, making it the busiest such office in the nation.

1836 – In the Treaty of Washington, Michigan Indians sign away the territory from the Grand River north to Lake Superior.

1837 – Michigan becomes a state. Also, the first Muskegon sawmill begins operation.

1839 – First peaches from Berrien County are shipped to Chicago.

1847 – The Rev. Albertus Van Raalte leads religious separatists from the Netherlands to West Michigan, where they found the city of Holland.

1849 – Virginian John Saunders frees his slaves and pays to build a cabin for each of the freed families in Cass County's Calvin Township.

1849 – Michigan finally has a cross-state railroad, as the Michigan Central reaches New Buffalo.

1861-65 – Michigan sends thousands of young men – and a few young women – to fight in the Civil War.

1867 – The Kalamazoo Paper Co. opens the first paper mill on the Kalamazoo River.

1871 – Much of Holland is destroyed by fire.

1876 – An elaborately crafted wooden bedroom suite from Grand Rapids is a hit at the Centennial Exposition in Philadelphia. The reputation of The Furniture City is born. Melville Bissell of Grand Rapids patents the carpet sweeper.

1877 – The Michigan Reformatory is built in Ionia.

1885 – The Upjohn Pill and Granule Co. opens in Kalamazoo.

1886 – Philo Beckwith manufactures the first Round Oak Stove in Dowagiac.

1911 – Grand Rapids furniture workers stage a bitter, but ultimately unsuccessful, strike against local furniture companies.

1912 – Female workers at the Kalamazoo Corset Co. picket for better pay and working conditions. They are partially successful.

1927 – The Fremont Canning Co. begins experimenting with a strained food product that will become Gerber Baby Food.

1927 – Oil is discovered in Muskegon County.

1928 – Newspaper editor Arthur Vandenberg of Grand Rapids is appointed to the U.S. Senate after the death of Sen. Woodbridge Ferris, of Big Rapids. Ferris had founded colleges in Muskegon and Big Rapids, earlier in his career. Vandenberg would go on to play a key role in the founding of the United Nations.

1929 – The stock market crash ushers in the Great Depression. West Michigan's industrial economy sheds thousands of jobs.

1941-45 – Thousands of West Michigan men are sent overseas to fight in World War II. Local factories shake off the Depression and produce war goods.

1945 – Grand Rapids becomes the first American city to introduce fluoride into its drinking water, in an effort to reduce tooth decay. Even after 60 years, fluoridation remains controversial, though the U.S. Centers for Disease Control calls it a safe, effective public health measure.

1957 – The first West Michigan segment of what will become I-96 opens in Ottawa County, between Coopersville and Marne. The freeway will be finished from Muskegon to Lansing in 1961.

1959 – Kalamazoo removes auto traffic from a downtown street, creating America's first downtown pedestrian mall.

1960 – US-131 expressway opens from Grand Rapids to Kalamazoo.

1961 – I-94 expressway completed from New Buffalo to Detroit.

1962 – Walker-based retailer Meijer opens its first Thrifty Acres market – the forerunner of today's "supercenters" – on 28th Street in Grand Rapids.

1963 – After several years of construction, the US-131 freeway is open from I-94 at Kalamazoo to I-96 at Grand Rapids.

1968 – Herman Miller Co. of Zeeland introduces the "Action Office," a panelized office system with interlocking desktops, storage and lighting. The system is designed so it can be customized to the needs of every employee. In the real world, it leads to the modern "cubicle" that passes for office space at many large corporations.

1969-71 – With the United States economy in a mild recession, Michigan loses some manufacturing jobs. It's a hint of things to come.

Arthur Vandenberg (U.S. Senate photo)

1973 – Oil Crisis. An oil embargo imposed by Arab members of the Organization of Petroleum Exporting Countries (OPEC) leads to recession in the United States, especially in auto-dependent Michigan.

Around this time, the term "Rust Belt" is coined.

1974 – Gerald R. Ford, former Republican Congressman from Grand Rapids, becomes President of the United States, following the resignation of the scandal-plagued Richard Nixon. Ford tells American, "Our long national nightmare is over."

1980-82 – Oil prices triple in the wake of the Iranian revolution. Again, the nation is plunged into recession. And again, Michigan is hardest hit.

1993 – The national "dot-com" boom – a dramatic expansion in computer-related businesses – results in a huge demand for office furniture. West Michigan furniture manufacturers reap the benefits, but are forced to downsize when the bubble bursts after 2000.

1996 – VanAndel Arena opens in downtown Grand Rapids and quickly becomes the region's top indoor venue for concerts and sports events. The VanAndel seats about 10,800 for hockey and basketball, and up to 13,000 for concerts.

1998 – Kalamazoo's downtown mall reopens to traffic.

2000 – West Michigan's population stands at nearly 2 million people.

NATURAL RESOURCES

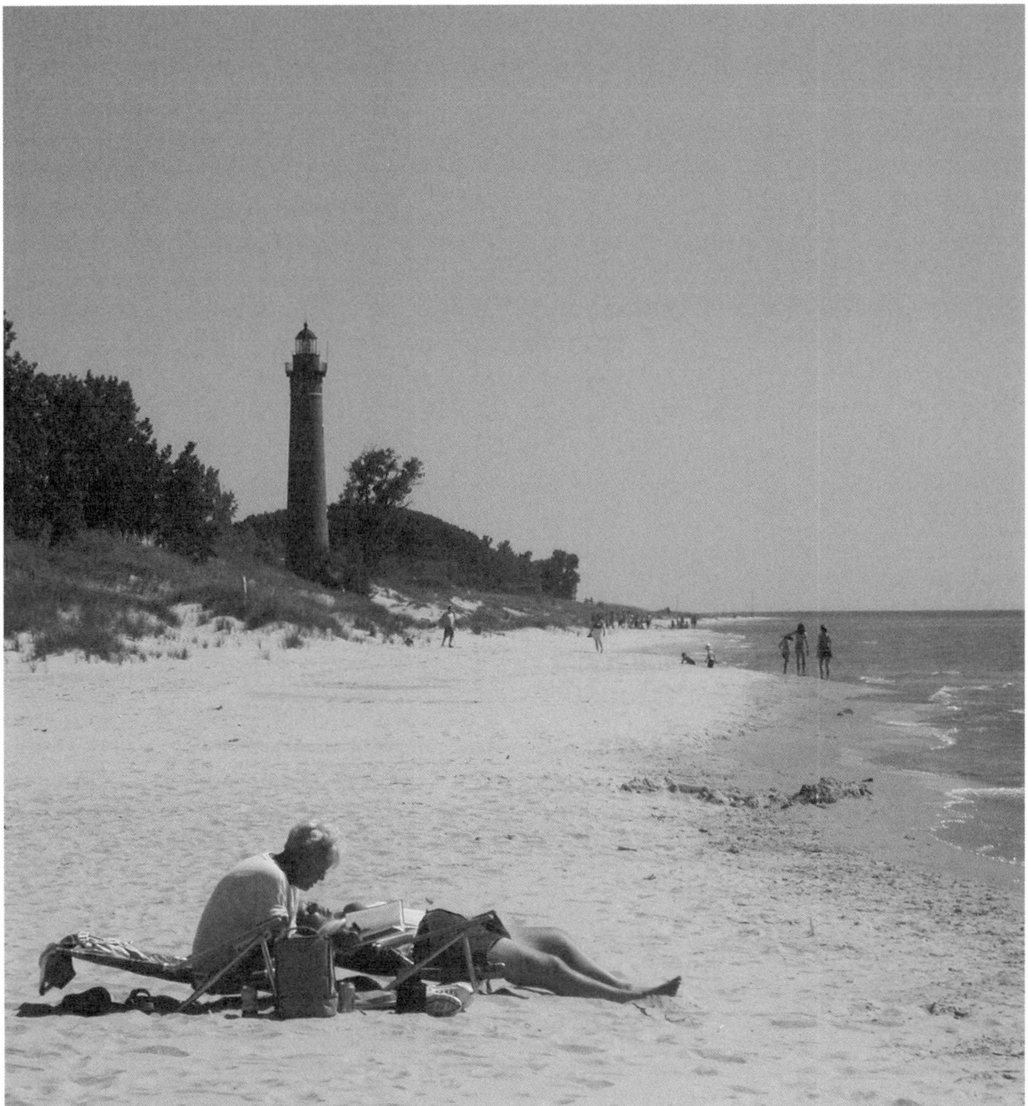

Photo on previous page: Ed Hoogterp

NATURAL RESOURCES

Fast facts about Lake Michigan:

Overall Length: 307 miles

Breadth: 118 miles

Water volume:
1,107 cubic miles

Surface area:
22,300 square miles

Average depth: 279 feet.

Deepest point: 925 feet

Average elevation above sea level: 579 feet

Our Great, Big Lake
The single most identifiable characteristic of our region is the long blue shoreline of Lake Michigan that forms our western boundary.

This huge body of water – the sixth largest freshwater lake in the world – affects our lives in more ways that we can count. It cools the summer breezes and warms the winter winds blowing east from the Great Plains. It creates one of America's great recreational resources for everything from charter-boat captains to beach volleyball players.

Its sandy beaches make a perfect summer destination for residents and tourists. The ample water runs through our factories, power plants, lawns and kitchens.

And, just as a bonus, it makes a setting for some of the greatest sunsets anywhere.

For all those endearing qualities, Lake Michigan also faces huge challenges. The water quality is threatened by industrial pollution, agricultural runoff, and the waste produced by the growing human population along its shores. The popular fishery is under assault from invasive species such as zebra mussels and round gobies, which can alter the habitat and crowd out native plants and animals. Cleaning up the lake has become a multi-billion-dollar task since governments began attacking the problem in the 1970s.

For many West Michigan communities, the Big Lake is both the source of drinking water and the ultimate destination of sewage. That's not as terrible as it may sound. Communities along the lake have invested hundreds of million of dollars and made huge strides in treating sewage and removing industrial wastes from the rivers that flow into Lake Michigan.

In Grand Rapids, for example, as recently as 1990, sewer pipes that carried a combination of sewage and rainwater dumped something like 350 million gallons of diluted-but-untreated sewage into the Grand River each year.

A project to separate those sewers and build a huge retention basin has eliminated more than 90 percent of that "combined sewer overflow," though heavy rains can still spill some waste into the river.

Pretreatment programs overseen by local government and the state Department of Environmental Quality have similarly reduced the levels of heavy metals and other industrial wastes that flow down the rivers into Lake Michigan.

But much more work remains.

The rivers that flow to the lake still drink in pollution from so-called non-point sources such as erosion, failing septic tanks and the tiles that run under farm fields. And stuff that gets in the air from auto exhaust and coal-burning power plants eventually settles into the lake. Of particular concern is mercury, which is toxic in minuscule amounts and has shown up in fish in every West Michigan waterway.

The 1987 Great Lakes Water Quality Agreement between the United States and Canada identified 43 "Areas of Concern" where the degraded environment was likely to harm aquatic life.

Three of those areas are in West Michigan, and a total of 10 are on Lake Michigan or connecting rivers.

The three West Michigan Areas of Concern are:

The Kalamazoo River where a century of wastes from paper mills have contaminated an 80-mile stretch of the river with PCBs. Most discharges of industrial waste have been eliminated, but contaminants continue to leach out into the water from PCB-laced sediments. Clean-up is underway or in the planning stages at a number of sites along the river.

White Lake, at the mouth of the White River in Muskegon County, was listed as an area of concern because contaminated groundwater below a former Hooker Chemical Co. plant was migrating into the lake water. White Lake also received contamination from a leather tannery and several other industries. The contaminated groundwater is now intercepted and treated before it gets to the lake. Tests of lake sediments show that water quality has been improving since the industrial discharges stopped in the 1970s, but levels of such contaminants as chromium, lead, mercury, chlordane and PCB's remain high.

Muskegon Lake was designated as result of the combined impact of industrial waste, municipal wastewater and such non-point sources as erosion along the Muskegon River and tributaries. As in other areas, industrial waste has been greatly reduced. Muskegon's wastewater treatment plant now uses its effluent to irrigate farmland. In late 2005, contractors began removing some 80,000 yards of contaminated sediment from Ruddiman Creek, which runs into Muskegon Lake. That project is funded by $10.8 million from the US Environmental Protection Agency and the Michigan Department of Environmental Quality.

Changing Lake Levels
Lake Michigan's natural outlet is at the Straits of Mackinac, where the water flows very gradually into Lake Huron. An artificial outlet at the Chicago Ship and Sanitary Canal allows Lake Michigan water (and Chicago sewage) to flow into the Mississippi River system. The amount of water allowed to flow through the canal is strictly controlled by a federal court order.

The lake level is constantly changing.

In an annual cycle determined by rain, snow and evaporation, the water typically hits a low level in February, then rises about a foot by July, before beginning to decline again. Over the past 80 years or so, the water level has varied by about 6 feet. The recorded low (based on monthly averages) was 576.05 feet above sea level, in March of 1964. The recorded high was in October of 1986 at 582.35.

So far in the 21st century, most readings have been a foot or more below the long-term average. Some experts believe global warming is causing a permanent decline in the levels. Others contend the recent low levels are part of a long-term cycle.

Beach Walking
In 2005, the Michigan Supreme Court ruled that the strip of Great Lakes beach between the water's edge and the "recent high water mark" is considered to be exposed lake bottom, and is held in public trust, even if the adjacent land is privately owned.

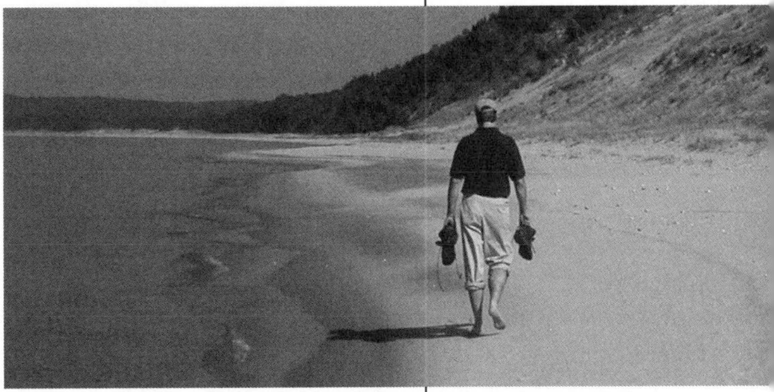

Walking the Lake Michigan beach is a pleasant – and legal – way to spend a summer day (photo: Ed Hoogterp)

What that means is that anyone has a right to walk along

the beach, so long as they stay close to the water.

The court said the high water mark should usually be a visible line of vegetation or debris deposited by waves. The best advice, if you're walking the beach in front of private property, is to stay near the water, be polite, and keep moving. Most experts believe the court ruling does not give the public a right to throw down a blanket or build a bonfire on the exposed lake bottom in front of private property.

Public Access to the Lake

The world's largest collection of freshwater sand dunes lies along the shore of Lake Michigan, from about Gary, Ind., to Petoskey, Mich. That sand, spread out along the beaches and piled into dunes several hundred feet high, draws millions of people to West Michigan's lakeshore every summer.

West Michigan has some of the world's most impressive sand dunes, including these in Oceana County (photo: Terry Phipps)

State and local governments provide scores of public access sites on the 160 miles of shoreline between the Indiana border and Pentwater. Here are some of the most popular, starting at the southern end:

New Buffalo Beach, on the north side of the Galien River in New Buffalo, has a parking area and sandy beach. It's within easy walking distance from downtown shops and restaurants.

Warren Dunes State Park, on Red Arrow Highway near Sawyer, has more than 2 miles of sandy beach, along with dunes to climb, forests to hike, and a 185-site campground where you can spend the night. It's easily the most popular Michigan beach near the south end of the lake, but there's enough shoreline to spread out the crowds.

Weko Beach, in Bridgman, is a city beach just north of Warren Dunes. It has a campground, modern beach house, board walk and other amenities. There's an admission charge for non-residents.

Grand Mere State Park, near Stevensville, has nearly a mile of shoreline on Lake Michigan, in addition to frontage on three inland lakes. The park is largely undeveloped. It has no campground and the beach is a short hike from the parking area. Back from the beach, the 985-acre park has a unique ecosystem of interdunal lakes and wetlands.

Silver Beach and the adjacent Lion's Club Beach at St. Joseph make one of the best urban beaches on the southern part of the lake. Silver Beach was once a popular amusement park that drew steamboat loads of visitors from Chicago. Today, in addition to the expanse of sand and surf, Silver Beach provides a view of the St. Joseph Harbor Lighthouse and access to the south breakwall at the mouth of the St. Joseph River. A short walk and a climb up a long flight of stairs will get you to downtown St. Joe.

Tiscornia Beach, also in St. Joseph, is on the north side of the river. It has a sandy beach for swimming, and access to the north harbor breakwall for fishing.

Benton Harbor's Jean Klock Park provides great swimming and sunning just a bit north of the St. Joseph River. The park is usually less crowded than Silver Beach. It has paved parking, a boardwalk, an observation tower, bathhouse, picnic shelter and concession area.

Berrien County's Rocky Gap Park, just north of Benton Harbor, has an observation platform on a bluff above the lake and access to 1,100 feet of beach down below.

Van Buren State Park has 220 campsites, nearly a mile of Lake Michigan beach and high dunes off Red Arrow Highway south of South Haven. The 400-acre park is adjacent to the Palisades nuclear power plant.

South Beach, at South Haven, provides access to the Big Lake and the South Haven Pierhead Light (photo: Ed Hoogterp)

South Beach, in South Haven, is another great city beach, with access to a breakwall and the South Haven Pierhead Light at the mouth of the Black River Harbor. The beach is in walking distance from the shops and restaurants in downtown South Haven.

North Beach, also in South Haven, extends public access to the north side of the harbor.

West Side County Park, in Allegan County just west of Ganges, has 600 feet of sandy beach. The park has modern restrooms and a fenced playground for little kids. The small Pier Cove park is about a mile to the north.

Saugatuck's famous Oval Beach is across the Kalamazoo River from the downtown's restaurants and gift shops.

You can get there by driving around the harbor, or by crossing the river on the town's unique chain ferry and walking a short distance to the beach.

Saugatuck Dunes State Park, just north of Saugatuck, has 2.5 miles of undeveloped and generally uncrowded beach. It's a walk of about a mile through wooded dunes to reach the water, and it's well worth the hike.

Holland State Park is tucked up against the north side of the Lake Macatawa Channel. The waterfront, known locally as Ottawa Beach, has fine, soft sand and a view across the channel to "Big Red," the Holland Harbor Lighthouse. Holland is Michigan's busiest state park. On a summer weekend you'll have to arrive early if you want space to spread your blanket.

Tunnel Park, just north of Holland State Park, is operated by Ottawa County. A tunnel through a sand dune leads from the parking lot to the beach. A popular network of bike trails links Tunnel Park with the state park and other attractions.

Kirk Park, midway between Holland and Grand Haven, is another Ottawa County Park. The 60-acre park has about one-third of a mile of Lake Michigan beach.

The Rosy Mound Natural Area is a 160-acre Ottawa County park with a 0.7 mile trail to a Lake Michigan Beach. The trail is both scenic and strenuous, with 1,000 feet of stairs up and down the dunes.

Grand Haven State Park, at the mouth of the Grand River, is regarded as one of America's great city beaches, drawing more than a million visitors a year. A boardwalk along the river links the sandy beach with downtown Grand Haven.

North Beach Park is a popular 20-acre spot on the shoreline in Ferrysburg, just north of Grand Haven. Ottawa County manages this small lakeshore park, and is in process of buying an additional mile of dunes back from the beach that would connect North Beach to Hoffmaster State Park, on the Ottawa-Muskegon County Line.

Hoffmaster State Park, between Grand Haven and Muskegon, has forested sand dunes, boardwalks, and 2.5 miles of fine beach. Also here is the E. Genevieve Gillette Sand Dune Visitor Center, with exhibits to help visitors understand the ecology of the dunes.

Pere Marquette Park in Muskegon is another of the region's great urban beaches.

The city-owned park butts up against the south side of the Muskegon Channel. It includes plenty of grassy picnic areas, in addition to the sandy beach.

Muskegon State Park has three miles of lakeshore on the north side of the Muskegon Channel. In addition to its beach, the park also has a winter sports area including a luge run where anyone can take a lesson and go for a slide.

Pioneer County Park, north of Muskegon State Park, has a campground and 2000 feet of sandy beach.

Duck Lake State Park, south of Whitehall, has frontage on both Lake Michigan and Duck Lake. The 700-acre park is day use only – no camping – and includes tall sand dunes as well as the beaches and a creek that runs across the sand from Duck Lake to Lake Michigan.

Meinert County Park is a Muskegon County park north of Montague. The 88-acre parcel has modern campsites and 2,000 feet of Lake Michigan shore. It also has sand dunes and a small creek.

Claybanks Township Park, west of Rothbury in Oceana County, extends about half a mile along Lake Michigan. It's a secluded spot with views of the unspoiled shoreline to the north and south.

Little Point Sable is part of Silver Lake State Park, though it's separate from the main body of the park. A tall, brick tower – all that remains from the Little Sable Light Station – overlooks a popular stretch of sandy beach.

Children play in the warm water of a creek at Golden Township Park (photo: Ed Hoogterp)

Golden Township Park is a tiny pocket park, partially surrounded by Silver Lake State Park, near Little Point Sable. It has a sandy beach and broad, shallow creek that's a great place for kids to play.

Silver Lake State Park has miles of shifting sand for hiking and dune buggy rides. The 3,000-acre park includes tall dunes that span from Silver Lake to Lake Michigan. The swimming is great in both lakes.

Cedar Point Park is a small Oceana County park between Silver Lake and Pentwater. It has restrooms, a picnic area, and a long stairway leading down the bluff to the Lake Michigan beach.

Charles Mears State Park is among the smallest in the system at only 50 acres. But it's a great spot that's far enough north that it's not usually too crowded. The park, at the mouth of the Pentwater River, is made up of beach, a sandy campground, and the "Old Baldy" dune. It's a few blocks from downtown Pentwater and is a great place for a swim.

Mottville Bridge is a historic triple-span "camelback" structure over the St. Joseph River (photo: Ed Hoogterp)

RIVERS

The rivers that flow into Lake Michigan have served as lifelines for the people of West Michigan for thousands of years.

Prehistoric Indians used the streams as highways into the interior. They took fish from the water and game from the riverbanks.

When the first Europeans arrived, they found native villages along the rivers – and ancient burial mounds often nearby.

White trappers and missionaries followed the example of the natives, and used rivers as highways. They also journeyed up even the tiniest creeks to trap the beaver, muskrat and mink whose furs were in high demand back in Europe.

The early settlers saw energy in the flowing water, and they erected dams to harness that power. Loggers used the water to float their product to mills downstream. And then the Industrial Revolution reached Michigan, employing hundreds of thousands of workers. Until electricity became available, factories used river water to turn flywheels, shafts and turbines. The same factories released their wastes to flow out of sight downstream. Farms, human sewage and garbage dumps in the floodplains added more gunk to the waterways.

The years of abuse led to the extinction of some species of fish, including the Grayling, and left other river creatures, such as freshwater clams, barely hanging on.

Today, West Michigan lives with the complicated legacy of river systems that are part of our cultural soul and industrial heart, but which still carry the poisons of past centuries. Clean-up began in the 1970s, and huge progress has been made. But toxins like chromium and mercury remain in some bottom sediments, and the state advises residents to limit the number of fish they eat.

Unwelcome pollution continues to reach the rivers from septic tanks, inadequate sewage systems, and run-off from farms, roadways and over-fertilized lawns.

For all that, our rivers have come a long way back. They're used for boating, fishing, even swimming. And in cities such as Grand Rapids, riverbanks that were once an embarrassment are now seen as a keystone for new development.

West Michigan's four major river systems – the St. Joseph, Kalamazoo, Grand and Muskegon – together gather water from about 15,000 square miles and funnel that water into Lake Michigan.

Smaller West Michigan streams that flow directly into Lake Michigan include the Galien River, at New Buffalo; the Black River, at South Haven; the Macatawa River at Holland; the White River at Whitehall and the Pentwater River at Pentwater.

Here's a primer on the four major rivers:

THE ST. JOSEPH RIVER:

Length: 210 miles

Source: Baw Beese Lake, Hillsdale County

Mouth: St. Joseph Harbor, Lake Michigan

Average flow (at Niles): 3,869 cubic feet per second

Watershed: 4,700 square miles in Michigan and northern Indiana.

Major tributaries: Prairie River; Coldwater River; Fawn River; Pigeon River; Little Elkhart River; Elkhart River; Dowagiac River; Paw Paw River.

Major cities: Hillsdale; Three Rivers; Constantine; Elkhart, Ind; South Bend, Ind; Niles; Benton Harbor; St. Joseph.

Native Americans and early explorers used the St. Joe as part of a route between the Great Lakes and the Mississippi River system. They could canoe upriver to about the present site of South Bend, Ind., then make a short portage to the Kankakee River, which joins the Illinois and, ultimately, the Mississippi River. Marquette and LaSalle both used that route on visits to the Illinois and Miami Indians who lived in the region.

This historic stream was also the site of a French Fort, at the present site of Niles, more than a century before there were settlers anywhere else in West Michigan.

Today, the St. Joseph flows mainly through agricultural areas. Phosphorus from fertilizer that runs off farmland is a major problem with the water quality.

Tourism and recreation groups in St. Joseph County have compiled a guide for canoeists and kayakers, describing historic sites and other interesting spots along the river. The River Country Heritage Water Trails guide is available from the River Country Tourism Bureau in Centreville (www.rivercountry.com).

Some of the good spots to visit on the river are the Langley Covered Bridge, near Centreville, and Scidmore Park in Three Rivers, where the Rocky River merges with the St. Joseph.

KALAMAZOO RIVER:

Length: 210 miles

Source: Moscow Township, Hillsdale County

Mouth: Saugatuck, Lake Michigan

Average flow (at Fennville): 1,629 cubic feet per second

Watershed: 2,020 square miles in parts of Allegan, Barry, Eaton, Van Buren, Kalamazoo, Calhoun, Jackson, Hillsdale, Kent and Ottawa counties.

Major tributaries: Rice Creek, Wabascon Creek, Battle Creek River, Augusta Creek, Portage Creek, Gun River, Sawn Creek, Rabbit River.

Major cities: Albion, Marshall, Battle Creek, Kalamazoo, Plainwell, Otsego, Allegan.

An 1839 history of Michigan described the Kalamazoo River as "A small, winding and transparent stream, flowing over a bed of limestone and pebbles."

The word "transparent" hasn't been applied to the Kalamazoo in the past 100 years or so. The river is heavily dammed, and much of its lower reaches have been contaminated with industrial wastes, especially from the paper mills that operated along the river beginning in 1867.

The lower river is designated both as a Great Lakes Area of Concern and a federal Superfund Site. Years of clean-up have taken place, and there are years more to go.

Still, the river has its good points. Its meandering path through the historic districts of Allegan add to the charm of that small city. And there is plenty of natural riverfront in the Allegan State Game Area and the Fort Custer State Recreation area. The *Star of Saugatuck* river boat offers cruises near the mouth of the river in Saugatuck.

GRAND RIVER:

Length: 260 miles

Source: Grand Lake, Jackson County

Mouth: Grand Haven, Lake Michigan

Average flow (at Grand Rapids): 4,346 cubic feet per second

Watershed: 5,570 square miles, encompassing parts of 19 counties.

Major tributaries: Red Cedar River, Looking Glass River, Maple River, Flat River, Thornapple River, Rogue River.

Major cities: Jackson, Lansing, Portland, Ionia, Grand Rapids, Grand Haven.

The Grand is West Michigan's largest stream, in terms of water flow, and the longest river in Michigan. The region's pioneers began putting dams across the broad stream almost as soon as settlement became legal, in the 1830s. The Grand was used for log drives, to sawmills in Grand Rapids and Grand Haven. Its water quality suffered terribly for much of the 20th century from city and farm run-off and from industrial discharges in Jackson, Lansing and Grand Rapids. The three cities had a concentration of plating and metalworking shops. As a result the Grand was contaminated by heavy metal wastes in the decades before the government began regulating pollution. Until a few years ago, the Grand Rapids sewer system overflowed with every heavy rain, sending sewage into the river and causing local health departments to advise against contact with the water.

Investment of hundreds of millions of dollars has reduced the discharges from both industry and the city, but toxic metals remain in the sediments.

The water below the Fourth Street Dam near downtown Grand Rapids is one of the state's most popular fishing spots. Spectators gather along the banks and near the fish ladder sculpture designed by Joseph Kinnebrew to watch the anglers. Another inviting riverfront location is in downtown Portland, where the Maple River enters the Grand in a public park. In Grand Haven, visitors can stroll a riverfront boardwalk from the rivermouth at Grand Haven State Park to the downtown shopping district.

MUSKEGON RIVER:

Length: 212 miles

Source: Houghton Lake and Higgins Lake, Roscommom County

Mouth: Muskegon Lake, Lake Michigan

Average flow (at Newaygo): 2,216 cubic feet per second

Watershed: 2,600 square miles

Major Tributaries: Hersey River; Little Muskegon River; Bear Creek

Major cities: Big Rapids, Newaygo, Muskegon

Unlike the rivers farther south, the Muskegon River runs through woodlands for much of its journey from Houghton Lake to Muskegon Lake. The river's watershed includes swatches of the Manistee National Forest, in addition to the Muskegon State Game Area.

Dams that once blocked the river's flow at Big Rapids and Newaygo have been removed. Three major dams remain in Newaygo and Mecosta counties, including the 100-foot tall Hardy Dam, the largest in the state. Hardy Pond is among West Michigan's largest lakes and is the site of Newaygo State Park.

The area around the city of Muskegon, where the river widens into Muskegon Lake, is historically one of Michigan's most concentrated industrial areas. The lake had 47 sawmills around it at the height of the lumbering era in the 1880s, and later was host to chemical, foundry and paper-making industries. Muskegon Lake is home port for the Lake Express ferry service, which crosses Lake Michigan to Milwaukee.

WEST MICHIGAN DAMS

West Michigan's early settlers began building dams almost from the moment they arrived here from their previous homes in New England.

A fisherman works the current below Lyons Dam on the Grand River (photo: Ed Hoogterp)

To survive in the Michigan "wilderness" the newcomers had to clear the trees off their land and and get crops into the ground.

Transportation was extremely difficult in those days, so every village needed at least one local mill to grind their grain into flour and saw the felled trees into useful building lumber. The best way to power those mills was to dam up the creek, and use the weight of the water falling through a millrace to turn the grindstones or move the saws.

Eventually, the dams got larger, powering factories, wagon-making shops and sawmills with scores of saws.

In 1880, a water-powered dynamo at a Grand Rapids factory was used to send electricity to 16 street lamps, and the age of hydro-electricity in Michigan was born. In 1898, the forerunner of Consumers Energy Co. built the Trowbridge Dam on the Kalamazoo River and began transmitting power to Kalamazoo.

The era of dam building lasted into the 1930s. By then, dams were generating electricity on all four of West Michigan's major rivers – the St. Joseph, Kalamazoo, Grand and Muskegon – as well as many smaller streams.

In recent years, many of the smaller dams have stopped producing electricity and been turned over to local governments or private owners to maintain the water levels on their backwater ponds. A few, including those at Newaygo and Big Rapids, have been removed altogether. Dams that once were considered a necessity are now seen as a mixed blessing.

The larger facilities continue to produce reliable, inexpensive electricity, without burning fossil fuels. And the backwater ponds often create great home sites and opportunities for water recreation.

On the other hand, a dam may block the movement of fish, cause silt to build up in the slack water behind the barrier, and warm the water so much that cold-water species such as trout can no longer thrive.

So, are dams good or bad? Darned if we know.

Here is a list of the West Michigan dams licensed to generate electricity.

Ada Dam
On Thornapple River at Ada, Kent County. Built 1926, 31 feet high, 318 acre pond

Adamsville Dam
On Christiann Creek at Adamsville in Cass County. Built in 1865, 10 feet high, 398 acre pond

Belding Dam
Flat River at Belding in Ionia County. Built in 1887, 15 feet high, 110 acre pond

Berrien Springs Dam
On St. Joseph River at Berrien Springs in Berrien County. Built in 1908, 36 feet high, 600 acre pond

Buchanan Dam
On St. Joseph River at Buchanan in Berrien County. Built in 1902, 28 feet high, 300 acre pond

Calkins Bridge Dam
On Kalamazoo River at Allegan in Allegan County. Built in 1930, 42 feet high, 1,587 acre pond

Cascade Dam
On Thornapple River in Cascade Township, in Kent County. Built in 1926, 31 feet high, 270 acre pond

Constantine Dam
On St. Joseph River at Constantine in St. Joseph County. Built in 1873, 30 feet high, 555 acre pond

Croton Dam
On Muskegon River near Newaygo in Newaygo County. Built in 1907, 53 feet high, 1,230 acre pond

Fallasburg Dam
On Flat River at Lowell in Kent County. Built in 1900, 40 feet high, 259 acre pond

French Paper Dam
On St. Joseph River at Niles in Berrien County. Built in 1887, 22 feet high, 80 acre pond

Hardy Dam
On Muskegon River near Newaygo in Newaygo County. Built in 1931, 114 feet high, 3,750 acre pond

Hart Hydro Dam
On South Branch of Pentwater River at Hart in Oceana County. Built in 1927, 39 feet high, 240 acre pond

Hubbardston Dam
On Fish Creek at Hubbardston in Ionia County. Built in 1850, 26 feet high, 35 acre pond

Irving Dam
On Thornapple River in Irving Township, Barry County. Built in 1939, 18 feet high, 25 acre pond

King Milling Co. Dam
On Flat River at Lowell in Kent County. Built in 1942, 15 feet high, 53 acre pond

LaBarge Dam
On Thornapple River at Caledonia in Kent County. Built in 1901, 32 feet high, 100 acre pond

Middleville Dam
On Thornapple River at Middleville in Barry County. Built in 1938, 16 feet high, 35 acre pond

Morrow Dam
On Kalamazoo River at Comstock in Kalamazoo County. Built in 1941, 25 feet high, 1,000 acre pond

Mottville Dam
On St. Joseph River at Mottville in St. Joseph County. Built in 1923, 20 feet high, 487 acre pond

Portland Dam
On Grand River at Portland in Ionia County. Built in 1896, 15 feet high, 104 acre pond

Rogers Dam
On Muskegon River at Big Rapids in Mecosta County. Built in 1906, 45 feet high, 340 acre pond

Sturgis Dam
On St. Joseph River at Mendon in St. Joseph County. Built in 1912, 41 feet high, 480 acre pond

Three Rivers Dam
On St. Joseph River at Three Rivers in St. Joseph County. Built in 1917, 16 feet high, 600 acre pond

Webber Dam
On Grand River at Lyons in Ionia County. Built in 1907, 33 feet high, 660 acre pond

White's Bridge Dam
On Flat River at Smyrna in Ionia County. Year unknown; 24 feet high, 300 acre pond

Fawn River Dam
On Fawn River, in Fawn River Township of St. Joseph County.

King Mill Dam
On Nottawa Creek at Leonidas in St. Joseph County.

(source: Michigan Department of Natural Resources)

THE LARGEST INLAND LAKES

Lake Michigan – with its lighthouses, whitecapped waves and endless sand dunes – is the scenic heart of West Michigan. But no one should forget the region's hundreds of inland lakes.

While the Big Lake is unsurpassed for beach-walking or salmon fishing, inland water bodies are often better suited for water-skiing, small-boat fishing, paddling a canoe or swimming with little kids.

Spots like Paw Paw Lake, near Coloma, and Diamond Lake at Cassopolis were popular resort areas for out-of-state visitors a century ago. They've since become prime real estate locations, as well as vacation destinations.

Other lakes – including Muskegon, White, Pentwater and Macatawa – offer channel access to Lake Michigan in addition to some of the advantages of inland water.

Still others – such as Gun Lake near Middleville or

Wabasis Lake near Rockford, have state or county parks that offer swimming, camping, boat launch facilities and hiking trails. In the northern part of the region, many lakes are ringed with undeveloped forest. In the more populated south, cottages and second homes are the norm.

A grassy shoreline makes for an instant playground on a Muskegon County lake (photo: Ed Hoogterp)

West Michigan's 25 largest inland lakes:

1) Muskegon Lake, Muskegon County, 4231 acres

2) Hardy Pond, Mecosta and Newaygo counties, 3750 acres

3) Gun Lake, Allegan and Barry counties, 2735 acres

4) White Lake, Muskegon County, 2535 acres

5) Lake Macatawa, Ottawa County, 2218 acres

6) Gull Lake, Barry and Kalamazoo counties, 2046 acres

7) Lake Allegan, Allegan County, 1695 acres

8) Martiny Lake, Mecosta County, 1663 acres

9) Spring Lake, Ottawa and Muskegon counties, 1251 acres

10) Croton Dam Pond, Newaygo County, 1235 acres

11) Austin Lake, Kalamazoo County, 1101 acres

12) Diamond Lake, Cass County, 1041 acres

13) Paw Paw Lake, Berrien County, 922 acres

14) Morrow Pond, Kalamazoo County, 919 acres

15) Klinger Lake, St. Joseph County, 834 acres

16) Chippewa Lake, Mecosta County, 791 acres

17) Fremont Lake, Newaygo County, 790 acres

18) Webber Lake, Ionia County, 766 acres

19) Hess Lake, Newaygo county, 764 acres

20) Indian Lake, Kalamazoo County, 758 acres

21) Crystal Lake, Montcalm County, 708 acres

22) Silver Lake, Oceana County, 672 acres

23) Pine Lake, Barry County, 660 acres

24) Mona Lake, Muskegon County, 656 acres

25) Upper Crooked Lake, Barry County, 644 acres

Trowbridge Hydro Pond,
Allegan County, 527 acres

Magician Lake, Cass and Van Buren counties, 521 acres

Portage Lake,
St. Joseph County, 510 acres

Long Lake,
Kalamazoo County, 500 acres

Palmer Lake,
St. Joseph County, 497 acres

Three Rivers Hydro Pond,
St. Joseph County, 490 acres

Mottville Hydro Pond,
St. Joseph County, 487 acres

Indian Lake,
Cass County, 486 acres

Jordan Lake,
Ionia County, 460 acres

Pentwater Lake,
Oceana County, 436 acres

Lower Crooked Lake,
Barry County, 433 acres

Otsego Hydro Plant,
Allegan County, 428 acres

Featherbed Marsh,
Mecosta County, 425 acres

Jordan Lake,
Barry County, 417 acres

Lincoln Lake,
Kent County, 416 acres

Thornapple Lake,
Barry County, 415 acres

Bear Lake, Muskegon County, 415 acres

Wabasis Lake,
Kent County, 404 acres

Bankson Lake,
Van Buren County, 393 acres

Eagle Lake,
Cass County, 379 acres

Long Lake,
Ionia County, 356 acres

Hutchins Lake,
Allegan County, 340 acres

Rogers Pond,
Mecosta County, 337 acres

West Lake, Kalamazoo County, 335 acres

Big Blue Lake,
Muskegon County, 335 acres

Fish Lake,
Cass County, 333 acres

Fisher's Lake,
St. Joseph County, 330 acres

Barton Lake,
Kalamazoo County, 329 acres

Miner Lake,
Allegan County, 328 acres

La Grange Mill Pond,
Cass County, 325 acres

Fine Lake,
Barry County, 323 acres

Inland lakes offer perfect conditions for small sailboats (photo: Terry Phipps)

Kalamazoo Lake,
Allegan County, 320 acres

Ada Dam Pond,
Kent County, 318 acres

Tamarack Lake,
Montcalm County, 316 acres

Jehnsen Lake,
Mecosta County, 315 acres

Morrison Lake,
Ionia County, 314 acres

Murray Lake,
Kent County, 312 acres

Mecosta Lake,
Mecosta County, 312 acres

Pickerel Lake,
Newaygo County, 307 acres

Duck Lake,
Montcalm County, 301 acres

Buchanan Lake,
Berrien County, 300 acres

Birch Lake,
Cass County, 300 acres

Horsehead Lake,
Mecosta County, 300 acres

Lake of the Woods,
Van Buren County, 300 acres

Green Lake,
Allegan County, 298 acres

Gravel Lake,
Van Buren County, 297 acres

Brooks Lake,
Newaygo County, 286 acres

Saddle Lake,
Van Buren County, 282 acres

Townline Lake,
Montcalm County, 280 acres

Stony Lake,
Oceana County, 278 acres

Fish Lake,
St. Joseph County, 275 acres

Silver Lake,
Allegan County, 274 acres

Cedar Lake,
Van Buren County, 274 acres

Algonquin Lake,
Barry County, 271 acres

Shavehead Lake,
Cass County, 270 acres

Cascade Hydro Pond,
Kent County, 270 acres

Baldwin Lake,
Cass County, 265 acres

Reed's Lake,
Kent County, 265 acres

Ryerson Lake,
Newaygo County, 262 acres

Long Lake,
Barry County, 261 acres

McLaren Lake,
Oceana County, 261 acres

Three Mile Lake,
Van Buren County, 261 acres

Mud Lake,
Kalamazoo County, 257 acres

Pleasant Lake,
St. Joseph County, 256 acres

Duck Lake,
Muskegon County, 254 acres

Van Auken Lake,
Van Buren County, 252 acres

Donnell Lake,
Cass County, 246 acres

Long Lake,
Cass County, 245 acres

Eagle Lake,
Van Buren County, 244 acres

Hart Lake,
Oceana County, 240 acres

Fair Lake,
Barry County, 238 acres

Silver Lake,
Kent County, 237 acres

Blue Lake,
Mecosta County, 235 acres

Cora Lake,
Van Buren County, 234 acres

Long Lake, St. Joseph County
(Colon Twp), 233 acres

Clear Lake,
St. Joseph County, 232 acres

Haymarsh Lake,
Mecosta County, 231 acres

Dickerson Lake,
Montcalm County, 227 acres

Eagle Lake,
Allegan County, 225 acres

Dewey Lake,
Cass County, 225 acres

Pigeon Lake,
Ottawa County, 225 acres

Wolf Lake,
Muskegon County, 224 acres

Crooked Lake, Cass and Van
Buren counties, 223 acres

Little Black Lake, Muskegon
and Ottawa counties, 223 acres

Gourdneck Lake,
Kalamazoo County, 222 acres

Bostwick Lake,
Kent County, 221 acres

Guernsey Lake,
Barry County, 218 acres

Dumont Lake,
Allegan County, 215 acres

Swan Lake,
Allegan County, 214 acres

Baseline Lake,
Allegan County, 211 acres

Long Lake, St. Joseph County
(Fabius Twp), 211 acres

Christie Lake,
Van Buren County, 211 acres

Lowell Pond,
Kent County, 210 acres

Long Lake,
Cass County, 208 acres

Sturgeon Lake,
St. Joseph County, 208 acres

Round Lake,
Van Buren County, 205 acres

Little Bankson Lake,
Van Buren County, 202 acres

Crooked Lake,
Allegan County, 200 acres

Bills Lake,
Newaygo County, 200 acres

STATE PARKS

The Michigan State Park system includes nearly 100 sites scattered through the Upper and Lower peninsulas. Of all those parks, four of the five busiest are situated along a 60 mile stretch of Lake Michigan shoreline in Ottawa, Muskegon and Oceana Counties.

Holland State Park is the state's busiest, followed by Grand Haven State Park, Island Lake Recreation Area in Metro Detroit, Muskegon State Park and Silver Lake State Park, near Hart. Island Lake is the only non-Lake Michigan park in the top five.

West Michigan's 10 busiest State Parks in 2004:

1. Holland: 1,238,397 visitors. Ranked No. 1 in Michigan.

2. Grand Haven: 1,102,073 visitors. Ranked No. 2 in Michigan.

3. Muskegon: 981,074 visitors. Ranked No. 4 in Michigan.

4. Silver Lake: 854,460 visitors. Ranked No. 5 in Michigan.

5. Yankee Springs: 804,888 visitors. Ranked No. 6 in Michigan.

6. Hoffmaster: 518,958 visitors. Ranked No. 11 in Michigan.

7. Warren Dunes: 436,574 visitors. Ranked No. 15 in Michigan.

8. Mears: 284,534 visitors. Ranked No. 23 in Michigan.

9. Ionia: 254,545 visitors. Ranked No. 32 in Michigan.

10. Van Buren: 241,658 visitors. Ranked No. 34 in Michigan.

A guide to the parks
Here's an all-too-brief guide to what you'll find at state parks in the region.
Entry to Michigan State Parks requires a motor vehicle sticker. The 2006 price for an annual sticker, which covers entry for the occupants of one vehicle all year, is $24 for Michigan residents and $29 for non-residents. Daily Permits are $6 per vehicle for residents and $8 for non-residents.

Campground reservations are available by phone at (800) 447-2757, or on-line through www.michigan.gov/dnr.

Bass River Recreation Area. Ottawa County. 1,665 acres. No camping

This is a newer, largely undeveloped park area along three miles of the Grand River. It's used for hiking, hunting, mountain biking and horse riding. Take M-45 to 104th Avenue, then north 2.5 miles to west park entrance.

Duck Lake State Park, Muskegon County, 728 acres. No camping.

Duck Lake is a day-use park with frontage on both Lake Michigan and Duck Lake. It has great swimming and dune-walking. The state acquired the property, which had been used as a boy scout camp, in 1974. Take the US-31 exit to Whitelake Drive and follow the signs to the park.

Fort Custer Recreation Area, Kalamazoo County, 3,033 acres. 219 campsites.

This former federal military site along the Kalamazoo River became state property in 1971. The park has three lakes. Much of the land is old farm fields, which are returning to forest or prairie conditions. Some of the state's best mountain-biking trails are here. The park entrance is off M-96 just east of Augusta.

Grand Haven State Park, Ottawa County, 48 acres. 174 campsites.

This is a traditional Lake Michigan city beach, at the mouth of the Grand River. It's one of the smallest sites in the state park system, and also one of the busiest. The reason is simple: a wonderful beach in a great town. The park is inside the city of Grand Haven, just a riverwalk stroll from the downtown district.

Grand Mere State Park, Berrien County, 985 acres. No camping.

The mile long Lake Michigan beach is a short walk from the parking area in this undeveloped park. The natural area back in the dunes includes three lakes and trails through a unique ecosystem of sand and water. Take the John Beers Road exit (exit 22) from I-94.

P.J. Hoffmaster State Park, Muskegon and Ottawa counties, 1,100 acres. 293 campsites.

Hoffmaster has more than 2 miles of sandy Lake Michigan beach, along with forested dunes for hiking. The E. Genevieve Gillette Sand Dune Visitor Center has programs and exhibits to explain the ecology of Michigan's great freshwater dunes. Take U.S. 31 to Pontaluna Road exit in Norton Shores, then go 3 miles west to the park.

Hoffmaster State Park has two miles of Lake Michigan beach (photo: Terry Phipps)

Holland State Park, Ottawa County, 142 acres. 319 campsites.

This Lake Michigan park, at the Lake Macatawa Channel, is the busiest in Michigan. It has campgrounds on Lake Macatawa and Lake Michigan and a broad sandy beach on the Big Lake. A network of bike paths links the park with the surrounding area. The state park is on Ottawa Beach Road, west of the city of Holland.

Ionia Recreation Area,
Ionia County, 4,500 acres.
149 campsites.

Ionia recreation area extends for four miles along the Grand River, and includes a swimming beach on Sessions Lake, which was created by damming Sessions Creek in the 1980s. The recreation area has forested trails for hiking and mountain biking. It's a popular site for field-dog competitions and for bird-watching. Take I-96 to Jordan Lake Road (exit 64) then 3 miles north to the park.

Charles Mears State Park,
Oceana County, 50 acres.
180 campsites.

This small park in the village of Pentwater features one sand dune, one beach and one harbor breakwall. That's enough to make it one great place on a summer afternoon. The park is a short walk from downtown Pentwater, and fits perfectly with the scale of the small resort town. Take US-31 to the Monroe Road (Pentwater) exit.

A lone bird searches for food in the waves at Muskegon State Park (photo: Terry Phipps)

Muskegon State Park,
Muskegon County, 1,165 acres. 239 campsites.

With miles of Lake Michigan beach, extensive sand dunes and a winter sports area that includes a luge run, Muskegon State Park is an all-season attraction. The park is on the north side of the Muskegon harbor, with frontage on Muskegon Lake and Lake Michigan. Take US-31 to the M-120 exit (North Muskegon) and follow the signs.

Newaygo State Park,
Newaygo County, 257 acres.
99 campsites.

This is primarily a boating and fishing area on a bluff above Hardy Pond, the lake formed on the Muskegon River behind Hardy Dam. The park's boat launch provides access to the waterway. Camp-sites are rustic and spacious. Take US-131 to exit 125. Go west 5 miles to Beech Street, then north to the park entrance.

Saugatuck Dunes State Park,
Allegan County, 1,000 acres.
No camping.

This park offers something that is very rare in the populated areas of West Michigan: Uncrowded access to a great Lake Michigan beach. The downside, if there is one, is that the lake is a mile away from the parking lot, on a sandy woodland trail. There's also a 300 acre natural area and miles of hiking trails. From I-196, take exit 41, then take 64th Street north to 138th Avenue, which goes west into the park.

Silver Lake State Park,
Oceana County, 2,936 acres. 200 campsites.

The huge, bare sand dune that stretches from Silver Lake to Lake Michigan gives this park a look like nowhere else in Michigan. It's one of the few places where people are permitted to drive off-road vehicles on the dunes. It's also great swimming and a popular spot for family camping trips. Take US-31 to either Hart or Shelby and follow the signs to the park.

Van Buren State Park,
Van Buren County, 400 acres. 220 campsites.

This park, added to the system in 1965, has high dunes and a mile of Lake Michigan beach. The park, on Ruggles Road off the Blue Star Highway, is south of South Haven, near the Palisades Nuclear Power Plant.

Warren Dunes State Park.
Berrien County, 1,952 acres. 185 campsites.

With two miles of Lake Michigan beach and sand dunes that rise 240 feet above the lake, Warren Dunes serves as the southern anchor of the line of state parks that extend up the shoreline. The area has miles of trails and also has a hang-gliding area. Take exit 16 from I-94, and go two miles south of Red Arrow Highway to the park.

Warren Woods State Park.
Berrien County, 311 acres. No camping.

This is a quiet, mostly undeveloped area along the Galien River. It includes one of the few remnants of southern Michigan's original beech-maple climax forest. From US-12 at Three Oaks, go north two miles on Three Oaks Road to Elm Valley Road, then west to the parking lot.

Yankee Springs State Recreation Area.
Barry County, 5,200 acres. 345 campsites.

This huge park has nine lakes within its boundaries, along with trails, natural areas and more. The modern campground and day use areas on Gun Lake are busy all summer, when Gun Lake is popular for swimming, fishing and recreational boating. The park is open year round and is used by hunters, snowmobilers and equestrians. From US-131 south of Grand Rapids, take exit 61, go east seven miles on M-179, then south on Briggs Road to the entrance.

Silver Lake State Park includes an area for private "dune buggies" (photo: Terry Phipps)

BACKYARD BIRDS

The diversity of West Michigan's landscape – big-water shoreline, deep woods, farms, suburbs, riverbanks and inland lakes – makes for an abundance of bird species in the region. Some serious bird-watchers, with support from the Audubon Society and Cornell University, help catalogue those species by keeping track of the birds that show up in back yards, parks and other spots.

Each winter, thousands of amateur ornithologists submit tally sheets that are compiled into state and national lists. Anyone with an interest in birds can participate. (For more information on taking part in the annual counts, contact your local Audubon chapter, or check the national website www.birdsource.org)

Here is a list of the 25 birds you're most likely to see on a February day in Western Michigan. It's based on 447 "Great Backyard Bird Count" checklists filed in 2003 and 2004 by birdwatchers in Kalamazoo, Muskegon, Grand Rapids, Holland and Niles.

1) Northern cardinal
2) Dark-eyed junco
3) Mourning dove
4) Black-capped chickadee
5) American goldfinch
6) Downy woodpecker
7) Blue jay
8) House sparrow
9) Tufted titmouse
10) House finch
11) White-breasted nuthatch
12) Red-bellied woodpecker
13) American crow
14) European starling
15) Hairy woodpecker
16) American tree sparrow
17) Red-breasted nuthatch
18) Song sparrow
19) Northern flicker
20) American robin
21) Wild turkey
22) Eastern bluebird
23) Carolina wren
24) Mallard
25) Canada goose

FISHING RECORDS

With more than 1,000 miles of rivers and streams and hundreds of inland lakes – not to mention the Big Lake – it stands to reason that West Michigan is an anglers' paradise. Whether it's dipping for suckers on the spring run in the Grand River, setting downriggers on Lake Michigan, casting flies on the Rogue River or watching a bobber on Paw Paw Lake, the region offers just about every kind of fishing. The Department of Natural Resources keeps track of the largest specimens caught from more than 50 species of fish.

Here is a list of the state-record fish caught in West Michigan waters.

Species Waterway/County	Year	Weight	Length
Black Buffalo Grand River/Ottawa	2004	33.25 lbs	36.5 in.
Black Bullhead Magician Lake/Cass	1999	3.44 lbs	17 in.
Black Crappie Lincoln Lake/Kent	1947	4.12 lbs	N/A
Brown Bullhead Kalamazoo County	1989	3.62 lbs	17.5 in.
Chinook Salmon Grand River/Kent	1978	46.06 lbs	43.5 in.
Flathead Catfish Maple River/Ionia	1943	47.5 lbs	44 in.
Freshwater Drum Muskegon Lake/Muskegon	1973	26 lb	37.5 in.
Green Sunfish Great Bear Lake/Van Buren	1988	1.31 lb	9.25 in
Hybrid Sunfish Doans Lake/Allegan	1991	1.44 lbs	11.75 in.
Largemouth Bass Big Pine Island Lake/Kent	1934	11.94 lbs	27 in.
Northern Muskellunge Thornapple Lake/Barry	2000	49.75 lbs	51 in.
Northern Hog Sucker St. Joseph River/Berrien	1994	2.54 lbs	19 in.

Gov. Jennifer Granholm hoists a king salmon in the harbor at Grand Haven. Someone else caught the fish. The Governor is being a good sport for photographers. (photo: Ed Hoogterp)

Species Waterway/County	Year	Weight	Length
Quillback Stony Lake/Oceana	2000	8 lbs	25.25 in.
Redear Sunfish Thompson Lake/St. Joseph	2002	1.97 lbs	12.75 in.
Redhorse Croton Pond/Newaygo	1991	12.89 lbs	29.95 in.
Round Whitefish-Menominee Lake Michigan/Ottawa	1992	4.06 lbs	21.5 in.
Warmouth Great Bear Lake/Van Buren	2001	1.38 lbs	11 in.
White Bass Hybrid Kalamazoo River/Allegan	1996	10.75 lb	27.5 in.

(source: Michigan DNR, 2005)

STATE WILDLIFE AREAS

Much of the public land in West Michigan is contained in state wildlife areas, managed by the Department of Natural Resources. The budget for purchasing and maintaining these areas comes from hunting and fishing licenses. The game areas are open for hunting and fishing, and also for such pursuits as hiking and bird-watching. The largest is the Allegan State Game Area, which covers nearly 50,000 acres (78 square miles) near the Kalamazoo River between Allegan and Fennville. Several small areas check in at less than 100 acres.

Here are the state game areas in West Michigan. Maps are available on-line at the Department of Natural Resources Website: **www.Michigan.gov/dnr**

Area Name	County	Acres
Allegan State Game Area	Allegan	49,852
Augusta Creek Fish and Wildlife Area	Kalamazoo	395
Barry State Game Area	Barry	16,759
Blendon Twp. State Game Area	Ottawa	172

Area Name	County	Acres
Boyle Lake State Wildlife Area	Berrien	407
Cannonsburg State Game Area	Kent	1,348
Crane Pond State Game Area	Cass	4,063
Edmore State Game Area	Isabella	3,236
Fabius State Game Area	St. Joseph	93
Flat River State Game Area	Montcalm	11,235
Fulton State Game Area	Kalamazoo	680
Gourdneck State Game Area	Kalamazoo	2,158
Grand Haven State Game Area	Ottawa	713
Grand River State Game Area	Ionia	870
Haymarsh Lake State Game Area	Mecosta	6,760
Keeler State Game Area	Van Buren	396
Kinney Wildlife Area	Van Buren	92
Langston State Game Area	Montcalm	3,100
Leidy Lake State Game Area	St. Joseph	93
Maple River State Game Area	Ionia	233
Martiny Lake State Game Area	Mecosta	6,307
Middleville State Game Area	Barry	4,437
Muskegon State Game Area	Muskegon	15,345
Olive Twp. State Game Area	Ottawa	247
Pentwater River State Game Area	Oceana	2,410
Portland State Game Area	Ionia	2,373
Rogue River State Game Area	Kent	6,135
Saranac-Lowell State Game Area	Ionia	1,863
Spring Creek State Game Area	St. Joseph	82
Stanton State Game Area	Montcalm	4,725
Three Rivers State Game Area	St. Joseph	2,126
Vestaburg State Game Area	Montcalm	2,933
Webster Lake State Game Area	Berrien	26

DEER HUNTING

When people think of deer hunting, they often have an image of a bunch of guys hanging out in a deer camp somewhere up north. There's plenty of that going on, of course, but West Michigan hunters also know there are a lot of deer around the farms and woods in this part of the state.

Department of Natural Resources figures show that, in a typical year, more than 20 percent of the deer "harvested" in the state come from right here in West Michigan. That's not even counting the animals our hunters bring home from those northern deer camps.

Here are the county-by-county estimates for the 2003 deer harvest in West Michigan:

2003 Deer Harvest	Antlered Bucks	Total
Allegan	3,309	6,551
Barry	5,766	11,772
Berrien	1,255	2,677
Cass	2,417	5,396
Ionia	5,774	10,848
Kalamazoo	2,896	6,691
Kent	4,395	8,675
Mecosta	5,422	10,323
Montcalm	7,074	13,145
Muskegon	2,049	4,750
Newaygo	6,195	12,098
Oceana	3,168	5,830
Ottawa	2,613	4,884
St. Joseph	2,444	5,347
Van Buren	2,796	5,421
West Michigan	57,573	114,408
State Total	254,473	499,747

BOATS AND SNOWMOBILES

As a leader in outdoor recreation, West Michigan naturally has a large number of boats and snowmobiles. And the numbers are growing. Here is a county-by-county list of boat and snowmobile registrations for the most recent year available and for 10 years earlier.

Boat/watercraft registrations	2005	1995
Allegan	13,632	11,369
Barry	10,975	9,260
Berrien	15,104	15,227
Cass	10,174	9,324
Ionia	6,170	5,497
Kalamazoo	20,840	20,587
Kent	51,176	46,389
Mecosta	6,054	5,082
Montcalm	8,468	7,313
Muskegon	17,102	15,999
Newaygo	8,220	6,983
Oceana	3,628	3,104
Ottawa	27,778	22,682
St. Joseph	10,047	9,328
Van Buren	9,926	8,960

Boats rest at the docks in Pentwater Lake (photo: Terry Phipps)

Snowmobile registrations	2005	1995
Allegan	6,258	2,841
Barry	3,411	1,582
Berrien	5,058	2,847
Cass	3,180	1,882
Ionia	2,857	1,240
Kalamazoo	5,449	2,869
Kent	16,625	8,747
Mecosta	2,674	1,099
Montcalm	3,820	1,605
Muskegon	8,260	3,392
Newaygo	4,303	1,846
Oceana	3,135	1,107
Ottawa	10,448	4,957
St. Joseph	1,727	946
Van Buren	4,011	1,910

(source: Michigan DNR)

COUNTIES

Photo on previous page: Ed Hoogterp

ALLEGAN COUNTY

Allegan County has it all. Well, almost all.

There are new housing developments, and districts of nationally recognized historic homes. There are orchards, wineries, state parks, and a 50,000 acre state game area.

There is some of Michigan's most productive farmland, to go along with heavy industry and 25 miles of tourist-friendly Lake Michigan shoreline.

There are cosmopolitan tourist destinations such as Saugatuck, where Chicago comes to party. And conservative communities like Hamilton, where it was big news in the 1980s when high school students persuaded the board of education to allow a dance in the school gym.

There is sparkling beauty, as on the Lake Michigan beach at Saugatuck Dunes State Park. And there is pollution, as in the Kalamazoo River Superfund Site, where toxic sludge remains from paper mills that provided jobs and prosperity for more than a century.

There is wealth, especially along the lakeshore and in the expanding suburban territory south of Grand Rapids. And there is poverty, most notably in Lee Township and Pullman, where median incomes are 30 percent below the state average.

Allegan County has all that and more. What it doesn't have, is a big city. Or even a city of 10,000 people.

Allegan County is home to some of Michigan's most productive farms (photo: Ed Hoogterp)

In fact, the biggest town in Allegan County is also the biggest in neighboring Ottawa County. Holland, with a total population of about 35,000, sits astride the county line, with 27,000 residents on the Ottawa side, and 7,248 in Allegan. The next largest municipality in Allegan County is Dorr Township, with 6,579 people.

The other cities, Allegan, Fennville, Otsego, Plainwell, Saugatuck and Wayland, each have between 1,000 and 5,000 residents. (South Haven, mostly in Van Buren County, also squeaks barely across the county line, with 14 residents in Allegan County, according to the 2000 census.)

Allegan County was established by the Michigan Territorial Legislature in 1831. That was 10 years after the signing of the Treaty of Chicago, in which American Indians ceded most of southwest Michigan including what's now Allegan County, to the United States.

The Douglas Union School has been converted to residential space (photo: Terry Phipps)

It's not clear whether the name "Allegan" has any original meaning. Some sources suggest it refers to an American Indian tribe called the "Allegawi." Most believe it's simply a word made up by Henry Rowe Schoolcraft, a geographer and linguist who served as Indian Agent for much of Michigan and was also a member of the territorial Legislature in the 1830s. A number of Michigan counties have names coined by Schoolcraft, who mixed syllables from Greek, Latin and Indian languages.

It was also about 1831 when white settlers began showing up to cut the timber, work the rich soil and harness the streams and rivers for water power. Those first settlers mostly came from New England states, reaching Detroit by boat and then traveling overland on what passed for roads, to West Michigan.

The earliest arrivals, such as Dr. Samuel Foster and his family, found land near the Kalamazoo River, in the southeast corner of the county. Money from eastern capital markets helped build dams and mills on the Kalamazoo River and its tributaries.

Fifteen years later, the opposite corner of the county, near Holland, saw a population boom as religious separatists from the Netherlands moved to Holland and nearby communities.

By 1880, half a century after the first settlers arrived, Allegan County had nearly 38,000 residents. Then, for the next 50 years, growth virtually stopped. From 1880 to 1930, Allegan gained only 1,000 residents, as Michigan's population growth shifted to urban centers.

Today, the county is growing again, especially in the northern tiers of townships near Grand Rapids and Holland. This time, people are moving out of urban areas into the uncrowded farmland.

The local economy has suffered in recent years from the closing of paper mills that once stood along the Kalamazoo River in Plainwell, Otsego and Allegan. About half of all employed people who live in Allegan County travel to jobs elsewhere, mostly in Kent, Ottawa and Kalamazoo counties.

Allegan is one of the state's richest agricultural areas. It leads Michigan counties in hog production, and is in the top five in production of corn, cattle, milk, blueberries and cucumbers.

ALLEGAN COUNTY FACTS

Population in 2000: 105,665

Land area (square miles): 827

Population density (people per square mile): 127.7

Estimated population in 2004: 112,477

Growth 2000-2004: 6.45 percent

2004 election results: Bush, 63.1 percent; Kerry 35.9 percent

County seat: Allegan

Largest cities: Holland (shared with Ottawa County); Allegan, Wayland, Otsego, Plainwell

Total Tax Base (State Equalized Valuation) 2005: $4.9 billion

Agricultural tax base: $568 million (11.6 percent)

Commercial tax base: $443 million (9.1 percent)

Industrial tax base: $225 million (4.6 percent)

Residential tax base: $3.3 billion (67.3 percent)

Traffic fatalities, 2000-2004: 103

Homicides (murder/ manslaughter) 2000-2004: 8

Major rivers: Kalamazoo, Macatawa, Rabbit

Largest lakes: Gun Lake (shared with Barry County), Lake Allegan, Trowbridge Hydro Pond, Otsego Hydro Pond, Hutchins Lake

Active farms in 2002: 1,489

Land in farms: 243,000 acres (45.9 percent of land in county)

ALLEGAN COUNTY IN 2000 CENSUS

White, non-hispanic population: 91 percent

Black population: 1.3 percent

American Indian population: 0.5 percent

Asian population: 0.6 percent

Persons reporting two or more races: 1.3 percent

Hispanic population (may be any race): 5.7 percent

Percent of population under age 18: 28.9 percent

Percent of population age 65 or older: 11.1 percent

Percent, age 25 and over, with four-year college degree: 15.8 percent

Average travel time to work (for workers age 16 and older): 23.4 minutes

Percent of workers who travel to jobs outside the county: 50.18 percent

Total number of homes and apartments (housing units): 43,292

Detached, single family homes: 31,645
 Percent of total housing units: 73.10 percent

Dwellings in structures with 10 or more units: 1,058
 Percent of total housing units: 2.44 percent

Mobile homes: 6,171
 Percent of total housing units: 7.57 percent

Home ownership rate: 82.9 percent

Median value of owner-occupied homes: $115,500

Median household income: $45,813

Income rank among Michigan's 83 counties: 14

Percent of households with income below poverty level: 7.3

LOCAL AREA GROWTH AND ECONOMIC STATISTICS (ALLEGAN COUNTY)

City / Township	2004 Population	2000–2004 Growth	Median Household Income (1999)	Median age of homes in 2000
Allegan city	4,959	2.5%	$39,539	57 years
Allegan township	4,604	13.6%	$40,760	32 years
Casco township	3,097	2.5%	$45,043	28 years
Cheshire township	2,443	6.9%	$40,405	28 years
Clyde township	2,144	0.8%	$42,717	27 years
Dorr township	7,379	12.2%	$60,446	21 years
Fennville city	1,465	3.8%	$39,013	20 years
Fillmore township	2,857	2.1%	$52,969	31 years
Ganges township	2,763	9.8%	$47,143	34 years
Gunplain township	6,193	6.4%	$53,495	24 years
Heath township	3,563	16.3%	$54,545	16 years
Holland city (part)	7,421	2.4%	$40,534	21 years
Hopkins township	2,826	6.6%	$46,296	44 years
Laketown township	5,984	9.7%	$60,893	20 years
Lee township	4,246	2.0%	$30,875	27 years
Leighton township	4,127	12.5%	$51,743	39 years
Manlius township	2,671	-1.1%	$51,653	15 years
Martin township	2,758	8.8%	$40,565	38 years
Monterey township	2,327	11.6%	$48,750	23 years
Otsego city	3,984	2.8%	$37,525	52 years
Otsego township	5,081	3.7%	$48,654	27 years
Overisel township	2,842	8.5%	$52,857	36 years
Plainwell city	4,011	6.6%	$39,590	46 years
Salem township	3,759	8.0%	$48,203	20 years
Saugatuck city	1,053	-4.0%	$44,318	43 years
Saugatuck township	4,031	13.3%	$43,771	24 years
South Haven city (part)	9	-35.7%	N/A	N/A
Trowbridge township	2,545	1.2%	$40,476	26 years
Valley township	1,927	5.5%	$48,672	14 years
Watson township	2,150	4.2%	$49,070	28 years
Wayland city	3,990	2.6%	$41,852	18 years
Wayland township	3,268	7.3%	$46,853	27 years

LOCAL AREA RACE AND ETHNIC POPULATIONS (ALLEGAN COUNTY)

City / Township	Population (2000 census)	White (non-Hispanic)	Black or African-American	Hispanic or Latino (of any race)
Allegan city	4,838	90.5%	4.6%	3.3%
Allegan township	4,054	95.3%	0.3%	2.6%
Casco township	3,021	83.0%	5.1%	10.3%
Cheshire township	2,285	93.5%	3.0%	0.0%
Clyde township	2,126	65.9%	1.4%	31.2%
Dorr township	6,579	95.9%	0.4%	2.5%
Fennville city	1,412	64.3%	4.5%	29.4%
Fillmore township	2,798	88.3%	1.4%	6.2%
Ganges township	2,516	85.6%	0.0%	13.7%
Gunplain township	5,821	96.0%	0.6%	0.2%
Heath township	3,063	95.5%	0.1%	2.6%
Holland city (part)	7,248	76.6%	3.1%	17.0%
Hopkins township	2,651	92.2%	0.2%	4.7%
Laketown township	5,453	94.1%	0.6%	4.7%
Lee township	4,164	66.1%	7.4%	22.2%
Leighton township	3,668	98.9%	0.0%	0.8%
Manlius township	2,700	87.7%	1.3%	10.5%
Martin township	2,536	94.4%	0.2%	3.4%
Monterey township	2,085	93.9%	0.4%	2.4%
Otsego city	3,876	96.7%	0.8%	0.5%
Otsego township	4,899	94.9%	0.8%	0.4%
Overisel township	2,620	93.5%	0.1%	4.6%
Plainwell city	3,761	95.5%	0.0%	2.6%
Salem township	3,480	96.4%	0.0%	1.6%
Saugatuck city	1,097	95.6%	1.2%	2.5%
Saugatuck township	3,558	92.0%	0.1%	6.7%
South Haven city (part)	14	100.0%	0.0%	0.0%
Trowbridge township	2,515	95.5%	1.1%	1.3%
Valley township	1,827	93.8%	2.2%	2.2%
Watson township	2,064	97.2%	0.1%	1.9%
Wayland city	3,889	95.1%	0.0%	4.3%
Wayland township	3,047	95.5%	0.0%	1.8%

BARRY COUNTY

Stand along M-37 in Thornapple Township on any workday morning, and you can witness an essential fact of life in Barry County.

That endless line of headlights snaking along the highway is a sign of the most powerful force in the local economy: Workers heading north out of Hastings, Middleville and surrounding areas to their jobs in Kentwood, Wyoming and Grand Rapids.

Nearly six of every 10 employed Barry County residents drive across the county line for work. And the money they bring home helps put Barry well above the state average in terms of household and family income.

Census Bureau estimates for 2003 place the median household income in Barry County at just over $48,000. That's about 4 percent above the statewide median. It's also the second highest in West Michigan, trailing only Ottawa County.

Barry County has a lower population than any of the adjacent counties. There's no large city, no daily newspaper, no television station. The county has little industry, no major shopping centers and not a single mile of expressway (though four expressways run just outside the boundaries).

So how can the residents be making higher incomes than the folks in supposedly more developed counties?

The answer lies in the old real estate cliché: Location, location, location.

While Barry is largely rural, it's surrounded by urban areas: Grand Rapids to the north, Lansing to the east, and Kalamazoo and Battle Creek to the south.

Charlton Park, on the Thornapple River, provides a glimpse of Barry County's past (photo courtesy of Charlton Park)

Residents drive to work in those cities, then return home each evening to their oasis of lakes, forests and farms.

Settlers who came to Barry County in the early 1830s found a number of small Indian villages on the lakes and rivers in the area. From about 1836 to 1852, the Baptist minister Leonard Slater had a mission in Prairieville Township. Chief Noonday, who had been leader of an Ottawa Village at Grand Rapids, was among those who moved to Prairieville with Slater.

Most of the native people were ultimately forced by the United States government to move out of Barry County. Ottawa were sent to a reservation in Oceana County, and Potawatomi relocated to Kansas.

The county is named for William T. Barry, who was United States Postmaster General in the administration of President Andrew Jackson. (Jackson was president in the 1830s, when the Michigan territory was trying to gain admission to the union. A number of counties were named for members of Jackson's cabinet.)

The first white settler in the county was Amasa Parker, who arrived in 1831. Hastings, the county seat, is named for a Detroit Banker, Eurotas P. Hastings, who sold the site to local developers in 1836.

Barry grew more slowly than some of its neighbors, in part because settlers were drawn to the emerging cities of Grand Rapids and Kalamazoo. The lack of a major river and the presence of heavy timber in some townships also made development a challenge.

Historian Roger Rosentreter, editor of *Michigan History Magazine,* wrote that the first railroad didn't reach Hastings until well after the Civil War, and cows were roaming the streets of the county seat as late as the 1880s.

By 1880, the county had about 25,000 residents. It stayed at about that level for the next 70 years, before resuming steady growth in the 1950s.

The county's largest employer is Bradford White Corp., a manufacturer of furnaces and water heaters, with about 1,000 workers at a plant in Middleville. Other major job-providers include Pennock Hospital in Hastings, with about 650 employees and Flex- Fab Horizons International, a supplier to aerospace and transportation industries, with about 500 workers.

About half the county's total land area is in agriculture, with much of that devoted to corn, soybeans and dairy farms. Barry's 43 dairy farms produced something over 250 million pounds of milk in 2003.

The Yankee Springs Recreation Area on Gun Lake is Michigan's sixth busiest state park, with more than 800,000 visitors a year. The park offers boating, swimming, camping, and miles of trails.

The Gilmore Car Museum at Hickory Corners is one of the

region's top automotive destinations, with 200 vintage cars in a restored farm setting.

Historic Charlton Park, a recreated village and museum on the Thornapple river near Hastings, gives visitors a feel for the region in the late 19th century.

One of Barry's newest attractions is the Pierce Cedar Creek Institute, an ecological education center in Baltimore Township, south of Hastings. The 600 acres of forest, wetland and prairies, operated by a private foundation, has a visitor center and miles of trails for hiking and skiing. It's used for ecological research by a consortium of colleges and universities.

BARRY COUNTY FACTS

Population in 2000: 56,755

Land area (square miles): 556

Population density (people per square mile): 102.1

Estimated population in 2004: 59,371

Growth 2000-2004: 4.61 percent

2004 election results: Bush, 61.6 percent; Kerry, 37.4 percent

County seat: Hastings

Largest cities: Hastings, Middleville, Nashville

Total Tax Base (State Equalized Valuation) 2005: $2.3 billion

Agricultural tax base: $299 million (12.8 percent)

Commercial tax base: $146 million (6.2 percent)

Industrial tax base: $18 million (0.8 percent)

Residential tax base: $3.3 billion (76.5 percent)

Traffic fatalities, 2000-2004: 70

Homicides (murder/manslaughter) 2000-2004: 6

Major rivers: Thornapple

Largest lakes: Gun Lake (shared with Allegan County), Gull Lake (shared with Kalamazoo County), Pine Lake, Upper Crooked Lake, Wall Lake.

Active farms in 2002: 1,053

Land in farms: 182,000 acres (51.1 percent of land in county)

DEMOGRAPHICS FROM 2000 CENSUS:

White, non-hispanic population: 96.5 percent

Black population: 0.2 percent

American Indian population: 0.5 percent

Asian population: 0.3 percent

Persons reporting two or more races: 1.1 percent

Hispanic population (may be any race): 1.5 percent

Percent of population under age 18: 27.2 percent

Percent of population age 65 or older: 11.8 percent

Percent of adult population (age 25-plus) with four-year college degree: 14.7 percent

Average travel time to work (for workers age 16 and older): 26.9 minutes

Percent of workers who travel to jobs outside the county: 59.24 percent

Total number of homes and apartments (housing units): 23,876

Detached, single-family homes: 19,891
  Percent of total housing units: 83.31 percent

Dwellings in structures with 10 or more units: 361
  Percent of total housing units: 1.51 percent

Mobile homes or house trailers: 2,372
  Percent of total housing units: 9.93 percent

Home ownership rate: 85.8 percent

Median value of owner-occupied homes: $107,100

Median household income: $46,820

Income rank among Michigan's 83 counties: 11

Percent of households with income below poverty level: 5.5 percent

LOCAL AREA GROWTH AND ECONOMIC STATISTICS (BARRY COUNTY)

City / Township	2004 Population	2000–2004 Growth	Median Household Income (1999)	Median age of homes in 2000
Assyria township	2,039	6.2%	$50,192	32 years
Baltimore township	1,970	6.3%	$45,761	30 years
Barry township	3,612	3.4%	$45,339	40 years
Carlton township	2,464	5.4%	$46,359	32 years
Castleton township	3,621	4.0%	$33,929	46 years
Hastings city	7,151	0.8%	$39,033	48 years
Hastings charter township	3,049	3.9%	$51,316	32 years
Hope township	3,431	4.3%	$41,983	33 years
Irving township	2,836	5.4%	$50,532	19 years
Johnstown township	3,181	3.6%	$50,216	37 years
Maple Grove township	1,595	7.8%	$51,200	45 years
Orangeville township	3,452	3.8%	$44,348	25 years
Prairieville township	3,455	8.1%	$51,071	31 years
Rutland charter township	4,023	9.4%	$52,065	26 years
Thornapple township	6,892	3.0%	$53,333	23 years
Woodland township	2,240	5.0%	$38,920	48 years
Yankee Springs township	4,360	3.2%	$52,661	20 years

LOCAL AREA RACE AND ETHNIC POPULATIONS (BARRY COUNTY)

City / Township	Population (2000 census)	White (non-Hispanic)	Black or African-American	Hispanic or Latino (of any race)
Assyria township	1,912	97.6%	0.8%	0.6%
Baltimore township	1,845	96.0%	0.0%	1.1%
Barry township	3,489	97.9%	1.2%	0.5%
Carlton township	2,331	96.7%	0.9%	1.5%
Castleton township	3,475	96.5%	0.2%	0.9%
Hastings city	7,095	96.4%	0.2%	1.8%
Hastings charter township	2,930	98.0%	0.0%	0.0%
Hope township	3,283	95.2%	0.3%	1.8%
Irving township	2,682	98.4%	0.1%	0.0%
Johnstown township	3,067	96.3%	0.8%	1.1%
Maple Grove township	1,471	98.1%	0.0%	0.3%
Orangeville township	3,321	95.9%	0.6%	1.8%
Prairieville township	3,175	98.2%	0.3%	1.1%
Rutland charter township	3,646	96.8%	0.2%	0.4%
Thornapple township	6,685	94.9%	0.0%	2.2%
Woodland township	2,129	96.9%	0.3%	1.4%
Yankee Springs township	4,219	96.1%	0.4%	0.4%

BERRIEN COUNTY

Berrien County, tucked up against Lake Michigan and the Indiana border in the state's far southwest corner, would seem to be just about a perfect place to live and work.

The county has 50 miles of sandy and scenic Lake Michigan shoreline. It has history dating back to the French explorers Marquette and LaSalle. It has agriculture and tourism that have combined to produce half a dozen new wineries. It has freeway and passenger rail connections to Chicago and Detroit. It has highly regarded museums and nature centers. It has plenty of open space. And it's only a 90-minute drive from downtown Chicago.

Despite all those attributes, Berrien has the slowest-growing population in West Michigan. In 2004 it had about the same number of people as in 1970.

Local officials say the area is just about ready to begin growing again. After all, the strength of the region has been established through 300 years of history.

Marquette came through here in the early 1670s, while returning to the Straits of Mackinac from his voyage of discovery to the Mississippi River. He passed through again a few years later to establish a mission for Indians in northern Indiana.

LaSalle made his appearance in 1679. He built a base called Fort Miami at the mouth of the St. Joseph River, explored the area, and later hiked across the Lower Peninsula to get back to Canada.

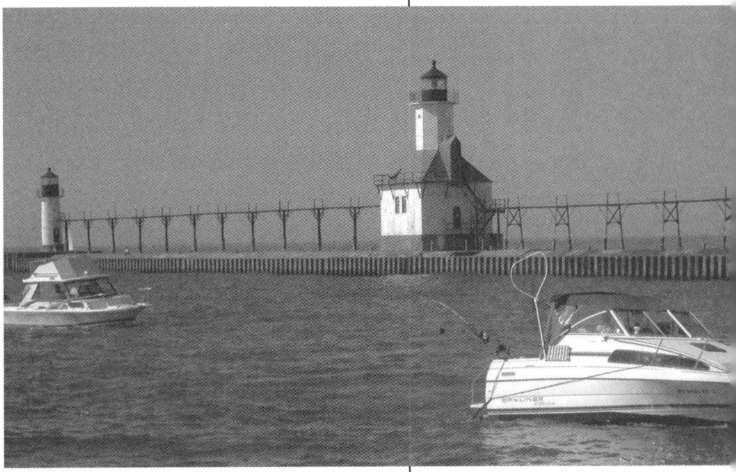

Fishing boats pass the lighthouse on the way into St. Joseph Harbor (photo: Ed Hoogterp)

The St. Joe River was the closest thing to a Michigan highway in those days. Explorers, trappers, missionaries, Indians and traders moved up and down the stream. The Catholic Mission of St. Joseph was established on the river at Niles in the 1680s, and a French military outpost, Fort St. Joseph, followed within a few years.

The fort came under British control following the French and Indian War, and was abandoned around the time of the American revolution.

Joseph Bertrand, with his Indian wife Madeleine, opened a trading post about 1807, near where the St. Joseph dips into present day Indiana. A new mission – this time staffed by Baptists – was set up at Niles after Indians ceded the area to the United States government in the 1821 Treaty of Chicago.

Permanent settlement began in 1823, when Squire Isaac Thompson arrived in Niles. By the 1830s, local farmers were shipping fruit to Chicago, and for the next 140 years or so, Berrien grew steadily. It was a prime farming district, a popular tourist destination for metro Chicago and, by the middle of the 20th century, a major manufacturing area. Whites from rural areas, and African Americans from Chicago and the South turned Benton Harbor into a boom town as they moved there to work in the local factories.

In the last third of the 20th century, Berrien faced more than its share of troubles. Highways, air travel, and changing tastes killed off many of the resorts that made up the heart of the tourist economy. Racial animosity in Benton Harbor spilled over into riots in the late 1960s. Thousands of factory workers lost their jobs when plants such as Clark Equipment Co. closed in the 1970s and later.

Today, beach towns like New Buffalo and St. Joseph are busy in summer. Much of the former resort economy has been transformed into a real estate market as metro Chicagoans buy second homes, condos and "dockominiums" on the waterfront.

Perhaps the most positive trend is the merging of farming and tourism into what is called "agri-tourism." Visitors come from Michigan and surrounding states to sample the wares of the local wineries. Farms such as Tree-Mendus Fruit Farm in Eau Clair are also popular destinations for travelers.

Local officials also hope the economy will get a push from a 10-year project to develop the waterfront north of the river in St. Joseph and Benton Harbor, and from a proposed casino near I-94. The Pokagon Band of Potawatomi Indians signed a state compact in 1998 allowing them to build a casino near New Buffalo. Opponents have held up construction with a series of legal challenges.

Berrien's climate is moderated by Lake Michigan, which makes it an ideal spot for fruit and other specialty crops. It's Michigan's top grape-producing county and is in the top five for apples, blueberries, tart cherries and asparagus.

Much of the lakeshore is occupied by resort villages such as Michiana, Grand Beach, Lakeside and Shoreham. But there remains considerable access, with Grand Mere and Warren Dunes state parks, along with public beaches at New Buffalo, Bridgman, Stevensville, Benton Harbor, St. Joseph, Hagar Township and Covert.

The county is named for John M. Berrien, who was president Andrew Jackson's attorney general.

BERRIEN COUNTY FACTS

Population in 2000: 162,453

Land area (square miles): 571

Population density (people per square mile): 284.5

Estimated population, 2004: 163,125

Growth 2000-2004: 0.41 percent

2004 election results: Bush, 55.0 percent; Kerry, 44.0 percent

County seat: St. Joseph

Largest cities: Niles, Benton Harbor, St. Joseph, Buchanan

Total Tax Base (State Equalized Valuation) 2005: $7.2 billion

Agricultural tax base: $446 million (6.2 percent)

Commercial tax base: $690 million (9.6 percent)

Industrial tax base: $667 million (9.3 percent)

Residential tax base: $4.9 billion (68.6 percent)

Traffic fatalities, 2000-2004: 128

Homicides (murder/ manslaughter) 2000-2004: 35

Major rivers: St. Joseph, Galien, Paw Paw, Dowagiac

Largest lakes: Paw Paw, Berrien Springs Hydro pond, Buchanan, Smith, Pipestone

Active farms in 2002: 1,093

Land in farms: 174,000 acres (47.6 percent of land in county)

DEMOGRAPHICS FROM 2000 CENSUS:

White, non-hispanic population: 78.1 percent

Black population: 15.9 percent

American Indian population: 0.4 percent

Asian population: 1.1 percent

Persons reporting two or more races: 1.6 percent

Hispanic population (may be any race): 3.0 percent

Percent of population under age 18: 26.0 percent

Percent of population age 65 or older: 14.4 percent

Percent of adult population (age 25-plus) with four-year college degree: 19.6 percent

Average travel time to work (for workers age 16 and older): 20.0 minutes

Percent of workers who travel to jobs outside the county: 18.60

Total number of homes and apartments (housing units): 73,445

Detached, single-family homes: 54,563
Percent of total housing units: 74.29 percent

Dwellings in structures with 10 or more units: 4,796
Percent of total housing units: 6.49 percent

Mobile homes or house trailers: 4,409
Percent of total housing units: 6.0 percent

Home ownership rate: 72.3 percent

Median value of owner-occupied homes: $94.700

Median household income: $38,567

Income rank among Michigan's 83 counties: 37

Percent of households with income below poverty level: 13.0 percent

LOCAL AREA GROWTH AND ECONOMIC STATISTICS (BERRIEN COUNTY)

City / Township	2004 Population	2000–2004 Growth	Median Household Income (1999)	Median age of homes in 2000
Bainbridge township	3,180	1.53%	$38,750	38 years
Baroda township	2,939	2.05%	$44,219	29 years
Benton charter township	16,102	-1.84%	$25,942	39 years
Benton Harbor city	10,851	-2.96%	$17,471	49 years
Berrien township	5,298	4.39%	$46,293	29 years
Bertrand township	2,480	4.20%	$55,183	41 years
Bridgman city	2,452	0.82%	$48,292	29 years
Buchanan city	4,575	-2.26%	$34,244	47 years
Buchanan township	3,616	3.02%	$40,503	32 years
Chikaming township	3,705	0.73%	$47,778	49 years
Coloma city	1,544	-3.20%	$38,882	45 years
Coloma charter township	5,254	0.71%	$40,029	35 years
Galien township	1,664	3.29%	$37,434	44 years
Hagar township	3,970	0.15%	$38,614	43 years
Lake charter township	3,219	2.39%	$49,764	30 years
Lincoln charter township	14,340	2.78%	$53,718	28 years
New Buffalo city	2,268	3.09%	$41,658	36 years
New Buffalo township	2,603	5.47%	$46,991	37 years
Niles city	11,867	-2.72%	$31,208	52 years
Niles township	13,501	1.32%	$37,794	39 years
Oronoko charter township	9,755	-0.89%	$35,980	33 years
Pipestone township	2,569	3.84%	$41,440	40 years
Royalton township	4,290	10.34%	$69,375	27 years
St. Joseph city	8,701	-1.00%	$37,032	53 years
St. Joseph charter township	10,022	-0.20%	$54,158	36 years
Sodus township	2,144	0.23%	$33,804	30 years
Three Oaks township	2,904	-1.53%	$36,989	50 years
Watervliet city	1,803	-2.17%	$38,681	48 years
Watervliet township	3,460	2.00%	$39,152	36 years
Weesaw township	2,049	-0.77%	$41,434	51 years

LOCAL AREA RACE AND ETHNIC POPULATIONS (BERRIEN COUNTY)

City / Township	Population (2000 census)	White (non-Hispanic)	Black or African-American	Hispanic or Latino (of any race)
Bainbridge township	3,132	85.6%	0.3%	12.8%
Baroda township	2,880	97.8%	0.1%	1.3%
Benton charter township	16,404	41.3%	53.4%	3.3%
Benton Harbor city	11,182	6.7%	91.7%	0.6%
Berrien township	5,075	83.6%	5.5%	6.8%
Bertrand township	2,380	97.0%	0.0%	0.7%
Bridgman city	2,428	94.0%	1.6%	1.8%
Buchanan city	4,681	84.7%	11.6%	1.9%
Buchanan township	3,510	98.3%	0.0%	0.2%
Chikaming township	3,678	95.2%	3.2%	0.4%
Coloma city	1,595	96.4%	0.7%	0.9%
Coloma charter township	5,217	94.3%	0.7%	2.1%
Galien township	1,611	96.0%	0.4%	0.7%
Hagar township	3,964	94.1%	1.2%	3.3%
Lake charter township	3,148	97.2%	0.9%	0.4%
Lincoln charter township	13,952	95.5%	0.8%	0.8%
New Buffalo city	2,200	96.0%	0.5%	1.6%
New Buffalo township	2,468	93.7%	3.0%	1.3%
Niles city	12,199	79.8%	11.5%	3.6%
Niles township	13,325	92.8%	3.3%	1.8%
Oronoko charter township	9,843	63.2%	17.5%	8.1%
Pipestone township	2,474	81.6%	4.6%	11.4%
Royalton township	3,888	92.2%	2.3%	2.4%
St. Joseph city	8,789	90.2%	5.3%	1.0%
St. Joseph charter township	10,042	84.0%	11.3%	2.0%
Sodus township	2,139	82.0%	6.5%	8.5%
Three Oaks township	2,949	94.1%	0.6%	1.9%
Watervliet city	1,843	95.2%	0.0%	1.0%
Watervliet township	3,392	94.8%	0.8%	3.5%
Weesaw township	2,065	96.0%	0.0%	1.3%

CASS COUNTY

Cass County is a land of lakes, farms and small towns a few miles inland from Lake Michigan on the Indiana border.

Cass has become somewhat isolated in recent decades because of a state expressway system that directs traffic around the edges of the county. I-94 runs through Van Buren County, just to the north, while a new US-31 expressway runs through Niles, just west of the county line.

The main two-lane road through the county is US-12, the historical Chicago Road that follows the path of ancient Indian trails between Detroit and Chicago.

Early white settlers found earthworks and other evidence that Indians had been farming the fertile soil here for hundreds, if not thousands, of years.

Uzziel Putnam, the county's first permanent settler, was something of a nomad, who had lived in five different states before moving his family to the Pokagon Prairie in 1825. By the time the Territorial Legislature officially created Cass County, in 1829, the population was up to about 900.

The county is named for Lewis Cass, who was Michigan's second territorial governor and later served as President Andrew Jackson's secretary of war. At 492 square miles, it is the smallest West Michigan county, in terms of land area.

A young naturalist walks the wildflower trail in Dowagiac Woods (photo courtesy of Michigan Nature Association)

The county seat is at Cassopolis. The largest town is Dowagiac.

Cass County's early history involved more than just white settlers moving in from other states.

The region had been opened for settlement after Indian tribes ceded the area to the U.S. government in the 1821 Treaty of Chicago. Twelve years later, the federal government forced most of the local Indians to move west to Kansas. One group that escaped that order was the band of Potawatomi led by Leopold Pokagon.

Pokagon's group was allowed to stay in Silver Creek Township, near Dowagiac, apparently because their leader had converted to Christianity and purchased land for his people. Their descendents, the Pokagon Band of Potawatomi Indians, won federal recognition as a tribe in the 1990s. They have state approval to build a casino near New Buffalo, in Berrien County. That plan has been held up for years because of legal challenges.

Cass County's Calvin Township was the site of one of the largest communities of African-American farmers in the northern United States. As early as 1836, local Quakers were providing aid to blacks who had either been freed or had escaped along routes of the Underground Railroad that passed through Michigan.

In 1849, John Saunders of Virginia freed his family's slaves and built a cabin for each of them in Calvin Township. The African American farmers became an important part of the county's economy. The community remained intact well into the second half of the 20th century. A few black-owned farms remain, and the 2000 census found that more than 20 percent of Calvin Township's population was black, an unusually high figure in rural Michigan.

For most of the 20th century, Cass County was known for small farms that produced field crops and hogs.

The pigs are still there – some 280,000 sold in 2002 – but the small farms are disappearing. Today, the market for pork is controlled by a few large companies. Farmers who stayed in the business often grow thousands of animals inside large buildings under contract with processing firms. That system makes for low-cost meat. But it has raised concerns because it tends to concentrate manure and odors in amounts that can be overpowering to nearby residents, and because antibiotics are routinely used as part of raising the animals in such close confinement.

A few long-time Cass County farmers have bucked the trend by raising small herds for such specialty food marketers as Whole Foods Market or Niman Ranch. Those companies pay a premium for animals raised with access to sunlight and pasture, and without the use of antibiotics or certain food supplements.

In addition to hogs, Cass County farmers produce corn, cucumbers, snap beans, potatoes and other crops. About 60 percent of the county's land is in agriculture.

Dowagiac was an industrial town early in the 20th century, with the famous Round Oak Stove Co. employing some 1,400 people. While some industry remains, more than six of every 10 workers drive to jobs outside the county. Many of those jobs are in northern Indiana, around Elkhart and South Bend.

Though it has a limited amount of public land, the county is home to a few impressive natural areas. At the Fred Russ Memorial Forest in Newton Woods in Volinia Township, Michigan State University watches over one of the few slivers of virgin hardwood forest left in southern Michigan.

And the Dowagiac Woods sanctuary, owned by the Michigan Nature Association, is considered one of the region's best spots for spring wildflowers.

CASS COUNTY FACTS

Population in 2000: 51,104

Land area (square miles): 492

Population density (people per square mile): 103.8

Estimated population, 2004: 51,761

Growth 2000-2004: 1.29 percent

2004 election results: Bush, 57.1 percent; Kerry, 42.0 percent

County seat: Cassopolis

Largest cities: Dowagiac is the only city in Cass County

Total Tax Base (State Equalized Valuation) 2005: $2.1 billion

Agricultural tax base: $337 million (15.8 percent)

Commercial tax base: $89 million (4.2 percent)

Industrial tax base: $37.7 million (1.8 percent)

Residential tax base: $1.6 billion (73.8 percent)

Traffic fatalities, 2000-2004: 65

Homicides (murder/ manslaughter) 2000-2004: 8

Major rivers: St. Joseph, Dowagiac, Rocky

Largest lakes: Diamond, Corey, Magician (shared with Van Buren County), Indian, Eagle

Active farms in 2002: 808

Land in farms: 189,000 acres (60.0 percent of land in county)

DEMOGRAPHICS FROM 2000 CENSUS:

White, non-hispanic population: 88.2 percent

Black population: 6.1 percent

American Indian population: 0.8 percent

Asian population: 0.5 percent

Persons reporting two or more races: 2.1 percent

Hispanic population (may be any race): 2.4 percent

Percent of population under age 18: 25.5 percent

Percent of population age 65 or older: 13.6 percent

Percent of adult population (age 25-plus) with four-year college degree: 12.1 percent

Percent of workers who travel to jobs outside the county: 61.44

Average travel time to work (for workers age 16 and older): 24.2 minutes

Total number of homes and apartments (housing units): 23,884

Detached, single-family homes: 19,711
Percent of total housing units: 82.53 percent

Dwellings in structures with 10 or more units: 466
Percent of total housing units: 1.95 percent

Mobile homes or house trailers: 2,565
Percent of total housing units: 10.74 percent

Home ownership rate: 81.9 percent

Median value of owner-occupied homes: $91,800

Median household income: $41,264

Income rank among Michigan's 83 counties: 23

Percent of households with income below poverty level: 9.9 percent

LOCAL AREA GROWTH AND ECONOMIC STATISTICS (CASS COUNTY)

City / Township	2004 Population	2000–2004 Growth	Median Household Income (1999)	Median age of homes in 2000
Calvin township	2,115	3.63%	$42,171	25 years
Dowagiac city	5,968	-0.96%	$29,926	53 years
Howard township	6,301	-0.13%	$41,477	35 years
Jefferson township	2,603	8.41%	$43,633	26 years
La Grange township	3,395	-2.39%	$35,566	45 years
Marcellus township	2,664	-1.77%	$39,306	44 years
Mason township	2,710	7.80%	$41,902	25 years
Milton township	2,881	8.88%	$53,750	29 years
Newberg township	1,678	-1.47%	$43,466	40 years
Niles city (part)	9	80.00%	N/A	N/A
Ontwa township	5,899	0.58%	$43,488	34 years
Penn township	1,855	-2.47%	$38,375	40 years
Pokagon township	2,242	2.75%	$38,850	39 years
Porter township	3,885	2.40%	$51,320	33 years
Silver Creek township	3,503	0.34%	$42,572	35 years
Volinia township	1,165	-0.77%	$38,900	40 years
Wayne township	2,888	0.94%	$42,816	34 years

LOCAL AREA RACE AND ETHNIC POPULATIONS (CASS COUNTY)

City / Township	Population (2000 census)	White (non-Hispanic)	Black or African-American	Hispanic or Latino (of any race)
Calvin township	2,041	68.7%	22.7%	1.1%
Dowagiac city	6,147	76.7%	13.8%	2.8%
Howard township	6,309	93.7%	3.2%	1.6%
Jefferson township	2,401	92.6%	4.5%	0.3%
La Grange township	3,340	70.8%	18.7%	3.2%
Marcellus township	2,712	97.0%	0.7%	0.9%
Mason township	2,514	97.5%	0.0%	0.4%
Milton township	2,646	93.6%	1.6%	2.3%
Newberg township	1,703	94.2%	1.1%	2.7%
Niles city (part)	5	N/A	N/A	N/A
Ontwa township	5,865	97.4%	0.1%	0.1%
Penn township	1,902	80.5%	14.4%	0.3%
Pokagon township	2,199	83.7%	7.1%	5.2%
Porter township	3,794	95.9%	0.2%	0.5%
Silver Creek township	3,491	87.5%	0.3%	10.8%
Volinia township	1,174	94.5%	2.3%	0.7%
Wayne township	2,861	92.2%	1.1%	3.3%

IONIA COUNTY

Ionia County is a square – 24 miles on a side – of flat and rolling farmland that serves as a transition between West Michigan and Mid-Michigan.

The county's western townships, around Saranac and Clarksville, look increasingly toward Grand Rapids for employment and "big-city" services such as health care and entertainment, while eastern townships near Portland and Pewamo look toward Lansing.

At the center is the city of Ionia itself – 33 miles from Grand Rapids and 38 from Lansing. The city of Ionia, with about 12,000 residents, is the county's largest town, and serves as the county seat. It has an economic base that includes both industry and a cluster of state prisons.

A number of buildings in and around the city are built with Ionia Sandstone, an attractive, colorfully grained rock that was quarried near the Grand River.

Most of the early settlers in this part of Michigan were farmers. Ionia County remains an agricultural region, with more than 60 percent of the land classed as farmland.

Ionia farmers plant some 75,000 acres of corn and 60,000 acres of soybeans each year, with the rich land providing crop yields that often rank among the top Michigan counties.

The county's dairy farms produced some 230 million pounds of milk in 2003, and Ionia ranked in the top five Michigan counties in the total number of cattle and calves. The county also has commercial egg farms and a significant number of hogs and pigs.

A pedestrian bridge crosses the Looking Glass River where it enters the Grand River in Portland (photo: Ed Hoogterp)

The county's agricultural showcase, the Ionia Free Fair, is one of the state's most popular summer events.

The most outstanding natural feature in the county is the Grand River, which bends north out of the Lansing area to flow through Danby and Portland townships, then turns west to meander through the county's midsection.

Archeologists have found evidence that Indians camped along the river as long as 10,000 years ago. Native American villagers were still farming and collecting maple syrup near the river when the first Europeans arrived in the region.

The towns of Saranac, Ionia, Lyons and Portland all lie along the Grand. Belding, the county's second largest city, is on the Flat River, which flows into the Grand.

The county was created by the Territorial Legislature in 1831, and named for a region of ancient Greece.

The first significant European settlement occurred two years later, when New York native Samuel Dexter led a party of 63 pioneers to land he had purchased on the Grand River at the present site of the city of Ionia. By 1834 the little settlement was on its way, with a sawmill, flour mill, grocery store, school and church.

Lucius Lyon, a government surveyor who had a hand in the early history of several West Michigan cities, began building the city of Lyons in 1836, six miles upstream from Ionia.

Lyon would become one of Michigan's first senators when the state was admitted to the Union in 1837. He envisioned his town as a major metropolis, and possibly even the state capital. But it was not to be. The honor of being county seat went to Ionia, the Legislature decided to place the state capital at Lansing, and the railroad skipped Lyons in favor of nearby Muir.

Lyons does have the distinction of being the site of the first bridge over the Grand River between Grand Haven and Jackson.

If the river was the main thoroughfare through Ionia County in the early years, today that function is handled by the I-96 expressway, which carries more than 30,000 vehicles a day through the county's rural areas.

The largest swath of public land is the Ionia State Recreation Area, which stretches along the Grand River and Sessions Lake near Saranac. The Flat River State Game Area and Portland State Game Area are also in the county.

Ionia's most affluent townships are those near the freeway and closest to the edges of the county, where it's convenient to commute to work in Grand Rapids or Lansing. About half of the county's employed residents work in other counties, according to the 2000 census.

IONIA COUNTY FACTS

Population in 2000: 61,518

Land area (square miles): 573

Population density (people per square mile: 107.3

Estimated population, 2004: 64,378

Growth 2000-2004: 4.65 percent

2004 election results:
Bush, 60.2 percent;
Kerry, 38.6 percent

County seat: Ionia

Largest cities:
Ionia, Belding, Portland

Total Tax Base (State Equalized Valuation) 2005: $1.8 billion

Agricultural tax base:
$351 million (19.9 percent)

Commercial tax base:
$143 million (8.1 percent)

Industrial tax base:
$32 million (1.8 percent)

Residential tax base:
$1.1 billion (64.6 percent)

Traffic fatalities, 2000-2004: 62

Homicides (murder/ manslaughter) 2000-2004: 3

Major rivers:
Grand, Maple, Flat

Largest lakes: Webber, Jordan, Long, Morrison, Sessions

Active farms in 2002: 1,146

Land in farms: 230,000 acres (62.7 percent of land in county)

DEMOGRAPHICS FROM 2000 CENSUS:

White, non-hispanic population: 93.2 percent

Black population: 4.6 percent

American Indian population: 0.6 percent

Asian population: 0.3 percent

Persons reporting two or more races: 1.5 percent

Hispanic population (may be any race): 2.8 percent

Percent of population under age 18: 26.9 percent

Percent of population age 65 or older: 10.0 percent

Percent of adult population (age 25-plus) with four-year college degree: 10.8 percent

Average travel time to work (for workers age 16 and older): 27.6 minutes

Percent of workers who travel to jobs outside the county: 51.8 percent

Total number of homes and apartments (housing units): 22,006

Detached, single-family homes: 16,009
Percent of total housing units: 72.75 percent

Dwellings in structures with 10 or more units: 811
Percent of total housing units: 3.69 percent

Mobile homes or house trailers: 3,240
Percent of total housing units: 14.72 percent

Home ownership rate: 80.0 percent

Median value of owner-occupied homes: $94,400

Median household income: $43,074

Income rank among Michigan's 83 counties: 19

Percent of households with income below poverty level: 8.7 percent

LOCAL AREA GROWTH AND ECONOMIC STATISTICS (IONIA COUNTY)

City / Township	2004 Population	2000–2004 Growth	Median Household Income (1999)	Median age of homes in 2000
Belding city	5,870	-0.12%	$32,878	44 years
Berlin township	1,949	6.62%	$48,158	33 years
Boston township	5,107	2.94%	$43,172	26 years
Campbell township	2,364	5.39%	$50,370	37 years
Danby township	2,830	4.97%	$55,662	27 years
Easton township	2,954	4.20%	$40,493	33 years
Ionia city	12,359	7.21%	$38,289	58 years
Ionia township	3,831	4.42%	$44,659	25 years
Keene township	1,784	7.47%	$50,114	23 years
Lyons township	3,587	4.09%	$38,750	36 years
North Plains township	1,481	8.42%	$39,833	40 years
Odessa township	4,165	3.20%	$40,625	46 years
Orange township	1,142	9.81%	$50,217	40 years
Orleans township	2,866	4.75%	$42,665	30 years
Otisco township	2,355	4.99%	$45,042	28 years
Portland city	3,806	0.45%	$45,656	47 years
Portland township	2,579	4.84%	$59,700	27 years
Ronald township	2,032	6.78%	$45,952	29 years
Sebewa township	1,317	9.57%	$47,065	51 years

LOCAL AREA RACE AND ETHNIC POPULATIONS (IONIA COUNTY)

City / Township	Population (2000 census)	White (non-Hispanic)	Black or African-American	Hispanic or Latino (of any race)
Belding city	5,877	96.6%	0.0%	1.9%
Berlin township	2,787	79.8%	15.2%	2.0%
Boston township	4,961	97.8%	0.3%	1.1%
Campbell township	2,243	97.4%	0.5%	1.7%
Danby township	2,696	98.1%	0.0%	0.2%
Easton township	2,835	96.0%	0.0%	1.5%
Ionia city	10,569	69.0%	21.2%	5.5%
Ionia township	3,669	97.1%	0.1%	1.5%
Keene township	1,660	94.8%	0.0%	2.5%
Lyons township	3,446	96.7%	0.1%	1.9%
North Plains township	1,366	94.8%	0.0%	2.1%
Odessa township	4,036	92.2%	0.4%	4.4%
Orange township	1,040	96.3%	0.2%	0.8%
Orleans township	2,736	97.3%	0.0%	1.2%
Otisco township	2,243	97.7%	0.0%	1.7%
Portland city	3,789	98.8%	0.3%	0.2%
Portland township	2,460	97.0%	0.0%	2.0%
Ronald township	1,903	94.0%	0.5%	3.6%
Sebewa township	1,202	98.5%	0.0%	1.1%

KALAMAZOO COUNTY

When outsiders think of Kalamazoo County, they inevitably focus on the central city of the same name. That's fine – the city of Kalamazoo has plenty to offer – but the outlying towns and rural areas also have their own stories to tell.

Kalamazoo County is a mix of industry and agriculture, with pleasant small towns like Richland, Augusta and Schoolcraft, many of them located on native prairies that were scattered around the region in pre-settlement days. It also is home to Western Michigan University, which, as the name implies, is West Michigan's largest institution of higher learning.

The county's first white settlers came in 1828, when Maryland native Bazel Harrison led a group of 21 people and assorted livestock to Prairie Ronde, near present-day Schoolcraft.

Within another year or two, a steady stream of settlers was entering the county. Most took up residence near the Kalamazoo River or on the open grasslands, of which Prairie Ronde was the largest.

Harrison, who lived to be more than 100 years old, was appointed as the county's first judge. He was the cousin of William Henry Harrison, the ninth president of the United States.

Another early settler was Titus Bronson, who bought land at the present site of Kalamazoo and founded a town which he named after himself.

Military grave markers stand in solemn rows at Fort Custer National Cemetery near Augusta (photo: Ed Hoogterp)

When the Territorial Legislature established Kalamazoo County in 1830, the village of Bronson was named as the county seat.

Local histories invariably refer to Bronson as "eccentric" – among other things he was accused of stealing a neighbor's cherry tree – and in 1836 the village's residents punished him by changing the name to Kalamazoo. Bronson's name remains on a downtown Kalamazoo park that he donated to the village before his neighbors turned against him.

The name Kalamazoo comes from an Indian word – possibly Ke-kenamazoo or Kikalamazoo – that described the river. It's often translated as "boiling water" or "reflecting water."

Like much of southwest Michigan, Kalamazoo County is a land of rolling hills, lakes and small streams. The Kalamazoo River flows in from the west and then turns north at the city of Kalamazoo.

Paper mills at Kalamazoo, Parchment and downstream communities in Allegan County provided thousands of jobs in the region through much of the 20th century. But they also poured so much pollution into the river that it is listed as a federal superfund site and an international "area of concern" on the Great Lakes.

The two largest cities, Kalamazoo and Portage, account for almost half of the county's population. The fastest growing areas in recent years are Oshstemo and Texas townships, immediately to the west of the central cities.

While those areas are experiencing rapid suburban growth, the eastern and southern tiers of townships have remained largely agricultural.

With about 41 percent of the county in agricultural production, Kalamazoo is among the state leaders in grapes and snap beans. The county is also among the top areas nationally in greenhouse production of bedding plants.

The paper industry is pretty much gone, and some areas have been cleaned up, though river sediments are still contaminated. The industry that remains has dramatically reduced the amount of pollution entering the river.

The I-94 expressway runs east and west through the county. The prime north-south artery is US-131, which is expressway from just south of Portage all the way north to Cadillac. For decades, local business interests have pressed the state to extend the freeway south to the Indiana border.

Kalamazoo County has an unusual system for naming its roads. East-west roads are designated by letters, starting with B Avenue near the north county line and ending with Z Avenue at the south county line. North-south roads are numbered, with 1st Street near the western boundary and 48th Street at the eastern county line.

The 3,000-acre Fort Custer Recreation Area, near Augusta, provides the county's largest piece of public land. It has popular mountain-biking trails, along with space for hiking, horse riding and other outdoor recreation. The Fort Custer National Cemetery is nearby.

The county has a number of West Michigan's favorite cultural and ecological attractions, including the Kalamazoo Nature Center, The Air Zoo, the State Theater, Western Michigan University's Miller Auditorium, the Barn Theater in Augusta and the Celery Flats Interpretive Center in Portage.

KALAMAZOO COUNTY FACTS

Population in 2000: 238,603

Land area (square miles): 562

Population density (people per square mile: 424.7

Estimated population, 2004: 240,724

Growth 2000-2004: 0.89 percent

2004 election results: Bush, 47.7 percent; Kerry, 51.3 percent

County seat: Kalamazoo

Largest cities: Kalamazoo, Portage, Galesburg, Parchment

Total Tax Base (State Equalized Valuation) 2005: $8.5 billion

Agricultural tax base: $203 million (2.4 percent)

Commercial tax base: $1.6 billion (18.4 percent)

Industrial tax base: $482 million (5.7 percent)

Residential tax base: $5.4 billion (64.0 percent)

Traffic fatalities, 2000-2004: 145

Homicides (murder/ manslaughter) 2000-2004: 45

Major rivers: Kalamazoo, Portage

Largest lakes: Gull Lake, Austin Lake, Morrow Pond, Indian Lake, Long Lake

Active farms in 2002: 808

Land in farms: 148,000 acres (41.2 percent of land in county)

DEMOGRAPHICS FROM 2000 CENSUS:

White, non-hispanic population: 83.5 percent

Black population: 9.7 percent

American Indian population: 0.4 percent

Asian population: 1.8 percent

Persons reporting two or more races: 2.2 percent

Hispanic population (may be any race): 2.6 percent

Percent of population under age 18: 24.1 percent

Percent of population age 65 or older: 11.4 percent

Percent of adult population (age 25-plus) with four-year college degree: 31.2 percent

Average travel time to work (for workers age 16 and older): 19.7 minutes

Percent of workers who travel to jobs outside the county: 14.34 percent

Total number of homes and apartments (housing units): 99,250

Detached, single-family homes: 63,017
Percent of total housing units: 63.49 percent

Dwellings in structures with 10 or more units: 15,781
Percent of total housing units: 15.90 percent

Mobile homes or house trailers: 4,565
Percent of total housing units: 4.60 percent

Home ownership rate: 65.7 percent

Median value of owner-occupied homes: $108,000

Median household income: $42,022

Income rank among Michigan's 83 counties: 21

Percent of households with income below poverty level: 12.0 percent

LOCAL AREA GROWTH AND ECONOMIC STATISTICS (KALAMAZOO COUNTY)

City / Township	2004 Population	2000–2004 Growth	Median Household Income (1999)	Median age of homes in 2000
Alamo township	3,925	2.75%	$50,409	23 years
Brady township	4,162	-2.37%	$52,202	33 years
Charleston township	1,922	6.01%	$50,707	36 years
Climax township	2,398	-0.58%	$47,620	41 years
Comstock township	14,909	7.64%	$46,140	29 years
Cooper township	9,737	11.23%	$47,004	35 years
Galesburg city	1,937	-2.57%	$34,663	30 years
Kalamazoo city	73,960	-4.13%	$31,189	44 years
Kalamazoo township	21,639	-0.17%	$37,463	39 years
Oshtemo township	19,139	12.56%	$38,433	21 years
Parchment city	1,832	-5.37%	$40,074	46 years
Pavilion township	5,722	-1.84%	$46,675	26 years
Portage city	45,210	0.70%	$49,410	28 years
Prairie Ronde township	2,097	0.53%	$65,385	17 years
Richland township	6,428	-0.97%	$59,432	25 years
Ross township	5,093	0.91%	$58,446	42 years
Schoolcraft township	7,037	-3.07%	$48,737	30 years
Texas township	12,125	11.04%	$69,854	15 years
Wakeshma township	1,452	2.69%	$52,328	49 years

LOCAL AREA RACE AND ETHNIC POPULATIONS (KALAMAZOO COUNTY)

City / Township	Population (2000 census)	White (non-Hispanic)	Black or African-American	Hispanic or Latino (of any race)
Alamo township	3,820	96.8%	0.4%	0.9%
Brady township	4,263	96.7%	0.3%	0.7%
Charleston township	1,813	95.6%	0.6%	1.9%
Climax township	2,412	95.4%	0.5%	1.5%
Comstock township	13,851	91.2%	3.8%	1.2%
Cooper township	8,754	95.5%	0.5%	0.9%
Galesburg city	1,988	95.7%	0.9%	0.4%
Kalamazoo city	77,145	69.4%	19.7%	4.4%
Kalamazoo township	21,675	81.9%	11.5%	2.5%
Oshtemo township	17,003	83.8%	7.8%	3.2%
Parchment city	1,936	91.4%	4.0%	1.1%
Pavilion township	5,829	94.9%	1.5%	1.0%
Portage city	44,897	89.9%	3.1%	2.1%
Prairie Ronde township	2,086	97.3%	0.1%	0.9%
Richland township	6,491	91.0%	3.4%	3.2%
Ross township	5,047	96.1%	0.6%	0.8%
Schoolcraft township	7,260	94.2%	0.7%	2.8%
Texas township	10,919	92.5%	1.8%	1.0%
Wakeshma township	1,414	96.7%	0.3%	1.0%

KENT COUNTY

Kent County had its beginning along the banks of the Grand River and slowly grew out from there. That was 170 years ago, and it's still happening.

With a population approaching 600,000, West Michigan's largest county is well on its way to becoming a solid expanse of suburbia surrounding the central city of Grand Rapids. While rural areas remain at the four corners of the county, most of the interior is rapidly filling with homes and businesses.

The Grand River flows in from the east, joins the Flat River at Lowell and the Thornapple at Ada, then bends to the north and comes back south through downtown Grand Rapids before resuming its westward journey to Lake Michigan.

The river, particularly the broad valley and swift, shallow water at what is now Grand Rapids, was a gathering place for human beings long before Europeans set foot in North America.

Native Americans of the Hopewellian culture were at the rapids about 2,000 years ago. They built two clusters of burial mounds along the river, including one near the present site of the Gerald R. Ford Museum and the Grand Valley State University campus in downtown Grand Rapids.

Decades of new home construction have transformed much of Kent County into suburbia (photo: Ed Hoogterp)

When the first French traders journeyed up the Grand, they found Ottawa Indian villages along the river. One early account indicated that Pontiac spoke to several thousand Indians at the rapids in the 1760s, as he was organizing his war against the British. In 1763, Pontiac's Indian warriers took over several British posts, including those at St. Joseph and Mackinaw City. The rebellion failed when he was unable to dislodge the British troops from Detroit.

Kent County's first permanent white settler was Rix Robinson, who came in 1821 to Ada, where the Grand and Thornapple rivers meet. Robinson took over a trading network from Madame Magdelaine LaFramboise, who had operated a seasonal post upstream at Lowell.

In the mid-1820s, Baptist preachers Isaac McCoy and Leonard Slater founded a mission to the Indians on the north side of the river at Grand Rapids. Louis Campau arrived in 1826 and is credited with founding Grand Rapids.

As settlers began to stream into the area in the 1830s, they quickly created the diverse agricultural and manufacturing economy that persists in Kent County to this day.

Lucius Lyon, who also had a hand in developing towns in Ionia and Kalamazoo counties, was busy building a water power canal alongside the river by 1836. Farms began to spring up as land was cleared of the heavy forest.

The county was formally organized in 1836 and was named for James Kent, a prominent New York lawyer.

The outlying townships, especially in the southern part of the county, were once prized for their prime farmland. But each year more of that land is converted to residential and commercial development.

Of Kent County's 21 townships, 10 recorded double-digit growth between 2000 and 2004, according to U.S. Census Bureau estimates.

Grand Rapids, meanwhile, hasn't gained population in decades. The largest suburban cities, Wyoming and Kentwood, grew rapidly in the 1970s and 80s, but leveled off in recent years as they became more developed.

Though farmland is diminishing in the face of urban sprawl, Kent remains the state's leader in apple production. The county's farms also produce significant amounts of corn, soybeans and milk.

West Michigan's most affluent areas are in the suburbs of Grand Rapids. Ada Township, Cascade Township and East Grand Rapids all had median household incomes above $80,000 in 1999, a figure that put them at least 75 percent above the statewide median.

Public land includes the Rogue River and Cannonsburg state game areas, along with popular county parks at Wabasis and Long lakes and on the Flat River at Fallasburg.

The county also operates a zoo at John Ball Park in Grand Rapids, and is continuing development of the 1,500-acre Millenium Park in Grand Rapids and Walker.

KENT COUNTY FACTS

Population in 2000: 574,335

Land area (square miles): 856

Population density (people per square mile): 670.8

Estimated population, 2004: 593,898

Growth 2000-2004: 3.41 percent

2004 election results: Bush, 58.9 percent; Kerry, 40.2 percent

County seat: Grand Rapids

Largest cities: Grand Rapids, Wyoming, Kentwood, Walker, Grandville, East Grand Rapids

Total Tax Base (State Equalized Valuation) 2005: $22.1 billion

- **Agricultural tax base:** $306 million (1.4 percent)
- **Commercial tax base:** $3.9 billion (17.8 percent)
- **Industrial tax base:** $1.8 billion (8.2 percent)
- **Residential tax base:** $14.2 billion (64.4 percent)

Traffic fatalities, 2000-2004: 341

Homicides (murder/ manslaughter) 2000-2004: 85

Major rivers: Grand, Thornapple, Rogue, Flat

Largest lakes: Lincoln, Wabasis, Murray, Reeds, Silver

Active farms in 2002: 1,212

Land in farms: 173,000 acres (31.6 percent of land in county)

DEMOGRAPHICS FROM 2000 CENSUS:

White, non-hispanic population: 80.3 percent

Black population: 8.9 percent

American Indian population: 0.5 percent

Asian population: 1.9 percent

Hispanic population (may be any race): 7.0 percent

Percent of population under age 18: 28.3 percent

Percent of population age 65 or older: 10.4 percent

Percent of adult population (age 25-plus) with four-year college degree: 25.8 percent

Average travel time to work (for workers age 16 and older): 20.7 minutes

Percent of workers who travel to jobs outside the county: 8.98 percent

Total number of homes and apartments (housing units): 224,000

Detached, single-family homes: 142,341
Percent of total housing units: 63.55 percent

Dwellings in structures with 10 or more units: 28,372
Percent of total housing units: 12.67 percent

Mobile homes or house trailers: 11,069
Percent of total housing units: 4.94 percent

Home ownership rate: 70.3 percent

Median value of owner-occupied homes: $115,100

Median household income: $45,980

Income rank among Michigan's 83 counties: 13

Percent of households with income below poverty level: 8.9 percent

LOCAL AREA GROWTH AND ECONOMIC STATISTICS (KENT COUNTY)

City / Township	2004 Population	2000–2004 Growth	Median Household Income (1999)	Median age of homes in 2000
Ada township	11,586	17.24%	$83,357	20 years
Algoma township	8,911	17.40%	$58,285	19 years
Alpine township	13,946	-0.21%	$42,484	17 years
Bowne township	2,909	6.05%	$60,909	27 years
Byron township	19,509	11.14%	$49,672	15 years
Caledonia township	10,578	18.01%	$63,032	20 years
Cannon township	13,083	8.35%	$70,925	16 years
Cascade township	16,286	7.80%	$87,290	22 years
Cedar Springs city	3,227	2.54%	$39,542	33 years
Courtland township	6,775	16.47%	$64,430	21 years
East Grand Rapids city	10,482	-2.62%	$84,772	48 years
Gaines township	22,813	13.43%	$48,482	15 years
Grand Rapids city	195,115	-1.36%	$37,224	49 years
Grand Rapids charter township	14,621	4.02%	$66,250	24 years
Grandville city	16,680	2.56%	$47,570	28 years
Grattan township	3,688	3.86%	$56,467	30 years
Kentwood city	46,538	2.84%	$45,812	21 years
Lowell city	4,128	2.87%	$42,326	37 years
Lowell township	5,971	14.41%	$58,639	23 years
Nelson township	4,569	8.99%	$50,521	20 years
Oakfield township	5,569	10.10%	$49,429	23 years
Plainfield township	31,348	3.82%	$55,181	23 years
Rockford city	4,954	6.95%	$50,562	27 years
Solon township	5,479	18.41%	$44,814	17 years
Sparta township	9,215	3.10%	$42,992	32 years
Spencer township	3,833	4.13%	$51,765	21 years
Tyrone township	4,438	3.11%	$48,006	28 years
Vergennes township	4,032	11.66%	$61,500	15 years
Walker city	23,315	6.74%	$44,818	22 years
Wyoming city	70,300	1.34%	$43,164	35 years

LOCAL AREA RACE AND ETHNIC POPULATIONS (KENT COUNTY)

City / Township	Population (2000 census)	White (non-Hispanic)	Black or African-American	Hispanic or Latino (of any race)
Ada township	9,882	94.5%	0.7%	1.1%
Algoma township	7,596	96.8%	0.0%	0.9%
Alpine township	13,976	87.1%	3.5%	6.4%
Bowne township	2,743	93.9%	0.0%	3.6%
Byron township	17,553	93.4%	1.6%	2.3%
Caledonia township	8,964	97.9%	0.2%	0.5%
Cannon township	12,075	97.9%	0.5%	0.2%
Cascade township	15,107	94.6%	1.3%	1.1%
Cedar Springs city	3,112	94.0%	0.6%	4.2%
Courtland township	5,817	97.5%	0.5%	1.1%
East Grand Rapids city	10,764	96.3%	0.9%	1.8%
Gaines township	20,112	87.3%	5.3%	3.4%
Grand Rapids city	197,800	62.4%	20.4%	13.0%
Grand Rapids charter township	14,056	95.8%	1.3%	1.0%
Grandville city	16,263	93.0%	2.0%	2.9%
Grattan township	3,551	94.9%	0.2%	2.9%
Kentwood city	45,255	79.1%	9.1%	3.8%
Lowell city	4,013	95.4%	0.0%	1.8%
Lowell township	5,219	97.4%	0.2%	1.1%
Nelson township	4,192	96.1%	0.4%	1.8%
Oakfield township	5,058	96.9%	0.6%	1.0%
Plainfield township	30,195	94.7%	1.4%	1.7%
Rockford city	4,626	95.1%	0.3%	1.9%
Solon township	4,662	96.5%	0.5%	1.2%
Sparta township	8,938	95.0%	0.6%	3.2%
Spencer township	3,681	93.9%	1.2%	1.9%
Tyrone township	4,304	93.3%	0.1%	5.2%
Vergennes township	3,611	96.8%	0.4%	2.2%
Walker city	21,842	93.0%	1.6%	2.7%
Wyoming city	69,368	80.5%	4.7%	9.7%

MECOSTA COUNTY

Mecosta County is about as far north and as far east as you can go, and still lay claim to being in West Michigan.

But while the county is close to the central Michigan city of Mount Pleasant and the northern Michigan town of Cadillac, history links it solidly with West Michigan. The county seat of Big Rapids is located on the Muskegon River, which meant that most early transportation in and out of Mecosta went to Lake Michigan. And the first railroad into the community came from Grand Rapids, 50 miles to the south.

Mecosta actually sits on the peninsular divide. The Muskegon River flows west into Lake Michigan, while on the east side of the county, the Chippewa River is part of the Saginaw River system that empties into Lake Huron.

The county today is largely rural, with Big Rapids the only city. The US-131 expressway runs through Mecosta's western townships, linking the county with Grand Rapids and Cadillac. The old north-south railroad grade is now the White Pine Trail, used by bicyclists, hikers and snowmobile riders.

One of the county's most prosperous spots is the Canadian Lakes resort area between Mecosta and Stanwood. The 7,000-acre development includes four golf courses, 2,000 year-round or seasonal homes and such amenities as a small shopping center, indoor pool, beaches and nature trails.

The Big Rapids RiverWalk makes nature accessible along the Muskegon River (photo courtesy of Mecosta County Chamber of Commerce)

European settlement in Mecosta county began as much as 30 years later than in areas farther south. Early settlers included John Davis, who brought his family to the Stanwood area in 1851, and John Parish, who built a cabin on the Muskegon River near Big Rapids the same year.

Parish eventually moved a few miles north to establish the town of Parish, which still exists (minus the "h") as Paris. A former state fish hatchery at Paris is now the site of a Mecosta County park.

Mecosta County was thick with white pine forests when the early settlers arrived, and the first sawmill went up at the present site of Big Rapids in 1857. While some logs from area forests were sawed into lumber at Big Rapids, many more were floated down the river to mills at Newaygo or Muskegon

The county was organized in 1859, and named for a Potawatomi chief whose name is said to mean Bear Cub. The region was largely isolated until 1870, when the first railroad reached north from Grand Rapids.

In 1884, Woodbridge Ferris founded the Ferris Industrial School at Big Rapids. The school is now Ferris State University, and the county's largest employer.

Ferris himself went on to serve two terms as governor of Michigan and one as a U.S. senator.

As the timber boom cooled, much of the cut-over land was converted to agriculture, at least for a time. At the dawn of the 20th century, Mecosta had more than 2,000 farms, including a number owned by African-Americans. A church headed by one of those black farmers, Thomas Cross, stands today in Wheatland Township, near Remus. Mecosta's rural areas are now populated almost exclusively by whites. The only African-American population of significant size is in Big Rapids.

Today, the county has fewer than 800 farms. About a third of the county's land is in agriculture

Much of the rest has returned to forest. A large share of the forest land is owned by people who live in other parts of Michigan and maintain property here for hunting or other recreational use.

Public land includes the Haymarsh Lake and Martiny Lake state game areas.

As recently as the 1990s Mecosta was a significant producer of Christmas trees, but acreage has diminished considerably.

There remains nearly 20,000 acres of corn fields, in addition to dairy operations that produced some 70 million pounds of milk in 2003.

Almost 20 percent of the dwellings in the county are trailers or mobile homes, though many of those are used as seasonal dwellings.

MECOSTA COUNTY FACTS

Population in 2000: 40,553

Land area (square miles): 556

Population density (people per square mile): 73.0

Estimated population, 2004: 42,394

Growth 2000-2004 (percent): 4.54 percent

2004 election results:
Bush, 55.2 percent;
Kerry, 44.0 percent

County seat: Big Rapids

Largest cities: Big Rapids is the only city in Mecosta County

Total Tax Base (State Equalized Valuation) 2005: $1.5 billion

- **Agricultural tax base:** $181 million (12.0 percent)
- **Commercial tax base:** $140 million (9.3 percent)
- **Industrial tax base:** $24 million (1.6 percent)
- **Residential tax base:** $1.1 billion (70.7 percent)

Traffic fatalities, 2000-2004: 51

Homicides (murder/ manslaughter) 2000-2004: 2

Major rivers: Muskegon, Little Muskegon, Chippewa

Largest lakes: Hardy Pond (shared with Newaygo) Martiny Lake, Chippewa Lake, Rogers Pond

Active farms in 2002: 794

Land in farms: 120,000 acres (33.7 percent of land in county)

DEMOGRAPHICS FROM 2000 CENSUS:

White, non-hispanic population: 91.9 percent

Black population: 3.6 percent

American Indian population: 0.6 percent

Asian population: 0.9 percent

Hispanic population (may be any race): 1.3 percent

Percent of population under age 18: 22.5 percent

Percent of population age 65 or older: 13.2 percent

Percent of adult population (age 25-plus) with four-year college degree: 19.1 percent

Average travel time to work (for workers age 16 and older): 24.4 minutes

Percent of workers who travel to a job outside the county: 31.05 percent

Total number of homes and apartments (housing units): 19,593

Detached, single-family homes: 13,389
Percent of total housing units: 68.34 percent

Dwellings in structures with 10 or more units: 719
Percent of total housing units: 3.67 percent

Mobile homes or house trailers: 3,374
Percent of total housing units: 19.06 percent

Home ownership rate: 73.7 percent

Median value of owner-occupied homes: $90,100

Median household income: $33,849

Income rank among Michigan's 83 counties: 60

Percent of households with income below poverty level: 16.1 percent

LOCAL AREA GROWTH AND ECONOMIC STATISTICS (MECOSTA COUNTY)

City / Township	2004 Population	2000–2004 Growth	Median Household Income (1999)	Median age of homes in 2000
Aetna township	2,172	6.26%	$34,571	25 years
Austin township	1,512	6.86%	$34,674	23 years
Big Rapids city	10,852	0.03%	$20,192	36 years
Big Rapids township	3,385	4.19%	$47,933	24 years
Chippewa township	1,296	4.60%	$33,859	32 years
Colfax township	2,083	5.47%	$46,071	26 years
Deerfield township	1,746	7.12%	$36,293	28 years
Fork township	1,763	5.07%	$28,750	33 years
Grant township	743	9.26%	$36,071	29 years
Green charter township	3,361	4.74%	$39,036	23 years
Hinton township	1,124	8.60%	$37,976	32 years
Martiny township	1,678	4.48%	$31,681	29 years
Mecosta township	2,557	5.01%	$37,287	28 years
Millbrook township	1,170	8.23%	$35,238	27 years
Morton township	3,949	9.79%	$41,422	21 years
Sheridan township	1,437	5.90%	$31,050	31 years
Wheatland township	1,566	6.24%	$33,654	30 years

LOCAL AREA RACE AND ETHNIC POPULATIONS (MECOSTA COUNTY)

City / Township	Population (2000 census)	White (non-Hispanic)	Black or African-American	Hispanic or Latino (of any race)
Aetna township	2,044	95.0%	0.6%	0.7%
Austin township	1,415	97.9%	0.9%	0.7%
Big Rapids city	10,849	82.6%	11.1%	1.7%
Big Rapids township	3,249	95.1%	1.1%	0.4%
Chippewa township	1,239	99.0%	0.0%	0.3%
Colfax township	1,975	97.0%	0.9%	0.0%
Deerfield township	1,630	93.2%	0.9%	2.7%
Fork township	1,678	96.1%	0.5%	1.6%
Grant township	680	96.9%	0.0%	0.8%
Green charter township	3,209	96.0%	0.8%	0.7%
Hinton township	1,035	94.8%	0.2%	3.1%
Martiny township	1,606	98.4%	0.3%	0.0%
Mecosta township	2,435	96.4%	0.5%	0.7%
Millbrook township	1,081	94.4%	0.2%	1.9%
Morton township	3,597	93.7%	1.3%	2.0%
Sheridan township	1,357	91.2%	1.7%	0.6%
Wheatland township	1,474	94.1%	1.0%	0.4%

MONTCALM COUNTY

Montcalm County is a sprawling swath of territory that extends from just north of Grand Rapids almost to the geographic center of the Lower Peninsula.

Its largest city, Greenville, has a rich commercial and industrial history, while much of the rural county has been productive farmland ever since it was stripped of its native timber in the 1870s and 1880s.

The county is named for the Marquis de Montcalm, a French military officer whose defeat on the Plains of Abraham at Montreal in 1759 was a decisive battle in the French and Indian War.

Montcalm, with its northern panhandle, extends 30 miles from east to west. That expanse of space was a factor in a series of early battles over the location of the county seat.

When county government was first organized, in 1850, Greenville served as the seat. But residents of eastern parts of the county pressed for a more central location. In 1860, county residents voted to move the county seat to a central location where four townships meet – even though there was no town there.

Stanton, the new county seat, was built on a 160-acre plot of land donated for that purpose.

The long distances also make Montcalm a transition county between West Michigan and Mid-Michigan.

Huge locomotive is part of the historical village at Montcalm Community College (photo: Ed Hoogterp)

Greenville, Gowen and Howard City are pretty much within the Grand Rapids orbit, while some Carson City residents commute to jobs in Lansing. The northeast corner of the county, near Edmore and Vestaburg, is in driving distance of Mount Pleasant or even Saginaw.

Montcalm in the 19th century was a heavily wooded land that developed much later than adjacent areas of Kent and Ionia counties.

A surveyor reported at least one family living in a cabin on the Flat River in 1837. John Green, the founder of Greenville, arrived in 1844.

But much of the county remained wilderness until after the Civil War and the coming of the railroads.

In the 1870s, the county was in the middle of the Michigan timber boom. Many of the trees harvested from Montcalm were floated down small streams to the Grand or Muskegon rivers, and on to mills in Grand Rapids and Muskegon. In addition, more than 100 local sawmills were operating in the county in the mid-1870s.

Oil was discovered in the Edmore and Crystal areas in the early 1930s. Later discovery of natural gas around Six Lakes continued the boom. Today, the Six Lakes field is one of several in Michigan used for storage of natural gas pumped from other sites.

Greenville was home to the Gibson Co., which made wooden iceboxes in the early 1900s and grew to become the nation's largest refrigerator manufacturer. During World War II, the plant made aircraft components and more than 1,000 Army Air Force gliders, including some that landed troops in Normandy in D-Day in 1944.

Mergers and acquisitions made Gibson part of the Swedish company, Electrolux AB in 1986. The company announced in 2004 that it would close the plant – eliminating 2,700 jobs – and move production to Mexico.

The city and county are still struggling to deal with the loss of jobs.

Also founded in Greenville was the Meijer grocery store chain, which is now West Michigan's largest private employer. Meijer moved its headquarters to Grand Rapids in the 1950s but maintains one of its signature grocery and general merchandise stores in Greenville.

The county has more than 1,100 active farms, covering more than 250,000 acres, or about 56 percent of the total land area. It produces a diverse mix of crops, including apples, corn, beans, potatoes, Christmas trees, milk and beef.

In addition to agriculture, rural Montcalm has a considerable number of cottages and seasonal homes around its 200 lakes. Public land in the county includes the Flat River, Edmore, Vestaburg and Stanton state game areas. A historical village at Montcalm Community College in Sidney offers a glimpse into the county's past, as does the Flat River Historical Museum in Greenville.

MONTCALM COUNTY FACTS

Population in 2000: 61,266

Land area (square miles): 708

Population density (people per square mile): 86.5

Estimated population, 2004: 63,627

Growth 2000-2004 (percent): 3.85 percent

2004 election results: Bush, 56.0 percent; Kerry, 42.9 percent

County seat: Stanton

Largest cities: Greenville, Stanton, Carson City

Total Tax Base (State Equalized Valuation) 2005: $2.1 billion

- **Agricultural tax base:** $366 million (17.2 percent)
- **Commercial tax base:** $174 million (8.2 percent)
- **Industrial tax base:** $134 million (6.3 percent)
- **Residential tax base:** $1.3 billion (62.0 percent)

Traffic fatalities, 2000-2004: 86

Homicides (murder/ manslaughter) 2000-2004: 3

Major rivers: Flat, Little Muskegon, Pine

Largest lakes: Crystal, Big Whitefish, Tamarack, Duck, Townline

Active farms in 2002: 1,139

Land in farms: 255,000 acres (56.3 percent of land in county)

DEMOGRAPHICS FROM 2000 CENSUS:

White, non-hispanic population: 93.5 percent

Black population: 2.2 percent

American Indian population: 0.6 percent

Asian population: 0.3 percent

Hispanic population (may be any race): 2.3 percent

Percent of population under age 18: 27.1 percent

Percent of population age 65 or older: 12.1 percent

Percent of adult population (age 25-plus) with four-year college degree: 10.8 percent

Average travel time to work (for workers age 16 and older): 28.2 minutes

Percent of workers who travel to jobs outside the county: 42.27 percent

Total number of homes and apartments (housing units): 25,900

Detached, single-family homes: 13,389
Percent of total housing units: 68.34 percent

Dwellings in structures with 10 or more units: 688
Percent of total housing units: 2.66 percent

Mobile homes or house trailers: 3,374
Percent of total housing units: 16.60 percent

Home ownership rate: 81.6 percent

Median value of owner-occupied homes: $84,900

Median household income: $37,218

Income rank among Michigan's 83 counties: 42

Percent of households with income below poverty level: 10.9 percent

LOCAL AREA GROWTH AND ECONOMIC STATISTICS (MONTCALM COUNTY)

City / Township	2004 Population	2000–2004 Growth	Median Household Income (1999)	Median age of homes in 2000
Belvidere township	2,513	3.08%	$33,477	34 years
Bloomer township	3,645	-0.19%	$36,488	37 years
Bushnell township	1,580	5.47%	$35,573	32 years
Carson City city	1,198	0.67%	$32,500	54 years
Cato township	2,998	2.67%	$35,919	33 years
Crystal township	2,896	2.55%	$34,421	36 years
Day township	1,352	5.46%	$35,500	48 years
Douglass township	2,462	3.58%	$44,309	27 years
Eureka township	3,566	12.53%	$50,566	26 years
Evergreen township	3,018	3.29%	$33,604	29 years
Fairplain township	1,919	5.09%	$42,955	27 years
Ferris township	1,461	5.95%	$35,820	23 years
Greenville city	8,282	3.05%	$30,453	38 years
Home township	2,795	3.21%	$30,590	37 years
Maple Valley township	2,156	3.50%	$36,583	41 years
Montcalm township	3,382	6.42%	$43,485	27 years
Pierson township	2,956	3.14%	$48,519	26 years
Pine township	1,725	4.29%	$41,583	27 years
Reynolds township	4,435	3.65%	$40,799	18 years
Richland township	2,971	3.59%	$34,847	32 years
Sidney township	2,658	3.71%	$40,682	28 years
Stanton city	1,528	1.60%	$29,286	40 years
Winfield township	2,131	4.00%	$44,524	20 years

LOCAL AREA RACE AND ETHNIC POPULATIONS (MONTCALM COUNTY)

City / Township	Population (2000 census)	White (non-Hispanic)	Black or African-American	Hispanic or Latino (of any race)
Belvidere township	2,438	95.6%	0.0%	1.0%
Bloomer township	3,039	62.9%	27.5%	3.7%
Bushnell township	2,111	79.6%	14.6%	4.3%
Carson City city	1,190	94.6%	0.7%	3.5%
Cato township	2,920	97.0%	0.0%	1.6%
Crystal township	2,824	95.3%	1.0%	0.6%
Day township	1,282	95.0%	0.1%	2.5%
Douglass township	2,377	95.9%	0.0%	2.0%
Eureka township	3,271	95.3%	0.1%	2.9%
Evergreen township	2,922	97.4%	0.1%	1.1%
Fairplain township	1,826	95.5%	1.0%	1.7%
Ferris township	1,379	97.7%	0.0%	1.6%
Greenville city	7,935	94.3%	0.3%	3.5%
Home township	2,708	94.7%	0.4%	3.1%
Maple Valley township	2,083	95.9%	0.3%	0.5%
Montcalm township	3,178	96.2%	0.0%	1.5%
Pierson township	2,866	95.2%	0.2%	1.8%
Pine township	1,654	96.1%	0.1%	0.2%
Reynolds township	4,279	92.9%	0.1%	2.2%
Richland township	2,868	96.4%	0.4%	2.0%
Sidney township	2,563	97.7%	0.0%	0.6%
Stanton city	1,504	94.5%	0.5%	3.6%
Winfield township	2,049	97.9%	0.1%	0.2%

MUSKEGON COUNTY

Of all West Michigan counties, Muskegon is the most difficult to fit into any category.

That's because this county is a little bit of everything, from forests, to industry, to pristine Lake Michigan beaches.

The southwest corner of the county is heavily urbanized, with Muskegon, four suburban cities and three adjacent townships accounting for more than 70 percent of the county's population.

In the far northeast corner, the townships of Blue Lake, Holton and Cedar Creek include thousands of acres of the Huron-Manistee National Forest, along with private retreats, summer camps and recreational property.

Southeastern townships, around Ravenna, form the county's farm belt, while the northwest townships, have a mix of industry and recreation around White Lake.

The county's Lake Michigan shoreline includes three state parks – Muskegon, Duck Lake and P.J. Hoffmaster – while Muskegon Lake is a deepwater port for both commercial and recreational vessels.

Since 2004, the Lake Express has provided high-speed ferry service between Muskegon and Milwaukee.

The name "Muskegon" comes from an Indian word meaning "swamp" or "marsh," a reference to the lake and wetlands near the mouth of the river. The name was applied first to the Muskegon River, and later to the city and county.

The White River Lighthouse, near Whitehall, has been converted to a museum (photo: Ed Hoogterp)

French explorers and traders passed through the Muskegon area as early as the 1600s, but there were no permanent non-Indian residents until Jean Baptiste Recollect and Pierre Constant set up trading posts around the year 1812.

Settlement began in earnest after 1836, when the Indians gave up this part of Michigan in the Treaty of Washington.

The first Muskegon Lake sawmill was built in 1837. In 1839, Muskegon's government was split between Ottawa and Oceana counties. It became a county on its own in 1859.

Montague is a popular tourist venue in northern Muskegon County (photo: Terry Phipps)

The area's development lagged in the early years. Muskegon County had fewer than 4,000 residents in 1860, and then exploded along with the national demand for white pine lumber in the 1870s and 1880s. According to some historians, Muskegon had more millionaires per capita than any other city in America during the 1880s. The Hackley and Hume mansions, preserved and managed as part of the Muskegon County Historical Museum, provide a hint of that great wealth.

When the timber business peaked and died, at the end of the 19th century, Muskegon's leaders worked to attract new business, and helped turn the city into an industrial powerhouse, making everything from engine castings to bowling balls.

In 1927, oil was discovered north of Muskegon, and another temporary boom was on. The Muskegon County oil fields were the largest discovered in Michigan up to that time. By the end of 1928 the Muskegon Chronicle reported that the area had 70 drill rigs operating pretty much round the clock and employing as many as 1,000 workers. In 1929, the Muskegon wells produced more than 3 million barrels of oil, along with significant quantities of natural gas.

Muskegon's industry remained healthy through the 1950s, but began fading after that, as Michigan's auto companies lost their dominance and midwest "smokestack" industries shrank. The companies that made chemicals, leather, paper and other products in past decades left a legacy of industrial pollution around Muskegon and White lakes. Even after decades of progress, contamination remains in sediments at the bottom of the lakes. More years of clean-up will be required.

Today, Muskegon County is reinventing itself again, trying to hang on to as much industry as possible, but also stressing culture, history and quality of life in an effort to attract business, tourists and residents.

The Michigan's Adventure theme park just north of Muskegon is a major attraction, as is the World War II submarine *USS Silversides,* which is docked in Muskegon Lake. Events such as the Summer Celebration and the Muskegon Air Fair draw visitors to the waterfront. The Lakes Mall in Fruitport Township has become a regional shopping center.

MUSKEGON COUNTY FACTS

Population in 2000: 170,200

Land area (square miles): 509

Population per square mile: 334.3

Estimated population, 2004: 174,401

Growth 2000-2004 (percent): 2.47 percent

2004 election results: Bush, 44.0 percent; Kerry, 55.1 percent

County seat: Muskegon

Largest cities: Muskegon, Norton Shores, Muskegon Heights

Total Tax Base (State Equalized Valuation) 2005: $5.1 billion

Agricultural tax base: $138 million (2.7 percent)

Commercial tax base: $739 million (14.62 percent)

Industrial tax base: $228 million (4.5 percent)

Residential tax base: $3.6 billion (70.6 percent)

Traffic fatalities, 2000-2004: 122

Homicides (murder/manslaughter) 2000-2004: 21

Major rivers: Muskegon, White, Crockery Creek, Black Creek

Largest lakes: Muskegon, White, Spring (shared with Ottawa County) Mona, Bear

Active farms in 2002: 545

Land in farms: 74,000 acres (22.7 percent of land in county)

DEMOGRAPHICS FROM 2000 CENSUS:

White, non-hispanic population: 79.5 percent

Black population: 14.2 percent

American Indian population: 0.8 percent

Asian population: 0.4 percent

Persons reporting two or more races: 2.0 percent

Hispanic population (may be any race): 3.5 percent

Percent of population under age 18: 27.5 percent

Percent of population age 65 or older: 12.9 percent

Percent of adult population (age 25-plus) with four-year college degree: 13.9 percent

Average travel time to work (for workers age 16 and older): 20.8 minutes

Percent of workers who travel to jobs outside the county: 25.08 percent

Total number of homes and apartments (housing units): 68,556

Detached, single-family homes: 52,120
Percent of total housing units: 76.03 percent

Dwellings in structures with 10 or more units: 3,974
Percent of total housing units: 5.80 percent

Mobile homes or house trailers: 5,311
Percent of total housing units: 7.75 percent

Home ownership rate: 77.7 percent

Median value of owner-occupied homes: $85,900

Median household income: $38,008

Income rank among Michigan's 83 counties: 39

Percent of households with income below poverty level: 11.4 percent

LOCAL AREA GROWTH AND ECONOMIC STATISTICS (MUSKEGON COUNTY)

City / Township	2004 Population	2000–2004 Growth	Median Household Income (1999)	Median age of homes in 2000
Blue Lake township	2,331	17.14%	$50,000	19 years
Casnovia township	2,756	3.92%	$41,711	31 years
Cedar Creek township	3,323	6.88%	$36,179	25 years
Dalton township	8,884	10.40%	$47,127	26 years
Egelston township	9,851	3.29%	$37,557	23 years
Fruitland township	5,475	4.58%	$53,977	28 years
Fruitport charter township	12,993	3.67%	$49,065	33 years
Holton township	2,602	2.76%	$37,813	28 years
Laketon township	7,712	4.74%	$50,913	30 years
Montague city	2,345	-2.58%	$40,677	41 years
Montague township	1,678	2.50%	$41,534	29 years
Moorland township	1,849	14.42%	$40,669	26 years
Muskegon city	39,954	-0.38%	$27,929	50 years
Muskegon township	18,500	4.30%	$38,634	30 years
Muskegon Heights city	11,807	-2.01%	$21,778	53 years
North Muskegon city	4,009	-0.55%	$55,063	45 years
Norton Shores city	23,287	3.37%	$45,457	33 years
Ravenna township	2,905	1.72%	$44,315	34 years
Roosevelt Park city	3,819	-1.83%	$37,035	35 years
Sullivan township	2,437	-1.61%	$46,447	30 years
Whitehall city	2,828	-2.21%	$37,641	41 years
Whitehall township	1,668	1.71%	$50,375	22 years
White River township	1,388	3.74%	$48,077	27 years

LOCAL AREA RACE AND ETHNIC POPULATIONS (MUSKEGON COUNTY)

City / Township	Population (2000 census)	White (non-Hispanic)	Black or African-American	Hispanic or Latino (of any race)
Blue Lake township	1,990	85.9%	6.3%	1.7%
Casnovia township	2,652	91.7%	0.0%	5.9%
Cedar Creek township	3,109	93.1%	0.9%	4.2%
Dalton township	8,047	92.3%	3.0%	1.6%
Egelston township	9,537	92.2%	0.7%	4.4%
Fruitland township	5,235	95.9%	0.5%	1.2%
Fruitport charter township	12,533	95.9%	1.1%	1.0%
Holton township	2,532	95.5%	0.0%	2.4%
Laketon township	7,363	94.9%	0.1%	2.9%
Montague city	2,407	96.9%	0.5%	0.6%
Montague township	1,637	95.6%	0.2%	1.6%
Moorland township	1,616	96.1%	0.0%	2.8%
Muskegon city	40,105	58.0%	31.0%	6.0%
Muskegon township	17,737	89.7%	4.8%	3.0%
Muskegon Heights city	12,049	16.3%	78.6%	3.4%
North Muskegon city	4,031	96.5%	0.8%	1.8%
Norton Shores city	22,527	93.4%	2.0%	2.3%
Ravenna township	2,856	95.4%	0.1%	2.8%
Roosevelt Park city	3,890	91.5%	2.4%	2.7%
Sullivan township	2,477	94.6%	0.3%	3.5%
Whitehall city	2,884	94.9%	1.7%	1.9%
Whitehall township	1,648	97.0%	1.0%	1.0%
White River township	1,338	94.0%	0.0%	3.7%

NEWAYGO COUNTY

Newaygo County has a much different history than areas of Western Michigan farther to the south.

While southern counties were mostly settled by farmers and merchants, Newaygo's first permanent non-Indian residents were timber speculators, who moved in to establish "squatters' rights" as soon as Indians gave up title to the region in the 1836 Treaty of Washington.

August Pennoyer and Jack McBride came up the Muskegon River in the summer of 1836 and erected a cabin at the present site of Newaygo. They built a water-powered sawmill and by the fall of 1837 began floating finished lumber downriver to the port at Muskegon.

A few years later, John Brooks set up a mill on Brooks Creek, at Newaygo. He is often considered to be the founder of the town.

The county was at the center of the Michigan lumber boom until the late 1880s, when the big trees were pretty much gone from this part of the state. In 1890, Newaygo county had more than 20,000 residents. That fell by more than 10 percent by 1900 and it would be another half century before the county population rebounded above 20,000. In recent decades, the county has grown at a steady, if not spectacular, pace to its current population of about 50,000.

The county was formally organized in 1851, when it had fewer than 1,000 residents. Newaygo may have been the name of a Chippewa leader, or an Indian word meaning "much water."

Historic railroad bridge crosses Muskegon River at Newaygo (photo courtesy of Newaygo Area Chamber of Commerce)

The area is mostly rolling forest land, cut by the Muskegon, White, Pere Marquette and Little Muskegon rivers, along with scores of creeks and tributaries.

This was the area where the hardwood forests of southern Michigan merged with the pinelands of the north. Today, it remains a transition zone, with the Huron-Manistee National forest occupying thousands of acres in the northern half of the county, while southern townships are a mix of woods, farms and homes.

White Cloud, the governmental seat and the geographic center of the county, bills itself as the place "Where the north begins, and the pure waters flow."

In addition to its forests of pine and hardwood, Newaygo orignally had several dry sand prairies. Farmers tried growing crops on those prairies, with little success, and in some cases left the land denuded of all vegetation. Wind erosion then piled the sand into dunes, and the "Big Prairie Desert" actually became something of a tourist attraction in the 1930s.

Ultimately, the federal government and private property owners succeeded in planting the "desert" with pine trees to stop the erosion.

Today, about 25 percent of the county's land is in agriculture. Products include corn, milk and Christmas trees.

The largest city is Fremont, with about 4,000 residents. The locally founded Gerber Products Co. is now part of the multinational Novartis Group and is headquarterd in New Jersey. But the Gerber Baby Food plant in Fremont is still filling those little jars. It remains Newaygo's largest employer. Fremont is also home to the highly rated Gerber Memorial Hospital.

The north end of the county is sparsely populated. Each of the eight northernmost townships has fewer than 1,000 residents. The smallest, Home and Troy twnships, each have fewer that 300 people, according to U.S. Census Bureau estimates in 2004.

Overall, Newaygo's County's population is about 95 percent non-hispanic whites. But there are pockets of diversity. Merrill township, which includes the former African-American resort community of Woodland Park, is about 18 percent black, while Ashland and Grant townships, at the south end of the county, are about 10 percent Hispanic.

Of Newaygo's 24 townships, only Ensley, near the Kent County line, and Dayton, north of Fremont, have household incomes above the state median.

Two major Muskegon River dams – Croton and Hardy – produce electricity for Consumers Energy, while also creating backwater ponds that are heavily used for recreation.

The 250-acre Newaygo State Park is on Hardy Pond.

NEWAYGO COUNTY FACTS

Population in 2000: 47,874

Land area (square miles): 842

Population density (people per square mile): 56.8

Estimated population, 2004: 49,892

Growth 2000-2004 (percent): 4.22 percent

2004 election results:
Bush, 59.5 percent;
Kerry, 39.6 percent

County seat: White Cloud

Largest cities: Fremont, Newaygo, White Cloud, Grant

Total Tax Base (State Equalized Valuation) 2005: $1.8 billion

- **Agricultural tax base:** $169 million (9.6 percent)
- **Commercial tax base:** $121 million (6.9 percent)
- **Industrial tax base:** $48 million (2.7 percent)
- **Residential tax base:** $1.3 billion (75.9 percent)

Traffic fatalities, 2000-2004: 57

Homicides (murder/ manslaughter) 2000-2004: 7

Major rivers: Muskegon, Little Muskegon, White, South Branch of Pere Marquette

Largest lakes: Hardy Pond (shared with Mecosta County) Croton Pond, Fremont Lake, Hess Lake, Pickerel Lake

Active farms in 2002: 902

Land in farms: 135,000 acres (25.1 percent of land in county)

DEMOGRAPHICS FROM 2000 CENSUS:

White, non-hispanic population: 94.8 percent

Black population: 1.1 percent

American Indian population: 0.6 percent

Asian population: 0.3 percent

Persons reporting two or more races: 1.5 percent

Hispanic population (may be any race): 3.9 percent

Percent of population under age 18: 29.1 percent

Percent of population age 65 or older: 12.8 percent

Percent of adult population (age 25-plus) with four-year college degree: 11.4 percent

Average travel time to work (for workers age 16 and older): 31.0 minutes

Percent of workers who travel to a job outside the county: 47.03 percent

Total number of homes and apartments (housing units): 23,202

Detached, single-family homes: 16,214
Percent of total housing units: 69.88 percent

Dwellings in structures with 10 or more units: 350
Percent of total housing units: 1.51 percent

Mobile homes or house trailers: 5,514
Percent of total housing units: 23.77 percent

Home ownership rate: 84.4 percent

Median value of owner-occupied homes: 88,700

Median household income: $37,130

Income rank among Michigan's 83 counties: 43

Percent of households with income below poverty level: 11.6 percent

LOCAL AREA GROWTH AND ECONOMIC STATISTICS (NEWAYGO COUNTY)

City / Township	2004 Population	2000–2004 Growth	Median Household Income (1999)	Median age of homes in 2000
Ashland township	2,658	3.42%	$42,151	26 years
Barton township	853	4.02%	$35,000	21 years
Beaver township	654	7.57%	$29,500	30 years
Big Prairie township	2,580	4.67%	$32,879	26 years
Bridgeton township	2,348	11.92%	$38,750	22 years
Brooks township	3,750	2.15%	$42,434	29 years
Croton township	3,354	10.26%	$41,596	24 years
Dayton township	2,062	3.00%	$44,770	41 years
Denver township	2,051	4.06%	$33,365	24 years
Ensley township	2,598	5.01%	$47,993	21 years
Everett township	2,070	4.28%	$35,000	26 years
Fremont city	4,271	1.11%	$32,246	36 years
Garfield township	2,524	2.44%	$38,548	31 years
Goodwell township	594	7.80%	$37,813	30 years
Grant city	888	0.79%	$30,972	44 years
Grant township	3,235	3.35%	$41,295	25 years
Home township	287	9.96%	$31,964	29 years
Lilley township	812	3.05%	$25,870	33 years
Lincoln township	1,386	3.59%	$35,739	28 years
Merrill township	614	4.07%	$22,917	29 years
Monroe township	351	8.33%	$30,156	25 years
Newaygo city	1,690	1.20%	$32,273	44 years
Norwich township	607	8.98%	$36,250	28 years
Sheridan charter township	2,471	1.98%	$41,875	43 years
Sherman township	2,266	4.96%	$40,163	33 years
Troy township	273	12.35%	$26,250	14 years
White Cloud city	1,436	1.13%	$24,313	37 years
Wilcox township	1,209	5.59%	$32,039	26 years

LOCAL AREA RACE AND ETHNIC POPULATIONS (NEWAYGO COUNTY)

City / Township	Population (2000 census)	White (non-Hispanic)	Black or African-American	Hispanic or Latino (of any race)
Ashland township	2,570	89.5%	0.1%	9.7%
Barton township	820	97.9%	0.0%	0.8%
Beaver township	608	89.5%	3.3%	4.5%
Big Prairie township	2,465	96.8%	0.4%	1.5%
Bridgeton township	2,098	93.0%	0.1%	3.1%
Brooks township	3,671	94.6%	0.4%	2.7%
Croton township	3,042	97.0%	0.0%	1.4%
Dayton township	2,002	94.9%	0.0%	3.0%
Denver township	1,971	93.8%	0.3%	3.2%
Ensley township	2,474	93.4%	0.4%	3.3%
Everett township	1,985	92.9%	2.7%	1.6%
Fremont city	4,224	95.5%	0.3%	1.7%
Garfield township	2,464	90.9%	0.0%	6.7%
Goodwell township	551	97.5%	0.0%	1.2%
Grant city	881	86.6%	0.5%	13.2%
Grant township	3,130	86.4%	0.1%	11.7%
Home township	261	99.6%	0.0%	0.0%
Lilley township	788	90.8%	5.8%	1.0%
Lincoln township	1,338	94.1%	1.4%	1.1%
Merrill township	590	71.4%	18.0%	4.4%
Monroe township	324	94.5%	0.6%	0.6%
Newaygo city	1,670	92.7%	0.6%	4.7%
Norwich township	557	93.3%	0.0%	4.8%
Sheridan charter township	2,423	95.8%	0.1%	3.2%
Sherman township	2,159	95.5%	0.2%	3.0%
Troy township	243	94.2%	0.0%	5.8%
White Cloud city	1,420	84.7%	8.0%	4.5%
Wilcox township	1,145	94.5%	1.7%	1.1%

OCEANA COUNTY

Oceana County is one of Michigan's favored vacation destinations, in addition to being a prime fruit-growing area. It's a largely rural county that stretches from spectacular sand dunes on the Lake Michigan shore to deep woods 25 miles inland.

It has the smallest population of any West Michigan county. The industry that exists here is mainly in food-processing plants.

Oceana's early settlement was chiefly accomplished by people who moved north along the lakeshore from what are now Ottawa and Muskegon counties in the 1840s and 50s. The first community was established in the late 1840s at the mouth of Whiskey Creek in what is now Claybanks Township, according to Roger Rosentreter, the editor of *Michigan History Magazine* and author of a series of articles on county histories.

The most prominent of Oceana's early developers were the timbermen who exploited the region's forest riches.

William M. Ferry, the founder of Grand Haven, bought extensive timberland about 1850 and set up Oceana's first sawmill at Stony Creek, with his son Thomas. A few years later, Charles Mears extended his own holdings north from the Whitehall area to include a mill at Pentwater.

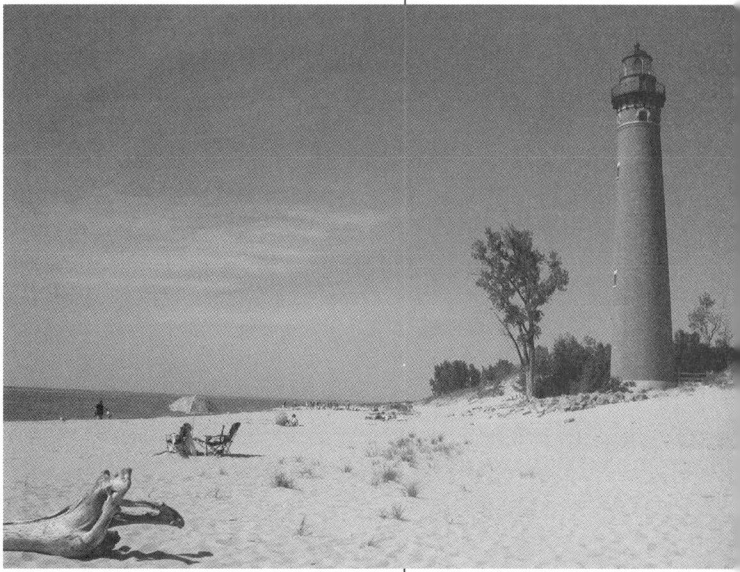

The Little Point Sable Light is an icon on Oceana County's Lake Michigan shoreline (photo: Ed Hoogterp)

Oceana County was formally organized in 1855. Most sources say the name refers to the "freshwater ocean" that is Lake Michigan.

The county's first orchards were planted in the early 1860s. By the end of that decade, peaches, plums and pears were being shipped out of Pentwater to Chicago. As the native pine forests came down, more land was planted to fruit.

In recent decades, some farms have removed their fruit trees in favor of asparagus. Oceana leads the state in production of that vegetable, and hosts the annual National Asparagus

Festival, which alternates between Hart and Shelby.

Many fruit orchards remain, however. State Agriculture Department statistics for 2003 showed Oceana was Michigan's No. 2 county for tart cherries and No. 5 for apples. The gentle terrain and blossoming orchards make for spectacular spring bicycle rides on the back roads around Hart and Pentwater.

Pentwater Lake provides moorings for hundreds of boats (photo: Terry Phipps)

Not everyone who came to Oceana County did so voluntarily. Under an 1855 Indian treaty, members of Grand River Ottawa bands were assembled at Grand Haven and brought north to an Oceana County reservation in 1857-58. The reservation, which included an area of Mason County as well as Crystal and Elbridge townships in Oceana, became home to as many as 1,300 Indians.

For a time, the reservation residents drew annual payments from the government. They also sold maple syrup and other forest products to their white neighbors. Eventually, the reservation was distributed to the Indian residents in 40 and 80-acre parcels. The new owners sold some of the property, and other parcels reverted to the government for unpaid taxes. Today, only about 1 percent of Oceana's population is Indian, according to the 2000 census.

An important prehistoric archeological site is on Dumaw Creek, not far from the former reservation. Researchers believe that ancestors of modern Michigan Indians farmed and hunted around a village at the Dumaw Creek site about 1600 A.D., before Europeans entered Michigan.

Today, the western part of the county, close to Lake Michigan, is devoted largely to tourism and farming. The eastern townships are a mix of woodlands and farms, including some dairies. The Huron-Manistee National Forest takes up thousands of acres in Greenwood, Otto, Crystal and Colfax townships.

Silver Lake State Park, with its towering sand dunes west of Hart, draws summer visitors from throughout the Midwest. It's one of the few places where private "dune buggies" are allowed on open dunes.

Pentwater, at the mouth of the Pentwater River, is a quiet resort village with a beach at Charles Mears State Park and harbor facilities that serve as home port for hundreds of recreational boaters.

The county seat is at Hart. The population has grown steadily in recent decades, but median incomes for year-round residents are far below the state average.

OCEANA COUNTY FACTS

Population in 2000: 26,873

Land area (square miles): 540

Population density (people per square mile): 49.7

Estimated population, 2004: 28,415

Growth 2000-2004 (percent): 5.74 percent

2004 election results: Bush, 54.3 percent; Kerry, 44.2 percent

County seat: Hart

Largest cities: Hart is the only city in Oceana County

Total Tax Base (State Equalized Valuation) 2005: $1.4 billion

Agricultural tax base: $175 million (12.4 percent)

Commercial tax base: $82 million (5.8 percent)

Industrial tax base: $23 million (1.7 percent)

Residential tax base: $1.1 billion (76.6 percent)

Traffic fatalities, 2000-2004: 47

Homicides (murder/ manslaughter) 2000-2004: 5

Major rivers: Pentwater, White

Largest lakes: Silver Lake, Pentwater Lake, Stony Lake, McLaren Lake, Hart Lake

Active farms in 2002: 648

Land in farms: 127,000 acres (36.8 percent of land in county)

DEMOGRAPHICS FROM 2000 CENSUS:

White, non-hispanic population: 85.8 percent

Black population: 0.3 percent

American Indian population: 1.0 percent

Asian population: 0.2 percent

Persons reporting two or more races: 1.9 percent

Hispanic population (may be any race): 11.6 percent

Percent of population under age 18: 28.2 percent

Percent of population age 65 or older: 14.0 percent

Percent of adult population (age 25-plus) with four-year college degree: 12.6 percent

Average travel time to work (for workers age 16 and older): 24.4 minutes

Percent of workers who travel to a job outside the county: 44.57 percent

Total number of homes and apartments (housing units): 15,009

Detached, single-family homes: 10,890
Percent of total housing units: 72.50 percent

Dwellings in structures with 10 or more units: 95
Percent of total housing units: 0.63 percent

Mobile homes or house trailers: 3,024
Percent of total housing units: 20.15 percent

Home ownership rate: 82.7 percent

Median value of owner-occupied homes: $82,500

Median household income: $35,307

Income rank among Michigan's 83 counties: 51

Percent of households with income below poverty level: 14.7 percent

Pentwater's Nickerson Inn has hosted generations of resorters (photo: Terry Phipps)

LOCAL AREA GROWTH AND ECONOMIC STATISTICS (OCEANA COUNTY)

City / Township	2004 Population	2000–2004 Growth	Median Household Income (1999)	Median age of homes in 2000
Benona township	1,591	4.67%	$44,375	27 years
Claybanks township	873	5.05%	$41,319	38 years
Colfax township	612	6.62%	$30,417	22 years
Crystal township	892	7.21%	$31,719	28 years
Elbridge township	1,304	5.76%	$31,838	32 years
Ferry township	1,388	7.10%	$35,170	27 years
Golden township	1,900	4.97%	$35,878	20 years
Grant township	3,183	8.56%	$37,594	24 years
Greenwood township	1,239	7.37%	$36,964	27 years
Hart city	2,005	2.82%	$25,855	55 years
Hart township	2,132	5.23%	$37,434	29 years
Leavitt township	911	7.81%	$30,179	31 years
Newfield township	2,629	5.88%	$30,547	30 years
Otto township	726	9.67%	$36,625	23 years
Pentwater township	1,564	3.37%	$42,574	32 years
Shelby township	4,124	4.38%	$35,078	43 years
Weare township	1,342	6.42%	$37,283	24 years

LOCAL AREA RACE AND ETHNIC POPULATIONS (OCEANA COUNTY)

City / Township	Population (2000 census)	White (non-Hispanic)	Black or African-American	Hispanic or Latino (of any race)
Benona township	1,520	86.9%	0.3%	12.3%
Claybanks township	831	92.2%	0.3%	5.7%
Colfax township	574	84.9%	4.3%	10.4%
Crystal township	832	65.2%	0.2%	31.5%
Elbridge township	1,233	68.8%	0.0%	26.9%
Ferry township	1,296	89.8%	2.2%	4.7%
Golden township	1,810	87.7%	0.0%	11.0%
Grant township	2,932	88.2%	0.2%	9.1%
Greenwood township	1,154	96.2%	0.0%	1.2%
Hart city	1,950	79.7%	0.4%	17.2%
Hart township	2,026	84.3%	0.0%	12.8%
Leavitt township	845	82.6%	0.2%	15.0%
Newfield township	2,483	96.4%	0.1%	2.5%
Otto township	662	94.9%	0.0%	3.8%
Pentwater township	1,513	95.0%	0.0%	2.7%
Shelby township	3,951	78.6%	0.2%	20.0%
Weare township	1,261	86.4%	0.0%	10.6%

OTTAWA COUNTY

Ottawa County, once considered a sleepy rural area populated by Dutch farmers and craftsmen, has been transformed over the past three decades into West Michigan's fastest-growing area, and one of the top economic engines in the state.

Its population has boomed past Berrien, Muskegon and Kalamazoo counties, making it the second-most populated county in West Michigan, behind only Kent.

It is home to such industrial giants as Herman Miller and Haworth. Its median household income is the highest of any West Michigan county, and fourth highest in the state.

Grand Valley State University, in Allendale, is the state's fastest growing public college, while Hope College, in Holland, is annually ranked among the best private institutions in the Midwest.

Meanwhile, plenty of farmers remain, producing apples, blueberries, vegetables, hogs and milk.

And, as if that's not enough, Ottawa's Lake Michigan shoreline has the two most visited sites in the Michigan state park system.

Ottawa County's early history centers on the Grand River, which flows diagonally through the county from Jenison to Grand Haven.

Archeology indicates that as long as 2000 years ago, native Americans were living at the site where Crockery Creek enters the Grand, in Crockery Township.

The DeZwaan windmill towers over Holland's Windmill Island (photo: Ed Hoogterp)

Trader Joseph LaFramboise had a trading post near the same site – and at other locations along the Grand – in the 1690s. LaFramboise was killed by a disgruntled Indian in the first decade of the 1700s. His wife, Magdelaine, continued to operate the posts until 1821, when she sold them to another West Michigan pioneer, Rix Robinson.

William Montague Ferry, the founder of Grand Haven,

arrived in 1834. Three years later, when the county was formally organized, Ferry's settlement at Grand Haven was named the county seat. The county is named for the Ottawa Indians, who lived along the river.

Grand Haven maintains a lively downtown for summer visitors (photo: Terry Phipps)

In 1847, the Rev. Albertus Van Raalte led a group of religious separatists from the Netherlands to West Michigan and founded the town of Holland, on Lake Macatawa. Thousands of Dutch immigrants followed those pioneers into the area, building churches, farms, schools and colleges.

Though the Dutch influence has diminished in the growth spurt of recent decades, the 2000 census reported that more than a third of the county's residents have some Dutch ancestry.

With six cities and 17 townships, Ottawa presents many faces to the world.

There's the sparkling Lake Michigan shoreline on the west side, with Holland and Grand Haven state parks each attracting a million or more visitors each year.

Just inland, there's flat agricultural land covered with blueberry fields, tree nurseries and greenhouses.

Further inland are cornfields, muck farms, apple orchards and small towns. And finally, on the eastern edge of the county near Grand Rapids, there is sprawling, bustling suburbia.

The median household income for Ottawa County residents is nearly 20 percent higher than the median for all Michigan residents. The most affluent areas are along the Lake Michigan shore and in the Grand Rapids suburbs.

The I-96 expressway traverses the northern part of the county, while I-196 runs through the southern townships. The state Transportation Department has a proposal to link those highways with a new expressway that would run from I-196 near Zeeland north to I-96 east of Grand Haven. The proposal would create a high-speed alternative to the existing US-31, allowing north-south traffic to bypass both Grand

Haven and Holland. Opponents of the plan fear it would destroy valuable farmland and spur even more residential and commercial growth.

The I-196 corridor, linking Grand Rapids and Holland, is West Michigan's most rapidly developing area, with Zeeland Township, Holland Township and Jamestown Township all adding about 15 percent to their populations between 2000 and 2004.

OTTAWA COUNTY FACTS

Population in 2000: 238,314

Land area (square miles): 566

Population density (people per square mile): 421.3

Estimated population, 2004: 252,351

Growth 2000-2004 (percent): 5.89 percent

2004 election results:
Bush, 71.6 percent;
Kerry, 27.6 percent

County seat: Grand Haven

Largest cities: Holland, Grand Haven, Hudsonville, Zeeland,

Total Tax Base (State Equalized Valuation) 2005: $10.3 billion

Agricultural tax base:
$543 million (5.2 percent)

Commercial tax base:
$1.2 billion (11.5 percent)

Industrial tax base:
$758 million (7.3 percent)

Residential tax base:
$7.2 billion (70.0 percent)

Traffic fatalities, 2000-2004: 152

Homicides (murder/ manslaughter) 2000-2004: 11

Major rivers: Grand, Macatawa, Pigeon

Largest lakes: Lake Macatawa, Spring Lake (shared with Muskegon County), Pigeon Lake, Little Black Lake, Stearns Bayou

Active farms in 2002: 1,291

Land in farms: 165,000 acres (45.7 percent of land in county)

DEMOGRAPHICS FROM 2000 CENSUS:

White, non-hispanic population: 88.6 percent

Black population: 1.0 percent

American Indian population: 0.4 percent

Asian population: 2.1 percent

Persons reporting two or more races: 1.5 percent

Hispanic population (may be any race): 7.0 percent

Percent of population under age 18: 28.7 percent

Percent of population age 65 or older: 10.1 percent

Percent of adult population (age 25-plus) with four-year college degree: 26.0 percent

Average travel time to work (for workers age 16 and older): 19.4 minutes

Percent of workers who travel to jobs outside the county: 37.55 percent

Home ownership rate: 80.7 percent

Median value of owner-occupied homes: $133,000

Median household income: $52,347

Income rank among Michigan's 83 counties: 4

Percent of households with income below poverty level: 5.5 percent

Total number of homes and apartments (housing units): 86,856

Detached, single-family homes: 61,292
Percent of total housing units: 70.57 percent

Dwellings in structures with 10 or more units: 5,211
Percent of total housing units: 6.00 percent

Mobile homes or house trailers: 6,540
Percent of total housing units: 7.53 percent

LOCAL AREA GROWTH AND ECONOMIC STATISTICS (OTTAWA COUNTY)

City / Township	2004 Population	2000–2004 Growth	Median Household Income (1999)	Median age of homes in 2000
Allendale township	15,790	21.07%	$48,669	15 years
Blendon township	5,811	1.57%	$56,094	25 years
Chester township	2,328	0.56%	$46,328	39 years
Coopersville city	4,114	5.22%	$48,875	24 years
Crockery township	3,816	0.90%	$42,399	32 years
Ferrysburg city	3,005	-1.15%	$53,622	25 years
Georgetown township	43,703	4.91%	$58,936	20 years
Grand Haven city	10,733	-3.90%	$40,322	44 years
Grand Haven township	14,838	11.75%	$62,380	18 years
Holland city	27,185	-2.37%	$42,994	43 years
Holland township	33,338	15.31%	$49,458	15 years
Hudsonville city	7,091	-0.96%	$46,961	23 years
Jamestown charter township	5,821	14.99%	$68,689	25 years
Olive township	4,775	1.79%	$48,526	20 years
Park township	18,228	3.69%	$65,328	22 years
Polkton township	2,431	4.11%	$53,929	34 years
Port Sheldon township	4,636	2.95%	$63,604	17 years
Robinson township	5,984	7.09%	$57,110	17 years
Spring Lake township	14,077	7.13%	$50,648	23 years
Tallmadge township	7,009	1.86%	$59,205	25 years
Wright township	3,282	-0.12%	$51,023	41 years
Zeeland city	5,588	-3.74%	$45,611	41 years
Zeeland charter township	8,768	15.17%	$52,079	12 years

LOCAL AREA RACE AND ETHNIC POPULATIONS (OTTAWA COUNTY)

City / Township	Population (2000 census)	White (non-Hispanic)	Black or African-American	Hispanic or Latino (of any race)
Allendale township	13,042	93.1%	2.4%	2.7%
Blendon township	5,721	98.3%	0.0%	0.8%
Chester township	2,315	92.4%	0.4%	5.9%
Coopersville city	3,910	96.2%	0.0%	2.9%
Crockery township	3,782	94.1%	0.8%	3.6%
Ferrysburg city	3,040	97.1%	0.2%	0.8%
Georgetown township	41,658	96.0%	0.7%	2.0%
Grand Haven city	11,168	95.1%	0.6%	1.3%
Grand Haven township	13,278	96.4%	0.0%	2.3%
Holland city	27,846	67.7%	2.3%	23.8%
Holland township	28,911	72.4%	2.2%	15.6%
Hudsonville city	7,160	96.2%	0.7%	2.1%
Jamestown charter township	5,062	96.0%	0.0%	2.3%
Olive township	4,691	82.1%	1.9%	12.9%
Park township	17,579	90.6%	0.3%	5.3%
Polkton township	2,335	93.3%	0.3%	5.4%
Port Sheldon township	4,503	90.4%	0.1%	5.5%
Robinson township	5,588	91.2%	0.2%	3.9%
Spring Lake township	13,140	96.1%	0.0%	2.6%
Tallmadge township	6,881	97.8%	0.7%	0.4%
Wright township	3,286	93.1%	0.2%	4.5%
Zeeland city	5,805	92.6%	0.2%	4.5%
Zeeland charter township	7,613	88.6%	0.2%	7.9%

ST. JOSEPH COUNTY

St. Joseph County is an attractive mixture of productive farmland and small towns along the Indiana border south of Kalamazoo.

It's known as one of Michigan's outstanding agricultural areas. It also possesses a significant amount of industry. There's even summer tourism, largely involving people from Indiana and Illinois who vacation on St. Joseph County lakes.

Early settlers found a gently rolling landscape of forests and prairies, dotted with Indian villages along the streams. The prairie openings, which the Indians had maintained through periodic burning, were especially valued by the settlers because the land could be planted to crops without first having to clear away trees.

Among the first settlers were John Sturgis, who came to the Sturgis area about 1827, and William Meek, who founded Constantine (then known as Meek's Mill) the following year.

The Territorial Legislature set up the county in 1829. It is named for the St. Joseph River, which enters near Colon, and meanders southwest through eight of the county's sixteen townships before flowing south into Indiana.

Along the way, the St. Joe grows into a much larger stream, picking up the waters of the Fawn River, Prairie River, Rocky River, and Portage River.

(After dipping into Indiana, the river bends back north into Michigan and empties into Lake Michigan at the city of St. Joseph, which is in Berrien County.)

The United States Land Office building in White Pigeon is among the oldest structures in West Michigan (photo: Ed Hoogterp)

The 1821 Treaty of Chicago, in which Indians ceded the area to the United States government, set aside a large reservation on the Mendon Prairie. By 1833, most of the local Potawatomi Indians had been forced to move to Kansas, and that former reservation was opened to settlers.

The first government land office in West Michigan was opened in 1831 at White

Pigeon. The land office building still exists, considered one of the oldest surviving structures in this part of the state.

It would be a stretch to call St. Joseph County wealthy, with median household income about $5,000 below the figure for the state as a whole. But such communities as Mendon, Three Rivers, Constantine and Sturgis have escaped the deterioration that affected many other Michigan small towns. They retain the look and feel of Middle America at its best.

The largest city is Sturgis, while the county seat is at the village of Centreville.

Large industrial plants such as Lear in Mendon, Summit Polymers in Sturgis, and American Axle & Manufacturing in Three Rivers provide a job base that allows most residents to find work without having to drive to other counties.

More than 70 percent of the land in St. Joseph County is in agriculture, the highest percentage in West Michigan. The southern part of the county, especially around Constantine, is a leading producer of seed corn, which is processed by national seed companies and resold to other farmers as the basis for the following year's crop. Seed corn production requires a higher investment than run-of-the-mill field corn – the cropland must be irrigated, for example – and it brings a higher return to growers.

St. Joe is also among Michigan's top five counties in production of cucumbers, snap beans and sheep, according to the 2002 census of agriculture.

In the early years of settlement, travel in St. Joseph County was mainly on the waterways or along territorial roads that followed approximately the present alignments of M-60 and US-12. Both of those roads followed ancient Indian trails. Railroads reached Sturgis and Three Rivers in the 1850s.

Today, St. Joseph has a network of two-lane and four-lane roads, but no expressway connections. US-131 enters the county from the north as a divided highway, but the median disappears at Three Rivers. Business groups have clamored for a US-131 expressway link to the Indiana Toll Road. A state study found in early 2006 that the highway didn't have enough traffic to warrant consideration as an expressway. But, under pressure from legislators and business leaders, transportation officials relented on that position. US-131 expansion is now back on the table, though without a concrete timetable.

ST. JOSEPH COUNTY FACTS

Population in 2000: 62,422

Land area (square miles): 504

Population density (people per square mile): 123.9

Estimated population, 2004: 62,964

Growth 2000-2004 (percent): 0.87 percent

2004 election results: Bush, 60.8 percent; Kerry, 38.2 percent

County seat: Centreville

Largest cities: Sturgis, Three Rivers

Total Tax Base (State Equalized Valuation) 2005: $2.1 billion

Agricultural tax base: $333 million (15.6 percent)

Commercial tax base: $169 million (7.9 percent)

Industrial tax base: $110 million (5.2 percent)

Residential tax base: $1.3 billion (62.2 percent)

Traffic fatalities, 2000-2004: 72

Homicides (murder/ manslaughter) 2000-2004: 11

Major rivers: St. Joseph, Portage, Prairie, Rocky, White Pigeon

Largest lakes: Klinger Lake, Corey Lake, Sturgis Pond, Constantine Hydro Pond, Portage Lake

Active farms in 2002: 907

Land in farms: 231,000 acres (71.5 percent of land in county)

DEMOGRAPHICS FROM 2000 CENSUS:

White, non-hispanic population: 91.3 percent

Black population: 2.6 percent

American Indian population: 0.4 percent

Asian population: 0.6 percent

Persons reporting two or more races: 1.5 percent

Hispanic population (may be any race): 4.0 percent

Percent of population under age 18: 27.5 percent

Percent of population age 65 or older: 13.0 percent

Percent of adult population (age 25-plus) with four-year college degree: 12.7 percent

Average travel time to work (for workers age 16 and older): 20.8 minutes

Percent of workers who travel to jobs outside the county: 28.72 percent

Total number of homes and apartments (housing units): 26,503

Detached, single-family homes: 20,010
Percent of total housing units: 75.5 percent

Dwellings in structures with 10 or more units: 1,108
Percent of total housing units: 4.18 percent

Mobile homes or house trailers: 2,915
Percent of total housing units: 11.0 percent

Home ownership rate: 76.9 percent

Median value of owner-occupied homes: $85,000

Median household income: $40,355

Income rank among Michigan's 83 counties: 28

Percent of households with income below poverty level: 11.3 percent

LOCAL AREA GROWTH AND ECONOMIC STATISTICS (ST. JOSEPH COUNTY)

City / Township	2004 Population	2000–2004 Growth	Median Household Income (1999)	Median age of homes in 2000
Burr Oak township	2,759	0.80%	$44,875	40 years
Colon township	3,380	-0.73%	$34,890	41 years
Constantine township	4,208	0.65%	$43,125	39 years
Fabius township	3,348	1.92%	$50,888	30 years
Fawn River township	1,648	1.79%	$41,852	33 years
Florence township	1,411	-1.74%	$45,288	37 years
Flowerfield township	1,679	5.46%	$46,897	25 years
Leonidas township	1,226	-1.05%	$42,417	53 years
Lockport township	3,987	4.24%	$43,931	29 years
Mendon township	2,821	1.66%	$41,324	28 years
Mottville township	1,499	0.00%	$43,421	31 years
Nottawa township	4,118	2.98%	$41,875	30 years
Park township	2,801	3.78%	$48,173	35 years
Sherman township	3,485	8.06%	$47,727	33 years
Sturgis city	11,120	-2.04%	$33,838	46 years
Sturgis township	2,381	-0.42%	$40,982	24 years
Three Rivers city	7,126	-2.61%	$32,460	53 years
White Pigeon township	3,967	3.12%	$42,908	37 years

LOCAL AREA RACE AND ETHNIC POPULATIONS (ST. JOSEPH COUNTY)

City / Township	Population (2000 census)	White (non-Hispanic)	Black or African-American	Hispanic or Latino (of any race)
Burr Oak township	2,739	97.4%	0.8%	1.1%
Colon township	3,405	96.9%	0.0%	0.4%
Constantine township	4,181	96.7%	0.2%	0.5%
Fabius township	3,285	96.2%	0.5%	0.2%
Fawn River township	1,648	93.6%	2.1%	3.2%
Florence township	1,436	92.4%	0.7%	5.1%
Flowerfield township	1,592	95.7%	0.8%	1.4%
Leonidas township	1,239	99.8%	0.0%	0.2%
Lockport township	3,814	86.1%	10.4%	0.3%
Mendon township	2,775	97.5%	0.5%	0.6%
Mottville township	1,499	97.2%	0.0%	1.2%
Nottawa township	3,999	96.5%	2.1%	0.4%
Park township	2,699	90.0%	2.7%	3.4%
Sherman township	3,248	94.0%	0.2%	2.0%
Sturgis city	11,285	82.6%	1.5%	13.0%
Sturgis township	2,403	91.8%	0.5%	5.0%
Three Rivers city	7,328	83.5%	9.6%	3.3%
White Pigeon township	3,847	95.9%	0.0%	1.5%

VAN BUREN COUNTY

Van Buren County, which stretches between Kalamazoo and Lake Michigan, is a traditional farm and orchard region that remains largely rural, except for fast growing townships adjacent to Kalamazoo.

This is a great fruit-growing land. It has 7,500 acres of blueberry fields, the most in Michigan, and is among the top three counties for grapes and apples.

Van Buren County was established by the Territorial Legislature in 1829, and named for Martin Van Buren, who was secretary of state at the time. Van Buren later was elected as the eighth president of the United States, serving from 1837-1841.

The county's first permanent settlers were Nancy and Dolphin Morris, who moved from Virginia to a homestead in Decatur Township in 1829.

The land filled rapidly with farmers and merchants. By the mid 1830s, Daniel Dodge's tavern in Paw Paw had become an important stopping off place for travelers on the Territorial Road. By 1837, when Michigan attained statehood, Epaphroditus Ransom was holding court as the county's first circuit judge.

Paw Paw was chosen over Lawrence as the county seat in 1840.

The early farmers planted apple orchards along with their other crops. The first vineyards were established in the 1860s near Lawton.

South Haven, on Lake Michigan in the county's northwest corner, is Van Buren's largest city, with just over 5,000 residents. But the county's center of population is shifting to the east, where the townships of Almena and Antwerp are becoming bedroom communities for the Kalamazoo metro area.

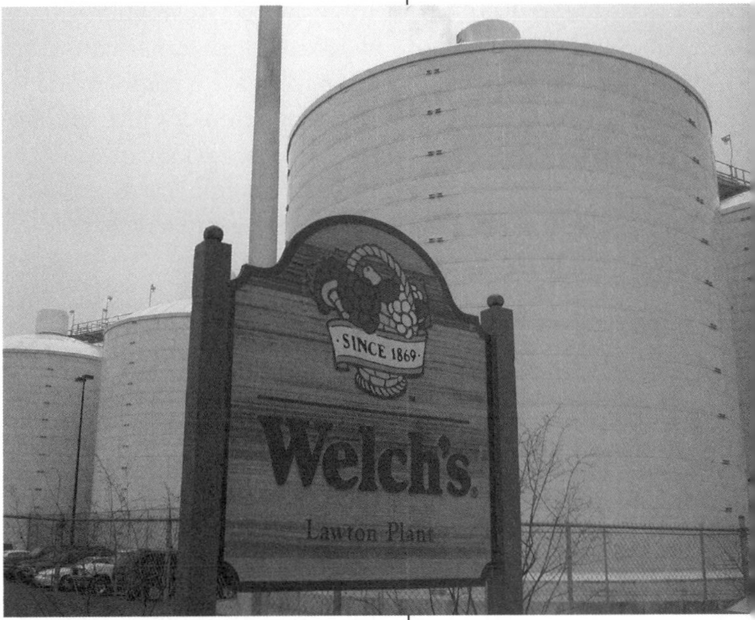

Huge tanks at Lawton hold the juice from grapes grown in the surrounding area (photo: Ed Hoogterp)

Antwerp, which includes the villages of Mattawan and Lawton, gained nearly 1,000 residents from 2000 to 2004, according to U.S. census estimates.

The townships close to Kalamazoo are also the most affluent. Median incomes in the eastern tier of townships are often 40 percent or more above those in the center of the county.

Covert Township, south of South Haven, is the only rural township in West Michigan where African Americans and Hispanics are a majority of the population. It's also among the poorest areas, with a median income less than half that of the state as a whole.

The St. Julian Winery in Paw Paw is the state's largest and oldest. It moved here from Canada soon after the end of prohibition. During its early history, St. Julian made its wines from the Concord and Niagara grapes that were grown in the area primarily for juice. More recently, the company has created highly regarded vintages from such traditional wine grapes as Merlot and Chardonnay.

Van Buren County is bisected by the Paw Paw River, which runs through the towns of Hartford, Lawrence and Paw Paw. The county's other major stream, the Black River, empties into Lake Michigan at South Haven.
Much of the county is rolling and attractive farmland.

There is little public land here, other than Van Buren State Park, on Lake Michigan. The Timber Ridge Ski area is in Pine Grove Township, in the county's northeast corner. Consumers Energy's Palisades Nuclear Power Plant is on Lake Michigan in Covert Township.

Among Van Buren's best known residents was ventriloquist Edgar Bergen (1903-1978), who grew up in Decatur. Bergen and his wooden dummies, Charley McCarthy and Mortimer Snerd, were among America's favorite entertainers in the first half of the 20th century.

South Haven was home to Liberty Hyde Bailey (1858-1954), a pioneer of American agricultural education. During his long career, Bailey wrote more than 60 books, and headed the horticulture departments at Michigan State University and Cornell University, two of the nation's best known agricultural colleges.

His family home in South Haven is a museum and also a state and national historic site.

Other museums in Van Buren County include the Poor House County Museum near Hartford and the Michigan Maritime Museum on the South Haven waterfront.
The Maritime Museum

South Haven's business district is characterized by solid, well-maintained structures (photo: Terry Phipps)

includes a research library and exhibits of watercraft. It is home to the tallship *Friends Good Will.*

VAN BUREN COUNTY FACTS

Population in 2000: 76,263

Land area (square miles): 611

Population density (people per square mile): 124.8

Estimated population, 2004: 78,541

Growth 2000-2004 (percent): 2.99 percent

2004 election results: Bush, 51.6 percent; Kerry, 47.3 percent

County seat: Paw Paw

Largest cities: South Haven, Hartford, Bangor

Total Tax Base (State Equalized Valuation) 2005: $3.2 billion

- **Agricultural tax base:** $289 million (9.0 percent)
- **Commercial tax base:** $237 million (7.4 percent)
- **Industrial tax base:** $267 million (8.3 percent)
- **Residential tax base:** $2.1 billion (66.2 percent)

Traffic fatalities, 2000-2004: 86

Homicides (murder/ manslaughter) 2000-2004: 17

Major rivers: Black, Paw Paw

Largest lakes: Magician Lake, Bankson Lake, Lake of the Woods, Gravel Lake, Saddle Lake

Active farms in 2002: 1,160

Land in farms: 176,000 acres (45.1 percent of land in county)

DEMOGRAPHICS FROM 2000 CENSUS:

White, non-hispanic population: 84.5 percent

Black population: 5.2 percent

American Indian population: 0.9 percent

Asian population: 0.3 percent

Persons reporting two or more races: 2.2 percent

Hispanic population (may be any race): 7.4 percent

Percent of population under age 18: 28.1 percent

Percent of population age 65 or older: 12.3 percent

Percent of adult population (age 25-plus) with four-year college degree: 14.3 percent

Average travel time to work (for workers age 16 and older): 23.6 minutes

Percent of workers who travel to jobs outside the county: 49.98 percent

Total number of homes and apartments (housing units): 33,975

Detached, single-family homes: 25,227
Percent of total housing units: 74.25 percent

Dwellings in structures with 10 or more units: 955
Percent of total housing units: 2.81 percent

Mobile homes or house trailers: 5,020
Percent of total housing units: 14.78 percent

Home ownership rate: 79.6 percent

Median value of owner-occupied homes: $94,200

Median household income: $39,365

Income rank among Michigan's 83 counties: 32

Percent of households with income below poverty level: 11.1 percent

LOCAL AREA GROWTH AND ECONOMIC STATISTICS (VAN BUREN COUNTY)

City / Township	2004 Population	2000–2004 Growth	Median Household Income (1999)	Median age of homes in 2000
Almena township	4,779	13.09%	$51,027	20 years
Antwerp township	11,798	9.11%	$50,556	23 years
Arlington township	2,112	1.78%	$36,847	35 years
Bangor city	1,896	-1.91%	$28,165	45 years
Bangor township	2,197	3.58%	$35,375	33 years
Bloomingdale township	3,494	3.86%	$40,488	26 years
Columbia township	2,796	3.02%	$34,389	31 years
Covert township	3,169	0.89%	$22,829	34 years
Decatur township	3,956	1.02%	$35,754	45 years
Geneva township	4,051	1.91%	$34,900	19 years
Gobles city	811	-0.49%	$26,917	48 years
Hamilton township	1,866	3.84%	$37,434	27 years
Hartford city	2,450	-1.05%	$32,879	45 years
Hartford township	3,212	1.68%	$35,741	28 years
Keeler township	2,570	-1.19%	$42,955	40 years
Lawrence township	3,399	1.74%	$36,944	35 years
Paw Paw township	7,067	-0.34%	$43,802	37 years
Pine Grove township	2,896	4.44%	$47,060	28 years
Porter township	2,438	1.33%	$48,491	32 years
South Haven city	5,135	2.43%	$35,731	48 years
South Haven township	3,987	-1.46%	$35,000	30 years
Waverly township	2,462	-0.20%	$51,100	25 years

LOCAL AREA RACE AND ETHNIC POPULATIONS (VAN BUREN COUNTY)

City / Township	Population (2000 census)	White (non-Hispanic)	Black or African-American	Hispanic or Latino (of any race)
Almena township	4,226	96.3%	1.6%	2.0%
Antwerp township	10,813	91.4%	1.1%	4.8%
Arlington township	2,075	87.0%	4.7%	7.7%
Bangor city	1,933	72.6%	13.0%	12.7%
Bangor township	2,121	81.8%	2.1%	13.2%
Bloomingdale township	3,364	90.4%	1.9%	5.7%
Columbia township	2,714	84.2%	3.1%	9.9%
Covert township	3,141	44.7%	36.1%	15.7%
Decatur township	3,916	86.9%	5.6%	4.1%
Geneva township	3,975	79.9%	11.1%	5.6%
Gobles city	815	89.3%	0.1%	4.5%
Hamilton township	1,797	73.9%	1.9%	21.1%
Hartford city	2,476	78.1%	0.4%	14.9%
Hartford township	3,159	82.6%	0.8%	13.9%
Keeler township	2,601	73.8%	0.0%	23.7%
Lawrence township	3,341	79.3%	4.1%	13.8%
Paw Paw township	7,091	91.6%	2.5%	3.6%
Pine Grove township	2,773	93.2%	0.7%	2.0%
Porter township	2,406	94.7%	0.0%	4.9%
South Haven city	5,013	80.7%	12.5%	3.3%
South Haven charter township	4,046	81.5%	12.8%	4.0%
Waverly township	2,467	93.4%	0.9%	3.4%

URBAN REGIONS

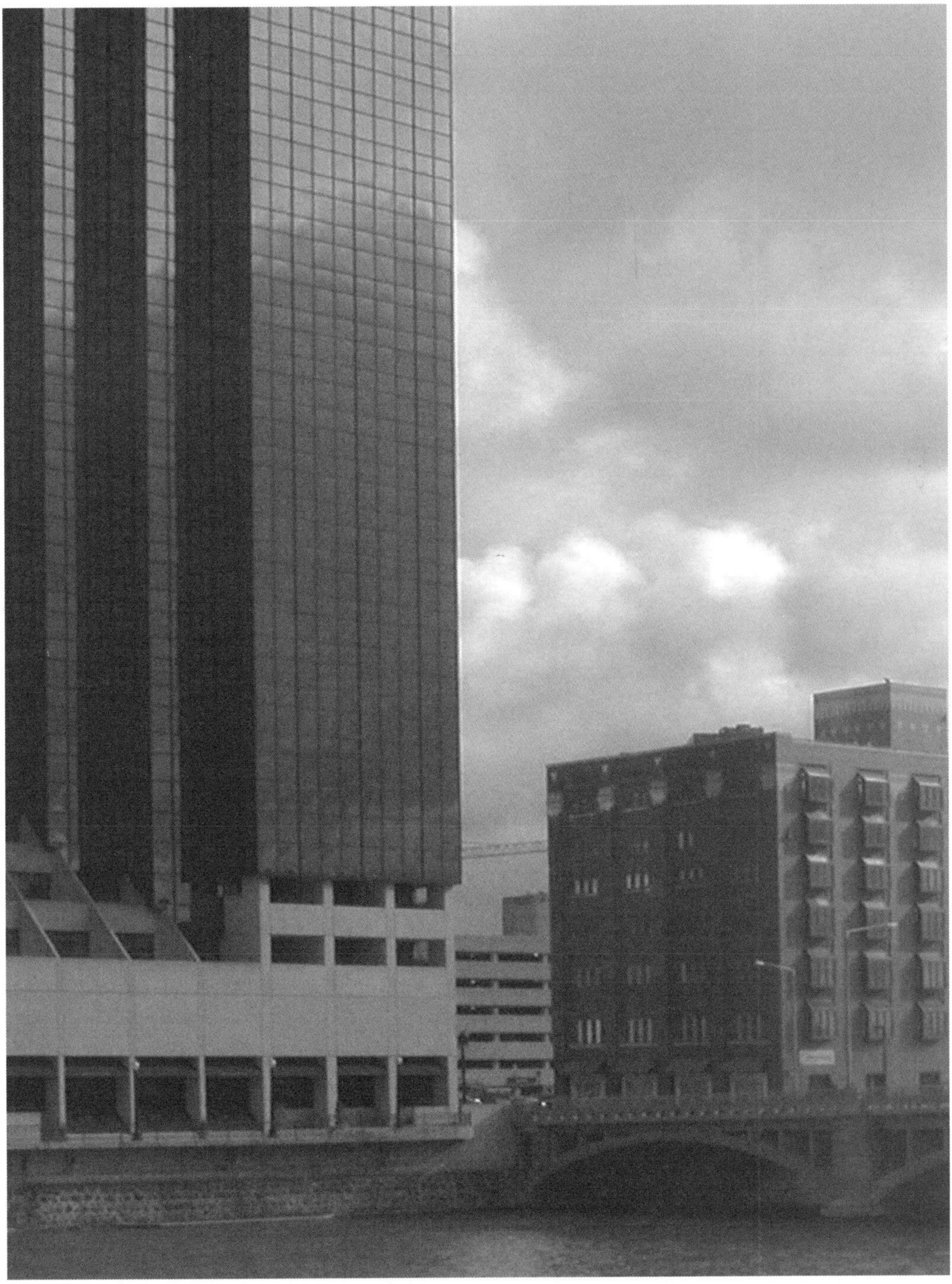

Photo on previous page: Ed Hoogterp

BENTON HARBOR/ ST. JOSEPH

2004 Population:

Benton Harbor: 10,022	
Saint Joseph: 8,701	
Benton Township: 16,102	
Saint Joseph Township: 10,851.	
Lincoln Township: 14,340	
Total 60,016	

In decades of media reports, this small urban area has been portrayed as a symbol of the American dichotomy: Benton Harbor, poor and black; St. Joseph wealthy and white.

The reality, as usual, is a bit more complicated.

While the St. Joseph River marks a clear economic and racial divide between the two towns, the surrounding urban townships are considerably more integrated.

And, far from being "wealthy," residents of the city of St. Joseph have median incomes about 15 percent below the level for Michigan as a whole.

What sets this region apart from everywhere else in Michigan is not the wealth of the surrounding area, but the poverty in the urban core of Benton Harbor. The city is the poorest in Michigan, with household incomes less than half the median for the rest of the state.

Economic development officials, including leaders of the Cornerstone Chamber of Commerce, have hope of better days in the near future.

An abandoned school reflects the deterioration of Benton Harbor (photo: Ed Hoogterp)

New housing is going up on the Benton Harbor side of the St. Joseph River, and plans are in the works for a huge development called Harbor Shores that would extend into St. Joseph, Benton Harbor and Benton Charter Township. The $500 million development, along the river and the Lake Michigan shoreline, could include as many as 1,000 homes as well as commercial buildings, a hotel and a Jack Nicklaus signature golf course.

The project, if it comes to fruition, would be a huge boost to a metro area that has seen little if any growth for half a century. If it doesn't fly, it is at least an indication that the region has both the space and the interest to resume growth in the future.

Benton Harbor was a steadily growing industrial and commercial center from about the time of the Civil War until the end of World War II. In the 1940s and 50s, jobs in the area's factories lured new residents, including whites from the rural South, and African-Americans from the South and from metro Chicago.

By 1960, Benton Harbor was a busy community of nearly 20,000 residents. About 75 percent were white, and 25 percent black.

In the next decade, whites left the city by the thousands, and blacks continued to move in. From 1960 to 1970, Benton Harbor's white population fell by half, while the black population more than doubled. By 2004, the city's population had fallen to about 10,000 and 95 percent of those who remained were African-Americans.

In other Michigan communities, so-called "white-flight" led to fast-growing suburbs just outside the central city. But here, instead of moving to the suburbs, many whites apparently moved out of the metro area altogether. The overall population of Berrien County has barely budged since 1960.

This community was devastated by factory closings that began in the 1960s and continued into the 1990s. Firms like Clark Equipment Co. disappeared from the landscape, taking with them many of Berrien County's blue-collar jobs. The area's remaining major employer, Whirlpool Corp, has reduced manufacturing employment, while keeping its world headquarters in Benton Township.

St. Joseph weathered the economic storm, with county government, Lakeland Hospital and a tourist-friendly downtown continuing to provide jobs. Benton Harbor simply collapsed, losing most of its local commerce along with its industrial base.

A long-running school desegregation order from a federal court gave the Benton Harbor schools extra money while allowing some of the city's students to attend suburban schools. But the school district continued to decline. Racial disturbances rocked Benton Harbor in the 1960s and again in 2003.

In recent years, the town has made tentative steps toward revival. Chicago sculptor Richard Hunt opened a studio in Benton Harbor, and a growing downtown arts district includes several studios and galleries, along with the Livery, a microbrewery and concert venue in a building once used as a stable.

GRAND RAPIDS

2004 Population:

Grand Rapids; 195,115

Walker: 23,315

Grandville: 16,680

Wyoming: 70,300

Kentwood: 46,538

East Grand Rapids: 10,482

Grand Rapids Township: 14,621

Total: 377,051

With more than 375,000 people living in a 12-mile-square area, Grand Rapids and its close-in suburbs make up by far the largest urban region in West Michigan.

Grand Rapids is West Michigan's largest city, and suburban Wyoming is poised to pass Kalamazoo as No. 2 in the next few years.

The urban area is growing strong, but it faces significant problems in a changing economy. Several of the largest manufacturers, notably Steelcase Inc., have cut back employment in recent years. That's been a blow to a town whose prosperity has long been tied to blue-collar jobs in such industries as auto parts, furniture and office systems.

Local economic developers are hoping that biotechnology, health care and higher education will take up some of the slack.

Growth in those fields is centered on Michigan Street, a few blocks from downtown Grand Rapids, where the Van Andel Institute, Spectrum Health (the former Butterworth Hospital) and Grand Valley State University all have major facilities. A Grand Rapids campus for Michigan State University's medical school could end up in the same area.

These days, downtown Grand Rapids seems a major success story.

Grand Rapids' modern skyline stands above the Grand River (photo: Ed Hoogterp)

Folks are living in high rise condominiums and in renovated factory buildings along the Grand River. The 12,000-seat Van Andel Arena is perhaps the most successful concert venue of its size anywhere in the country. The old Heartside District near the arena has morphed into a quirky and popular nightclub district.

The Grand Rapids Civic Theater and Grand Rapids Art Museum are in the midst of expansions. Grand Valley State, Western Michigan and Ferris State universities all have facilities downtown.

But that success came only after about three decades of trying to get it right. Downtown Grand Rapids was a bustling retail center into the 1960s. The main thoroughfare, Monroe Avenue, had three large locally owned department stores – Wurzburg's, Herpolsheimer's and Steketee's – along with four national chain "dime stores." There also were movie theaters, restaurants and a selection of jewelers, apparel shops and other specialty stores.

Local teen-agers came downtown by the hundreds on weekend nights to drive "The Circuit," and both Kennedy and Nixon spoke to huge crowds outdoors on Campau Square during the 1960 presidential election campaign.

But things were already changing. Urban renewal projects in the 60s leveled half a dozen blocks to create a new government and financial center. The I-196 and US-131 expressways were built through the center of town, making it easy for motorists to enter – or leave – the central city.

The first Meijer Thrifty Acres store opened on the outskirts of town in 1962. By the late 60s there were three enclosed shopping centers on 28th Street: Rogers Plaza in Wyoming; Eastbrook Mall in Grand Rapids and Woodland Mall in Kentwood.

In the 1970s, the area's defacto main street was no longer Monroe Avenue, but the five-lane 28th Street that had once served as a "Belt Line" marking the southern margin of the urban area.

The 1981 opening of a new convention center, along with the Gerald R. Ford Presidential Museum and the Amway Grand Plaza Hotel, kept some activity downtown. But the shopping district continued its slow decline.

Monroe Avenue was converted to a pedestrian mall and renamed Monroe Center, but that barely slowed the exodus. One-by-one, the department stores closed. A few smaller shops held on, but most went out of business or moved to the suburbs.

The latest revival began in the 1990s, when the opening of Van Andel Arena helped to spur the formation of the lively club and restaurant district.

There's still precious little retail downtown, but there's hope. In late 2005, a new bookstore opened in a renovated section of the old Steketee's store, and planners say more shops are possible.

The urban area's main retail centers now are at Woodland Mall in Kentwood, Rivertown Crossings in Grandville and Alpine Avenue in Walker. The M-6 expressway, which opened in 2004 as the new south beltline, is drawing some development to its wide-open exits. A shopping center with a Meijer store and a multi-plex theater is up and running at the Kalamazoo Avenue exit, and Metro Health is building a new hospital at the Byron Center Road exit in Wyoming.

Like most central cities, Grand Rapids often has a testy relationship with its smaller neighbors. The cities of Wyoming, Kentwood, and Walker all incorporated about 1960 to halt annexations by Grand Rapids.

Several northern townships are banding together to build their own sewer system, largely because they didn't like the prospect of Grand Rapids restricting sewer expansion to control their growth.

Some of that animosity has eased in recent years. Kent County helped spur the downtown revival by taking part in financing such facilities as the Van Andel Arena and DeVos Place convention center. Voters in the region agreed to tax themselves to support the bus system, known as The Rapid. And the Grand Valley Metro Council has helped communities work together on common issues.

Perhaps the most serious problem facing the region is the Grand Rapids Public School system, which is plagued by falling enrollment, aging facilities and chronic budget shortfalls.

KALAMAZOO

2004 Population:
Kalamazoo: 73,960
Portage: 45,210
Kalamazoo Township: 21,639
Parchment: 1,832
Oshtemo: 19,139
Texas Township: 12,145
Comstock Township: 14,909
Total: 188,834

Downtown Kalamazoo includes an interesting mix of modern and historic buildings (photo courtesy of Jennifer Giesey)

Kalamazoo has never been what you'd call a typical community.

For more than 100 years, Kalamazoo has built itself around big institutions and big industries. It wasn't merely a farming town in the early days, it was a national center for production of its two main agricultural products, celery and mint.

The paper industry, which first appeared on the Kalamazoo River in 1867, employed thousands of workers. In later years, Western Michigan University, Upjohn Pharmaceuticals and the city's two highly regarded hospitals – Bronson and Borgess – became the engines of employment.

From the 1850s until the 1970s, the Kalamazoo State Hospital housed thousands of mental patients, and employed nearly that many staff. The state began downsizing the hospital in the 1970s, when more humane and effective treatments for mental illness became available. The hospital's 175 foot tall brick water tower still stands as one of Kalamazoo's most recognizable landmarks.

Corporate mergers made Upjohn part of Pfizer, Inc., which remains a major employer in Kalamazoo.

The paper industry, which provided prosperity for nearly 100 years, is largely gone. Unfortunately, it left a legacy of pollution in the Kalamazoo River and at mill sites up and down the stream. Plans for cleaning up those sites – and the river itself – could help to enable future development.

Kalamazoo's downtown pedestrian mall was a cutting-edge idea in 1959 that seemed to breathe vitality into the downtown district for two decades or more. But it was a tired concept by 1998, when the streets were redesigned and opened back up to limited auto traffic.

A master plan for downtown Kalamazoo calls for new commercial buildings and possibly an arena and convention center. Economic development agencies and Western Michigan University have quietly assembled property in that area that could provide the core of those new developments, but as of early 2006 there was no solid plan.

The Kalamazoo city school district is engaged in a grand experiment that could reverse the decline in city population. In a program called The Kalamazoo Promise, students who go from kindergarten through high school graduation in the Kalamazoo Public Schools are promised full tuition at any Michigan public university. Enrollment in city schools began rising soon after the program was announced in 2005.

The greater Kalamazoo area has a number of Michigan's top tourist and educational attractions. The Kalamazoo Nature Center is a paradise for birders, and one of the largest such institutions in the Midwest. The Air Zoo, has displays on the history of aviation, and may soon add a space center. Northeast of town, near Hickory Corners, are the Gilmore Car Club automotive museum, and the W.K. Kellogg Manor House and Biological Station, managed by Michigan State University.

Bronson Park, at the center of town on land donated by Kalamazoo's founder, is hailed in the book "Buildings of Michigan" as the finest public square in the state. The park's centerpiece is a fountain designed by Alfonso Iannelli.

An abandoned railroad line stretching from Kalamazoo west to Lake Michigan at South Haven was converted to a bike path in the 1980s and christened the Kal-Haven Trail. The 35-mile route passes through farmland, forest, small towns and blueberry fields and is a popular ride in summer and fall.

Until Grand Rapids began expanding its downtown facilities in the 1980s, Kalamazoo was the unquestioned cultural capital of

West Michigan. Wings Stadium was the top venue for rock and pop music acts, while WMU's Miller Auditorium hosted theater productions.

The State Theater may be the region's most inviting hall for smaller concerts when acoustics and intimacy are valued more highly than crowd size.

WMU also is the site of West Michigan's only Division 1 football and basketball program.

The Crossroads Mall, on S. Westnedge Ave near I-94 in Portage, is the main regional shopping center.

While Kalamazoo and Portage form the heart of this urban area, much of the growth in recent decades has been directed toward Oshtemo Township, west of US 131, and to the Westwood area of Kalamazoo Township. Now, that growth is beginning to spill across the Van Buren County line into Mattawan.

MUSKEGON

2004 Population:
Muskegon, 39,954
Norton Shores: 23,287
North Muskegon, 4,009
Roosevelt Park, 3,819
Muskegon Heights, 11,807
Laketon Township 7,712
Muskegon Township 18,500
Fruitport Township 12,993
Total: 122,081

Take one look at the scene of destruction that occupies much of downtown Muskegon, and it's clear that – to put it kindly – this is a city in transition.

But that shouldn't be a surprise. The people of Muskegon and the surrounding communities have been responding to changes almost since the first sawmill went up on Muskegon Lake 170 years ago.

It's been a fur-trading outpost, a wealthy lumbering center, a Great Lakes shipping hub, an oil boomtown, and an industrial city. These days, community leaders are working toward a future with a more diverse economy. They hope to develop a blend of higher-tech industry, tourism, health services and regional retail centers.

That's the dream of every "rust-belt" city, of course. But Muskegon has a few things in its favor, including a history of coming back from adversity, a great natural harbor, and a location that puts residents close to miles of public Lake Michigan access.

The Frauenthal Theater overlooks a scene of devastation that may be the first stage of renewal in downtown Muskegon (photo: Ed Hoogterp)

Fur traders were working around the mouth of the Muskegon River as early as 1810, and the first sawmill began cutting lumber on Muskegon Lake in 1837. But the region's real growth began after the Civil War.

Michigan's endless forest of white pine timber provided the raw material for the explosive growth of Chicago and other towns to the west, and Muskegon was in a prime location for sawing the pine logs into usable lumber.

Muskegon County's population grew by 166 percent in the six years from 1864 to 1870. By the mid-1880s, as many as 47 sawmills crowded around Muskegon Lake.

In just another decade, that endless forest was gone, and Muskegon began to stumble. The region's business leaders, including Charles Hackley, came up with a plan to pay a "bonus" of up to $100 per employee to factories that relocated to Muskegon. The plan worked, and Muskegon's economy and population were expanding nicely, until the Depression put an end to industrial growth.

The downturn in the region was softened somewhat by another natural resource. In 1927, oil was discovered a few miles north of the city. It was the first big oil strike in Michigan, and it kept as many as 1,000 people working into the lean years of the Great Depression.

When World War II finally revived the nation's economy, Muskegon's industry bounced back with vigor. Jobs were plentiful well into the 1950s at the area's factories, foundries and paper mills. And then, Muskegon's economy began to fade along with the rest of the Midwest's heavy industry.

The job drain continued in 2005, as Brunswick Corp. announced it would move the production of bowling balls from Muskegon to Mexico, and Sappi Papers revealed plans to close its Muskegon pulp mill.

Back in the 1970s, Muskegon built a roof over several downtown streets to convert the shopping district into an enclosed mall. It seemed like a good idea at the time, with downtowns across Americas losing their stores to the suburbs. But the street-to-mall strategy never worked particularly well here or elsewhere.

And when The Lakes Mall opened in Fruitport Township at the dawn of the 21st century, Muskegon saw the writing on the mall, as it were.

To make way for future development, the city began demolishing several blocks, creating a huge, dusty hole where the downtown stores used to be. While it's in the demolition/construction mode, the work leaves a distinct feeling that Muskegon has no downtown at all. Fast food restaurants and their parking lots sit alongside City Hall and the Muskegon County buildings.

That first impression isn't quite fair. Muskegon's cultural heart is still beating at the venerable L.C. Walker Arena and the meticulously restored Frauenthal Theater. Also nearby are the Hackley and Hume mansions, elaborate Queen Anne style homes that are part of the Muskegon County Historical Museum.

Meanwhile the center of retail activity for the Muskegon urban area – and much of the surrounding countryside – has switched to The Lakes Mall area on Sternberg and Quarterline roads, at the boundary between Norton Shores and Fruitport Township. In addition to the enclosed mall, that business strip features all the big box discounters, chain restaurants and fast food joints.

The unique strength of the Muskegon area lies in its waterfront. In addition to a natural harbor for recreational and commercial vessels, the community has more public beach access than almost any other urban area on Lake Michigan.

From P.J. Hoffmaster State Park on the Ottawa - Muskegon County line, through the city's Pere Marquette Park and Muskegon State Park, residents and visitors can enjoy miles of shoreline without having to peek around condominiums or private homes.

Ferry service was revived in 2004, after being idle for decades, when *The Lake Express* began carrying autos and passengers across Lake Michigan. The high-speed ferry, which runs from spring to fall, reaches Milwaukee in about 2 ½ hours.

TOWN PROFILES

Photo on previous page: Ed Hoogterp

TOWNS

My, how we've changed.

West Michigan, at the middle of the 20th century, was a land of a few cities and a lot of small villages, with mostly farmland in between.

A million people lived here then, including 300,000 in the bustling central cities of Grand Rapids, Kalamazoo, Muskegon and Benton Harbor.

The cities and large towns were just about reaching their peak as manufacturing centers. Villages were mostly agricultural outposts, where a farmer could come to sell his crops or to buy a cup of coffee, a haircut or a Ford 8N tractor.

World War II was a fresh memory. Railroads and radios were everywhere. Cars, paved roads and telephones were becoming more common by the day. The oldest members of the Baby Boom generation were just about ready to start school; their moms were mostly full-time homemakers.

Jump forward 50 years, and we find the four cities still have about 300,000 residents (actually, 326,314; the increase is almost entirely in areas annexed to the city of Grand Rapids in the 50s and 60s). But the entire region is now home to 2 million people.

Put another way: In half a century, our central cities gained almost no residents, while the countryside around them gained a million.

What happened?

Two words: Subdivisions and highways.

Thousands of acres of farmland have been converted to residential suburbs, shopping centers and industrial plants. And despite all the moaning about potholes and traffic jams, West Michigan's highway system has made it a simple matter to live in one town and work in another.

No one thinks twice about driving daily from Newaygo to Muskegon, Three Rivers to Kalamazoo or Lake Odessa to Grand Rapids.

When West Michigan was being settled, from about 1825 to 1875, townsites were usually chosen for one of two reasons: water power or railroad access. Those factors, in the 21st century, are pretty much irrelevant. Instead, developers look for abundant land close to expressways.

Each year, thousands of new homes are built on what used to be the farmland that separated one community from another. That so-called urban sprawl, especially in the townships around Grand

Rapids, has literally swallowed some villages in a sea of suburbia, and blurred the boundary between "urban" and "rural."

In Kent County alone, 25,000 acres of farmland were converted to other uses between 1997 and 2002, according to the 2002 U.S. Census of Agriculture.

Some communities have thrived despite the march of time, finding tourism or new industry to make their place in the changing world.

Others are barely hanging on.

Many rural villages have followed a familiar pattern: Railroads disappeared. Farms became fewer and larger. Freeways bypassed the towns, with 70 mph traffic far too intense for the slow pace of village life. Today's village residents often drive 30 miles or more to work in larger towns.

Gradually, commerce moved out to the highway exits, leaving traditional downtowns filled with gift shoppes, antique stores and professional offices. Or, worse, with empty buildings.

Still, many West Michigan villages remain pleasant places to live. Schools are often excellent (though students usually ride a bus, rather than walking to a village school).

The streets are lined with ancient shade trees. The downtowns often maintain at least hardware and convenience stores. Village lots are big enough for a garden, an above ground pool, a satellite dish and other trappings of working-class affluence.

And Meijer, Wal-Mart and The Mall are seldom more than half an hour up the highway.

Here's a snapshot of 200 West Michigan communities – all those that have their own post office, or are incorporated as a city or village.

Read quickly. They're changing all the time...

(Population and income figures are from the 2000 census, unless otherwise noted. Sources for information on community names and early settlement include *Michigan History Magazine,* local historical societies, community Internet sites and Walter Romig's indispensible 1973 book *Michigan Place Names*)

TOWN PROFILES

ADA, 49301

Unincorporated village and township in Kent County. Township population, 9,882. Median household income, $83,357, or 187 percent of the statewide median.

Western Michigan pioneer Rix Robinson became Kent County's first permanent settler in 1821, when he took over a trading post at the present site of Ada, where the Thornapple and Grand rivers run together. That was five years before Louis Campau founded Grand Rapids a few miles down the Grand.

While Campau's trading post grew into a major metropolitan center, Ada remained small. And no one's complaining. Today, Ada is home to Amway and its corporate parent Alticor, whose world headquarters, production facilities and warehouses stretch for a full mile along M-21. The township's rolling hills and winding roads make for some of the most desirable residential addresses in West Michigan. Ada village boasts a thriving collection of upscale shops and restaurants, as well as a park with a covered bridge.

ALLEGAN, 49010

County seat of Allegan County. Population, 4,838. Median household income, $39,539, or 89 percent of the statewide median. The city on the Kalamazoo River traces its beginnings to 1833, when investors from Kalamazoo and Marshall bought property here from the government land office.

The town today is a fine place to live or visit, though the shutdown of paper mills along the Kalamazoo River has cut deeply into the area's employment base. Allegan maintains a historic district, listed on the National Register of Historic Places, and a pleasant downtown marked by a one-lane trestle bridge and a pattern of streets that meet at odd angles.

Allegan's downtown is filled with historic buildings and angled streets (photo: Ed Hoogterp)

The business district has its share of antique shops and professional offices, but it also has the Old Regent Theatre, which still shows up-to-date movies. There's a mix of shops that any downtown would welcome, including a Pizza Hut and a bookstore on the same block. What big city can top that?

ALLENDALE 49401

Unincorporated village and township in Ottawa County. Township population, 13,141. Median household income, $48,669, or 109 percent of the statewide median.

This rural community 12 miles west of Grand Rapids was transformed beginning in 1963, when Michigan opened Grand Valley State College on what had been woods, cornfields and ravines along the Grand River. At the time, Allendale was an agricultural area and one of the few "dry" townships in Michigan, which meant the new students and professors couldn't buy a beer at the local bowling alley.

The college has since matured into a university, with more than 20,000 students. And Allendale has grown right along with it. Much of the land remains in agriculture, but residential development has blossomed in recent decades. M-45, the old two-lane road that linked the community to Grand Rapids, is now a boulevard, with twin bridges across the Grand River and decorative lighting that makes it look like a permanent parade route. Local officials have plans for a new "Town Center" to enhance the area.

In addition to the university, Allendale's location makes it a convenient bedroom community for residents who work in Grand Rapids, Muskegon or Holland.

ALTO, 49302

Unincorporated village in Kent County, southeast of Grand Rapids. Still an agricultural area, but increasingly a residential suburb. Camp O'Malley, a summer camp for city kids run by Youth Commonwealth of Grand Rapids, is on the Thornapple River nearby.

Alto, which sets on the line between Bowne and Lowell townships, was a station on the Detroit, Grand Rapids and Western Railroad. The station took its name from the fact it was the highest point between Grand Rapids and Detroit, according to Walter Romig in his 1973 book *Michigan Place Names.* (Republished in 1986 by Wayne State University Press)

Today, the village is an appealing scatter of old and new homes and small businesses on a hilly section of land just off the M-50 exit from I-96. Most of the commercial businesses are out on the highway, but the old business district retains a general store, post office and lumber company.

AUGUSTA, 49012

Village in Kalamazoo County. Population, 901. Median household income, $44,375, or 99 percent of the statewide median. Dr. Solomon King built his log cabin here about 1832, and later added an inn. The housing stock in the village is older than most, with half the homes built before 1948.

The Barn Theatre, housed in a 1943 dairy barn just outside the village, is a long-running summer entertainment venue and the home of Michigan's oldest resident summer-stock theater. This is a lively little town, about midway between Kalamazoo and Battle Creek. The state's Fort Custer Recreation Area is just across the Kalamazoo River from the village.

Downtown, in addition to the normal run of businesses, has the McKay Dole Library, the Knappen Milling Co. and the Barking Frog Pub and Grub.

BAILEY, 49303

Unincorporated village in Casnovia Township in Muskegon County's "panhandle." Township population, 2,633. Median household income, $41,711, or 93 percent of the statewide median. Like much of this region it was developed as a timbering center in the late 19th century, and took the name of a local logger.

For decades, travelers heading north on M-37 have stopped for a sticky bun and coffee at Hilltop Bakery, across from the Bailey General Store.

Bailey has a township fire barn, and a few small businesses. The residential area is a cluster of homes ranging from old house trailers to nice, modern homes.

BANGOR, 49031

City in Van Buren County. Population, 1,933. Median household income, $28,165, or 63 percent of the statewide median. The town was founded in 1837 and named for Bangor, Maine, the home of an early settler.

Bangor is home to the Freestone Pickle Co., which gives a distinctive tang to the city's air. The CSX railroad tracks through town are still active, and Amtrak's Pere

Marquette train stops here en route between Chicago and Grand Rapids. The city's old passenger depot was restored at a cost of $670,000 and reopened in May of 2005 to serve rail passengers.

The central business district, along M-43, includes a couple of banks, an antique mall, hardware stores and even a downtown McDonald's restaurant.

BARODA, 49101

Village in Berrien County. Population, 867. Median household income, $36,250, or 81 percent of the statewide median. The village was founded around 1880 by M.B. Houser, who named it after himself. The post office rejected that name, and Houser renamed his town Baroda, after a city in India.

The village, about five miles from Lake Michigan, is in a prime fruit-growing region. Four wineries – Tabor Hill, Round Barn, Domaine Berrien and Lemon Creek – are located within a few miles of town, though only Round Barn has a Baroda address.

The business district, stretched out along one gently winding road, is a mix of commercial and light industrial businesses. There's not a lot of retail, other than the Baroda City Mills, which offers supplies for feeding birds and four-footed animals.

The old village school building is closed. Housing is supplied by a large trailer park and several streets of nice homes. The surrounding township, also named Baroda, is somewhat more affluent than the village itself.

BARRYTON, 49305

Village in the northeast corner of Mecosta County. Population, 403. Median household income, $23,333, or 52 percent of the statewide median. The settlement was founded in 1894 on the Detroit, Grand Rapids and Western Railroad. It was named for grocer Frank Barry.

Today, it sits astride highway M-66, where two branches of the Chippewa River come together. The small community is somewhat isolated in an area of mixed farm and forest. It has more businesses than most villages of its size, including hardware and auto parts stores, a bank and the Barryton Elevator Co.

Residential streets have well-kept small houses, mobile homes and even a few apartments. Barryton is part of the Chippewa Hills School District.

BELDING, 48809

City in Ionia County. Population, 5,877. Median household income, $32,878, or 74 percent of the statewide median. The town was founded in the late 1830s along the Flat River. It was once known as Patterson's Mills, and was renamed in 1871 to honor Hiram Belding, patriarch of a family of silk merchants.

The Belding family built a silk-weaving mill here in the 1880s. The Belding Silk Mills operated until 1932, under several names, and employed as many as 1,200 people. One of the old mill buildings has been converted to modern apartments.

Today, Belding is a vibrant city with a number of fine, old homes on tree-lined streets. Its location in the northwest corner of Ionia County places it only a few miles from Greenville, in Montcalm County, where many residents work and shop.

Historical photos at the Alvah N. Belding Library show a busy Main Street lined with stores and hotels. That version of downtown Belding disappeared three decades ago as part of an urban renewal project.

In 1966, an elderly woman was crushed to death by masonry that fell from an upper floor of a dilapidated downtown building. The town responded with a renewal project in keeping with the trends of the time.

More than 60 downtown buildings were demolished, to be replaced by a small indoor shopping center, parking lots, and freestanding grocery and hardware stores.

The Covered Village shopping center is still open, though it has a number of vacancies. Leppink's supermarket continues to do a good business, bringing shoppers into the central city.

BELMONT, 49306

Unincorporated community in Kent County's Plainfield Township. Township population, 30,104. Median household income, $55,181, or 124 percent of the statewide median.

The community sets north of a big bend in the Grand River, which separated it from Grand Rapids and kept it largely rural for 100 years after its founding in the 1860s. Belmont succumbed to the suburban building boom around Grand Rapids in the 1970s. A new Jupiter Avenue Bridge across the Grand River provides a direct link into the city.

The few remaining older homes in Belmont are now surrounded by new construction. The old village area includes Plainfield Township offices, a modern post office, an elementary school and a commercial office park.

BENTON HARBOR, 49022

City in Berrien County. Population, 11,240. Median household income, $17,471, or 39 percent of the statewide median.

This is Michigan's poorest, and in many ways most troubled city. It's lost nearly half its population since 1960, and its boarded-up downtown buildings have been cited as a metaphor for the abandonment of America's urban areas.

Racially charged riots brought state attention in 2003. The 1998 book *The Other Side of the River* by Alex Kotlowitz, highlighted conflicts that separate Benton Harbor, mostly black and poor, from the neighboring town of St. Joseph, which is prosperous and predominantly white.

Benton Harbor grew rapidly in the years following the Civil War, after developers dredged a canal from St. Joseph Harbor into the business district. It was a healthy manufacturing center through the 1960s, and is still home to the world headquarters of Whirlpool Corp, the nation's largest maker of home appliances.

Attempts at revitalization have met with little success, though some substantial downtown buildings remain and there has been a movement of artists into the community in recent years.

Not everything is bad in Benton Harbor. There is an attractive waterfront along the St. Joseph River, a large library, and a determination by state and local officials to redevelop and revitalize the community.

Still, if you get out along the residential streets, you'll see blighted homes with sagging roofs, peeling paint, shattered curbs and drooping porches. The impression is of intractible and debilitating poverty.

BERRIEN CENTER, 49102

Unincorporated crossroads in Berrien County's Berrien Township. Township population, 5,075. Median household income, $46,293, or 104 percent of the statewide median.

This is a rural area in the fruit belt between Niles and Benton Harbor-St. Joseph. There's not a lot of business here at the junction of M-140 and Deans Hill Road. The small local grocery store carries both Mexican and Anglo products.

BERRIEN SPRINGS, 49103

Village in Berrien County. Population, 1,864. Median household income, $32,396, or 73 percent of the statewide median. The village was founded around 1829 and originally called "Wolf Prairie," according to Walter Romig.

Berrien Springs was the county seat until 1894, when county government moved to St. Joseph. The carefully restored 1839 courthouse, together with the surrounding public square, is now a museum that focuses on county and regional history.

The village sets above a broad bend in the St. Joseph River, where an American Electric Power Co. hydroelectric dam creates Lake Chapin. There is limited retail downtown, other than a village hardware store. Several wineries are in the surrounding countryside. Berrien Springs is also home to Andrews University, a private institution run by the Seventh Day Adventist Church.

BIG RAPIDS, 49307

City in Mecosta County. Population, 10,616. Median household income, 20,192, or 45 percent of the statewide median.

This picturesque town, founded in 1853 along the Muskegon River, serves as the county seat and is home to Ferris State University (the low household income figure is due largely to the presence of thousands of college students).

Anyone driving through Big Rapids on the US-131 business route might think they've seen the whole town: Big box stores near the freeway, fast food, gas stations, a bit of the university. But there's more to Big Rapids. Off the beaten path are some nice neighborhoods, with well-preserved older homes on tree-shaded streets. The downtown strip is made up of two- and three-story buildings, with most of the storefronts occupied. There's even a downtown movie house.

The "rapids" that gave the town its name were hidden behind a dam for many years. The dam was taken out in 2001 and the free-flowing river is now accessible along a three-mile walkway from the downtown area.

BITELY, 49309

Unincorporated village in Newaygo County's Lilley Township. Township population, 764. Median household income, $25,870, or 58 percent of the statewide median. The Bitely brothers had a sawmill here on the Chicago and Western Michigan Railroad about 1890. The railroad is still in place.

Today, Bitely is an isolated outpost in the northwoods, just west of highway M-37. The village is surrounded by several small lakes and close to thousands of acres of Manistee National Forest. Businesses include the Bitely Tavern and the Up North Gift Shop. There's also a township hall, a fire barn, and a head-start program operated by 5-CAP Inc.

Much of the housing is distinctly cottage style: Ancient cabins, trailers, modern modulars and a few A-frames. Fewer than half the dwellings in the township are used as year-round homes.

BLOOMINGDALE, 49026

Village in Van Buren County. Population, 504. Median household income, $35,714, or 80 percent of the statewide median. The village was founded about 1855 and named for the flowers blooming in the valley, according to Walter Romig.

Oil was discovered here in the 1930s, leading to a short-lived drilling boom.

Today, this is a pleasant town set on county roads four miles from M-40, the nearest state highway. The Bloomingdale school district covers much of the surrounding area, in an economically challenged region of northern Van Buren County. The Kal-Haven Trail runs on an abandoned railroad grade through town.

BRADLEY, 49311

Unincorporated community in Allegan County's Wayland Township. Township population, 3,047. Median household income, $41,852, or 105 percent of the statewide median.

Named for David Bradley, the community's first postmaster, this is a sparsely developed area between Grand Rapids and Kalamazoo, dotted with farms and a few small businesses.

Many West Michigan residents know the town only as the name on the US-131 expressway exit that takes them to the Gun Lake beach in Yankee Springs State Recreation Area. Bradley could get a lot busier in coming years, if the Gun Lake Band of Potawatomi Indians succeeds in its effort to open a casino at the freeway exit.

BREEDSVILLE, 49027

Village in Van Buren County. Population, 244. Median household income, $32,917, or 74 percent of the statewide median.

Silas Breed built a water-powered sawmill on the Black River here in 1835.

The town has seen its better days. There's still space for angle parking in front of the two-story wooden structures that once formed a small business district. But the buildings are now vacant. A dam and millpond are at the center of a quiet park behind the buildings.

BRIDGMAN, 49106

City in Berrien County. Population, 2,445. Median household income, $48,292, or 108 percent of the statewide median. This town on Lake Michigan was founded in the 1850s as a lumber shipping center and named for George Bridgman, an early settler.

The Donald C. Cook nuclear power plant is just north of town, providing considerable tax base for the Bridgman Public Schools. Warren Dunes State Park butts up against the southern city limits. Weko Beach provides public access to the Big Lake inside the city limits.

The city is cut in half by I-94, with traditional residential areas on the east side of the freeway, and a shaded, summer resort feel to the streets between the highway and Lake Michigan. The downtown area sprawls out along Shawnee Road close to I-94 and the Red Arrow Highway.

BROHMAN, 49312

Unincorporated village in Newaygo County's Merrill Township. Township population, 595. Median household income, $22,917, or 51 percent of the statewide median. Brohman was founded as a railroad station in the 1890s, and named for the owner of a local hotel.

The tracks are still here, and there is a small commercial district, including a hardware store, a restaurant and a rustic-sided post office along M-37.

The busiest place is the Brohman One-Stop, a gas station and convenience store where you can get anything from diesel to doughnuts.

Off the highway, Merrill Township is mostly woods. More than half of the land is Manistee National Forest. At the north end of the township, Woodland Lake is surrounded by nice cottages, mostly owned by African-Americans who live in Grand Rapids and other urban areas. The community of Woodland Park, on the north side of the lake, has a bar, Woody's, that is popular with white deer hunters. It also has dozens of small, aging homes, mostly occupied by poverty-stricken African-Americans.

BUCHANAN, 49107

City in Berrien County. Population, 4,921. Median household income, $34,244 or 77 percent of the statewide median. Named for James Buchanan, 15th president of the United States.

Buchanan has suffered as much as any city from the decline of heavy industry in Michigan. The town was home to the Clark Equipment Co, a manufacturing giant which provided hundreds of office and factory jobs until the 1980s, when the company began closing plants. Clark ultimately moved its headquarters to South Bend and was absorbed by other manufacturers.

Buchanan maintains a pleasant and historic downtown. A local group has preserved the 1853 Pears Mill, complete with its millrace and wooden overshot water-wheel. Across the well-kept town commons, another group produces live theater in a former tin shop that dates from 1866.

Downtown is well-preserved, though too many storefronts are empty. The residential streets have a number of fine old homes. The city has attracted some new jobs to its industrial park and the old factory areas.

For all that, acres of empty parking lots and abandoned factory buildings give testimony that Buchanan hasn't recovered the affluence it had 30 years ago.

BURNIPS, 49314

Unincorporated community in Allegan County's Salem Township. Township population, 3,480. Median household income, $48.203, or 108 percent of the statewide median.

The town was founded in the 1850s and named for store owner James Burnip. The area is still mainly agricultural, though Sandy Pines, one of Michigan's largest private campground resorts, is in Salem Township.

The village of Burnips consists of a small number of homes, along with a church, post office, grocery, gas station and a few other businesses. The area is close to the burgeoning I-196 corridor between Grand Rapids and Holland, but the closest freeway exit is eight miles from Burnips, and the community has so far been generally spared from urban sprawl.

BURR OAK, 49030

Village in St. Joseph County. Population, 783. Median household income, $34,792, or 78 percent of the statewide median. It was named for trees that grew in the area in the 1830s, when the village was founded.

Today, the great trees that line the village streets are mainly maples. The Prairie River angles through town. The commercial district has several well-preserved buildings and a boulevard streetscape. Unfortunately, many of the storefronts are empty. Burr Oak is home to the R-11 Classic Car Museum, which has a collection of more than 350 vehicles.

BYRON CENTER, 49315

Unincorporated village in Kent County's Byron Township. Township population, 17,611. Median household income, $49,672, or 111 percent of the statewide median.

The town dates from about 1836. For most of its years, it was a rural village serving farmers who worked the rich cropland south of Grand Rapids. A few farms remain, but much of the township is being converted to residential subdivisions. The township's northern border butts up against Wyoming, West Michigan's largest suburban city.

Byron Center itself remains a recognizable village, with schools, churches and commercial businesses near the busy crossroads. The M-6 freeway, completed in 2004 through the northern part of the township, is likely to spur even more urban sprawl.

CALEDONIA, 49316

Village and township in Kent County. Village population, 1,122 and median household income, $50,724, or 114 percent of the statewide median. Township population, 8,964 and median household income $63,032 or 141 percent of the statewide median.

The area was settled in the late 1830s and named for Caledonia NY, where an early settler was born. The township's rich farmland still supports agriculture, but suburban housing is now the main crop here.

The village retains an active downtown, with a grain elevator and small businesses, most notably "Sam's Joint," a popular local eatery.

Much more business, including several strip malls, is on the outskirts of town along M-37, the busy highway that links Grand Rapids and Battle Creek.

CANNONSBURG, 49317

Unincorporated village in Kent County's Cannon Township. Township population, 12,086. Median household income, $70,925, or 159 percent of the statewide median.

The area was settled around 1837 and named for LaGrand Cannon, a New York financier. Today, the village site is an attactive crossroads (How could the intersection of rural byways named "Cannonsburg Road" and Honey Creek Avenue" be anything but attractive?) with a restaurant, a convenience store and an old township hall that's been converted to a museum.

Cannon Township, a fast-growing suburb northeast of Grand Rapids, is also the site of Cannonsburg Ski Area, one of West Michigan's busiest winter sports centers. In addition to entertaining skiers, the ski area is host to the Grand Rapids Symphony's Summer Pops series.

CARSON CITY, 48811

City in Montcalm County. Population, 1,174. Median household income, $32,500, or 73 percent of the statewide median. The town was the site of a sawmill in 1866, and was named for Carson City, Nev. The name is the inspiration for the city's annual Frontier Days celebration.

Carson City is actually closer to Lansing than to any of the West Michigan urban centers. Many residents of the homes along the village's tree-lined streets work in the state capital city.

The Rusty Nail Restaurant is a well-known business, and the town also supports a lumber company, farm and garden store, antique and gift shops, a hardware store and a four-lane bowling alley. There's also a library and the Carson City Hospital.

CASNOVIA, 49318

Village in Muskegon County. Population, 299. Median household income, $42,019, or 94 percent of the statewide median. The village was settled around 1850, and the name is a variant of "Casa Nova" which means new home. Ironically, today it has some of the oldest housing stock in the region, with half the homes built in 1939 or before.

It's a town of old, frame houses on curbless village streets. Even the trees are showing their age, with majestic old maples slowly dying and being replaced by younger, smaller specimens. Along Probasco Street, on the edge of the village, cornfields push hard against back yards. For how long is anybody's guess: The land is marked for sale as an industrial site.

CASSOPOLIS, 49031

County seat of Cass County. The incorporated village had a 2000 population of 1,740 and a median household income of $28,696, or 64 percent of the statewide median. It was settled in 1829 and named (like the county) for Lewis Cass, who served as Michigan's territorial governor and was also a member of President Andrew Jackson's cabinet.

The downtown district is home to the impressive Cass County Courthouse. Despite the low income statistics, Cassopolis has a number of nice, century-old homes to go along with some smaller homes and mobiles.

The wide downtown street, M-62, is lined with solid buildings, including several made of stone. Parking for shoppers is provided behind the stores. Hayden Hardware, in business here for more than 120 years, offers a little bit of everything, from doorknobs to ammunition.

The Cass County Courthouse dominates the public square in the village of Cassopolis (photo: Ed Hoogterp)

CEDAR LAKE, 48812

Unincorporated village in Montcalm County's Home Township. Township population, 2,690. Median household income, $30,590, or 68 percent of the statewide median. The town on M-46, near tiny Cedar Lake, has only a few residents and businesses. It is home to the Great Lakes Adventist Academy, a school affiliated with the Cedar lake Seventh Day Adventist Church.

CEDAR SPRINGS, 49312

City in northern Kent County. Population, 3,163. Median household income, $39,542, or 89 percent of the statewide median. The town was named for the trees and springs found around the site when it was settled in the 1850s. It now bills itself as the Red Flannel Capital, with a festival each October to celebrate the warm, red long johns.

Cedar Springs, at the intersection of Northland Drive (old US-131) and 17 Mile Road is near the northern edge of the urban sprawl that emanates from Grand Rapids. The surrounding townships, Nelson and Solon, both have somewhat higher income and newer housing than does Cedar Springs.

Still, the area remains much less crowded than the townships closer to Grand Rapids. Cedar Springs Mill and Supply serves area farmers. The town has a lot of small, older houses, along with a few newer ones. The city's Morley Park is billed as "A Nice Place to Play," and a local drama group produces plays at the Kent Theatre downtown.

Most of the retail and restaurant business has moved to the outskirts, especially near the 17 Mile Road exit from the US-131 expressway, just west of town.

CENTREVILLE, 49032

County seat of St. Joseph County. Village population, 1,513. Median household income, $33,929 or 76 percent of the statewide median.

Centreville, at the center of St. Joseph County, has been the county seat ever since Thomas Langley built a tavern here in 1831. The well-kept downtown district is arranged around the courthouse square, with businesses like the Round-Up Bar and Grill and the Horseless Carriage Antique and Ice Cream Emporium.

The county courthouse is a Romanesque revival structure, built in 1900, with five-foot-tall clock faces on each side of the central tower.

The Langley Covered Bridge, built in 1887, still carries traffic in a single lane across the St. Joseph River just north of town. The 282-foot structure is the longest of Michigan's few remaining covered bridges.

The St. Joseph County Fairgrounds in Centreville are the site of several annual antique markets, a summer car show, and the county fair in September.

Glen Oaks Community College is just south of town.

Langley Covered Bridge carries one lane of traffic over the St. Joseph River near Centreville (photo: Ed Hoogterp)

CHIPPEWA LAKE, 49320

Unincorporated community in Mecosta County's Chippewa Township. Township population, 1,229. Median household income, $33,859, or 76 percent of the statewide median.

The Detroit, Grand Rapids and Western Railroad had a station here around 1870, when the Chippewa Lake Lumber Company operated a sawmill on the lake of the same name.

Today, the lake is a popular recreational spot surrounded by cottages. The village area includes the Chippewa Lake Bar and Grill, and the east Bay General Store. The Haymarsh Lake State Game Area is just west of Chippewa Lake.

CLARKSVILLE, 48815

Village in Ionia County. Population, 290. Median household income, $35,313, or 79 percent of the statewide median.

The village was founded in 1840 and named for a local storekeeper, Clark Howard.

Today, it has a blinker light and a few homes and small businesses, surrounded by agricultural land. Michigan State University's Clarksville Agricultural Experiment Station is among the state's most important sites for research on apples and other fruits.

CLIMAX, 49034

Village in Kalamazoo County. Population, 811. Median household income, $44,464, or

100 percent of the statewide median. New York native Daniel Eldred is said to have named the place in 1831, when he arrived at the small native prairie and declared it to be the climax of his search of a home.

Eldred's house, built in 1835, has a state historical marker. Climax also has local markers to commemorate the site of Michigan's first rural free delivery mail service, in 1896, and the farms where inventor Hiram Moore operated the first mechanical grain harvester. Moore's 16-horse contraption apparently worked just fine, but it couldn't compete with the simpler reaper invented by Cyrus McCormick.

Today, Climax sets along the busy Grand Trunk Railroad, surrounded by irrigated farm fields. Downtown is pretty much irrelevant, except for the independent Climax Telephone Co. and the impressive stone building that houses the Lawrence Memorial Library. But the residential streets are attactive, with nicely maintained homes.

Along the edge of town, flat agricultural fields and a faraway treeline give a hint – but only a hint – of what Daniel Eldred saw at the climax of his search 170-some years ago.

CLOVERDALE, 49035

Unincorporated village in Barry County's Hope Township. Township population, 3,271. Median household income, $41,983, or 94 percent of the statewide median. The village of Hope moved in 1885 to what was then a clover-filled valley in order to take advantage of a location on the Chicago, Kalamazoo and Saginaw Railroad, according to Walter Romig.

The community on M-43 sits between two lakes – Long and Wilkinson – and local businesses cater to boaters and other users of the water.

COLOMA, 49038

City in Berrien County, population, 1,619. Median household income, $38,882, or 87 percent of the statewide median. The settlement was first called Dickerville. The village was platted in 1855 by Stephen Gilson, who changed the name to Coloma, the name of a flower and also the name of a California town where Gilson had lived briefly during the California Gold Rush.

In its heyday during the first half of the 20th century, this was a busy tourist town, welcoming summer vacationers to nearby Paw Paw Lake.

Most of the visitors came from the Chicago area. Ray Kroc, founder of the McDonald's Restaurant empire, had a job playing piano in a Paw Paw Lake resort around 1920. Today, many of the resort businesses have been replaced by single family homes on the lake, which stretches between Coloma and Watervliet.

Local fundraising helped to build the Coloma Public Library in 2004 (photo: Ed Hoogterp)

Deer Forest, a petting zoo and animal attraction just north of town, is among the surviving tourist businesses.

Coloma remains an attractive small town, with tidy homes and an active, if somewhat dated, downtown district. A splendid downtown library that opened in 2004 is the result of a $2.5 million bond issue, approved by voters, and a $400,000 private fund drive.

COLON, 49040

Village in St. Joseph County. Population, 1,222. Median household income, $29,417, or 66 percent of the statewide median.

The town's name is something of a mystery, though the prevailing explanation is that an early leader thought the twisting geography of the local waterways resembled a drawing of the human digestive organ.

Colon calls itself the Magic Capital of the World. Harry Blackstone, the Chicago-born prestidigitator, lived here most of his adult life. He used the town as the off-season base where he perfected many of the tricks he used in vaudeville and in theaters around the world.
In the 1930s, Blackstone helped Percy Abbott found the Abbott Magic Co., of Colon, which makes equipment for performing magicians. The company continues to turn out tricks in a simple, black building in town. Each August, as many as 1,000 magicians gather here for Abbott's annual get-together.

In keeping with the theme, the town has businesses such

as "The MagiCafe," "Magic Net," and "Hair Illusions."

Colon also has a fine downtown library and a St. Joseph County Park on Palmer Lake.

COMSTOCK, 49041

Unincorporated village and township in Kalamazoo County. Township population, 13,822. Median household income, $46,140, or 103 percent of the statewide median. The community was named for Gen. Horace Comstock. The first grist mill on the Kalamazoo River was built here in 1832.

Today, Comstock's residential area butts up seamlessly against the eastern city limits of Kalamazoo.

Comstock has hundreds of acres of greenhouses, and is home to the Kalamazoo Valley Plant-Growers Co-op. The Kalamazoo River and I-94 run through the center of the township. Kalamazoo County's River Oaks Park is on Morrow Lake.

COMSTOCK PARK, 49321

Unincorporated area in Alpine Township, near the Grand River and just north of Grand Rapids. Township population, 14,088. Median household income, $42,484, or 95 percent of the statewide median.

Daniel North built a mill here in the 1830s, and the area was called North Park. It was renamed in 1906 for U.S. Rep. Charles Comstock. The US-131 expressway now separates the old village area from the Grand River. The old commercial strip along West River Drive has survived, with businesses and local government offices filling many of the buildings. Newer structures, including the expected string of fast food restaurants and gas stations, extend along the same road east of the old village.

Comstock Park is also home to the Fifth-Third Ballpark and the West Michigan Whitecaps, a Class A minor league baseball team affiliated with the Detroit Tigers.

CONKLIN, 49403

Unincorporated village in Ottawa County's Chester Township. Township population, 2,303. Median household income, $46,328, or 104 percent of the statewide median.

The site in the northeast corner of Ottawa County was a railroad station in the 1880s. It's named for Oscar Conklin.

Today, the village's small residential district includes a few very impressive older homes, on streets quiet enough that kids put their basketball hoops right next to the pavement.

Downtown has Dykstra's Elevator and Fenian's Irish Pub. Some of the old commerical buildings are in an advanced state of disrepair.

CONSTANTINE, 49402

Village in St. Joseph County. Population, 2,116. Median household income, $40,428, or 91 percent of the statewide median. It once was called "Meek's Mill" after Judge William Meek, who built a grist mill here in the 1820s. The first postmaster was John S. Barry, who opened a store here in 1834 and later served three terms as Michigan's governor.

Constantine remains a solid village amid the farmland north of the Indiana border. Gov. Barry's home is a local museum.

The village has a number of impressive old homes, and the downtown is listed on the National Register of Historic Places.

The farmland around Constantine grows as much as 20 percent of America's seed corn – that is, the carefully pollinated hybrid corn that is sold to farmers and planted to grow the next year's crop. Two large seed-processing operations are located here.

In 2003, the Michigan Senate declared Constantine as the Seed Corn Capital of the World.

COOPERSVILLE, 49404

City in Ottawa County. Population, 3,910. Median household income, $48,875, or 109 percent of the statewide median. Benjamin Cooper bought 640 acres here in 1845.

The surrounding area is still largely agricultural, but Coopersville has grown in recent years, in part because if its location. The town's southern boundary is I-96, which gives residents an easy drive to jobs in Grand Rapids or Muskegon.

The downtown strip includes two historical attractions – the Coopersville Historical Museum and the Coopersville Farm Museum – along with antique stores, bars, restaurants, and Coopersville Hardware and Farm Supply.

A Delphi Corp. plant that has employed several hundred workers in Coopersville is targeted for closure as part of the auto supplier's bankruptcy reorganization.

Fast food and highway service businesses are clustered around the 68th Avenue exit from the freeway.

CORAL, 49322

Unincorporated hamlet in Montcalm County's Maple Valley Township. Township population, 2,102. Median household income, $36,583, or 82 percent of the statewide median. The village dates back to the Stumptown Sawmill, built in 1882. Walter Romig wrote that an early developer, Charles Parker, chose the name Coral because it was easy to spell.

Today, it's a small town in farm country, with more than its share of big old country homes, some of which are very well maintained.

Businesses include the Coral Elevator Co., and Jody's Coral Market. The Maple Valley Township Hall is also here.

COVERT, 49043

Unincorporated village and township in Van Buren County. Township population, 3,141. Median household income, $22,829, or 51 percent of the statewide median. The town was founded about 1866 as a sawmill site. It was named for a local farmer.

The township, along Lake Michigan about midway between Benton Harbor and South Haven, is now a largely depressed rural area. It has an ethnically diverse population, about 50 percent white, 35 percent black and 15 percent Hispanic.

Consumers Energy's Palisades nuclear power plant is on the lakeshore in the northern part of the township, as is Van Buren State Park.

The Covert business district, including small stores and several churches, spreads out along M-140. There's also a district library and a local museum. The township has a number of blueberry farms.

CRYSTAL, 48818

Unincorporated village and township in eastern Montcalm County. Township population, 2,849. Median household income, $34,421, or 77 percent of the statewide median. The community was founded as Crystal Lake in the 1850s when Enos Drake built a lumber mill on the lake of that name.

Today, the lake is largely ringed with private cottages. A green and shady township park provides both access and a great view of the clear water.

The village area has a library, elementary school, a variety of old and new homes, and a choice of waterfront bars.

DECATUR, 49045

Village in southern Van Buren County. Population, 1,775. Median household income, $30,550, or 68 percent of state median. This was a railroad town in a heavily agricultural area, named for naval hero Stephen Decatur.

Decatur is off the beaten path, six miles south of I-94 and about 15 miles southwest of Kalamazoo.

It was the boyhood home of ventriloquist Edgar Bergen (1903-1978), who developed his own skills and those of his wooden alter-ego, Charlie McCarthy, while growing up here. One of Decatur's main roads is called Edgar Bergen Boulevard.

The Hayloft Ice Cream Parlor on the edge of town and Hard Times Family Restaurant in the compact downtown are among Decatur's businesses.

DELTON, 49046

Unincorporated village in Barry County's Barry Township. Township population, 3,501. Median household income, $45,339, or 102 percent of the statewide median.

The community in the lake country of southern Barry County was founded about 1840 and apparently named for Adelbert "Del" Monroe, an early storekeeper and postmaster.

The town lacks the multi-story brick buildings that are typical of the central business districts of West Michigan villages, but you can still get a bite to eat at a downtown restaurant.

The Bernard Historical Museum on Delton Road includes several historical buildings that display artifacts from the early years of southwest Barry County.

DORR, 49323

Township and unincorporated village just south of Grand Rapids in Allegan County. Township population, 6,579. Median household income, $60,446, or 135 percent of the state median.

Frank Neuman built a wagon shop here in the 1850s, to serve

the township's farmers. The village still boasts a hardware store, feed store, bars, restaurants and an ice cream shop.

A vacant, grassy lot at the center of town is lined with old farm machinery and flower boxes. It often bears hand-lettered signs accusing township officials of corruption. The whole thing results from a long-standing dispute between property owners. Trust us, you don't want to know the details.

Dorr is Allegan County's most populous township. The farmland is attractive for residential development because of its proximity to US-131. This is a community where you can see cows grazing in fields within sight of new housing subdivisions.

DOUGLAS, 49406

Village in Allegan County. Population, 1,202. Median household income, $41,250, or 92 percent of state average. The town was founded around 1851, and possibly named for famed orator Stephen Douglas, who debated Abe Lincoln in the 1850s (though not here).

The village has an attractive downtown area, and frontage on both the Kalamazoo River and Lake Michigan. It's adjacent to the southern boundary of its more famous neighbor, Saugatuck.

The two towns together, with their abundance of inns, restaurants and shops, make a popular upscale getaway destination for tourists from Chicago and West Michigan.

DOWAGIAC, 49047

City in Cass County. Population, 6,129. Median household income, $29,926, or 67 percent of the statewide median. The settlement dates from 1847, and is named for the Dowagiac River. The name comes from the Potawatomi and means foraging ground.

In the late 19th century, Dowagiac was home to the huge Round Oak Stove Co, which employed some 1,400 people in the manufacture of wood-burning stoves.

Still existing in town are two impressive stone homes, called "The Maples" and "The Rockery" built by family members of Round Oak founder Philo Beckwith.

Dowagiac is also the town where a local beekeeper, James Heddon, invented the artificial fishing lure. Heddon's story, and some of his company's lures, can be seen at the Heddon Museum here.

Dowagiac has lost much of its industry, but remains the largest community in Cass County. Borgess-Lee Memorial Hospital is here, as is Southwestern Michigan College. Ameriwood, Inc. employs more than 300 workers making ready-to-assemble furniture. There's also an Amtrak train station near the Victorian-style downtown district.

DOWLING, 49050

A crossroads community in Barry County's Baltimore Township. Township population, 1,819. Median household income, $45,761, or 102 percent of the statewide median. The village was known as Baltimore in the 1840s. The name was officially changed to Dowling about 1880.

The small post office is a center of activity in Dowling (photo: Ed Hoogterp)

Today, the village is little more than a few businesses and a post office along M-37 between Hastings and Battle Creek. The Pierce Cedar Creek Institute, a 660-acre ecological education center, is in Baltimore Township just west of Dowling.

EAST GRAND RAPIDS, 49506 (included in Grand Rapids ZIP code area)

City in Kent County. Population, 10,783. Median household income, $84,772, or 190 percent of the statewide median.

The city founded by Lou and Ezra Reed in the early 1830s is an old-money suburb of Grand Rapids. It wasn't always that way. From the late 19th century until the 1940s, the town on Reeds Lake was a well-known resort destination and home to the popular Ramona Park amusement park.

Today, it's a compact city where sidewalks are always full of people, walking, jogging and pushing baby strollers. The lakeside location, good schools, small but attractive business district and safe streets make this one of Michigan's most sought-after addresses.

EAU CLAIRE, 49111

Village in Berrien County. Population, 671. Median household income, $38,750, or 87 percent of the statewide median. The name comes from French words meaning "clear water," a reference to the clear-flowing streams that settlers found here in the 1850s.

This is an agricultural village in the midst of Southwest Michigan's orchards and vineyards.

The small downtown has the Eau Claire Fruit Exchange, along with hardware and lumber stores and a laundromat.

The nearby Tree-Mendus Fruit Farm is one of Michigan's top farm-tourism attractions and is the site of the annual National Cherry-Pit-Spitting championship.

EDMORE, 48829

Village in northern Montcalm County. Population, 1,258. Median household income, $24,926, or 56 percent of the statewide median. The town was founded in the 1870s as a railroad station and named for real estate man Edwin Moore.

Today, Edmore is a nice village with fine old trees and a mix of large and small homes on side streets along M-46, the main east-west artery through central Michigan. Despite the low median income, Edmore looks more prosperous than many of the villages this far north in Michigan.

The downtown strip is a row of two-story brick buildings housing such businesses as the Phoenix Bar and Grill, a bank, hardware, and auto parts store.

McDonald's, Burger King, the Gold Star outlet store and Jorgensen's supermarket are spread out along the highway. The Edmore State Game Area is nearby.

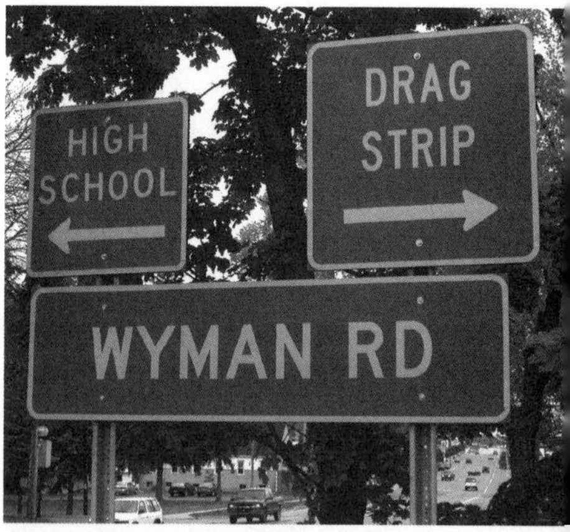

Road sign in Edmore seems to offer a choice of lifestyles (photo: Ed Hoogterp)

Edmore lost its largest employer in 2005, when Hitachi Magnetics closed a factory that had made magnets for speakers and other electronic devices. The plant had been in operation for decades under Hitachi and previous owners. It employed as many as 800 workers in past years. The work force was down to about 100 at the time it closed.

EDWARDSBURG, 49112

Village in Cass County. Population 1,144. Median household income, $33,359, or 75 percent of the statewide median. The area was first settled in 1828 by Ezra Beardsley, and named for an early merchant, Thomas Edwards.

The village limits are only a mile from the Indiana border. Business such as McDonald's and Taco Bell are spread out along M-62 toward the state line.

First impression is that this is a beat-up little town, doing its best to hang on. The housing stock is a mix of everything from large, well-maintained homes, to old house trailers. There's an attractive Cass District Library in the old commercial area, which also has the Real Deal Resale Shop. A small park provides access to Pleasant Lake inside the village limits.

The best-known business here is Lunker's, an outdoor sports store that features a restaurant and pub inside, and a huge, rotating statue of a fish atop its sign on US-12.

FENNVILLE, 49408

City in Allegan County. Population, 1,412. Median household income, $39,013, or 87 percent of the statewide median. Elam Fenn built a sawmill here in 1862. The city hosts an annual festival called Goose Fest, calling attention to waterfowl in the nearby Fennville State Game Refuge and Allegan State Game Area.

Downtown businesses like the Blue Goose Café follow the loosey-goosey theme. Bird's Eye Foods has a frozen-food plant here.

The town has a historic feel to it, with bed-and-breakfast inns and commercial businesses along the well-maintained main street. Signs on the way into town hail Fennville as the home of Rich Jordan, a diminutive athlete who starred in four sports and averaged 44 points a game in1964-65 for the Fennville High School basketball team.

Jordan was the first Michigan resident named to the National High School Sports Hall of Fame.

FENWICK, 48834

An unincorporated crossroads community in Montcalm County on the line between Fair Plain and Bushnell townships, east of Greenville. It was founded in the 1870s and named for the founder's former hometown in Canada.

There's not much "town" left here any more, though several large country homes hint at a level of bygone prosperity. There are also some newer modular homes. The general store is closed, and the post office seems to be the only activity center left in town.

FERRYSBURG, 49409

City in Ottawa County. Population, 3,010. Median household income, $53,622, or 120 percent of the statewide median. The town was developed in the 1850s by Col. William M. Ferry, whose father was one of the founders of nearby Grand Haven. This attractive small town is tucked along Spring Lake, the Grand River and Lake Michigan, between the city of Grand Haven and P.J. Hoffmaster State Park.

There's no real downtown area, but the Town Square strip mall has groceries, a drugstore and other essentials. A section of Grand Haven adjacent to the north side of the Grand River can be reached only by driving through Ferrysburg, via the scenic North Shore Drive. Ferrysburg's city government acts as trustee for the Lindquist Dunes Preserve, which extends into both cities.

Ottawa County officials are working to increase the area's public land by purchasing a mile-long strip of dunes, back from the beach, between North Beach Park, in Ferrysburg, and Hoffmaster State Park.

FREEPORT, 49325

Village in Barry County. Population, 415. Median household income, $42,708, or 96 percent of the statewide median. Named for Freeport, Ohio, the previous home of the Roush brothers, who founded the village in the 1870s.

Freeport has a surprising vitality for a small town far off the beaten path. The town sets well off the state highway in a farming area just south of the point where Kent, Ionia and Barry counties come together. Its downtown has a bank, library, hardware, general store and village hall, along with the Freeport Elevator Co.

A wooden building nearby houses the Chesebrough

Wooden Rake Co., which has been in business since 1872 making various styles of wooden rakes, first for farmers and now mostly for grooming golf course sand traps.

The Freeport Elevator Co. serves farms in Barry, Kent and Ionia counties (photo: Ed Hoogterp)

FREMONT, 49412

City in Newaygo County. Population, 4,301. Median household income, $32,246, or 72 percent of the statewide median. Daniel Joslin built a log cabin here in 1854. The town is named for John C. Fremont, a Civil War general.

Fremont, located where M-82 makes a big bend around Fremont Lake, is the largest city in Newaygo County. It's home to the Gerber Baby Food Co.

The town is more than 20 miles from the nearest freeway, about as far as you can get in West Michigan.

It has a bustling downtown of well-maintained two-story brick buildings, and an impressive modern library. Wal-Mart and a string of fast-food restaurants are in a commercial district on M-82 west of the city.

FRUITPORT, 49415

Village and township in Muskegon County. Village population, 1,170. Median household income, $48,125, or 108 percent of the statewide average. The village was a stop on the Pere Marquette Railroad in the 1870s, and got its name from the volume of fruit shipped on the railroad.

Today, the village and township make up a prime residential and commercial area near the junction of the I-96 and US-31 expressways. Fruitport Township has nearly 13,000 residents and is home to The Lakes Mall, a regional enclosed shopping center.

This tall station wagon is a commercial landmark in Fruitport village (photo: Ed Hoogterp)

The mall area, just east of US-31 at Sternberg and Harvey roads, has become the main retail center for much of the Muskegon and Grand Haven area.

FULTON, 49052

Crossroads in Kalamazoo County's Wakeshma Township. Township population, 1,417. Median household income, $52,328, or 117 percent of the statewide median. The town of Gardner's Corners was moved a mile south to this location about 1860. The town was named after Fulton County, NY. The Fulton State Game Area is nearby.

This is a strange and beautiful community in the farmland at the southeastern corner of Kalamazoo County. Several large, brick or wood-frame houses with broad, gracious porches spread out along the roads from what is mostly a boarded up downtown at the 4-way stop where W. Avenue meets 42nd Street.

About all that's left, says a resident, is a store, a restaurant, a post office, and "nice people."

GALESBURG, 49053

City in Kalamazoo County. Population, 1,988. Median household income, $34,633, or 78 percent of the statewide median. The town is named for George Gale, who settled here along the Kalamazoo River in 1835.

This remains an attractive, if not especially prosperous, small city. Big, old homes, some with two-story carriage houses in back, sit along streets shaded by ancient oak and maple trees. The Congregational Church has been little altered since it was built in 1861.

A historical museum and city offices are in a sprawling city park that traces the Kalamazoo River's edge along the southern city limits.

Downtown, the old city hall building is boarded up, but professional offices, an ice cream store, and Billy's Bike Shop are among those still doing business in the aging brick buildings.

GALIEN, 49113

Village in Berrien County. Population, 581. Median household income, $35,250, or 79 percent of the statewide median.

Locals pronounce the name "Guh-LEEN," whether referring to the Galien River, Galien Township or the village of Galien two miles north of the Indiana border. George Blakeslee bought a mill here on the Galien River in 1853.

Today, it's a neat little town, surrounded by fertile farmland. The residential areas are modest, with modulars comprising most of the newer dwellings. On Cleveland Avenue, downtown, most of the storefronts are either empty or contain antique shops.

The old brick train depot is in an advanced state of disrepair.

GLENN, 49416, AND GANGES (included in Fennville ZIP code)

Unincorporated villages in Allegan County's Ganges Township. Township population, 2,516. Median household income, $47,143, or 106 percent of the statewide median.

The township is split, with an affluent western region along the Lake Michigan shore and a less-well-off interior. Aging tourist businesses extend along the Red Arrow Highway, which parallels I-196 through much of the township.

Ganges is home to several religious institutions, including the Vivekananda Monastery and Retreat, which was founded by a Chicago Hindu group.

The Fenn Valley Vineyards winery is located in the township, with a Fennville address.

GOBLES, 49055

City in Van Buren County. Population, 807. Median household income, $26,917, or 60 percent of the statewide median. The town is named for John Goble, who owned a hotel here in the 1860s.

This region of Van Buren County seems a bit downtrodden economically. Gobles, on M-40 northwest of Kalamazoo, has a downtown that once was much busier than it is today. It still maintains such businesses such as Jan's Trailside Café, a popular stop for riders on the Kal-Haven Trail.

The Timber Ridge Ski Area is in Pine Grove Township, with a Gobles address.

GOWEN, 49326

Unincorporated community on the line between Kent and Montcalm counties. This former lumbering town was platted in the 1870s by Col. James Gowen. Today it's a cluster of homes and trailers near the Flat River, north of Greenville.

The surrounding area – including Kent County's Spencer Township and Montcalm County's Montcalm Township –

is experiencing modest population growth, but remains largely a mix of agricultural and recreational property.

GRAND BEACH, (included in New Buffalo's 49117 ZIP code)

Resort village on Lake Michigan in Berrien County. Population, 227. Median household income, $61,875, or 139 percent of the statewide median. This resort town between New Buffalo and the Indiana border was incorporated in 1934, so that property owners could retain more control.

There is little or no commerce here. A few residents live in Grand Beach year-round, but most go to Florida or elsewhere for the winter. A majority of the property owners have ties to the Chicago area.

GRAND HAVEN, 49417

City in Ottawa County. Population, 11,161. Median household income, $40,322 or 90 percent of the statewide average.

Rix Robinson had a trading post here in the early 1830s. By the end of that decade, Robinson, William Ferry and others had begun developing the city, which is named for its location at the mouth of the Grand River.

Today, Grand Haven is quite simply one of America's great beach towns. A boardwalk meanders along the riverfront from the lively downtown to the breakwall at the river-mouth. Grand Haven State Park, at the mouth of the river, is among the state's most popular beaches. The "campsites" here are little more than marked spaces (with full hook-ups, of course) where campers park their motor homes on a paved parking lot. But they're close to the beach and the pier, and they're full all summer.

The town's one negative is the US-31 highway that runs a gantlet of fast-food joints, filling stations and other businesses through the center of town. A drawbridge crossing the Grand River can sometimes create havoc in an already chaotic traffic situation.

The Michigan Department of Transportation has plans for a bypass freeway that would run through townships east of Grand Haven and Holland. The proposal has met stubborn opposition because of the cost (One billion dollars – that's billion with a "B") and because it might destroy farmland and encourage urban sprawl.

The project will likely take decades to complete. The first step may be a new bridge over the Grand River.

GRAND JUNCTION, 49056

Unincorporated community in Van Buren County's Columbia Township. Township population, 2,740. Median household income, $34,389, or 77 percent of the statewide median.

The town was named in the 1860s for its location at the junction of two railroads. The CSX tracks running north and south through town are still active, while the east-west railroad grade has been converted to slower travel as the Kal-Haven Trail.

There's not much town here, but it is home to the Michigan Blueberry Growers Association and to Grand Junction Elementary School (part of the Bloomingdale School District) which promises to "gently, joyously educate kindergarten to third grade students."

GRAND RAPIDS, 49501-59504

City in Kent County. Population, 197,846. Median household income, $37,227, or 83 percent of the statewide median. Trader Louis Campau gets credit for founding Grand Rapids in 1826, though a Native American village and a struggling Baptist mission were here before him.

Today, G.R. is the second largest city in the state, county seat of Kent County and the metropolitan center of Western Michigan. For more on Grand Rapids, see the Urban Regions section.

GRANDVILLE, 49418

City in Kent County, Population, 16,263. Median household income, $47,570, or 107 percent of the statewide median.

Grandville, a few miles downstream from Grand Rapids, was settled in 1832, and maintained an identity distinct from its larger neighbor.

Today, Grandville is home to Rivertown Crossings, one of West Michigan's largest indoor shopping malls. The city retains a hint of its former downtown, along Chicago Drive (M-21) and Wilson Avenue, but many of the business and local government buildings are new.

Quiet streets, affordable housing and good schools make Grandville's older residential sections a popular choice for young families.

GRANT, 49327

City in Newaygo County. Population, 911. Median household income, $30,972, or 69 percent of the statewide median. Andrew Squier built a sawmill here in 1832. The town is named for Ulysses S. Grant.

Entering town from the south, on M-37 just north of the Muskegon County line, a motorist may feel he's accidentally driven into a farm auction. Businesses such as Trade-A-Rama Used Equipment display their machinery for sale or rent on either side of the highway.

Once you get past that, Grant is a nice, compact town, with a short downtown business district. Grant High School includes an attractive glass-fronted Fine Arts Center. The Ryan Benson Memorial Skate Park offers a selection of half-pipes for skateboards and in-line skates. The park is named for a local youth who died in a 2001 traffic accident.

GREENVILLE, 48838

City in Montcalm County. Population, 7,876. Median household income, $30,453, or 68 percent of the statewide median.

The town, named for early resident John Green, started as a station on the Detroit, Grand Rapids and Western Railroad. The Meijer retail chain got its start here. Greenville's largest employer was an Electrolux (formerly Gibson) refrigerator plant that announced plans in 2004 to close shop and move its operation to Mexico for lower costs. The town is still searching for ways to recover from that loss.

The downtown business district consists of several blocks of solid commercial buildings, including the Winter Inn, a downtown hotel and restaurant that has had a number of owners over the years.

The area's retail center is now along M-57, west of town, where Meijer, Wal-Mart and Target all have stores. Meijer, which began as a local grocery story, opened one of its early Thrifty Acres supermarkets in the 1960s on M-91 at the north end of Greenville. That building was left empty when the company, now based in Walker, built its new store on M-57.

Also on M-57 west of town is Klackle Orchards, a major apple-grower with an autumn farm market that rivals many small-town carnivals.

HAMILTON, 49419

Unincorporated community in Allegan County's Heath Township. Township population, 3,063. Median household income, $54,545, or 122 percent of the statewide median. The community was first called Rabbit River when it was settled around 1835 by Charles Butler.

For many years, this agricultural area was populated predominantly by Dutch Calvinists who settled in nearby Holland. Students were not allowed to sponsor dances at the school until the 1980s. The population is becoming more diverse as the fast-growing area changes into a bedroom suburb of Holland and Grand Rapids.

The business district straddles M-40, which cuts an angle through town. An old dam and wooden railroad trestle over the Rabbit River create a local scenic attraction. The Allegan State Game Area is also nearby.

A wooden rail trestle crosses the Rabbit River above an old dam in Hamilton (photo: Ed Hoogterp)

HARBERT, 49115

Crossroads commercial district on the Red Arrow Highway in Berrien County's Chikaming Township. Township population, 3,678. Median household income, $47,778, or 107 percent of the statewide median.

The community, on the two-lane that was once the main road up the Lake Michigan shore from Chicago and Indiana, retains the charm of an old-time tourist region. A popular stop for travelers is the Harbert Swedish Bakery on Red Arrow Highway.

The poet and historian Carl Sandburg lived in Harbert while writing much of his authoritative biography of Abraham Lincoln.

The shops here are mostly upscale, offering art, gifts and antiques. The Harbert Market Garden Center has a huge selection of plants and landscape supplies, which are well-used by homes in the area. Many of the older homes are small. Much larger and more expensive homes are going up here and there along the back roads.

HART, 49420

City in Oceana County. Population, 1,958. Median household income, $25,855, or 58 percent of the statewide median. Hart, which is the Oceana County seat of government, was founded in 1856 and is named for pioneer Wellington Hart.

It sits within the northern Michigan fruit belt, with county growers producing cherries, peaches, apples, asparagus and other specialty crops.

Hart Lake, formed by a hydroelectric dam on the Pentwater River, sits just off the town's main street.

The popular Silver Lake Sand Dunes area is just to the west. Hart and nearby Shelby alternate annually as sponsors of the National Asparagus Festival.

The Chadwick-Munger House in Hart is headquarters for the Oceana County Historical Society (photo: Ed Hoogterp)

HARTFORD, 49057

City in Van Buren County. Population, 2,526. Median household income, $32,879 or 74 percent of the statewide median.

The former Van Buren County poorhouse near Hartford is now a museum (photo: Ed Hoogterp)

The town's founder wanted to name it "Hartland" after his former hometown in New York. But Michigan already had a Hartland (in Livingston County) so he settled on Hartford.

The town, on the north side of the I-94 freeway, is surrounded by agricultural land, and is home to Hilltop Orchards and Nurseries, one of the Midwest's top commercial fruit tree nurseries.

Today, the downtown business district seems a bit forlorn, with several empty buildings in addition to a hardware store and other businesses.

Fast food and gas stations are located out near the I-94 interchange.

HASTINGS, 49058

City in Barry County. Population, 7,309. Median household income, $39,033, or 88 percent of the statewide median. Hastings is Barry County's seat of government and largest city.

The town was founded in 1836 and named for Detroit banker Eurotas P. Hastings. The Thornapple River passes through town. A few miles away, also on the river, restored buildings in Charlton Park

A mural depicting old-time movie stars covers a wall of a theater in downtown Hastings (photo: Ed Hoogterp)

provide a glimpse into the region's history.

The downtown area is hanging on, with a movie house, hardware store and impressive county courthouse. Wal-Mart, K-mart and a choice of chain restaurants are spread out along M-37 on the outskirts of town.

Pennock Hospital serves the surrounding area. Several major employers, including Hastings Manufacturing and Flex-Fab have operations in Hastings.

HESPERIA, 49421

Village in Oceana and Newaygo counties. Population, 962. Median household income, $27,460, or 61 percent of the statewide median.

John Cook and Daniel Weaver built a sawmill here in 1866, near the White River. Cook's daughter named the settlement Hesperia because the setting resembled a garden, according to Walter Romig. (In Greek mythology, Hesperia was a nymph who lived in a beautiful garden.)

Today, standing on a footbridge that leads to islands in the mill pond behind Hesperia Dam, it's easy to see why the name was chosen. Much of the land around the village remains in a natural setting, as part of the Manistee National Forest. Kellogg's canoe livery rents canoes for trips down the river.

Despite the scenic beauty, Hesperia faces economic challenges common to the state's isolated communities. Many of the town's aging homes need attention, and downtown buildings are in need of repair. An apparent exception is Angelo's & Riccardo's Dining & Spirits, a popular downtown restaurant.

HICKORY CORNERS, 49060

Unincorporated community in Barry County's Barry Township. Township population, 3,501. Median household income, $45,339, or 102 percent of the statewide median.

The town, northwest of Gull Lake near the Barry-Kalamazoo county line, was settled in the 1830s and named for a large hickory tree on the schoolhouse grounds. It's not much more than a crossroads today, but it's home to the Gilmore Car Museum, with a collection of classic autos and impeccable, farm-like grounds.

Also nearby is Michigan State University's W.K. Kellogg Biological Station, which includes a bird sanctuary, and a restored mansion once owned by cereal magnate W.K. Kellogg.

HOLLAND, 49422-24

City in Ottawa and Allegan counties. Population, 35,211. Median household income, $42,291, or 95 percent of the statewide median. Holland was formed as a Dutch "Kolonie" in 1847 when the Rev. Albertus C. VanRaalte brought a group from the Netherlands to this site on Lake Macatawa.

VanRaalte and the other founders were members of a Calvinist protestant sect seeking a place where they could live according to their strict religious code. The Dutch dominated the city and surrounding area for more than a century, and their nose-to-the-grindstone work ethic helped bring prosperity to the region.

The Dutch heritage remains evident in the town's churches and such tourist attractions as the DeZwaan Windmill, an authentic mill imported from the Netherlands. But Holland's population has grown more diverse in recent decades. It has one of West Michigan's largest Hispanic communities.

Today, Holland has a lively downtown area and several fine parks. About 28,000 people live in the Ottawa County portion of the city, while 7,200 live in the Allegan

County sector. That makes Holland the biggest city in each county. The annual Tulip Time festival draws hundreds of thousands of visitors each May. Holland is also home to Hope College.

Holland State Park, on Lake Michigan just west of town, holds the distinction of being the busiest unit in the Michigan State Park system.

HOLTON, 49425

Unincorporated village and township in Muskegon County's Holton Township. Township population, 2,537. Median household income, $37,813, or 85 percent of the statewide median.

The village was named for Henry Holt, who was Michigan's lieutenant governor from 1873-76. Holton sits in a forested township within the boundaries of the Manistee National Forest.

In many ways, it has the feel of a Northern Michigan village. Small homes and businesses spread out on both sides of M-120 and several side streets. Railroad tracks run through town at an angle.

There's a library, the Severt Swenson Township Park, a fire barn, and a party store that prominently displays a sign advertising Walt's Crawlers.

HOPKINS, 49328

Village in Allegan County. Population, 595. Median household income, $38,462, or 86 percent of the statewide median.

The town was a railroad depot on the line between Grand Rapids and Kalamazoo in the 1870s. The area remains mostly agricultural. Despite being only 25 miles south of Grand Rapids and near the US-131 expressway, Hopkins and the surrounding township of the same name have so far escaped suburbanization.

The village has some of the oldest housing stock in West Michigan, with most homes built before 1940. The small business district includes a bank, restaurant, hardware and convenience store, along with a library, post office, school and township park.

HOWARD CITY, 49329

Village in Montcalm County. Population, 1,615. Median household income, $34,556, or 77 percent of the statewide median. The community became a stop on the Detroit, Grand Rapids and Western Railroad in the 1860s. It was named for a railroad attorney.

Today, the White Pine Trail follows the old railroad route through town. Howard City once sat astride the two-lane US-131 highway that ran between Grand Rapids and Cadillac. The freeway built in the 1970s runs a few miles to the west.

The "Gettin' Picky" music store and Great Northern Music Hall host musical jam sessions every Friday in the downtown area, which has a number of fine, but generally underutilized commercial buildings.

Much of the town's retail has moved out toward the expressway exit, or to M-46 just north of town.

HUBBARDSTON, 48845

Village in Ionia and Clinton counties. Population, 387. Median household income, $36,458, or 82 percent of the statewide median. A dam and mill went up on Fish Creek here in the 1830s. Thomas Hubbard bought the mill in 1852 and the village bears his name.

Today, it's a nice hilly village built around the dam and mill pond. The local historical society has a museum room in the old St. John's Parish School.

The town values its history as an Irish enclave, with such stores as the Celtic Path gift shop. Shiels Tavern downtown claims to be the first Michigan drinking establishment licensed after the end of prohibition in 1933.

HUDSONVILLE, 49426

City in Ottawa County. Population, 7,336. Median household income, $46,961, or 105 percent of the statewide median.

The community on the line between Georgetown and Jamestown townships was once called South Georgetown. It's named for its first postmaster, Homer Hudson.

Until the 1970s, this was a quiet hamlet surrounded by muck farms and cornfields. Many of the farms remain, and Hudsonville still calls itself "The Salad Bowl City." But today it stands at the heart of one of Michigan's fastest-growing residential areas: The busy I-196 corridor between Grand Rapids and Holland.

There's no real downtown here. Commerce spreads out along Chicago Drive, the four-lane boulevard that was the main road through this part of Ottawa County until the I-196 expressway opened in the 1960s.

A retail plaza just off that road provides all the necessities, including groceries, hardware, pizza and a Michigan Secretary of State office.

IONIA, 48846

City in Ionia County. Population, 10,653. Median household income, $38,289, or 86 percent of the statewide median. Ionia, on the Grand River midway between Grand Rapids and Lansing, was settled by Samuel Dexter, who led a group from New York here in 1833. It is named for the Greek province of the same name.

The town is the Ionia County seat of government and is home to a complex of state prisons, which provide stable employment. Much of the downtown area is beautifully restored, with brick streets and some buildings made of locally quarried Ionia sandstone. Still, local leaders acknowledge that the district needs more business. The 1904 Hall-Fowler Library is among the most impressive buildings. Ionia is surrounded by agricultural land, and the Ionia Free Fair, on grounds along the Grand River, is among the most popular fairs in the state.

Ionia's Hall-Fowler Library is crafted from local sandstone (photo: Ed Hoogterp)

JAMESTOWN, 49427

Township and unincorporated village in Ottawa County. Township population, 4,977. Median household income, $68,689, or 154 percent of the statewide median. According to Walter Romig, the town got its name because four out of 12 voters at an organizational meeting in 1843 had the first name of James.

Much of the township's rolling, picturesque land remains as agriculture, despite its proximity to Grand Rapids. The new M-6 freeway, which opened in 2004, has its western terminus in the township, and population growth is expected.

The village is a winsome crossroads (Riley Street and 24th Avenue) with a wedding chapel, antique shop and general store, along with an elementary school that backs up to farmland.

JENISON, 49428-29

Unincorporated community and school district in Ottawa County's Georgetown Township. Township population, 41,161. Median household income, $58,936, or 132 percent of the statewide median.

The community on the south bank of the Grand River, just downstream from Grand Rapids and Grandville, traces its history to 1864, when twin brothers Lumen and Lucius Jenison built a grist mill here.

The surrounding area and township are among the fastest growing in the state. Jenison Public Schools has grown from a rural district into one of the largest suburban school systems in West Michigan.

Georgetown is the region's most populous township, and is Ottawa County's largest municipality. The I-196 expressway runs through the southern part of the township, while the Grand River extends along the northern boundary, from the Kent County line almost to Grand Valley State University.

The Jenison business district, just off a confusing and dangerous I-196 expressway exit, features Meijer, Target and other retail giants. The Michigan Department of Transportation is planning to rebuild the intersection, though no date has been set for the work.

JONES, 49061

Unincorporated community in Cass County, on the line between Porter and Newberg townships, near where M-60 intersects with M-40.

Riders pass slowly through downtown Jones (photo: Ed Hoogterp)

The Crane Pond State Game Area occupies scattered parcels north and west of Jones. The Bair Lake Bible Camp and the Hickory Inn restaurant are on Bair Lake in Jones. Swiss Valley Ski Area is in

Newberg Township just north of the village, as is a highly rated Bed and Breakfast Inn, the Sanctuary at Wildwood.

There is still a small amount of commerce in Jones, but at times the "downtown" looks a bit like a ghost town from a Western movie. There are a number of empty, unpainted buildings and an aging "Opera House" that appears as though it's being held together by the ivy growing up the walls.

KALAMAZOO, 49001-49009

County seat of Kalamazoo County. Population, 77,092. Median household income, $31,189, or 69 percent of the statewide median. Kalamazoo is West Michigan's second largest city. It was founded by Titus Bronson in 1829, and known for a time as Bronson.

The "Kalamazoo" name comes from an Indian word thought to mean "boiling water." The city is home to Kalamazoo College, Western Michigan University and two of the nation's top-rated hospitals. (For more about Kalamazoo, see the Urban Regions section.)

KENDALL, 49062

Unincorporated community in Van Buren County's Pine Grove Township. Township population, 2,802. Median household income, $47,060, or 105 percent of the statewide median. The site was once a sawmill and railroad station. Today the Kal-Haven Trail follows the former railroad bed.

Kendall is now a pleasant crossroads northwest of Kalamazoo with, among other attributes, one of West Michigan's nicest-looking post offices.

A stone monument pays tribute to C.A. Wilkinson, a country doctor who served the area from 1891 to 1940. The Timber Ridge winter sports area is in Pine Grove Township.

Kendall has one of West Michigan's most attractive post office buildings (photo: Ed Hoogterp)

KENT CITY, 49330

Village in northern Kent County. Population, 1,034. Median household income, $35,341, or 75 percent of the statewide median. Kent City was founded as an agricultural village in the 1870s, and remains a quiet community near the intersection of M-37 and M-46.

Meanwhile, the surrounding townships have gained population as people move out beyond the older suburbs on the north end of the Grand Rapids urban area.

The old business district on 17 Mile Road (M-46) has seen some deterioration over the years, in part because shoppers can buy just about anything they want a dozen miles away in a major shopping district along M-37 (Alpine Avenue) in the Grand Rapids suburb of Walker. One local success story is the Valley Ridge Bank, formerly Kent City State Bank, which has nine locations in four counties, including a headquarters built in 1998 in Kent City.

KENTWOOD. 49518, (Part of Grand Rapids ZIP code area)

City in Kent County. Population, 45,239. Median household income, $45,812, or 103 percent of the statewide median.

Kentwood was incorporated in the 1960s from part of the original Paris Township on the outskirts of Grand Rapids. (The rest of the township had already become part of the central city.)

The fast-growing suburb is now one of West Michigan's largest cities. It contains everything from factories to trailer parks to million-dollar homes. It also has a portion of the 28th Street business strip and Woodland Shopping Center, one of the region's largest enclosed malls.

LACOTA, 49063

Unincorporated village in Van Buren County's Geneva Township. Township population, 3,949. Median household income, $34,900, or 78 percent of the statewide median.

This agricultural village, surrounded by peach orchards and blueberry fields, was first called Irvington. The name was changed in the 1890s at the behest of the Michigan Central Railroad, which had other stops with similar names. A local committee chose "Lacota" the name of an Indian heroine in a 19th century novel.

The railroad through town has been converted to the Kal-Haven Trail, which passes an empty store and a long-closed gas station on the way through what once was

An abandoned service station overlooks the Kal-Haven Trail in Lacota (photo: Ed Hoogterp)

downtown Lacota.
Like many rural villages, Lacota is barely hanging on. Here's how local resident Barbara Wood put it in her 1997 history of the village:

"It was a little cluster of homesteads that grew slowly and surely into a productive and healthy, country village, that stayed the course for about fifty years, and then just as slowly and surely began to fade."

LAKE ODESSA, 48849

Village in Ionia County. Population, 2,225. Median household income, $34,896, or 78 percent of the statewide median. The village of Bonanza was moved a mile and given the present name about 1880, when the Pere Marquette Railroad came through the area.

The village extends along the north shore of Jordan Lake, in Odessa Township. It's surrounded by agricultural land, and is the site of a well-attended livestock auction.

Most of the traffic through town follows M-50 along the shore of the lake. Just off that route, the two-block downtown is still going strong, with a tavern, bank, antique shop, and library.

A veterans' memorial stands on the Jordan Lake shore in Lake Odessa (photo: Ed Hoogterp)

LAKESIDE, 49116

Unincorporated village on Lake Michigan, in Berrien County's Chikaming Township, just north of New Buffalo and Union Pier. The village was the site of a sawmill and a pier in the 1850s. It is now part of a string of small communities along the Red Arrow Highway near the lakeshore in Michigan's far southwest corner.

LAKEVIEW, 48850

Village in Montcalm County. Population, 1,158. Median household income, $33,611, or 75 percent of the statewide median. The area was first settled in the late 1850s. A railroad station opened on Tamarack Lake in 1879 and took the name Lakeview.

Today, the town wraps around three sides of the lake, near the junction of M-46 and M-91. It's a quiet village, with stately trees, big country homes and churches along the residential streets.

Spectrum Health's United Memorial Hospital, Kelsey Campus, is here, along with a number of medical offices.

Downtown features old-style angle parking in front of a row of well-preserved brick commercial buildings. Much of the real commerce is located at the south end of the village along busy M-46.

LAMONT, 49430

Unincorporated village in Ottawa County's Tallmadge Township. Township population, 6,881. Median household income, $59,205, or 133 percent of the statewide median.

This location on the north side of the Grand River was known as Steele's Landing, in honor of brothers Harry and Zine Steele, who settled there in 1833. In 1855, Lamont Chubb of Grand Rapids traded a road scraper for the right to attach his name to the place.

Lamont remains an attractive residential community, with tall trees and a boulevarded median along the main thoroughfare, Leonard Street. The surrounding township retains a rural feel, though it is succumbing to urban sprawl, like much of the area around Grand Rapids.

LAWRENCE, 49064

Village in Van Buren County. Population, 987. Median household income, $29,583, or 66 percent of the statewide median. The site was first settled in 1835 and was called Brush Creek. The name was changed in the 1840s to match the township where it's located.

The town is on the Paw Paw River, on the north side of I-94. Despite its relatively low median income, Lawrence retains a nice, small-town flavor with big old homes shaded by ancient trees.

Today, it's a town dominated by grapes. The surrounding farmland is taken up by vineyards, and a Welch's juice plant provides employment in town.

The residential areas have a mix of older and modern homes on streets shaded by huge trees. Downtown has a number of restaurants, including the Vineyard Café, the Old Hat Brewery and Grill, and the Big T. Tavern.

LAWTON, 49065

Village in Van Buren County. Population, 1,857. Median household income, $36,250, or 81 percent of the statewide median. The settlement was first called South Paw Paw when it was founded in 1848. The name changed when the Michigan Central Railroad came through, and Nathan Lawton gave land for the station.

Lawton's old train depot is made from Michigan fieldstone (photo: Ed Hoogterp)

LEONIDAS, 49066

Unincorporated village and township in St. Joseph County. Township population, 1,253. Median household income, $42,417, or 95 percent of the statewide median.

George Matthews and his family from New York settled on nearby Nottawa Creek in 1831. The present townsite dates from 1846. It's named after an ancient king of the Greek city-state of Sparta.

According to one story, the early settlers chose to name their township "Leoni," while at the same time, a township in Jackson County submitted the name "Leonidas." A state bureaucrat accidentally switched the names, so Jackson County got Leoni Township, while

St. Joseph County received Leonidas. The names stuck.

A quiet cemetery on the north edge of town has weathered headstones dating from the time of the first settlers. Downtown, where the town once had several hotels and a busy train depot, there's now an antique shop, a tavern, a farm equipment store and a post office.

LOWELL, 49331

City in eastern Kent County. Population, 3,853. Median household income, $42,326, or 95 percent of the statewide median. Daniel Marsac built a trading post on the south bank of the Grand River in 1831. He bought land on the north side, at the present townsite in the 1840s.

The Lowell showboat lies at rest on the Flat River in downtown Lowell (photo: Ed Hoogterp)

Magdelaine LaFramboise was in the area even earlier, probably by 1806. After the death of her fur-trader husband that year, she operated a trading post near where the Flat River enters the Grand. She apparently spent winters along the Grand and summers on Mackinac Island. Madame LaFramboise sold her Lowell business in 1821 to Rix Robinson, who moved the operation downstream to the present site of Ada.

Today, Lowell's beautiful brick downtown has restaurants, antique and gift shops, and the King Milling Co. Other commerce spreads out along Highway M-21.

A dam where the highway crosses the Flat River creates a lazy millpond in downtown Lowell. The Lowell Showboat is permanently docked there, next to a stage that is used for local concerts during the summer. The surrounding township, once completely rural, is seeing more residential subdivisions, while the village retains its small-town appeal.

LYONS, 48851

Village in Ionia County. Population, 703. Median household income, $39,191, or 88 percent of the statewide median. This community, at the site of a former Indian village on the Grand River, was platted by Lucius Lyon in 1836. Two years later, the town had a hotel and the only bridge over the Grand River between Jackson and Grand Haven.

Lyon, a surveyor and entrepreneur who had a hand in developing several West

Michigan communities, envisioned his namesake town as a major commercial center and, possibly, the capital of the new state.

That never came to be. The town was bypassed by the railroad in 1856 and never grew much more. Lucius Lyon did right well for himself, however. When Michigan became a state in 1837, he was selected as one of the state's first U.S. senators.

MACATAWA, 49434

Unincorporated resort community in Ottawa County, on the south shore of Lake Macatawa, across from Holland State Park.

The site was a religious settlement in the 1850s, and became a non-sectarian resort around the 1880s. Macatawa comes from an Ottawa word meaning "black," which described the dark waters of the lake.

The community today is a tony resort that includes a post office, and a collection of beach houses, marinas and upscale shops.

MARCELLUS, 49067

Village in Cass County. Population, 1,165. Median household income, $38,958, or 87 percent of the statewide median. The town was a railroad station in 1870. The railroad still cuts through town, near the M-40 business district.

Businesses include the cleverly named Dog In Suds pet grooming salon, a bank, grocery store, the Pork Chops Diner and the Pit Stop Bar and Grill.

This village is in an area that once supported numerous small hog farms. Many of those farms have ceased operation as the pork industry consolidated into a system of fewer, and much larger farms.

Like many southwest Michigan villages, Marcellus has some impressive older homes, especially west of the business district, along with some smaller and less-well-maintained houses.

A few miles west of town, on Marcellus Road in Volinia Township, is Newton's Woods, also known as Russ Forest. The property, owned by Michigan State University, includes a museum and one of the state's few remaining virgin forest preserves.

MARNE, 49435

Unincorporated village in Ottawa County's Wright and Tallmadge townships. Wright Township population, 3,298. Median household income, $51,023, or 114 percent of the statewide median. The community was known as Berlin for 80 years, from its founding in 1839 until 1919. During World War I, it seemed a bad idea to live in a town named after the capital city of America's enemy. So, the name was changed to Marne, commemorating a major battle along the Marne River in France.

Marne continues to host the Berlin Fair and Berlin Raceway, both on the fairgrounds in the village. No one seems to mind the German connection.

Marne itself remains a quiet village, though there has been considerable development on I-96, which runs along the north end of town.

MARTIN, 49070

Village in Allegan County. Population, 453. Median household income, $41,389, or 93 percent of the statewide median. The first settlers arrived here in 1836. The village is named for President Martin Van Buren.

Martin sits along the old highway that linked Grand Rapids and Kalamazoo. Since the 1960s it's been the site of the popular drag racing competition at US-131 Motorsports Park, formerly called the Martin Dragway.

The village is less than a mile off the US-131 expressway. Working farmland extends into the village limits. The old downtown includes a hardware store and pharmacy.

MATTAWAN, 49071

Village in Van Buren County. Population, 2,488. Median household income, $42,241, or 95 percent of the statewide median. The site was settled in the 1840s and later became a station on the Michigan Central Railroad, six miles west of Kalamazoo.

Despite its location on I-94 and its proximity to Kalamazoo, Mattawan retains a small town, rural feel.

Population is growing in surrounding Antwerp Township, which has nearly 11,000 residents and is by far the most populous township in Van Buren County. But a good slice of the land is still forested. The township also has apple orchards and vineyards.

MCBRIDE, 48852

Village in Montcalm County. Population, 218. Median household income, $30,568, or 68 percent of the statewide median. In 1874 Alexander McBride built a sawmill here. The railroad station was known as McBride's Mill, which was later shortened to McBride. It's still occasionally called "McBride's."

This is a really small town, in potato-farming country two miles east of M-66. The 2000 Census counted 87 homes here, half of them built before 1940.

Despite its size, McBride is doing just fine. Its small neighborhoods have a mix of older homes, mobiles, and some newer dwellings. Many have big yards.

The town is home to Sackett Farm Equipment and the Crowe's Nest Bar. The Fred Meijer Heartland Trail runs through on an old railroad grade.

Just south of town is the Mid-Michigan Motorplex, formerly know as Central Michigan Dragway.

MEARS, 49436

Unincorporated village in Oceana County's Golden Township. Township population, 1,815. Median household income, $35,878, or 80 percent of the statewide median.

The land here was platted into village lots in 1873 by lumber baron Charles Mears, who had a sawmill on the site. It's now a country village, with a hardware store, restaurant and other small businesses on the road to the Silver Lake Sand Dunes.

The Oceana County Historical Society maintains a historical park here, and Mears is also the site of a unique race track, the West Michigan Sand Dragway.

MECOSTA, 49332

Village in Mecosta County. Population, 459. Median household income, $32,857, or 74 percent of the statewide median. The village was platted in 1879, the same year the Detroit, Lansing and Northern Railroad came through, by Edwin Moore, of Edmore and Giles Gilbert of Stanton.

Mecosta is from the Potawatomi word for "Big Bear." the name of a signer of the 1836 treaty of Washington.

You can drive through this town on M-20, east of Big Rapids, without really noticing. But it's bigger than it seems, with neighborhoods spreading out away from the two-block business district.

Mecosta was the home of noted conservative political theorist Russell Kirk, who died in 1994. His work is carried on by the Russell Kirk Center for Cultural Renewal, also based here.

MENDON, 49072

Village in St. Joseph County. Population, 904. Median household income, $40,000, or 90 percent of the statewide median. This is a substantial country town on the St. Joseph River. French traders were here in the 1820s, and probably much earlier.

St. Edward's Catholic Church in Mendon is a prime example of fieldstone architecture (photo: Ed Hoogterp)

Mendon figured prominently in relations between early settlers and American Indian tribes who lived along the St. Joseph River. The explorer Louis Hennepin is thought to have met with native people here in the late 1600s.

The 1821 Treaty of Chicago designated a large Potawatomi reservation that included Mendon and much of the surrounding prairie. By the 1830s, settlers streaming into the county had their eyes on the Indians' rich farmland. A new treaty dissolved the reservation in the 1830s and required the Potawatomi to move west of the Mississippi River.

Some of the Indians returned to Michigan. Their descendants now make up the Nottawaseppe Band of Huron Potawatomi, a federally recognized tribe that is seeking to build a casino near Battle Creek.

Mendon became a busy mill town in the 1830s. A 1916 fire destroyed most of downtown. The Bistro Rio restaurant is in one of the riverside buildings that survived. Also in town is the Mendon Country Inn, in an 1873 building on a site that was originally a stagecoach stop. St. Edward's Catholic Church, built in 1908, is an impressive example of fieldstone architecture.

MICHIANA, 49117 (included in New Buffalo ZIP code)

Village in Berrien County. Population, 184. Median household income, $75,984, or 170 percent of the statewide median. This small and affluent resort village lies along the Lake Michigan shore just on the Michigan side of the Indiana border. A sister community called Michiana Shores is adjacent to it on the Indiana side.

The village has no business

district. Most of the residents have ties to the Chicago area, and most live along Michiana's narrow, shaded streets only in the summer.

MIDDLEVILLE, 49333

Village in Barry County. Population, 2,731. Median household income, $41,917, or 94 percent of the statewide median. New York native Calvin Hill bought 400 acres on the Thornapple River here in 1834.

Today, commuters from Middleville and the surrounding township crowd M-37 each morning as they head north to jobs in Grand Rapids and Kentwood.

For those who stick around, the river and Stagecoach Park help create a pleasant setting for a downtown that features restaurants and gift shops. The Paul Henry Trail begins at the park and extends five miles along the Thornapple River.

MOLINE, 49335

Unincorporated village in Allegan County's Dorr Township. Township population (including the communities of Dorr and Moline), 6,579. Median household income, $60,466, or 135 percent of the statewide median.

This is a fast-growing area south of Grand Rapids, where farmland is rapidly being converted to residential subdivisions. Moline has little commercial business, but remains an attractive residential community, with small, nicely kept homes and a township library.

The Moline Milling Co-op is here, as is a branch of a local bank. The public elementary school is closed, but Moline Christian School still operates.

MONTAGUE, 49437

City in Muskegon County. Population, 2,421. Median household income, $40,677, or 91 percent of the statewide median. The site was first settled in 1855. It is named for William Montague Ferry, one of the town's founders.

It lies along the north side of White Lake, across from its "twin" city of Whitehall. The two towns are linked by a bridge across the mouth of the White River, which feeds White Lake.

One of Montague's most recognizable businesses is the Weathervane Inn, on the lake shore. Nearby is a 4,300 pound aluminum weathervane, in the form of a sailing ship. The local Chamber of Commerce says it's the largest weathervane in the world.

Montague features a traditional small-town business district (photo: Terry Phipps)

Big, old homes along Old Channel Trail command a great view of the lake and surrounding forest.

MORLEY 49336

Village in Mecosta County. Population, 512. Median household income, $31,442, or 70 percent of the statewide median. Morley was a station in the Grand Rapids and Indiana Railroad in 1869.

The village on the Little Muskegon River was bypassed in the 1970s by the US-131 expressway, which runs two miles to the west. A number of empty buildings stand along the old highway.

The Frank Deyo Dam and millpond make a picturesque sight along the old road. The Mecosta Pines Campground, a private facility on the river, is popular with summer visitors.

MUIR, 48860

Village in Ionia County. Population, 647. Median household income, $30,096, or 67 percent of the statewide median.

The town was settled in the 1850s as a sawmill site on the Maple River. It's named for H.K. Muir, a railroad superintendent who brought tracks through this town, instead of through the neighboring village of Lyons.

Muir appears to be an economically struggling community. The block-long downtown has village offices and a hardware store, but little else. On the residential streets, house trailers sit close by hundred-year-old homes. Muir's residential areas are separated from Lyons by the Maple River and acres of farm fields.

MUSKEGON, 49440-49445

City and county seat of Muskegon County. Population, 40,136. Median household income, $27,929, or 63 percent of the statewide median. Louis Baddeau had a trading post here in 1834, and other traders frequented the mouth of the Muskegon River for decades before that.

When the 1836 Treaty of Washington opened the area to settlement and logging, Muskegon's location made it a major sawmill and shipping center. For much of the 20th century, it was an industrial city that made everything from engines to bowling balls. That manufacturing base has been eroded in recent decades. Muskegon is home to a cross-lake ferry service to Milwaukee, established in 2004. (For more about Muskegon, see the Urban Regions section.)

MUSKEGON HEIGHTS, 49444 (included in Muskegon ZIP codes)

City in Muskegon County. Population, 11,999. Median household income, $21,778, or 49 percent of the statewide median.

"The Heights," at Muskegon's southern city limits, began as a forward-looking plan to bolster the local economy. In 1890, as the lumber boom was ending, a group of community leaders formed the Muskegon Improvement Co. They bought 1,000 acres of what is now Muskegon Heights and divided it into residential lots. Money from the sale went to subsidize new industry.

At the time it seemed a success. In recent decades, however, Muskegon Heights has seen nothing but hard times. Tax base has fallen and the city government struggles to pay for services to its residents, most of whom are black and poor. Both residential areas and commercial districts show the effects of years of poverty and deterioration.

NASHVILLE, 49073

Village in Barry County. Population, 1,680. Median household income, $32,857, or 74 percent of the statewide median. The town was platted in 1865 on farmland owned by George and Robert Gregg. It was named for George Nash, a Michigan Central Railroad construction engineer who helped bring the railroad here in the 1860s.

Nashville sets on the line between Barry and Eaton counties, which means it's in a transition zone between western and central Michigan.

Today, the railroad service is gone, but the community sits astride the busy M-66 highway. Commercial buildings – but not much commerce – remain in the downtown area. A Thornapple River dam and millrace help create a nice, small-town atmosphere in Putnam Park downtown.

NAZARETH, 49074

Kalamazoo County religious community, on the outskirts of the city of Kalamazoo.

In 1889 a group of Catholic nuns came to Michigan, at the request of the Detroit Diocese, to open a hospital in Kalamazoo. Soon after founding what is now Borgess

Medical Center, the nuns established their mother house on the east side of Kalamazoo and became known as the Sisters of St. Joseph of Nazareth.

They also operated a school and orphanage. Nazareth College was on the site for more than a century, until it closed in 1992.

A familiar sight on M-43 is the headquarters of the Sisters of St. Joseph of Nazareth (photo: Ed Hoogterp)

The Sisters remain active among themselves and in the community. Their huge limestone building, behind low stone walls and broad green lawns, is a familiar sight along M-43 near the Kalamazoo city limits. The Nazareth Post Office is inside.

NEW BUFFALO, 49117

City in Berrien County. Population, 2,200. Median household income, $41,658, or 93 percent of the statewide median. A seafarer from Buffalo, NY, named Wessel Whitaker was blown ashore here in 1834. The next year he brought a group of settlers and founded the town, which he named after the place they had left.

Today, New Buffalo has a fine recreational harbor and a touristy downtown, between the US-12 highway and Lake Michigan.

New Buffalo's harbor was one of the first in Michigan to develop housing and boat slips in the same area. Today, hundreds of condominiums line the marinas along the mouth of the Galien River. More modest homes of long-time residents are on the east side of the highway, away from Lake Michigan. The Pokagon Band of Potawatomi Indians has signed a state compact that includes permission to build a casino on I-94 just outside of town. The plan has been delayed for years by legal action.

NEW ERA, 49466

Village in Oceana County. Population, 470. Median household income, $45,909, or 103 percent of the statewide median.

This village in the West Michigan fruit belt was a railroad stop in the 1870s. Walter Romig says the name was coined by a physician who hailed from Erie, PA. Apparently New Era was the closest the good doctor could come to New Erie.

In any case, the town is a quiet village on the old two-lane highway that was bypassed by the US-31 expressway in the 1970s. A new downtown "streetscape" with brick pavers and antique-look streetlights was installed in 2005.

It's home to the New Era Canning Co., which processes more than 100 million pounds of beans, apples and other produce each year. Also nearby is the Country Dairy farm and store, which produces and sells milk, meat, ice cream and other products from its own 500-cow herd.

NEW TROY, 49119

Small, unincorporated village in Berrien County's Weesaw Township. Township Population, 2,077. Median household income, $41,434, or 93 percent of the statewide median.

New Troy is one in a cluster of small towns in Michigan's far southwest corner, near Lake Michigan and the Indiana border. Local signs declare this hamlet as "The Center of the World."

The settlement got its name, according to Walter Romig, from a nearby railroad station that was called "Troy." When a community grew up around the Gould Brothers' sawmill in the 1830s, it became "New Troy." The original Troy station, two miles to the west, is now the village of Sawyer.

NEWAYGO, 49,337

City in Newaygo County. Population, 1,696. Median household income, $32,273, or 72 percent of the statewide median. The first sawmill in this area of native white pine lumber was built on Pennoyer Creek in 1837 by a group that included Augustus Pennoyer.

The village of Newaygo was founded on banks above the Muskegon River a few years later by John A Brooks. The town and county are named for a Chippewa Indian chieftain. A 19th century dam in the downtown area provided enough water power to run a sawmill with 120 saws, thought to be the largest in Michigan at the time. The dam was removed in the 1960s, leaving a scenic and swift-flowing river through the heart of town.

Much of the daily local commerce is now conducted at the south end of town, where the north-south highway M-37 meets east-west M-82.

Downtown Newaygo, which parallels the south bank of the river, remains a substantial and busy district, with well maintained buildings and a pair of classic outdoor sports establishments: Parsley's Sport Shop and Powers Outdoor Supply.

NILES, 49120

City in Berrien County. Population, 12,150. Median household income, $31,208, or 70 percent of the statewide median. This community on the St. Joseph and Dowagiac rivers may be the most historic in West Michigan.

Roman Catholic Jesuit missionaries founded a mission here about 1685 to minister to local Indians. The Rev. Claude Jean Allouez, one of the best known of the missionaries in New France, is thought to have died and been buried at the mission in 1689. France established Fort St. Joseph near the mission site a few years later. It would be nearly 140 years before white settlers began streaming into most of West Michigan.

Before it was abandoned, in 1781, the fort came under control of the British and, briefly a Spanish party. That gives Niles its claim to being "The City of Four Flags," since the banners of France, Great Britain, Spain and the United States have flown here. (The area was also controlled by the Miami and Potawatomi Indians, but apparently the Native Americans didn't have flags.)

Another mission, this one staffed by Baptists, was formed here in 1821, but lasted only a few years.

Permanent settlement began in 1828. The town is named for Hezekiah Niles, who published a Whig Party newspaper on the East Coast.

There are no visible remains of the fort or missions, though archeologists from Western Michigan University recently uncovered the fort site, near the banks of the St. Joseph River.

Niles was the boyhood home of carmakers John and Horace Dodge, mail-order pioneer Montgomery Ward, and writer Ring Lardner, Jr.

Simplicity patterns for home sewing projects are made here.

The town has a number of gracious old homes, including the Chapin mansion, which has been converted to serve as City Hall. The mansion's former carriage house is a local museum. The downtown district is barely holding its own. Many local residents do their shopping a few miles south in South Bend, Ind.

NORTH MUSKEGON, 49445 (Included in Muskegon ZIP codes)

City in Muskegon County. Population, 4,097. Median household income, $55,053, or 123 percent of the statewide median. This former lumber boomtown on the north side of Muskegon Lake was originally called "Reedsville." It was renamed North Muskegon in 1872.

Today, it is a fine residential area, and the most affluent of Muskegon's suburbs, based on median income.

North Muskegon's Waterfront Sports Park offers a clear view across the lake to Muskegon's downtown district. There's an active commercial area on Lake Avenue, near the Veterans' Memorial Causeway, which links to suburb to the city of Muskegon.

NORTON SHORES, 49441 (Included in Muskegon ZIP codes)

City in Muskegon County. Population, 22,524. Median household income, $45,457, or 102 percent of the statewide median. The town is named for Amos Norton, who opened a sawmill near here in 1846.

It's considered to be a prosperous residential suburb to Muskegon, with frontage on Lake Michigan and Mona Lake. Muskegon County Airport is located here. Norton Shores has about half the population of the city of Muskegon, but covers considerably more land area.

Homes are small in the northern sections of town, adjacent to Muskegon, with larger dwellings nearer the outskirts of town.

Norton Shores' eastern boundary, near Sternberg Road, is a busy commercial district with big box stores across the street from the Lakes Mall.

NOTTAWA, 49075

Unincorporated village and township in St. Joseph County. Township population, 3,979. Median household income, $41,875, or 94 percent of the statewide median. The town is named for the Nottawa-Seppe band of Potawatomi Indians. Another hamlet in the township is called Wasepi. Centreville, the St. Joseph County seat, is on the township's western border.

St. Joseph County's Nottawa Park offers camping, a beach and boat launch on Sand Lake. Buildings in the village include a bank, farm supply store, party store, and old stone schoolhouse.

NUNICA, 49448

Unincorporated community in Ottawa County's Crockery Township. Township population, 3,782. Median household income, $42,399, or 95 percent of the statewide median. The site was settled about 1836 and first called Crockery Creek. "Nunica" comes from an Indian word for a type of clay used for making pottery.

The village, just off I-96 a few miles east of Grand Haven, has a small business district that includes a bar, a store, and Goenick's Hardware and Elevator.

Drivers headed from Grand Rapids to the beach at Grand Haven often take the Nunica exit from I-96, but few go through the town itself.

ORLEANS, 48865

Unincorporated community in Ionia County's Orleans Township. Township population, 2,746. Median household income, $42,665, or 96 percent of the statewide median. This agricultural community was known as Wheatland until 1868, when the name was changed. "Orleans" was in honor of Orleans County, NY, the former home of some early settlers.

Much of the land remains in farming. The Flat River State Game Area extends into the northern portion of the township.

Like other small communities in the agricultural areas of Ionia and Montcalm counties, Orleans appears as if its best days are behind it. The village has several large and impressive older homes, but also a number of house trailers – including some with attached pole barns.

There is a community library and a new township hall and fire station.

OSHTEMO, 49077

Unincorporated community and township in Kalamazoo County. Township population, 17,005. Median household income, $38,433, or 86 percent of the statewide median.

The township, just west of the city of Kalamazoo, is the fastest-growing municipality in the county, according to U.S. Census estimates.

Despite the growth, much of the township retains a surprisingly rural feel, with farms and forests along many of the hilly streets.

The US-131 expressway runs just inside the township's eastern edge. Businesses are spread out along Stadium Drive on both sides of the expressway.

OTSEGO, 49078

City in Allegan County. Population, 3,876. Median household income, $37,545, or 84 percent of the statewide median. It is named for Otsego, NY.

The town on the Kalamazoo River was the site of a millrace, dam and sawmill built by Horace Comstock in 1836. Today, the surrounding township, also named Otsego, has a larger and more affluent population than the city. Median household income in the township is $11,000 higher than in the city.

A new streetscape with planters, benches and trees gives a fresh look to the downtown area, and Otsego Memorial Park sports an authentic M60 tank, courtesy of the Veterans of Foreign Wars, post 3030. Much of the retail business, including big-box discount stores, is out along a commercial strip on M-89 near the US-131 freeway exit.

Otsego's major employer, a Menasha Corp. paper mill, closed in late 2005. A subsidiary of United States Gypsum Co. announced plans in 2006 to buy the mill and give it a new life manufacturing the paper coating for gypsum wallboard.

A military tank guards the playground in an Otsego park (photo: Ed Hoogterp)

PALO, 48870

Unincorporated community in Ronald Township in Ionia County. Township population, 1,893. Median household income, $45,952 or 103 percent of the statewide median. Palo was named for Palo Alto, where Gen. Zachary Taylor won the first battle of the Mexican War in 1846.

The community is isolated in the countryside 10 miles north of the city of Ionia. Some of the streets are paved; some are dirt. There is a stone church and a few nice homes. Residents of the village can pick up their mail at the post office inside Joe's Market on Judevine Street.

PARCHMENT, 49004
(Included in Kalamazoo ZIP codes)

City in Kalamazoo County. Population, 1,936. Median household income, $40,074, or 90 percent of the statewide median.

Jacob Kindleberger founded a paper mill, the Kalamazoo Vegetable Parchment Co. along the Kalamazoo River in 1909. He helped develop a model village around the mill site. The city was incorporated in the 1930s, and took the name of the paper company.

The mill closed in 2000. The city is working to redevelop the 85-acre riverfront site. One proposal is for a commercial and residential development worth nearly $150 million. Before that can happen, 91 years of mill waste will have to be cleaned up.

The city today has a number of nice homes and a few businesses along Riverview Drive. There's no real downtown, since Parchment is adjacent to the city of Kalamazoo.

PAW PAW, 49079

Village in Van Buren County. Population, 3,268. Median household income, $38,750, or 87 percent of the statewide median. The village, which is the Van Buren County seat of government, was founded in 1832 as a sawmill town on the Paw Paw River.

The town and river are named for the paw paw, a native fruit tree that grew along the

Wine shoppers enter the St. Julian tasting room in Paw Paw (photo: Ed Hoogterp)

stream. St. Julian, the state's oldest and largest winery, is located here, as is the Warner Vineyards winery.

Paw Paw sets just north of I-94, with plenty of gas stations and fast food joints on the M-40 exit from the freeway. The downtown retains considerable activity, with the feel of a small city, though it's technically a village.

The Reitz Flea market, on Red Arrow Highway between Paw Paw and Lawrence, is one of the largest in the state.

PENTWATER, 49443

Village in Oceana County. Population, 951. Median household income, $38,542, or 86 percent of the statewide median. Andrew Rector and Edwin Cobb built a sawmill here in the early 1850s. Lumber baron Charles Mears followed in 1856 with a mill and a boarding house. Mears also improved the harbor.

Today, Pentwater is among the nicest small beach towns on the Great Lakes. The protected harbor on Pentwater Lake, with a channel to Lake Michigan, is home to hundreds of recreational boats. The downtown strip hosts a selection of eateries and gift shops, while still maintaining its small-town charm.

In summer, the community band plays each Thursday in the band shell on the village green. Rural roads in the surrounding countryside are ideal for bike riding, especially in spring when the Oceana County fruit orchards are in blossom.

The historic Nickerson Inn is one of several places for tourists to bed down for the night. Charles Mears State Park, at the channel mouth, provides a broad, sandy beach and access to the Big Lake.

PEWAMO, 48873

Village in Ionia County. Population, 576. Median household income, $39,500, or 88 percent of the statewide median. The village, on the border between Ionia and Clinton counties, was a railroad station in the 1850s. It's named for an Indian chief. The town has changed little in recent years. Half of its houses were built before 1944.

Though it's in Ionia County, Pewamo's location on the county line puts it closer to Lansing than to any West Michigan metro area. Several businesses, including a bank, the Oakwood Lounge, and the Good Time Bar and Grill are near the downtown intersection of Main and State streets.

PIERSON, 49339

Village in Montcalm County. Population, 211. Median household income, $37,500, or 84 percent of the statewide median. The area was first settled in the 1850s, when David Pierson bought 40 acres. The village is on the White Pine Trail.

Just to the west is the US-131 expressway, which bypassed the town in the 1970s. The Central Sanitary Landfill rises like the silhouette of a huge dune near the Pierson exit from the expressway.
In the village, there's still plenty of traffic on the old two-lane highway, which has a few businesses including a convenience store and the Village Inn Restaurant. Homes stretch out along gravel roads on both sides of old highway.

PLAINWELL, 49080

City in Allegan County. Population, 3,761. Median household income, $39,590, or 89 percent of the statewide median. This city on the Kalamazoo River was founded in the 1830s by Dr. Cyrenius Thompson.

Despite the loss of major employers such as Plainwell Paper Co., the town retains an impressive historical district and park system where a millrace creates an island along the Kalamazoo River.

Much of Plainwell's retail commerce is directed along M-89 near the exit from the US-131 freeway that runs along the western city limits.

Plainwell, Otsego and Allegan are all cities of similar size located along a 10-mile stretch of the Kalamazoo River and linked by M-89. Residents of all three cities use the commercial district near the expressway exit.

POKAGON, 49120
(included in Niles postal area)

Unincorporated village and township in Cass County. Township population, 2,233. Median household income, $38,850, or 87 percent of the statewide median. Named for Leopold Pokagon, a Potawatomi leader from the area. The township is largely agricultural.

The largest landmark in the village is the former church where the Rev. George Bennard, an itinerant preacher and song-writer, is said to have first performed the popular hymn "The Old Rugged Cross." A local group is raising money to restore the building, which was built as a barn, converted to a church, and then left vacant for decades.

PORTAGE, 49081

City in Kalamazoo County. Population, 44,926. Median household income, $49,410, or 111 percent of the statewide median. Settled around 1830 and originally called "Sweetland," this suburban area south of Kalamazoo was renamed for Portage Creek, which flows through town.

Portage Township was incorporated as the City of Portage in 1963.

Today, Portage is among West Michigan's largest cities. It completely encompasses Austin, West and Hampton lakes. The Gourdneck State Game Area is also within the city limits.

Portage has a number of excellent neighborhoods, and a high level of education, with more than a third of its adult residents holding a bachelor's degree or higher. It also has considerable industry, and retail.

S. Westnedge Avenue is locally famous for its classic suburban mix of fast food, strip malls, waterbed stores and other accoutrements of automotive commerce.

PORTLAND, 48875

City in Ionia County. Population, 3,688. Median household income, $45,656, or 102 percent of the statewide median. Portland was settled in the 1830s, where the Looking Glass River enters the Grand River.

A twisted beam from the World Trade Center is displayed as a memorial near the Looking Glass River in Portland (photo: Ed Hoogterp)

The name comes from what settlers perceived as the possibilities of river travel. Today, most of the travel is along I-96 to Lansing, where many of Portland's residents are employed. The Portland exit, with a selection of fast food stores and gas stations, is a regular rest stop for freeway travelers between West Michigan and the capital area.

The junction of the two rivers in downtown Portland is today occupied by a pleasant park with a pedestrian bridge crossing the Looking Glass River.

PULLMAN, 49450

Unincorporated community in Allegan County's Lee Township. Township population, 4,164. Median household income, $30,875, or 69 percent of the statewide median.

This is an economically challenged area of woods and blueberry farms near the line between Allegan and Van Buren counties. The dusty crossroads near the CSX railroad tracks features a grocery store, hair salons and the Pullman Tavern.

Also here is Pullman Elementary School, part of the Bloomingdale School District.

RAVENNA, 49451

Village in Muskegon County. Population, 1,241. Median household income, $47,167, or 106 percent of the statewide median. In 1847, Benjamin Smith moved to the townsite on Crockery Creek, just across the line from Kent County. Smith purchased a sawmill that had been built three years earlier.

Today, the village and township of the same name are a prosperous country area within commuting distance of both Grand Rapids and Muskegon. Village streets are lined with nice homes and several churches.

Ravenna is near the midpoint of the Musketawa Trail, which runs from Marne to Muskegon.

The Swenson Pickle Co. is on the outskirts of town. Downtown buildings include a bank, pharmacy, pub and the Ravenna Township Museum and Library. Conklin Park has athletic fields and a paved walking trail.

REMUS, 49340

Unincorporated village in Mecosta County's Wheatland Township. Township population, 1,538. Median household income, $33,654, or 75 percent of the statewide median.

Wheatland Church of Christ, near Remus, was built by African-American Christians in the 19th century (photo: Ed Hoogterp)

This is a substantial village at the intersection of two major two-lane highways, M-20 and M-66. It's surrounded by farm and forest, and is best known as the home of the Wheatland Festival, which annually attracts thousands of visitors the weekend after Labor Day to celebrate traditional music, art and dance.

The business district includes gift shops, a drugstore, the Remus Tavern and the Wheatland Corners Trading Post. The surrounding area is marked by diverse farms, producing milk, beef, wool and other crops.

Wheatland Church of Christ, just north of town, has a state historical marker designating it as one of the earliest churches built by and for the area's 19th century black population.

RICHLAND, 49083

Village in Kalamazoo County. Population, 562. Median household income, $50,983, or 114 percent of the statewide median. Settled in the early 1830s, the hamlet was originally called Gull Corners, for its location near Gull Lake. The name was changed to match that of Richland Township. It's a prosperous and growing area northeast of Kalamazoo. There's plenty of traffic and bustle along M-43 and M-89, the main roads through town. But just a block off those roads, it becomes a quiet village with well-shaded streets and solid homes.

A downtown park forms a green public square near the Richland Community Library and the 1861 First Presbyterian Church.

RIVERSIDE, 49084

Small, unincorporated community in Berrien County's Hagar Township. Township population, 3,964. Median household income, $38,614, or 86 percent of the statewide median.

Riverside grew up near the Paw Paw River, north of Benton Harbor. Today, the I-96 freeway runs through town, cutting off most of it from the riverside. The Hagar Township Hall is here, but few other offices or businesses.

ROCKFORD, 49341

City in Kent County. Population, 4,626. Median household income, $50,562, or 113 percent of the statewide median. This town on the Rogue River north of Grand Rapids was founded in 1843 by Smith Lapham and originally called Laphamville. It was renamed Rockford in the 1860s.

Today, the town is at the center of the fast growing suburbs in northern Kent County. Its school district, which extends far beyond the city limits, is highly regarded.

Rockford has managed the nearly impossible task of redefining itself, without losing what was already there. Its downtown district along Squire Street is busy and bustling, as is a paved section of the White Pine Trail, which runs near the river through downtown.

The Corner Bar is well-known for its Hot Dog Hall of Fame (Current record: 42 chili dogs in four hours.) Wolverine World Wide, the company that makes Hush Puppies shoes, has its headquarters and its tannery operation here.

RODNEY, 49342

Unincorporated hamlet on the line between Colfax and Martiny townships in Mecosta County. This was a railroad station in the 1870s. It was named for Rodney Hood, an owner of the Hood and Gale Lumber Company. Today it's little more than a wide spot on M-20 east of Big Rapids, a wide spot with a tavern and post office, that is.

ROOSEVELT PARK, 49441

City in Muskegon County. Population, 3,890. Median household income, $37,035, or 83 percent of the statewide median.

This community sandwiched between Muskegon and Norton Shores, was incorporated as a city in 1946 and grew rapidly in the years after World War II. It is named for President Franklin D. Roosevelt.

Today, it's a middle-class residential community of small, mostly well-kept homes. A district of shops and restaurants extends along Henry and Broadway streets.

ROTHBURY, 49452

Village in southern Oceana County. Population, 372. Median household income, $30,357, or 68 percent of the statewide median. This is a small, rural village on a two-lane stretch of old US-31 that was bypassed by expressway in the 1970s.

A small business district is clinging to life on the old highway. Many village homes are set back from the village streets under fine, old trees. The Hart-Montague Trail runs through the village park. The Double JJ Ranch and Golf Resort is nearby. The village is only a few miles north of the Muskegon County line. Residents do much of their shopping in the Whitehall and Muskegon areas.

ST. JOSEPH, 49065

City in Berrien County. Population, 8,671. Median household income, $37,032, or 83 percent of the statewide median. "St. Joe" is the seat of government for Berrien County.

The French explorer LaSalle visited this spot at the mouth of the St. Joseph River in 1679 and built Fort Miami. The French soon abandoned the fort, though fur traders remained active on the river until the 1820s, when farmers and other settlers began to arrive.

In the early part of the 20th Century, St. Joseph's lakefront at Silver Beach was a well-known amusement park that drew steamship loads of visitors from Chicago and other cities. Today, the public beach is a traditional sandy lakefront, with no carnival rides, but plenty of swimmers and sunbathers.

The city's downtown area, filled with cafés, gift shops and restaurants, sits on a bluff overlooking the lake and the river mouth. It's a lively district that is often contrasted with the devastation in downtown Benton Harbor, just across the St. Joseph River.

SAND LAKE, 49343

Village on the north Kent County line. Population, 491. Median household income, $31,875, or 71 percent of the statewide median. In 1869, this village on the shore of Sand Lake was a stop on the Grand Rapids and Indiana Railroad.

Today, it maintains a few downtown businesses and also draws some summer visitors to the lake.

The paradise Cove Travel Trailer Resort is a busy summer venue on the lake. The old downtown has a grocery store, ice cream shop and a few other businesses, such as Gary and Sue's T.L.C. (Tanning, Laundry and Coffee).

SARANAC, 48881

Village in Ionia County. Population, 1,367. Median household income, $31,350, or 70 percent of the statewide median. The town on the south bank of the Grand River was settled in the 1830s. It was named Saranac in hopes of attracting settlers familiar with the resort town of

Tidy, tree-lined streets help to make St. Joseph a great place to visit (photo: Terry Phipps)

Saranac, NY, according to Walter Romig. The two-block downtown has local government offices, a bar, pizza place and a gas station.

Stone monument in Saranac pays tribute to highway official Lewis C. David (photo: Ed Hoogterp)

A stone monument pays tribute to Lewis C. David, an Ionia County official who died in 1929. David Highway, the main road heading east out of Saranac, is named for him.

Most of the surrounding land is still in agriculture. The Ionia State Recreation Area, which includes Sessions Lake, is just east of town, between David Highway and the Grand River.

SAUGATUCK, 49453

City in Allegan County. Population, 1,097. Median household income, $44,318, or 99 percent of the statewide median. Saugatuck, at the mouth of the Kalamazoo River, was settled around 1830 by William Gray Butler. The name comes from a Potawatomi word for river mouth.

Today, with its Oval Beach on Lake Michigan, an unmatched collection of gift and craft shops, and a popular chain ferry across the Kalamazoo River, Saugatuck is among West Michigan's most popular tourist towns.

The gift shops are set along shaded city streets that make browsing a pleasure even on hot days. Restaurants and night spots are arrayed along the riverfront. The town has a reputation as a gay-friendly community. But straight folks, including families, also feel right at home.

Saugatuck Dunes State Park is just north of town. Lake Michigan frontage on both sides of the Kalamazoo River

has remained largely undeveloped, unlike most river mouths in southern Michigan. The city and the state Department of Natural Resources have sought for years to come up with enough money to purchase the property as a preserve.

SAWYER, 49125

Unincorporated village in Berrien County's Chikaming Township. Township population, 3,678. Median household income, $47,778, or 107 percent of the statewide median. The site was settled in the 1840s and known as Troy. It was renamed in 1854 for mill owner Silas Sawyer.

The town, just east of I-94 near the southern end of Warren Dunes State Park, is one in a string of villages near the Indiana border and Lake Michigan. The surrounding area welcomes tourists and second-home owners from northern Indiana and metro Chicago.

Among the businesses here are a huge truck stop and a local hardware store.

SCHOOLCRAFT, 49087

Village in Kalamazoo County. Population, 1,587. Median household income, $45,380, or 106 percent of the statewide median.
The town was built in the 1830s on the edge of Prairie Ronde, the largest of Kalamazoo County's native prairies. It was founded by Lucius Lyon, a surveyor, developer, and later one of Michigan's first U.S. Senators. Lyon named the village after his friend, Henry Rowe Schoolcraft.

Fairly or unfairly, Schoolcraft means only one thing for travelers heading south from Kalamazoo: Traffic headaches. The US-131 expressway ends abruptly a few miles north of town, and southbound traffic is funneled right onto north Grand Street in downtown Schoolcraft.

That's a shame. It's a nice downtown with places like Prairie Home Antiques. But who can stop...

SCOTTS, 49088

Unincorporated crossroads on the line between Climax and Pavilion townships, in Kalamazoo County. Samuel Scott came here in 1847 and built a dam and mill. The settlement was known initially as Scott's Crossing.

Today, Scott's Mill County Park occupies the original mill site, and visitors can tour the working, water-powered mill that dates from the 1860s. The picturesque mill site is also a popular spot for weddings.

The village itself is a small collection of homes and businesses along the Grand Trunk Railroad tracks. Downtown has a general store and ice cream shop. The old Grange Hall, which once housed an IGA grocery store, has been converted to apartments.

SHELBY, 49455

Village in Oceana County. Population, 1,949. Median household income, $28,710, or 64 percent of the statewide median.

The village was founded in the 1860s and named for Isaac Shelby, a War of 1812 general. Shelby is in Oceana County's fruit-growing belt. Peterson Farms, one of the region's largest food processors, employs more than 300 people here, processing apples, blueberries, asparagus and other products. Shelby and nearby Hart alternate as hosts of the National Asparagus Festival, held annually in late spring.

The Hart-Montague bike trail runs through town, a block from the downtown business strip. Until the 1970s, motorists passed through Shelby en route to the Silver Lake Sand Dunes, 10 miles away on Lake Michigan. Now, the US-31 freeway takes cars west of town on their way to the dunes.

SHELBYVILLE, 49334

Unincorporated community on the border between Martin and Wayland townships in Allegan County. The railroad station here was named for a station agent about 1870. The "ville" was added a few years later to distinguish the post office from the village of Shelby in Oceana County.

Today, the village site is little more than a few homes and empty commercial buildings. The surrounding townships have a growing rural population, with many of the residents working in Grand Rapids or Kalamazoo.

SHERIDAN, 48884

Village in Montcalm County. Population, 713. Median household income, $30,556, or 68 percent of the statewide median. The village was originally a sawmill community, founded in the 1850s by John Winsor and named for Philip Sheridan, a Civil War general. This village on M-66 is home to Sheridan Community Hospital and several medical offices, which serve much of the surrounding area.

Businesses in Sheridan include the Hog's Head Saloon, Bush's Hardware, Little Tommy's IGA and more. Not bad for a town of only about 700 people. The mature trees and big, old homes indicate this is a town that's been here awhile and will still be here for a long time to come.

SHOREHAM, 49085
(Included in St. Joseph ZIP code area)

Village in Berrien County. Population, 835. Median household income, $51,333, or 115 percent of the statewide median.

This residential community along Lake Michigan, just south of St. Joseph, was incorporated in 1930. It stretches for nearly a mile along a high Lake Michigan bluff, and has few businesses. The bluff was subject to erosion in the past, but has been stable in recent years, in part because of low water levels.

SIDNEY, 48885

Unincorporated village and township in Montcalm County. Township population, 2,527. Median household income, $40,682, or 91 percent of the statewide median.

The village was founded by Phineas Swift in 1854, and named for Sidney, Ohio. Montcalm Community College is located in Sidney. The college grounds include a "Heritage Village" with restored buildings such as an 1860s log cabin and the old train depot from McBride, complete with a 1920s steam engine.

Sidney itself is a crossroads surrounded by farm land. Businesses include the D.L. Petersen General Store and Sidney State Bank. The Fred Meijer Heartland Trail carries bicyclists and hikers through town.

A log cabin is part of Montcalm County's Heritage Village in Sidney (photo: Ed Hoogterp)

SISTER LAKES, 49047
(included in Dowagiac postal area)

Unincorporated resort community on the line between Cass and Van Buren counties. The area around Round, Crooked and Hemlock lakes has been a summer resort since at least the 1870s.

South Haven's downtown is a busy district within walking distance of the waterfront (photo: Terry Phipps)

It remains popular with families from the Chicago area, but is little known to Michigan residents.

SIX LAKES, 48886

Unincorporated village in Montcalm County's Belvedere Township. Township population, 2,374. Median household income, $33,447, or 75 percent of the statewide median. The village was settled in the 1870s and named for six small lakes, which are now connected by channels and named (strange but true!) 1st, 2nd, 3rd, 4th, 5th and 6th lake.

The town has a mix of year-round and seasonal homes. A township park provides camping and lake access. The village at the junction of two major mid-Michigan highways, M-46 and M-66, is also home to a popular summer flea market.

SODUS, 49126

Unincorporated village and township in Berrien County. Township population, 2,147. Median household income, $33,804, or 76 percent of the statewide median. The first settler here was David Rector, who arrived in 1835 and named the community for his native town of Sodus, NY.

This is fruit country, just southeast of Benton Harbor. The St. Joseph River bisects the township, and a new section of the US-31 expressway passes just west of the village. The town is spread out along Pipestone and Naomi roads. It merges quickly into orchards, vineyards and cornfields.

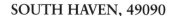

SOUTH HAVEN, 49090

City in Van Buren County. Population, 4,951. Median household income, $35,885, or 80 percent of the statewide median. The community at the mouth of the Black River was first settled about 1831. By 1850, Joseph Sturgis had built a sawmill here.

The downtown shopping area, on a hill above the busy recreational harbor, is filled with restaurants and gift shops. The harbor breakwall, lighthouse and South Beach are an easy downhill walk. It's an exciting, busy, vibrant town. South Haven, in the Lake Michigan fruit belt, was home to famed botanist Liberty Hyde Bailey, whose home has been turned into a local museum. The city is also home to the Michigan Maritime Museum, one of the best sources for information about sailing on the Great Lakes. *Friends Good Will*, a tallship replica built for the museum, is based in the harbor.

SPARTA, 49345

Village in Kent County. Population, 4,142. Median household income, $39,047, or 87 percent of the statewide median.

The village north of Grand Rapids was settled around 1850 and originally known as Sparta Center, for its location at the center of Sparta Township.

It is the hub of a traditional fruit growing area known locally as "The Ridge," which includes some of Michigan's most productive apple orchards. Old Orchard Brands LLC, one of the nation's top producers of bottled and frozen fruit juice products, is located here. Parts of the Ridge are coming under pressure from residential subdivisions, but there are continuing efforts to preserve the valuable agricultural land.

Sparta's location, at M-37 and 13 Mile Road, puts it only a 10 minute drive from the Alpine Avenue shopping district in Walker. Strip malls still do a decent local business but there's not a lot of activity in the old downtown.

SPRING LAKE, 49456

Village in Ottawa County. Population, 2,379. Median household income, $37,889, or 85 percent of the statewide median. Benjamin Hopkins built a mill on Spring Lake in 1837, and the site was known as Hopkins' Mill or Mill Point. The village name was changed to Spring Lake in 1869.

Today, it's an attractive community that stretches between the Grand River and Spring Lake just east of Grand Haven. The waterfront is lined with marinas and boat slips.

A popular route from Grand Rapids to the beach at Grand Haven leads through downtown Spring Lake and across the US-31 drawbridge. Some downtown businesses cater to this beach traffic, as well as to local residents.

STANTON, 48888

City in Montcalm County. Population, 1,518. Median household income, $29,286, or 66 percent of the statewide median. Stanton, the Montcalm County seat of government, was founded in 1860 to settle a dispute in which representatives of townships from the eastern part of the county insisted that the county seat be moved away from Greenville, in the far west. Stanton was chosen as a central site.

An Ionia man, Fred Hall, donated land for the new town, and county officials initially planned to name the place "Fred." Hall apparently talked them out of that idea, and in 1863, at the height of the Civil War, it was renamed in honor of Secretary of War Edwin Stanton.

The town has an impressive three-story county courthouse, a mix of housing and the Fred Meijer Heartland Trail for bike riders.

The main road, M-66, makes a jog through the downtown area, which has some nicely restored brick buildings as well as McDonald's, Subway and other businesses.

STANWOOD, 49346

Village in Mecosta County. Population, 212. Median household income, $39,000, or 87 percent of the statewide median. Stanwood was a stop on the Grand Rapids and Indiana Railroad in 1870. Walter Romig says it was named for the fine stand of woods in the area. Today, the old railroad grade through Stanwood is the White Pine Trail, a bike path that extends from Grand Rapids to Cadillac.

The town was bypassed by the US-131 expressway in the 1980s. The business district on the old highway includes a modern post office, a party store, pizza shop and other businesses, including a farm store named "Stanwood Feeds and Needs."

The town has about 80 residences, mostly on big lots along hilly streets set back from the old highway.

STEVENSVILLE, 49127

Village in Berrien County. Population, 1,190. Median household income, $42,569, or 95 percent of the statewide median. Around 1870, Thomas Stevens donated land here as a right of way for the Pere Marquette Railroad. The village is near Lake Michigan, just north of Grand Mere State Park. The railroad still runs through town, and the I-94 expressway forms the western village limits. From the high ground, you can see Lake Michigan, about a mile away.

Stevensville has a mix of old and new homes. Business is mostly near the junction of Red Arrow Highway and I-94.

STURGIS, 49091

City in St. Joseph County. Population, 11,355. Median

household income, $33,838, or 76 percent of the statewide median. One of the first settlers in the area was John Sturgis, who would later become a St. Joseph County judge. Other early residents platted villages called "Sherman" and Ivanhoe" along the Chicago Road. In 1857, the two were combined and renamed Sturgis.

The town, just north of the Indiana border, is St. Joseph County's largest city. Big box stores, fast food restaurants and gas stations stretch out along M-66 to the state line.

Downtown Sturgis has a pleasant, though somewhat dated, feel to it. Some of the brick facades remain covered with metal siding from 1950s or 60s remodeling projects.

The main street, Chicago Road (US-12), is a broad four lanes, with two additional lanes for parking. The Strand Theatre shows movies on four screens. Retailers offer everything from western wear to furniture. The local coffee shop, Great Lakes Chocolate Co., roasts its own coffee.

The Sturges-Young Civic Center is a popular entertainment and cultural venue. A string of great historic homes lines the brick-paved S. Nottawa Avenue.

THREE OAKS, 49128

Village in Berrien County. Population, 1,827. Median household income, $34,120, or 76 percent of the statewide median. The town, just north of the Indiana border, was founded around 1850 and named for a cluster of white oaks in the village site.

A metal sculpture on the old Featherbone factory invites patrons to the Acorn Theater in Three Oaks (photo: Ed Hoogterp)

At the turn of the 20th century, it was home to the Warren Featherbone Co., which employed as many as 400 people, making corset stays from turkey feathers. The nearby Warren Woods and Warren Dunes state parks are named for company founder Edward K. Warren, who donated park land to the state.

Today, Three Oaks is home to the Three Oaks Spokes Bicycle Museum and of the Apple Cider Century, a popular bike tour along area back roads. Smoked hams from Drier's Meat Market in Three Oaks are a holiday tradition for folks as far away as Chicago. The 1989 movie "Prancer" was shot partly on location in Three Oaks.

THREE RIVERS, 49093

City in St. Joseph County. Population, 7,543. Median household income, $32,460, or 73 percent of the statewide median. The town site was first laid out in 1831 by George Buck, and was known briefly as Bucks. It was changed to Three Rivers because (obviously) three rivers run through it: The St. Joseph, the Portage and the Rocky.

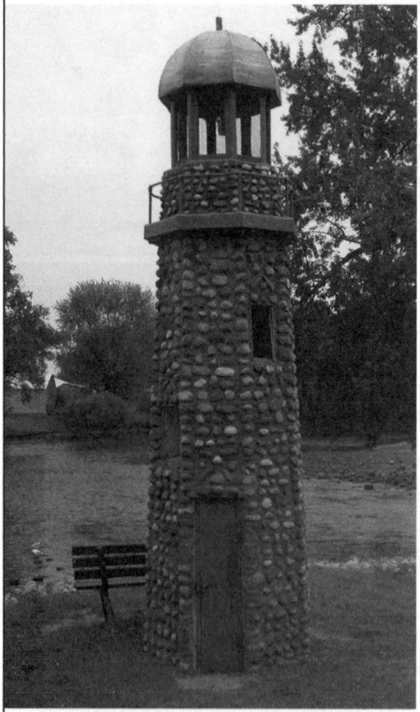

Small stone lighthouse stands at the confluence of the St. Joseph and Rocky rivers in Three Rivers (photo: Ed Hoogterp)

According to legend, the junction of the three rivers was the site of fierce Indian battles about 1800, when the Shawnee Tribe, under Chief Elkhart, attacked a Potawatomi village here. The Potawatomi eventually prevailed, with help from Ottawa and Chippewa bands farther north in Michigan.

The city's Scidmore Park, on the St. Joseph and Rocky rivers, includes a small petting zoo and a miniature stone lighthouse that is a local landmark.

Three Rivers' attractive downtown has too many empty buildings. Local leaders are trying to change that, including an effort to restore the closed Riviera movie theater. The Sue Silliman House, on a bank above the St. Joseph River, has been converted to a museum, and the Carnegie Library functions as a cultural center.

TRUFANT, 49347

Unincorporated village in Montcalm County's Maple Valley Township. Township population, 2,012. Median household income, $36,583, or 82 percent of the statewide median. The village is named for Emery Trufant, who built a sawmill here in 1871.

Today, businesses in the town near Muskellunge Lake, just north of the Kent County line, include Christensen's Farm and Home Center, and The Office Bar and Grill.

Signs proclaim this hamlet as "The Stump Fence Capital." But in fact there are no more stump fences here than in other rural Michigan towns.

Years ago, farmers often cleared land of trees, and then lined up the stumps as field borders. Those fences, once a common sight in rural Michigan, are gradually rotting away.

TWIN LAKE, 49457

Unincorporated community in Muskegon County's Dalton Township. Township Population, 8,043. Median household income, $47,127, or 106 percent of the statewide median.

At the time the area was settled, about 1866, there were two lakes here, hence the name. Water levels have since fallen, and now Twin Lake has four bodies of water. It's an area of mixed residential and recreational property, with thousands of acres of public land nearby in the Manistee National Forest and the Muskegon State Game Area.

Twin Lake County Park is in the village. Blue Lake County Park is nearby, as is the Blue Lake Fine Arts Camp, which operates summer programs for gifted students in performance, visual arts, music and dance.

There are a few commercial businesses along M-120, but it's mainly a residential area.

UNION, 49130

Unincorporated hamlet in Cass County's Porter Township. Township population, 3,794. Median household income, $51,320, or 115 percent of the statewide median. The town was founded in the 1830s and moved to its present location, on the Chicago Road (US-12), about 1853.

The town site is on the former Baldwin Prairie, two miles north of the Indiana line. It's closer to Elkhart than to any urban center in Michigan, and many residents cross the state line to work. Union should not be confused with Union City, Unionville, Union Lake or Union Pier, which are all communities elsewhere in Michigan.

UNION PIER, 49129

Unincorporated village in Berrien County's Chikaming Township. Township population, 3,676. Median household income, $47,778, or 107 percent of the statewide median.

This is one in a string of affluent villages along the Lake Michigan shore just north of the Indiana line. The name comes from an 1870 agreement in which a group of businessmen united to build a sawmill and pier near the line between Chikaming and New Buffalo townships.

The town has a number of mostly upscale inns and gift boutiques. The Inn at Union Pier is highly regarded by its Chicago clientele.

A local antique mall, at the Union Pier exit off I-94, features a building with ceiling murals that re-create Michelangelo's Sistine Chapel paintings.

VANDALIA, 49095

Village in Cass County. Population, 432. Median household income, $30,417, or 68 percent of the statewide median. Stephen Bogue and Charles Ball built a sawmill here in the 1840s. The site became a stop on the Michigan Central Railroad in 1871.

It's best known as a junction of the Underground Railroad, the network of safe houses and trails that brought escaped slaves to freedom in northern states and Canada in the years before the Civil War. Hundreds of African Americans settled in Cass County, especially in Calvin Township south of Vandalia, and created a unique community that lasted well into the 20th century.

Today, there is little business in the village, along M-60, and evidence of poverty is widespread. The village is home to the Wat Lao Buddhist Temple, which serves Buddhists, many of Laotian descent, from southwest Michigan and northern Indiana.

VESTABURG, 48891

Unincorporated village in Montcalm County's Richland Township. Township population, 2,881. Median household income, $34,847, or 78 percent of the statewide median. Founder George O'Donnell named the village for his wife, Vesta.

Today, Vestaburg is off the beaten path, just south of M-46. The Fred Meijer Heartland Bike Trail runs along an old railroad grade through town. Businesses include a bank, pizza shop, and Peasley's Hardware.

There's also a Richland Township Library, a veterans' memorial and an electricity generating plant operated by Wolverine Power Supply Cooperative.

Downtown Vicksburg has several well-preserved buildings (photo: Ed Hoogterp)

VICKSBURG, 49097

Village in Kalamazoo County. Population, 2,322. Median household income, $41,780, or 94 percent of the statewide median. The town was founded by John Vickers about 1830. It was incorporated in 1871 as Brady (it's on the line between Schoolcraft and Brady Townships) and renamed Vicksburg the same day.

Vicksburg today has a pleasant downtown for strolling or window-shopping. There's a community center in a restored former bank building, and a nice mix of specialty shops, like Rosewood Flowers and Gifts, where you can step inside on the vintage wood floors, or stand on the sidewalk and watch the huge cat lounging in the window. Older residential streets near the center of town are lined with solid two-story brick and wood-frame homes.

Summer evening concerts in Clark Park feature a mix of musical styles ranging from punk to Christian.

WABININGO, 49463

Unincorporated resort community in Muskegon County. The resort, on Lake Michigan just south of White Lake, was founded in the 1880s. It's named after an Ottawa Indian chief.

It was given a post office in the late 19th century, and the Postal Service still conducts

The Wabiningo Post Office stands on the shore of White Lake (photo: Ed Hoogterp)

business there – in the original clapboard-sided building – during the summer months. Mail is handled through the Whitehall Post Office in winter, when most of the cottagers have gone to warmer climes.

WALKER, 49504 (Included in Grand Rapids postal area)

City in Kent County. Population, 21,795. Median household income, $44,818, or 100 percent of the statewide median. This former township wraps around the north and west boundaries of Grand Rapids.

Parts of the original township were annexed to the central city over the years.
In 1959, Grand Rapids annexed land that included the township offices. Three years later, in 1962, with talk of more annexation in the air, Walker Township residents approved a charter creating the city of Walker.

Today, Walker has prime residential areas and two busy commercial centers, one in Standale along M-45 west of Grand Rapids, and the other on Alpine Avenue (M-37) north of GR.

Walker is home base for the Meijer retail chain, which has its corporate office and warehouse here. Kent County's 1,500-acre Millennium Park is largely within Walker's city limits, in an area formerly used for gravel mining near the Grand River.

WALKERVILLE, 49459

Village in Oceana County. Population, 295. Median household income, $27,083, or 61 percent of the statewide median. Walkerville, near the Oceana-Newaygo Line, was founded in 1883 by Fayette Walker. It was at the far end of the 27-mile Mason and Oceana Railroad.

Today, the small village is isolated in a sparsely populated area of mixed farm and woodland inside the boundaries of the Manistee National Forest. The site in eastern Oceana County is outside the county's prime Lake Michigan fruit belt, but still has some orchards, along with cornfields and cattle.

The residential streets have many mobile homes and older dwellings in obvious need of repair. Despite the absence of wealth, the village has the feel of a good place to live.

The Walkerville schools are right in the downtown area, where other services include a bank, grocery and tavern.

WATERVLIET, 49098

City in Berrien County. Population, 1,855. Median household income, $38,681, or 87 percent of the statewide median. The first sawmill appeared here in 1833, and Isaac Moffatt opened the first store in 1836. The settlement was named after a city in New York. The Paw Paw River runs through town. I-94 is at the southern city limits.

This town "where the waters meet" has the look of a nice, working-class community, with small homes on both sides of the railroad that bisects the city.

Paw Paw Lake, which stretches between Watervliet and nearby Coloma, was a popular destination for tourists from Indiana and Illinois during the first two-thirds of the 20th century. Today, the lake is mostly surrounded with large private homes.

Flaherty Park, in downtown Watervliet, offers a cool, shaded spot for a summer picnic.

WAYLAND, 49348

City in Allegan County. Population, 3,889. Median household income, $41,852, or 94 percent of the statewide median. The town grew up in the 1850s along the plank road that linked Grand Rapids and Kalamazoo.

The city is at the corner of four historically agricultural townships — Dorr, Hopkins, Wayland and Leighton. As that area in northeastern Allegan County has grown in population, Wayland has remained a center of activity.

Much of the region is served by Wayland Union Public Schools. Wayland also has churches, parks, medical offices and other services for the local area.

The traditional downtown has lost much of its retail business to the highway strip near the US-131 freeway exit.

WEST OLIVE, 49460

Unincorporated community in Ottawa County's Olive Township. Township population, 4,793. Median household income, $48,526, or 109 percent of the statewide median. The site, near the line between Olive and Port Sheldon Townships, was a railroad station in the 1880s.

Today, it's not so much a town as an address for residents and businesses on both sides of US-31 between Holland and Grand Haven.

Consumers Energy's huge James H. Campbell generating plant, which turns coal into electricity, sets on Lake

Michigan in Port Sheldon Township and has a West Olive address.

WHITE CLOUD, 49349

City in Newaygo County. Population, 1,431. Median household income, $24,313, or 54 percent of the statewide median. The settlement on the White River was called Morgan Station in the early 1870s, after Sextus Wilcox and Lester Morgan opened a lumber company there. It was renamed White Cloud in 1877.

White Cloud is the county seat of Newaygo County. For years, travelers heading north on M-37 have smiled at the sign branding the town as the place "Where the North Begins and the Pure Water Flows."

The downtown street was rebuilt in 2005 to give a boost to the central business district that includes a hardware store, bank and antique shops, in addition to the county government buildings.

WHITE PIGEON, 49099

Village in St. Joseph County. Population, 1,644. Median household income, $41,292, or 92 percent of the statewide median. The first permanent settlers came to the White Pigeon Prairie, just north of the Indiana border, in 1827. Within a year, the town had a post office and a tavern.

In 1831, the federal government opened a land office here to sell southern Michigan lands that had been procured in treaties with Indian tribes. In just three years, the White Pigeon Land Office sold 328,000 acres at the going rate of $1.25 an acre. Included was the prime real estate that makes up the heart of Grand Rapids and Kalamazoo.

Tasty Nut Shop occupies part of a former Masonic Temple in White Pigeon (photo: Ed Hoogterp)

The land office building still stands, as a local museum. It is considered to be one of the oldest surviving structures in West Michigan.

The town's name comes from an Indian named Wahbememe, or "White Pigeon." According to legend, Chief White Pigeon died of exhaustion after running 150 miles from Detroit to warn local settlers of an impending attack by hostile Indians. A monument honoring him is located on US-12.

The town's best-known business is the Tasty Nut Shop, in a downtown building that once served as the local Masonic Temple. Owner Marjorie Hamminga ships roasted nuts around the country through mail order, and also does a good business, especially in summer, from behind the old-time soda fountain in the store.

WHITEHALL, 49461

City in Muskegon County. Population, 2,881. Median household income, $37,641, or 84 percent of the statewide median. Lumber baron Charles Mears built his first sawmill here, at the mouth of the White River. Mears platted a town on the site in the 1850s and called it Mears, but when the village was incorporated in 1867, the name chosen was Whitehall.The town sets on the southeast side of White Lake, linked to nearby Montague by a causeway bridge that crosses the lake. The Howmet Theatre is operated by the Blue Lakes Fine Arts Camp.

Marinas line much of the lakefront inside the city limits. The downtown strip, on a US-31 business loop, has a nice variety of specialty stores. In addition to using the lake and river, many visitors make the short drive to see the White River Lighthouse, on the channel that links White Lake with Lake Michigan.

The White Lake area has historically supported considerable industry. The largest employer, Howmet Industries, employs more than 2,000 at several sites in Whitehall.

WOODLAND, 48897

Village in Barry County. Population, 509. Median household income, $32,222, or 72 percent of the statewide median. The site had its first white settlers about 1837, and became a railroad stop 50 years later. It was named for its location in a wooded area. Today, it might better be called "Farmland," since it's surrounded by more cornfields than woodlots.

Still, there are some great trees lining the residential streets. Businesses include the Woodland Townehouse Tavern. The small village is hanging on to its old housing stock, with more than half the homes dating to 1940 or before.

The historic Woodland Town Hall dates from 1867 (photo: Ed Hoogterp)

WYOMING, 49509
(Included in Grand Rapids ZIP Code area)

City in Kent County. Population, 69,366. Median household income, $43,164, or 97 percent of the statewide median.

The former Wyoming Township incorporated as a city in 1959, largely to keep the adjacent city of Grand Rapids from annexing more township land.

Wyoming is West Michigan's third largest city, after Grand Rapids and Kalamazoo. Its wide variety of housing includes neighborhoods of small, 1950-era homes, mobile home communities, huge apartment complexes such as Ramblewood, and large new "McMansions."

Wyoming was home to West Michigan's first indoor shopping mall, Rogers Plaza, and one of the nation's first multi-screen movie theaters, Studio 28.

It also has a considerable amount of industry, including a General Motors Plant. Metro Health is building a new hospital in Wyoming, near the M-6 expressway. When construction is complete, in 2007, the hospital expects to move some 1,800 employees from its former location in Grand Rapids.

ZEELAND, 49464

City in Ottawa County. Population, 5,894. Median household income, $45,611, or 103 percent of the statewide median. Zeeland was founded in 1847, when the Rev. Cornelius Vander Meulen led a group of immigrants here from the Dutch province of Zeeland. The town's Dutch roots still remain, but it's become much more diverse over the years.

It has many attractive streets with tidy houses, along with a row of large and impressive homes along Central Avenue.

The downtown is one of West Michigan's more attractive business districts. Antique street lights and brick pavers welcome shoppers to a Main Street with a nice variety of shops.

Zeeland also is home to the Herman Miller Furniture Co.

EDUCATION & RELIGION

Previous page: A bronze statue of Woodbridge Ferris, who founded colleges in Muskegon and Big Rapids, stands on the campus of Ferris State University. (Photo: Ed Hoogterp)

EDUCATION

West Michigan doesn't have a pure college town, like Ann Arbor or East Lansing. What we have is more than 20 colleges and universities which together enroll more than 100,000 students.

Several of the well-known institutions have their roots in religious education. That's true of such schools as Andrews University, Hope College and Aquinas College, all of which have broad offerings in arts and science, in addition to their religious traditions.

Three members of the state university system are distributed throughout the region, with Western Michigan University in Kalamazoo, Grand Valley State University in Allendale, near Grand Rapids, and Ferris State University in Big Rapids. Together, the three public institutions have more than 50,000 students.

The region also has several colleges which see their mission as religious training, and several that concentrate on business and economic education.

Here's a quick look at West Michigan's institutions of higher learning. The tuition and fee estimates are for full-time students who are residents of the appropriate district.

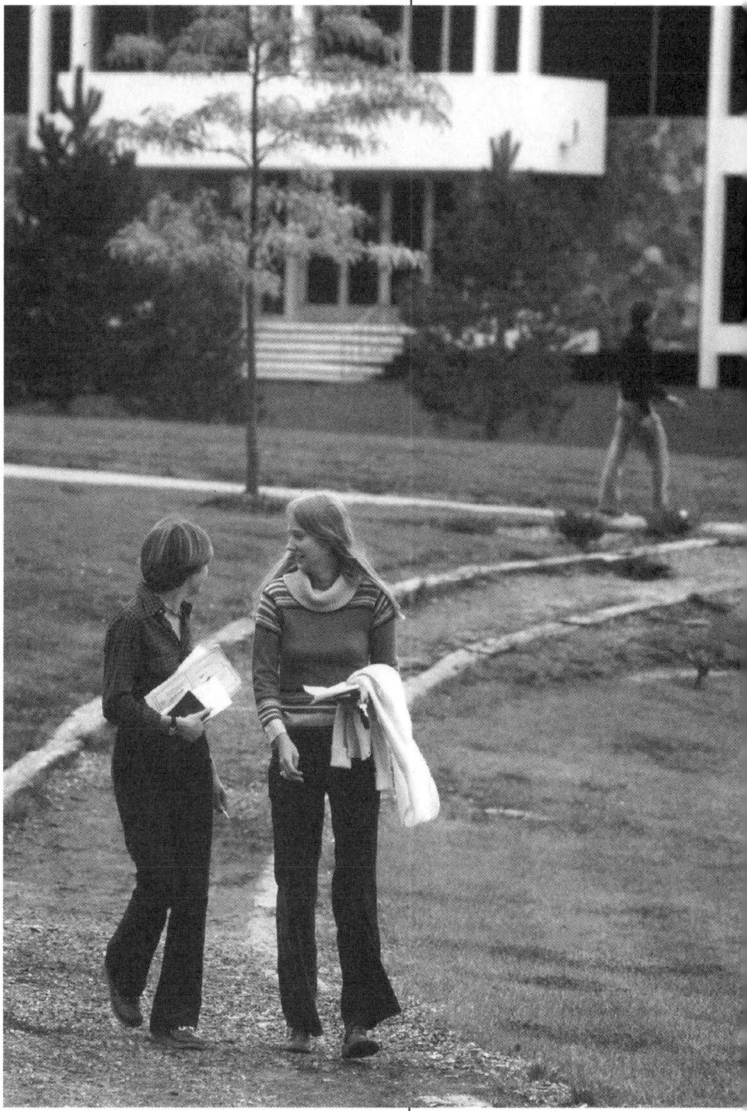

Students stroll on campus, about 1970 (photo courtesy of Grand Valley State University)

ANDREWS UNIVERSITY

Andrews University, in Berrien Springs, is affiliated with the Seventh Day Adventist Church. The university has about 3,000 students enrolled in undergraduate, graduate and seminary education programs. It offers more than 80 undergraduate and 50 graduate majors, and is among a handful of Michigan schools that offer degrees in architecture. Andrews was founded in Battle Creek in 1874, and moved to Berrien Springs in 1901. In the early years, it was called Emmanuel Missionary College. The name was changed in 1960 to honor John Nevins Andrews, the Adventist Church's first overseas missionary. The college is known for its international programs, which offer study in nine countries. Andrews has a diverse student body. Nearly 30 percent of the students are citizens of foreign lands. Andrews also has the distinction of being one of the few American colleges with an all-vegetarian cafeteria.

Estimated annual tuition and fees for 2005-2006: $16,500

Andrews University
Berrien Springs, MI 49104
www.andrews.edu

AQUINAS COLLEGE

Aquinas College was founded by the Dominican Sisters of Grand Rapids in 1886. The Grand Rapids institution continues to follow Dominican and Catholic tradition, though many other religions are represented among the 2,300 students. The college is named for St. Thomas Aquinas, a 13th century Catholic philosopher. (The college's sports teams were once called the Tommies; now they're known as the Saints.) Aquinas also operates a popular non-credit "Emeritus College" that offers enrichment courses for senior citizens. The 104-acre campus on the east side of Grand Rapids is filled with trees and green areas. It's a popular hiking spot both for students and neighborhood residents.

Estimated annual tuition and fees for 2005-2006: $17,900

Aquinas College
1607 Robinson Road
Grand Rapids, MI 49506
www.aquinas.edu

BAKER COLLEGE

Baker College of Muskegon was founded as Muskegon College in 1888 by Woodbridge Ferris. It was dedicated to training students for industrial jobs. In 1965 Muskegon College came under joint ownership with Baker Business University of Flint, which had a similar job-training mission. The two colleges began offering associate's degrees in 1974, and merged to form the Baker College system in 1985. Today, the system has campuses throughout Michigan, with more than 30,000 full- and part-time students. Baker College of Muskegon moved to a new 40 acre site in 1997. The college offers programs leading to professional certification, associate's degrees and bachelor's degrees. An extension operation in Fremont allows Newaygo County residents to take courses closer to home.

Estimated annual tuition and fees for 2005-2006: $6,300

Baker College of Muskegon
1903 Marquette Ave.
Muskegon, MI 49442
www.baker.edu

CALVIN COLLEGE

Calvin College was founded in Grand Rapids in 1876. It is now one of North America's largest Christian colleges, with an enrollment of 4,300. The college is affiliated with the Christian Reformed Church, and is named for John Calvin, a 16th century protestant scholar. In the 1960s, Calvin moved from a cramped urban campus to a tree-lined site on the Knollcrest farm on the outskirts of town. That campus has continued to grow. Calvin is a comprehensive liberal arts college, with more than 70 academic programs ranging from mathematics to Medieval Studies. Calvin Theological Seminary is at the same site, with some 300 students.

Estimated annual tuition and fees for 2005-2006: $19,900

Calvin College
3201 Burton St. SE
Grand Rapids MI 49546
www.calvin.edu
www.calvinseminary.edu

CORNERSTONE UNIVERSITY

Cornerstone University was founded in 1941 as the Baptist Bible Institute at Wealthy Street Baptist Church in Grand Rapids. It grew to become Baptist Bible College, and moved in 1964 to its present 132-acre campus. It was accredited as a degree-granting college of arts and sciences in the 1970s. It adopted the Cornerstone name in 1994, after merging with Grand Rapids School of the Bible and Music. Today, Cornerstone has 2,400 students. In addition to graduate and undergraduate arts and sciences programs, the university offers advanced theological training through the Grand Rapids Theological Seminary, on the same site. Cornerstone also operates a radio ministry.

Estimated annual tuition and fees for 2005-2006: $15,500

Cornerstone University
1001 East Beltline NE
Grand Rapids, MI 49525
www.cornerstone.edu

DAVENPORT UNIVERSITY

Davenport University began in 1866 in Grand Rapids as a business institute. Through much of the 20th century it was known for programs that trained secretaries, typists and other clerical workers. Today, it's a fully accredited university with programs in business, technology and health professions. Davenport offers short-term diploma programs, in addition to bachelor's degrees and a Master of Business Administration (MBA). The university moved its headquarters to its new W.A. Lettinga Campus at M-6 and M-37, just south of Grand Rapids, in the fall of 2005.

Estimated annual tuition and fees for 2005-2006: $8,800

Davenport University
6191 Kraft Ave. SE
Grand Rapids, MI 49512
www.davenport.edu

FERRIS STATE UNIVERSITY

Ferris State University was founded as the Big Rapids Industrial School in 1886 by Woodbridge N. Ferris, who would later serve Michigan as governor (1912-16) and U.S. senator (1922-28). The name of the private school was changed to Ferris Institute before the turn of the 20th century. It became a state college in 1949, and was renamed Ferris State University in 1987. It continues to offer career-oriented programs, along with a general liberal arts and sciences curriculum. Today, the university has an 880-acre main campus in Big Rapids, along with a center in downtown Grand Rapids. Ferris has more than 11,000 students in 170 graduate and undergraduate educational programs. It is also affiliated with Kendall College of Art and Design, in Grand Rapids.

Estimated annual tuition and fees for 2005-2006: $6,686

Ferris State University
1201 S. State St.
Big Rapids, MI 49307
www.ferris.edu

GLEN OAKS COMMUNITY COLLEGE

Glen Oaks Community College received state approval to offer classes in 1965. It serves the St. Joseph County Community College District. The 120-acre campus is on the former Hagen family farm, donated to the district in 1965 by Nora Hagen, who described herself as the family's "last survivor."

The college offers associate's degree programs and has about 1,500 students.

Estimated annual tuition and fees for 2005-2006: $2,516

Glen Oaks Community College
62249 Shimmel Road
Centreville, MI 49032
www.glenoaks.edu

GRACE BIBLE COLLEGE

Grace Bible College was founded in 1939 as the Milwaukee Bible Institute, which was designed as a training center for lay people and Sunday School teachers. The institution moved to Grand Rapids in 1961. Today, it offers two- four- and five-year degrees. Bachelor's degree students take some classes at Cornerstone or Davenport universities, through cooperative arrangements with those schools. Grace has an enrollment of about 160 students.

Estimated annual tuition and fees for 2005-2006: $10,900

Grace Bible College
P.O. Box 910
1101 Aldon St. SW
Grand Rapids, MI 49509
www.gbcol.edu

GRAND RAPIDS COMMUNITY COLLEGE

Grand Rapids Community College was founded in 1914 as Grand Rapids Junior College, a two-year institution operated by the local Board of Education. The first classes were held in Grand Rapids Central High School. Voters in Kent County approved creation of a Community College district in 1991, and the junior college became Grand Rapids Community College, with an independent, elected board of trustees.

Today, GRCC has an eight-block campus in downtown

Grand Rapids as well as several satellite sites where courses are offered. The college has 14,000 students in liberal arts courses and occupational programs.

Estimated annual tuition and fees for 2005-2006: $2,085

Grand Rapids
Community College
143 Bostwick Ave. NE
Grand Rapids, MI 49503
www.grcc.edu

GRAND VALLEY STATE UNIVERSITY

Grand Valley State University was chartered by the Michigan Legislature in 1960, and opened in 1964 on a 1,200 acre campus along the Grand River. It has been the state's fastest-growing college pretty much ever since. Enrollment now is more than 20,000. Grand Valley was originally considered a commuter college, but now provides housing for more than 5,000 students. In addition to the Allendale Campus, GVSU has a large

Grand Valley State has a large presence in downtown Grand Rapids (photo courtesy of Grand Valley State University)

presence in downtown Grand Rapids, 15 miles to the east. It offers 69 undergraduate and 25 graduate degrees. Its Annis Water Resources Institute is among the most active research organizations tracking the health of the Great Lakes.

Estimated annual tuition and fees for 2005-2006: $6,200

Grand Valley State University
1 Campus Drive
Allendale, MI 49401
www.gvsu.edu

HOPE COLLEGE

Hope College traces its beginning to 1851, when the founders of the Dutch colony of Holland established a pioneer school to serve the four-year-old community. The school was chartered as Hope College in 1866. It is affiliated with the Reformed Church in America. Today, Hope is among the top rank of America's private liberal-arts colleges. It has about 3,000 students, and offers more than 80 majors leading to bachelor's degrees. The campus blends easily into the city neighborhoods near downtown Holland. The college owns the Knickerbocker Theater, which hosts lectures and other events, in addition to showing classic and foreign films in downtown Holland. Western Theological Seminary offers advanced divinity degrees at the Hope College site.

Estimated annual tuition and fees for 2005-2006: $21,500

Hope College
141 E. 12th Street
Holland, MI 49422
www.hope.edu

KALAMAZOO COLLEGE

Kalamazoo College, founded by a group of Baptists in 1833 as the Michigan and Huron Institute, is the oldest site of higher education in Michigan. The college's early leaders, James and Lucinda Stone, established an academic reputation that endures today. K-College is now an independent, private institution with 1,300 students. It is noted both for its strong academic programs and for its "Kalamazoo Plan" which offers internships and opportunities for study at off-campus locations in the United States and abroad. As many as 80 percent of Kalamazoo's students take advantage of foreign-study plans.

Estimated annual tuition and fees for 2005-2006: $25,600

Kalamazoo College
1200 Academy Street
Kalamazoo, MI 49006
www.kzoo.edu

KALAMAZOO VALLEY COMMUNITY COLLEGE

Kalamazoo Valley Community College was established in 1966. It serves Kalamazoo County and the Mattawan School District in Van Buren County. Its two campuses – one in downtown Kalamazoo and the other in Texas Township near I-94 and US-131 – have a total enrollment of more than 10,000 students. The Texas Township campus was designed by architect Alden Dow. The downtown campus, known as Arcadia Commons, was built in 1994. It includes classroom space, as well as the Kalamazoo Valley Museum. KVCC offers two-year associate's of arts and science degrees, as well as certificate programs that can lead to careers in such fields as technology, industry and health care.

Estimated annual tuition and fees for 2005-2006: $1,900

Kalamazoo Valley
Community College
PO Box 4070
Kalamazoo, MI 49003
www.kvcc.edu

KENDALL COLLEGE OF ART AND DESIGN

Kendall College of Art and Design, now a branch of Ferris State University, was founded in 1931 as a two-year school that focused on furniture design. It was financed from the estate of David Wolcott Kendall, a renowned Grand Rapids furniture designer who died in 1928. It was accredited to offer bachelor's degrees in 1981. Kendall merged with Ferris State University in 2000. It has about 900 students, who study in renovated buildings in downtown Grand Rapids, and continues to offer bachelor's and master's degrees. It is officially known as Kendall College of Art and Design of Ferris State University.

Estimated annual tuition and fees for 2005-2006: $11,000

Kendall College of Art
and Design
17 Fountain St. NW
Grand Rapids MI 49503
www.kcad.edu

LAKE MICHIGAN COLLEGE

Lake Michigan College is a two-year community college serving Berrien County, along with the South Haven and Covert areas of Van Buren

County. It was founded in 1946 and now serves as many as 7,000 students a year, in corporate and academic training programs. The main campus, on Napier Avenue in Benton Harbor, is a 260-acre site that includes classrooms, labs and administrative offices. Also on the main campus is the Mendel Center, where the 1,500-seat Mainstage Theater serves as a regional performing arts venue. Other college sites are in Niles and South Haven.

Estimated annual tuition and fees for 2005-2006: $2,535

Lake Michigan College
2755 E. Napier Ave.
Benton Harbor, MI 49022
www.lakemichigancollege.edu

MONTCALM COMMUNITY COLLEGE

Montcalm Community College was established by a public vote in 1965. The 240-acre campus in Sidney includes several general-use facilities, in addition to the academic buildings.

The Montcalm County Heritage Village, on the college campus, includes a number of historic buildings moved here from around the area. The Barn Theater on campus is used for student productions and visiting performing artists. Montcalm Community College has an enrollment of about 2,300 students. It offers associate's degrees, and has partnership agreements with a number of four-year institutions to ease the process of going on for a bachelor's degree.

Estimated annual tuition and fees for 2005-2006: $2,085

Montcalm
Community College
2800 College Dr.
Sidney, MI 48885
www.montcalm.edu

MUSKEGON COMMUNITY COLLEGE

Muskegon Community College was founded as Muskegon Junior College by the Muskegon Board of Education in 1926. It was initially housed in Muskegon High School. Muskegon County votors approved a county-wide community college district in 1963, and MCC moved to its present 111-acre campus at Quarterline and Marquette streets, in 1967. MCC has an "open door" policy that welcomes application from anyone who wants to attend. It has about 5,000 students in its programs leading to associate's degrees or occupational certification. Western Michigan, Ferris State and Grand Valley

State universities offer upper-level courses on the MCC campus.

Estimated annual tuition and fees for 2005-2006: $1,800

Muskegon Community College
221 S. Quarterline Road
Muskegon, MI 49422
www.muskegoncc.edu

REFORMED BIBLE COLLEGE

Reformed Bible College was founded in 1939 as an institute designed to train lay people for work in the missions and churches of the Christian Reformed and Reformed denominations. In 1970 it gained a state charter to grant four-year degrees. Today, RBC is located on a 34-acre wooded campus 15 minutes from downtown Grand Rapids. It has about 300 students enrolled in 17 undergraduate programs. Some courses are offered in consortium with nearby Cornerstone University.

Estimated annual tuition and fees for 2005-2006: $11,500

Reformed Bible College
3333 East Beltline, NE
Grand Rapids, MI 49525
www.reformed.edu

SOUTHWESTERN MICHIGAN COLLEGE

Southwestern Michigan College, in Dowagiac, is a community college serving a district that includes Cass County and Keeler and Hamilton townships in Van Buren County. The college offers three associate's degrees, and also has a number of programs that lead to occupational certification. Western Michigan University offers upper-level courses at SWMC's two locations, in Dowagiac and in Milton Township near Niles. Enrollment is about 2,750 students.

Estimated annual tuition and fees for 2005-2006: $2,500

Southwestern Michigan College
58900 Cherry Grove Road
Dowagiac, MI 49047
www.swmich.edu

WESTERN MICHIGAN UNIVERSITY

Western Michigan University was authorized by the Legislature in 1903 under the name Western Michigan Normal School. The name was changed to Western State Teachers College in 1927, and to Western Michigan University in 1957. WMU's 550-acre main campus in Kalamazoo has 125 buildings, including housing for about 6,000 students. With total enrollment of more than 25,000, it is the largest university in West Michigan and No. 4 in the state. It offers more than 250 graduate and undergraduate degree programs.

In addition to the main campus, Western operates the new 26-acre Parkview Campus with engineering, applied sciences and business technology programs. The university also offers classes at a number of off-campus sites, including Grand Rapids, Holland, Muskegon and Benton Harbor.

Estimated annual tuition and fees for 2005-2006: $6,500

Western Michigan University
1903 W. Michigan Ave.
Kalamazoo, MI 49008
www.wmich.edu

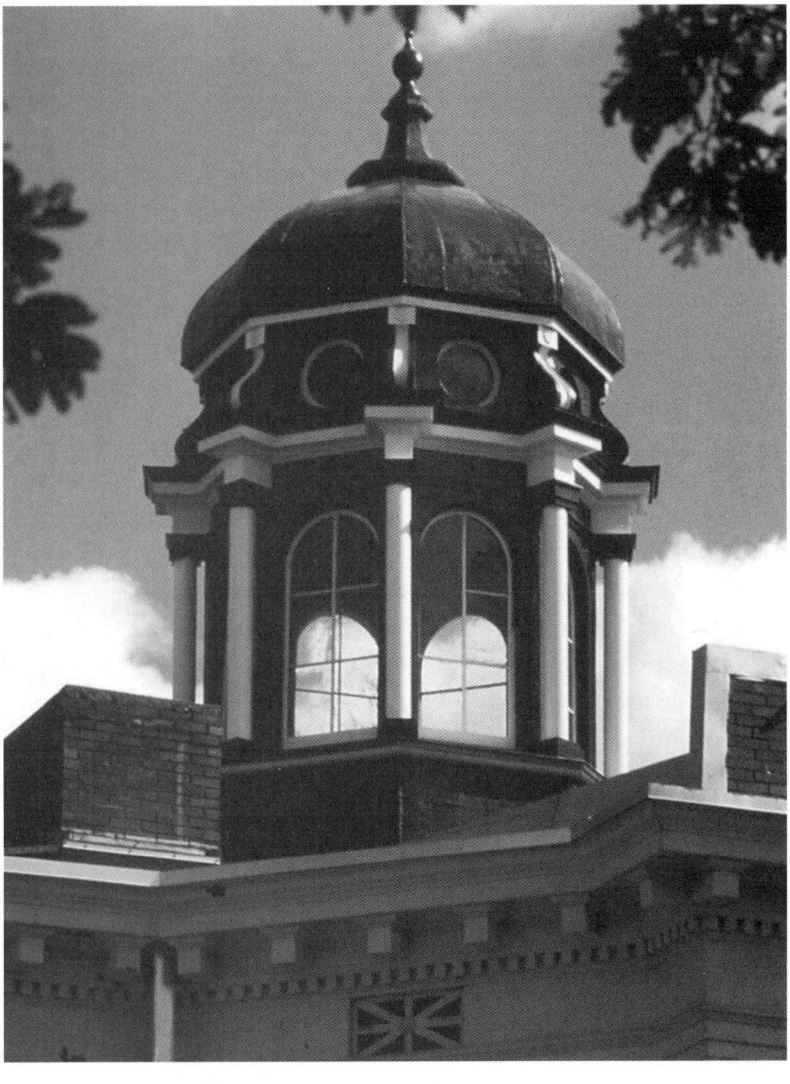

The cupola atop East Hall is a landmark at Western Michigan University (photo courtesy of Western Michigan University)

PRIVATE ELEMENTARY AND SECONDARY SCHOOLS

Western Michigan has more than 200 private elementary and secondary schools, with total enrollment of nearly 40,000 children. These schools range from large, long-established high schools, to tiny elementary schools such as the parish school in Montcalm County that serves 25 Amish children.

Most, but not all, of the private schools are sponsored by religious groups.

Here is a list of the 25 largest private schools in West Michgan. The statistics, from 2004, are provided by the Michigan Department of Education.

1. Grand Rapids Christian High School, 1,065 students
2. Hudsonville Christian School, 944 students
3. Holland Christian High School, 909 students
4. Zeeland Christian School, 881 students
5. Catholic Central High School, Grand Rapids, 827 students
6. Unity Christian High School, Hudsonville, 821 students
7. South Christian High School, Grand Rapids, 783 students
8. Ada Christian School, 664 students
9. Northpointe Christian School, Grand Rapids, 632 students
10. West Catholic High School, Grand Rapids, 631 students
11. Kalamazoo Christian West Elementary School, 503 students
12. Byron Center Christian School, 488 students
13. West Side Christian School, Grand Rapids, 480 students
14. Calvin Christian High School, Grandville, 473 students
15. Hackett Catholic Central, Kalamazoo, 468 students
16. Rose Park Christian School, Holland, 463 students
17. Kalamazoo Christian High School, 457 students
18. St. Monica School, Kalamazoo, 453 students
19. Immaculate Heart of Mary School, Grand Rapids, 445 students
20. Dutton Christian School, Caledonia, 444 students
21. St. Anthony of Padua School, Grand Rapids, 441 students
22. Heritage Christian School, Hudsonville, 441 students
23. Cutlerville Christian School, Grand Rapids, 434 students
24. Jenison Christian School, 409 students
25. Holy Spirit School, Grand Rapids, 405 students

PUBLIC SCHOOL DISTRICTS

Here is a list of West Michigan public school districts that offer classes in kindergarten through 12th grade. Enrollment and graduation rate statistics are from the Michigan Department of Education. District poverty estimates are for children age 5-17 who live within the district boundaries. Those statistics are provided by the United States Census Bureau. The districts are listed according to intermediate school districts.

ALLEGAN COUNTY

Allegan Public Schools

Total district enrollment (2004): 2,960
Total district enrollment (1994): 2,910
School-age children in poverty (2003): 11.77%
Reported graduation rate (2004): 95.24%

Fennville Public Schools

Total district enrollment (2004): 1,470
Total district enrollment (1994): 1,521
School-age children in poverty (2003): 14.93%
Reported graduation rate (2004): 88.91%

Hopkins Public Schools

Total district enrollment (2004): 1,495
Total district enrollment (1994): 1,363
School-age children in poverty (2003): 8.71%
Reported graduation rate (2004): 98.71%

Martin Public Schools

Total district enrollment (2004): 695
Total district enrollment (1994): 858
School-age children in poverty (2003): 14.35%
Reported graduation rate (2004): 91.34%

Otsego Public Schools

Total district enrollment (2004): 2,261
Total district enrollment (1994): 2,435
School-age children in poverty (2003): 6.88%
Reported graduation rate (2004): 97.11%

Plainwell Community Schools
Total district enrollment (2004): 2,830
Total district enrollment (1994): 2,515
School-age children in poverty (2003): 8.54%
Reported graduation rate (2004): 96.4%

Wayland Union School District
Total district enrollment (2004): 3,190
Total district enrollment (1994): 2,896
School-age children in poverty (2003): 5.19%
Reported graduation rate (2004): 90.85%

BARRY COUNTY

Delton-Kellogg School District
Total district enrollment (2004): 2,005
Total district enrollment (1994): 2,070
School-age children in poverty (2003): 12.04%
Reported graduation rate (2004): 84.93%

Hastings Area School District
Total district enrollment (2004): 3,392
Total district enrollment (1994): 3,336
School-age children in poverty (2003): 8.17%
Reported graduation rate (2004): 95.26%

BERRIEN COUNTY

Benton Harbor Area Schools
Total district enrollment (2004): 4,612
Total district enrollment (1994): 6,301
School-age children in poverty (2003): 39.59%
Reported graduation rate (2004): 66.97%

Berrien Springs Public Schools
Total district enrollment (2004): 1,600
Total district enrollment (1994): 1,522
School-age children in poverty (2003): 14.09%
Reported graduation rate (2004): 90.76%

Brandywine Community Schools (Niles)
Total district enrollment (2004): 1,478
Total district enrollment (1994): 1,585
School-age children in poverty (2003): 8.22%
Reported graduation rate (2004): 87.2%

Bridgman Public Schools
Total district enrollment (2004): 1,026
Total district enrollment (1994): 916
School-age children in poverty (2003): 9.72%
Reported graduation rate (2004): 95.7%

Buchanan Community Schools
Total district enrollment (2004): 1,758
Total district enrollment (1994): 1,733
School-age children in poverty (2003): 9.43%
Reported graduation rate (2004): 95.08%

Coloma Community Schools
Total district enrollment (2004): 2,213
Total district enrollment (1994): 2,445
School-age children in poverty (2003): 7.28%
Reported graduation rate (2004): 80.11%

Eau Claire Public Schools
Total district enrollment (2004): 856
Total district enrollment (1994): 868
School-age children in poverty (2003): 11.26%
Reported graduation rate (2004): 56.69%

Galien Township School District
Total district enrollment (2004): 177
Total district enrollment (1994): 543
School-age children in poverty (2003): 12.32%
Reported graduation rate (2004): N/A

Lakeshore School District (Stevensville)
Total district enrollment (2004): 2,838
Total district enrollment (1994): 2,941
School-age children in poverty (2003): 2.68%
Reported graduation rate (2004): 97.92%

New Buffalo Area Schools
Total district enrollment (2004): 687
Total district enrollment (1994): 661
School-age children in poverty (2003): 5.62%
Reported graduation rate (2004): 92.44%

Niles Community School District
Total district enrollment (2004): 4,032
Total district enrollment (1994): 3,856
School-age children in poverty (2003): 11.38%
Reported graduation rate (2004): 80.1%

River Valley School District
Total district enrollment (2004): 1,002
Total district enrollment (1994): 1,322
School-age children in poverty (2003): 8.50%
Reported graduation rate (2004): 86.72%

St. Joseph Public Schools
Total district enrollment (2004): 2,804
Total district enrollment (1994): 2,695
School-age children in poverty (2003): 4.48%
Reported graduation rate (2004): 89.94%

Watervliet School District
Total district enrollment (2004): 1,417
Total district enrollment (1994): 1,221
School-age children in poverty (2003): 8.92%
Reported graduation rate (2004): 90.96%

CASS COUNTY

Cassopolis Public Schools
Total district enrollment (2004): 1,322
Total district enrollment (1994): 1,457
School-age children in poverty (2003): 14.77%
Reported graduation rate (2004): 86%

Dowagiac Union Schools
Total district enrollment (2004): 2,693
Total district enrollment (1994): 3,073
School-age children in poverty (2003): 17.28%
Reported graduation rate (2004): 80.27%

Edwardsburg Public Schools
Total district enrollment (2004): 2,342
Total district enrollment (1994): 1,958
School-age children in poverty (2003): 9.16%
Reported graduation rate (2004): 94.43%

Marcellus Community Schools
Total district enrollment (2004): 1,064
Total district enrollment (1994): 1,058
School-age children in poverty (2003): 11.01%
Reported graduation rate (2004): 100%

IONIA COUNTY

Belding Area School District
Total district enrollment (2004): 2,412
Total district enrollment (1994): 2,486
School-age children in poverty (2003): 12.49%
Reported graduation rate (2004): 85.72%

Ionia Public Schools
Total district enrollment (2004): 3,279
Total district enrollment (1994): 3,260
School-age children in poverty (2003): 14.72%
Reported graduation rate (2004): 92.05%

Lakewood Public Schools
Total district enrollment (2004): 2,480
Total district enrollment (1994): 2,823
School-age children in poverty (2003): 7.57%
Reported graduation rate (2004): 95.4%

Portland Public Schools
Total district enrollment (2004): 2,066
Total district enrollment (1994): 1,786
School-age children in poverty (2003): 5.40%
Reported graduation rate (2004): 83.01%

Saranac Community Schools
Total district enrollment (2004): 1,233
Total district enrollment (1994): 1,228
School-age children in poverty (2003): 7.13%
Reported graduation rate (2004): 96.57%

Pewamo-Westphalia Community School District (Clinton ISD)
Total district enrollment (2004): 619
Total district enrollment (1994): 612
School-age children in poverty (2003): 2.43%
Reported graduation rate (2004): 92.58%

KALAMAZOO COUNTY

Climax-Scotts Community School District
Total district enrollment (2004): 726
Total district enrollment (1994): 716
School-age children in poverty (2003): 4.31%
Reported graduation rate (2004): 86.33%

Comstock Public Schools
Total district enrollment (2004): 2,885
Total district enrollment (1994): 2,742
School-age children in poverty (2003): 12.83%
Reported graduation rate (2004): 96.57%

Galesburg-Augusta Community Schools
Total district enrollment (2004): 1,314
Total district enrollment (1994): 1,165
School-age children in poverty (2003): 10.81%
Reported graduation rate (2004): 94.22%

Gull Lake Community School District
Total district enrollment (2004): 2,984
Total district enrollment (1994): 2,829
School-age children in poverty (2003): 4.96
Reported graduation rate (2004): 93.27%

Kalamazoo Public Schools
Total district enrollment (2004): 10,232
Total district enrollment (1994): 12,285
School-age children in poverty (2003): 25.26%
Reported graduation rate (2004): 83.07%

Parchment School District
Total district enrollment (2004): 2,022
Total district enrollment (1994): 1,702
School-age children in poverty (2003): 10.75%
Reported graduation rate (2004): 96.55%

Portage Public Schools
Total district enrollment (2004): 9,005
Total district enrollment (1994): 8,469
School-age children in poverty (2003): 5.33%
Reported graduation rate (2004): 95.39%

Schoolcraft Community Schools
Total district enrollment (2004): 1,212
Total district enrollment (1994): 1,047
School-age children in poverty (2003): 3.73%
Reported graduation rate (2004): 100%

Vicksburg Community Schools
Total district enrollment (2004): 2,776
Total district enrollment (1994): 2,616
School-age children in poverty (2003): 5.29%
Reported graduation rate (2004): 95.51%

KENT COUNTY

Byron Center Public Schools
Total district enrollment (2004): 3,016
Total district enrollment (1994): 2,003
School-age children in poverty (2003): 2.87%
Reported graduation rate (2004): 95.16%

Caledonia Community Schools
Total district enrollment (2004): 3,466
Total district enrollment (1994): 2,605
School-age children in poverty (2003): 3.24%
Reported graduation rate (2004): 93.44%

Cedar Springs Public Schools
Total district enrollment (2004): 3,406
Total district enrollment (1994): 2,792
School-age children in poverty (2003): 8.39%
Reported graduation rate (2004): 76.97%

Comstock Park Public Schools
Total district enrollment (2004): 2,380
Total district enrollment (1994): 1,690
School-age children in poverty (2003): 9.03%
Reported graduation rate (2004): 89%

East Grand Rapids Public Schools
Total district enrollment (2004): 2,886
Total district enrollment (1994): 2,516
School-age children in poverty (2003): 4.13%
Reported graduation rate (2004): 98.82%

Forest Hills Public Schools
Total district enrollment (2004): 9,438
Total district enrollment (1994): 6,563
School-age children in poverty (2003): 2.94%
Reported graduation rate (2004): 98.88%

Godfrey-Lee Public Schools
Total district enrollment (2004): 1,559
Total district enrollment (1994): 1,187
School-age children in poverty (2003): 15.47%
Reported graduation rate (2004): 87.83%

Godwin Heights Public Schools
Total district enrollment (2004): 2,334
Total district enrollment (1994): 2,266
School-age children in poverty (2003): 6.80%
Reported graduation rate (2004): 91.39%

Grand Rapids Public Schools
Total district enrollment (2004): 21,602
Total district enrollment (1994): 25,267
School-age children in poverty (2003): 21.0%
Reported graduation rate (2004): 86.14%

Grandville Public Schools
Total district enrollment (2004): 6,130
Total district enrollment (1994): 5,071
School-age children in poverty (2003): 4.18%
Reported graduation rate (2004): 89.23%

Kelloggsville Public Schools
Total district enrollment (2004): 2,108
Total district enrollment (1994): 2,075
School-age children in poverty (2003): 11.01%
Reported graduation rate (2004): 88.36%

Kenowa Hills Public Schools
Total district enrollment (2004): 3,646
Total district enrollment (1994): 2,757
School-age children in poverty (2003): 4.97%
Reported graduation rate (2004): 91.46%

Kent City Community Schools
Total district enrollment (2004): 1,405
Total district enrollment (1994): 1,503
School-age children in poverty (2003): 8.36%
Reported graduation rate (2004): 68.56%

Kentwood Public Schools
Total district enrollment (2004): 8,990
Total district enrollment (1994): 7,733
School-age children in poverty (2003): 9.41%
Reported graduation rate (2004): 93.44%

Lowell Area Schools
Total district enrollment (2004): 3,855
Total district enrollment (1994): 3,257
School-age children in poverty (2003): 5.99%
Reported graduation rate (2004): 94.32%

Northview Public Schools
Total district enrollment (2004): 3,328
Total district enrollment (1994): 3,198
School-age children in poverty (2003): 6.03%
Reported graduation rate (2004): 97.21%

Rockford Public Schools
Total district enrollment (2004): 7,682
Total district enrollment (1994): 6,094
School-age children in poverty (2003): 4.13%
Reported graduation rate (2004): 96.89%

Sparta Area Schools
Total district enrollment (2004): 2,979
Total district enrollment (1994): 2,692
School-age children in poverty (2003): 4.58%
Reported graduation rate (2004): 96.17%

Thornapple Kellogg School District
Total district enrollment (2004): 2,891
Total district enrollment (1994): 2,500
School-age children in poverty (2003): 4.34%
Reported graduation rate (2004): 98.54%

Wyoming Public Schools
Total district enrollment (2004): 5,585
Total district enrollment (1994): 5,602
School-age children in poverty (2003): 9.79%
Reported graduation rate (2004): 95.36%

MECOSTA COUNTY

Big Rapids Public Schools
Total district enrollment (2004): 2,122
Total district enrollment (1994): 2,233
School-age children in poverty (2003): 13.91%
Reported graduation rate (2004): 98.71%

Chippewa Hills School District
Total district enrollment (2004): 2,601
Total district enrollment (1994): 2,498
School-age children in poverty (2003): 16.73%
Reported graduation rate (2004): 86.41%

Morley Stanwood Community Schools
Total district enrollment (2004): 1,628
Total district enrollment (1994): 1,559
School-age children in poverty (2003): 18.87%
Reported graduation rate (2004): 90.20%

MONTCALM COUNTY

Carson City-Crystal Area Schools
Total district enrollment (2004): 1,278
Total district enrollment (1994): 1,389
School-age children in poverty (2003): 14.37%
Reported graduation rate (2004): 95.54%

Central Montcalm Public Schools
Total district enrollment (2004): 2,053
Total district enrollment (1994): 2,292
School-age children in poverty (2003): 16.50%
Reported graduation rate (2004): 82.64%

Greenville Public Schools
Total district enrollment (2004): 3,808
Total district enrollment (1994): 3,948
School-age children in poverty (2003): 11.68%
Reported graduation rate (2004): 87.89%

Lakeview Community Schools
Total district enrollment (2004): 1,816
Total district enrollment (1994): 1,745
School-age children in poverty (2003): 10.8%
Reported graduation rate (2004): 78.41%

Montabella Community Schools
Total district enrollment (2004): 1,062
Total district enrollment (1994): 1,236
School-age children in poverty (2003): 17.65%
Reported graduation rate (2004): 71.36%

Tri County Area Schools
Total district enrollment (2004): 2,362
Total district enrollment (1994): 2,030
School-age children in poverty (2003): 9.2%
Reported graduation rate (2004): 91.57%

Vestaburg Community Schools
Total district enrollment (2004): 768
Total district enrollment (1994): 719
School-age children in poverty (2003): 10.13%
Reported graduation rate (2004): 95.56%

MUSKEGON COUNTY

Fruitport Community Schools
Total district enrollment (2004): 3,207
Total district enrollment (1994): 3,320
School-age children in poverty (2003): 9.69%
Reported graduation rate (2004): 89.29%

Holton Public Schools
Total district enrollment (2004): 1,104
Total district enrollment (1994): 1,110
School-age children in poverty (2003): 14.17%
Reported graduation rate (2004): 98.8%

Mona Shores Public School District
Total district enrollment (2004): 4,231
Total district enrollment (1994): 3,668
School-age children in poverty (2003): 5.28%
Reported graduation rate (2004): 94.46%

Montague Area Public Schools
Total district enrollment (2004): 1,438
Total district enrollment (1994): 1,617
School-age children in poverty (2003): 12.16%
Reported graduation rate (2004): 98.89%

Muskegon City School District
Total district enrollment (2004): 6,678
Total district enrollment (1994): 6,892
School-age children in poverty (2003): 28.82%
Reported graduation rate (2004): 83.9%

Muskegon Heights School District
Total district enrollment (2004): 2,221
Total district enrollment (1994): 2,577
School-age children in poverty (2003): 42.56%
Reported graduation rate (2004): 95.58%

North Muskegon Public Schools
Total district enrollment (2004): 878
Total district enrollment (1994): 833
School-age children in poverty (2003): 3.06%
Reported graduation rate (2004): 94.82%

Oakridge Public Schools
Total district enrollment (2004): 2,003
Total district enrollment (1994): 1,840
School-age children in poverty (2003): 15.69%
Reported graduation rate (2004): 84.83%

Orchard View Schools
Total district enrollment (2004): 2,927
Total district enrollment (1994): 2,456
School-age children in poverty (2003): 13.45%
Reported graduation rate (2004): 94.17%

Ravenna Public Schools
Total district enrollment (2004): 1,197
Total district enrollment (1994): 1,202
School-age children in poverty (2003): 5.68%
Reported graduation rate (2004): 86.52%

Reeths-Puffer Schools
Total district enrollment (2004): 4,209
Total district enrollment (1994): 4,250
School-age children in poverty (2003): 6.27%
Reported graduation rate (2004): 89.05%

Whitehall District Schools
Total district enrollment (2004): 2,285
Total district enrollment (1994): 1,978
School-age children in poverty (2003): 11.93%
Reported graduation rate (2004): 98.22%

NEWAYGO COUNTY

Fremont Public School District
Total district enrollment (2004): 2,569
Total district enrollment (1994): 2,529
School-age children in poverty (2003): 14.7%
Reported graduation rate (2004): 94.17%

Grant Public School District
Total district enrollment (2004): 2,516
Total district enrollment (1994): 2,149
School-age children in poverty (2003): 11.76%
Reported graduation rate (2004): 100%

Hesperia Community Schools
Total district enrollment (2004): 1,122
Total district enrollment (1994): 1,116
School-age children in poverty (2003): 20.81%
Reported graduation rate (2004): 100%

Newaygo Public School District
Total district enrollment (2004): 2,033
Total district enrollment (1994): 1,840
School-age children in poverty (2003): 11.38%
Reported graduation rate (2004): 94.51%

White Cloud Public Schools
Total district enrollment (2004): 1,411
Total district enrollment (1994): 1,541
School-age children in poverty (2003): 20.53%
Reported graduation rate (2004): 88.23%

OCEANA COUNTY

Hart Public School District
Total district enrollment (2004): 1,392
Total district enrollment (1994): 1,578
School-age children in poverty (2003): 20.01%
Reported graduation rate (2004): 100%

Shelby Public Schools
Total district enrollment (2004): 1,836
Total district enrollment (1994): 1,788
School-age children in poverty (2003): 16.25%
Reported graduation rate (2004): 92.72%

Walkerville Rural Community School District
Total district enrollment (2004): 472
Total district enrollment (1994): 381
School-age children in poverty (2003): 24.23%
Reported graduation rate (2004): 75.32%

Pentwater Public School District
Total district enrollment (2004): 279
Total district enrollment (1994): 400
School-age children in poverty (2003): 11.92%
Reported graduation rate (2004): 92.86%

OTTAWA COUNTY

Allendale Public School District
Total district enrollment (2004): 2,062
Total district enrollment (1994): 1,372
School-age children in poverty (2003): 5.45%
Reported graduation rate (2004): 94.45%

Coopersville Public School District
Total district enrollment (2004): 2,421
Total district enrollment (1994): 2,378
School-age children in poverty (2003): 7.37%
Reported graduation rate (2004): 98.40%

Grand Haven Area Public Schools
Total district enrollment (2004): 5,999
Total district enrollment (1994): 5,921
School-age children in poverty (2003): 2.59%
Reported graduation rate (2004): 96.17%

Hamilton Community Schools
Total district enrollment (2004): 2,667
Total district enrollment (1994): 2,134
School-age children in poverty (2003): 6.68%
Reported graduation rate (2004): 97.02%

Holland City School District
Total district enrollment (2004): 5,014
Total district enrollment (1994): 5,644
School-age children in poverty (2003): 11.14%
Reported graduation rate (2004): 73,18%

Hudsonville Public School District
Total district enrollment (2004): 4,972
Total district enrollment (1994): 3,669
School-age children in poverty (2003): 3.60%
Reported graduation rate (2004): 100%

Jenison Public Schools
Total district enrollment (2004): 4,759
Total district enrollment (1994): 4,518
School-age children in poverty (2003): 5.92%
Reported graduation rate (2004): 92.78%

Saugatuck Public Schools
Total district enrollment (2004): 849
Total district enrollment (1994): 690
School-age children in poverty (2003): 14.0%
Reported graduation rate (2004): 100%

Spring Lake Public Schools
Total district enrollment (2004): 2,285
Total district enrollment (1994): 1,891
School-age children in poverty (2003): 4.82%
Reported graduation rate (2004): 99.47%

West Ottawa Public School District
Total district enrollment (2004): 8,125
Total district enrollment (1994): 5,782
School-age children in poverty (2003): 8.51%
Reported graduation rate (2004): 90.39%

Zeeland Public Schools
Total district enrollment (2004): 5,084
Total district enrollment (1994): 3,694
School-age children in poverty (2003): 6.22%
Reported graduation rate (2004): 95.67%

ST. JOSEPH COUNTY

Burr Oak Community School District
Total district enrollment (2004): 352
Total district enrollment (1994): 309
School-age children in poverty (2003): 13.44%
Reported graduation rate (2004): 100%

Centreville Public Schools
Total district enrollment (2004): 992
Total district enrollment (1994): 873
School-age children in poverty (2003): 11.15%
Reported graduation rate (2004): 80.53%

Colon Community School District
Total district enrollment (2004): 876
Total district enrollment (1994): 1,003
School-age children in poverty (2003): 14.61%
Reported graduation rate (2004): 91.14%

Constantine Public School District
Total district enrollment (2004): 1,510
Total district enrollment (1994): 1,648
School-age children in poverty (2003): 12.62%
Reported graduation rate (2004): 83.51%

Mendon Community School District
Total district enrollment (2004): 760
Total district enrollment (1994): 733
School-age children in poverty (2003): 13.25%
Reported graduation rate (2004): 97.44%

Sturgis Public Schools
Total district enrollment (2004): 3,129
Total district enrollment (1994): 3,065
School-age children in poverty (2003): 14.87%
Reported graduation rate (2004): 89.03%

Three Rivers Community Schools
Total district enrollment (2004): 3,038
Total district enrollment (1994): 2,960
School-age children in poverty (2003): 16.02%
Reported graduation rate (2004): 86.63%

White Pigeon Community Schools
Total district enrollment (2004): 923
Total district enrollment (1994): 1,165
School-age children in poverty (2003): 13.8%
Reported graduation rate (2004): 90.55%

VAN BUREN COUNTY

Bangor Public Schools
Total district enrollment (2004): 1,524
Total district enrollment (1994): 1,637
School-age children in poverty (2003): 22.4%
Reported graduation rate (2004): 85.30%

Bloomingdale Public School District
Total district enrollment (2004): 1,417
Total district enrollment (1994): 1,325
School-age children in poverty (2003): 21.35%
Reported graduation rate (2004): 80.28%

Covert Public Schools
Total district enrollment (2004): 703
Total district enrollment (1994): 806
School-age children in poverty (2003): 44.23%
Reported graduation rate (2004): 91.03%

Decatur Public Schools
Total district enrollment (2004): 1,171
Total district enrollment (1994): 1,223
School-age children in poverty (2003): 21.26%
Reported graduation rate (2004): 86.87%

Gobles Public School District
Total district enrollment (2004): 1,050
Total district enrollment (1994): 945
School-age children in poverty (2003): 8.51%
Reported graduation rate (2004): 85.90%

Hartford Public School District
Total district enrollment (2004): 1,494
Total district enrollment (1994): 1,394
School-age children in poverty (2003): 16.3%
Reported graduation rate (2004): 95.77%

Lawrence Public School District
Total district enrollment (2004): 766
Total district enrollment (1994): 812
School-age children in poverty (2003): 18.13%
Reported graduation rate (2004): 92.89%

Lawton Community School District
Total district enrollment (2004): 1,104
Total district enrollment (1994): 1,175
School-age children in poverty (2003): 12.2%
Reported graduation rate (2004): 82.43%

Mattawan Consolidated School
Total district enrollment (2004): 3,504
Total district enrollment (1994): 2,842
School-age children in poverty (2003): 4.61%
Reported graduation rate (2004): 94.65%

Paw Paw Public School District
Total district enrollment (2004): 2,366
Total district enrollment (1994): 2,077
School-age children in poverty (2003): 11.45%
Reported graduation rate (2004): 91.92%

South Haven Public Schools
Total district enrollment (2004): 2,345
Total district enrollment (1994): 2,680
School-age children in poverty (2003): 11.27%
Reported graduation rate (2004): 84.92%

RELIGION

Religion has played a part in West Michigan life for longer than anyone can remember.

A Catholic priest, Pere Marquette, was among the first Europeans to set eyes on the area. He canoed up the Lake Michigan shore in 1675, after ministering to Indians in Illinois, and named the St. Joseph River after the patron saint of New France.

Long before Marquette – even before the present Indian tribes moved into the Great Lakes region – the people we know as Hopewell were building earthen mounds and burying their dead in what must have been a religious or spiritual ceremony.

Religion also played a part in West Michigan's transition from Indian land to white settlement.

The 1821 Treaty of Chicago, in which Ottawa and Potawatomi tribes gave up most of their land south of the Grand River, called for the creation of two missions to the Indians.

The Carey Mission, founded at Niles by the Baptist minister Isaac McCoy in 1822, served virtually as the capitol of the West Michigan wilderness in the early years. A subsequent Indian treaty was signed there in 1828.

McCoy also set up a second mission on what is now the West Side of Grand Rapids. That mission was less successful at first, because the Grand River Indians were somewhat hostile about the whole idea of giving up their land.

Eventually, McCoy's associate, the Rev. Leonard Slater, persuaded the leader of the largest Grand River Indian village, Chief Noonday, to convert to Christianity.

St. Joseph's Catholic Church in Oceana County is typical of Michigan's rural congregations (photo: Ed Hoogterp)

The Baptist Mission was in operation at the Grand River several years before the arrival of Louis Campau, the trader who set up shop across the river in 1827 and is credited with founding the city.

Campau, a French Catholic, apparently had little use for Slater's Baptist religion. When a Catholic priest, the Rev. Frederic Baraga, arrived on the Grand to open another mission in the early 1830s, Campau made sure the Catholic house of worship was moved to his side of the river.

Baraga stayed less than two years. He spent the rest of his life ministering to native people in northern Michigan and

Wisconsin. He was called "The snowshoe priest" because of his extensive travels on foot, and became the first bishop of Marquette, where he died in 1868. Catholics in the Upper Peninsula have petitioned the Vatican to declare Bishop Baraga as a saint.

Slater stayed at the Grand River Mission until 1836, then moved with Noonday and about 50 other Indians to a new site at Prairieville, in Barry County. By that time, West Michigan was undergoing a population boom. And the newcomers from New England began building churches almost as soon as they arrived.

A Methodist preacher was in Constantine (then known as Meek's Mill) as early as 1829, and Constantine United Methodist Church was organized in 1831.

The Trinity Episcopal and Wesley United Methodist congregations in Niles both date from 1832. Both congregations worship today in churches built before or during the Civil War.

In 1836, Jeremiah Hall organized the first Baptist congregation in Kalamazoo. Baptists also chartered the institution that is now Kalamazoo College in 1833.

A Catholic Church was built at Bertrand, south of Niles, in 1837. The Sisters of the Holy Cross opened a school there in 1844. The church in Bertrand was under the direction of the Rev. Edward Sorin, who founded Notre Dame University at South Bend, Indiana, about five miles south of Bertrand. The Bertrand school later moved to South Bend and became St. Mary's College.

An African-American congregation was organized in Cass County's Calvin Township as early as 1838. In the 1850s, the members built the Chain Lake Baptist Church there.

Another early church built by and for African-Americans was the Wheatland Church of Christ in Mecosta County. The congregation was organized about 1870. Members built a church, which is still standing, about 1898.

In 1847, the Rev. Albertus Van Raalte led a group of conservative Dutch Protestants to Lake Macatawa in Ottawa County, where they created the new community of Holland. The immigrants also founded surrounding villages such as Zeeland, Graafschap and Overisel, and built impressive churches.

Many of the Dutch congregations affiliated with the Reformed Church in America. But in 1857 several congregations seceded from that denomination and formed the Christian Reformed Church.

Today, the Christian Reformed Church and Reformed Church in America remain as two of the largest denominations in West Michigan.

Hope College, in Holland, is affiliated with the Reformed Church. The Christian Reformed Church has Calvin College, in Grand Rapids.

Robert H. Schuller, an early television preacher and founder of the Crystal Cathedral in California, received his training at Western Theological Seminary in Holland. In 2006, Schuller passed the leadership of the Crystal Cathedral to his son, Robert A. Schuller, another Western Theological graduate.

Robert A. Schuller and Robert H. Schuller, of California's Crystal Cathedral, are graduates of Western Theological Seminary in Holland (photo courtesy of Crystal Cathedral)

Among the oldest surviving Dutch churches in West Michigan are the Ninth Street Christian Reformed Church in Holland, built in 1856; Graafschap Christian Reformed Church, built in 1862, and Overisel Reformed Church, which opened in 1866.

One of the region's most fascinating religious stories was the creation of the Israelite House of David colony in Benton Harbor in 1903. The colony, with up to 1,000 members, preached celibacy and vegetarianism, but also placed itself at the center of the cultural life of southwest Michigan. In the early part of the century its barnstorming baseball team played throughout the country, and its Eden Springs Amusement Park was one of the leading tourist venues in the Midwest.

One of the community's founders, Mary Purnell, reorganized the community in the 1930s. Today, what's left of Mary's City of David is open for tours in the summer.

West Michigan was the boyhood home of Cardinal Edmund Szoka, the former archbishop of Detroit who served Pope John Paul II as administrator of Vatican City. Szoka was born in Grand Rapids in 1927 and grew up in Muskegon.

Muskegon was also home to televangelist Jim Bakker, whose PTL Club broadcasts with wife Tammy Faye raked in millions of dollars in donations during the 1980s. Bakker's business/ministry came crashing down in a series of scandals involving sexual escapades and financial fraud. Jim Bakker served 10 years in prison and has since resumed a much more low key ministry.

While West Michigan residents are predominantly Christian, other religions of the world also found their way here.

Hindus meet at the Vivekananda center in Ganges, in Allegan County, while Vandalia, in Cass County is home to the Wat Lao Buddhist Temple. Both Grand Rapids and Kalamazoo have Islamic Centers.

Kalamazoo's first Jewish resident, Mannes Israel, settled there in 1844. His son, Edward, was a scientist on America's first Polar expedition, and died on Ellesmere Island in 1884. Edward Israel's burial site in Kalamazoo has a state historical marker.

Another early Jewish resident was Julius Houseman, who arrived in Grand Rapids in 1852. Temple Emanuel, which Houseman helped to form in 1857, is recognized as one of the oldest reform Jewish congregations in America. He later served as mayor of Grand Rapids and as U.S. congressman.

Despite the area's conservative reputation, it also provided a platform for one of America's leading liberal ministers, the Rev. Duncan Littlefair, who headed Fountain Street Church in Grand Rapids from 1944-1979.

Littlefair seldom spoke of the supernatural and once said he used the term "God" poetically. Yet, he was among West Michigan's most influential leaders. During his 35-year ministry Fountain Street hosted such guests as Eleanor Roosevelt, Robert Frost and Duke Ellington.

More recent trends have seen some predominantly white congregations move to suburban areas, while their old church buildings are taken over by urban black congregations. That happened in Grand Rapids, where Bishop William Abney presides over the venerable Bethel Pentecostal Church in the stone building that once housed Bethany Reformed Church.

Recent years have also seen the rise of so-called megachurches – which often cater to young families who had either given up on older denominations or who grew up with no religious tradition at all.

The Mars Hill Bible Church in Grandville is the best known of the new breed of churches in West Michigan. It draws up to 10,000 worshipers to services in a converted shopping center.

RELIGIOUS DENOMINATIONS IN WEST MICHIGAN

A national survey of religious denominations and church membership in 2000 identified 1,800 congregations or parishes in West Michigan, split up among about 90 separate denominations. The churches in the survey reported having some 845,000 adherents (generally defined as church members and their families). Not identified in the 2000 survey, were some non-denominational Christian churches, which are thought to take in 10 percent or more of church-goers. The survey also did not report data for historically African-American churches, which have significant membership in several West Michigan cities.

When researchers set out to count the number of church members in America, they can either contact churches and ask about the size of each congregation, or they can apply statistical tools to surveys that ask individual families what church, if any, the family attends.

In surveys, about 80 percent of Americans identify themselves with specific denominations, or with unspecified Christian religion. But estimates derived from membership reported by the churches are closer to 60 percent.

Presumably, that means a lot of people stay away from church, even though they identify themselves with religion.

Considering those factors, the total numbers reported in the survey of churches are necessarily inexact. The statistics for major denominations, however, are considered to be the most accurate available. The data comes from the Association of Statisticians of American Religious Bodies. It is published by Glenmary Research Center, and is used with permission.

Here are the denominations that reported more than 10,000 adherents in West Michigan:

Catholic Church: 144 parishes; 279,610 adherents

Christian Reformed Church in North America: 196 churches; 103,153 adherents

Reformed Church in America: 129 congregations; 77,431 adherents

United Methodist Church: 210 congregations; 50,368 adherents

Lutheran Church, Missouri Synod: 70 congregations; 35,773 adherents

General Assembly of Regular Baptist Churches: 81 congregations; 23,744 adherents

Wesleyan Church: 45 congregations; 22,685 adherents

Evangelical Lutheran Church in America: 51 congregations; 21,699 adherents

United Church of Christ: 54 congregations; 18,939 adherents

Seventh-day Adventist Church: 64 congregations; 16,442 adherents

Presbyterian Church (USA): 38 congregations; 16,356 adherents

Assemblies of God: 59 congregations; 15,762 adherents

Other groups of churches include:

Independent charismatic churches: 5 congregations; 13,550 adherents

Independent non-charismatic churches: 17 congregations; 20,090 adherents

African-American Baptist congregations (1990 estimate): 44,000 adherents

Here is a list of the leading denominations in each West Michigan county:

ALLEGAN COUNTY

Catholic Church: 11,992

Christian Reformed Church: 10,223

Reformed Church in America: 4,439

United Methodist Church: 3,294

Wesleyan Church: 1,265

County total: 119 congregations; 40,221 adherents

BARRY COUNTY

Catholic Church: 3,830

United Methodist Church: 2,464

Reformed Church in America: 849

Evangelical Lutheran Church in America: 676

Presbyterian Church (USA): 664

County total: 46 congregations; 12,374 adherents

BERRIEN COUNTY

Catholic Church: 25,336

Lutheran Church, Missouri Synod: 8,960

Seventh-day Adventist Church: 8,937

United Methodist Church: 5,175

Wisconsin Evangelical Lutheran Synod: 4,176

African-American Baptist congregations (1990 est.): 8,914

County total: 186 congregations; 76,180 adherents

CASS COUNTY

Catholic Church: 7,974

United Methodist Church: 1,561

Wisconsin Evangelical Lutheran Synod: 531

Seventh-day Adventist Church: 417

Christian Churches & Churches of Christ: 380

County total: 46 congregations; 13,528 adherents

IONIA COUNTY

Catholic Church: 13,868

United Methodist Church: 1,844

Lutheran Church, Missouri Synod: 911

General Assoc. of Regular Baptist Churches: 738

Christian Reformed Church: 561

Assemblies of God: 536

County total: 63 congregations; 22,031 adherents

KALAMAZOO COUNTY

Catholic Church: 21,159

Reformed Church in America: 9,538

United Methodist Church: 7,292

Christian Reformed Church: 5,708

African-American Baptist churches (1990 est.): 6,986

Independent, non-charismatic churches: 6,350

County total: 176 congregations; 84,216 adherents

KENT COUNTY

Catholic Church: 114,716

Christian Reformed Church: 48,973

Reformed Church in America: 17,633

African-American Baptist churches (1990 est.): 14,821

General Assoc. of Regular Baptist Churches: 11,562

United Methodist Church: 10,497

County total, 442 congregations; 303,574 adherents

MECOSTA COUNTY

Catholic Church: 3,067

United Methodist Church: 1,523

Lutheran Church, Missouri Synod: 1,167

United Church of Christ: 591

Wesleyan Church: 590

County total: 52 congregations; 11,007 adherents

MONTCALM COUNTY

Catholic Church: 5,958

United Methodist Church: 1,974

Evangelical Lutheran Church in America: 1,429

Lutheran Church, Missouri Synod: 1,347

Wesleyan Church: 1,325

County total: 84 congregations; 19,636 adherents

MUSKEGON COUNTY

Catholic Church: 19,950

African-American Baptist churches (1990 est.): 7,882

Reformed Church in America: 5,435

United Methodist Church: 4,211

Evangelical Lutheran Church in America: 3,947

Lutheran Church Missouri Synod: 3,228

County total: 144 congregations; 59,533 adherents

NEWAYGO COUNTY

Catholic Church: 4,757

Christian Reformed Church: 2,438

Reformed Church in America: 1,522

United Methodist Church: 1,390

Wesleyan Church: 1,084

County total: 49 congregations; 15,805 adherents

OCEANA COUNTY

Catholic Church: 2,947

United Methodist Church: 1,079

Wesleyan Church: 854

General Assoc. of Regular Baptist Churches: 780

United Church of Christ 576

County total: 42 congregations; 8,688 adherents

OTTAWA COUNTY

Reformed Church in America: 36,461

Christian Reformed Church: 30,490

Catholic Church: 27,110

Wesleyan Church: 9,614

Lutheran Church, Missouri Synod: 6,560

County total: 208 congregations; 133,495 adherents

ST. JOSEPH COUNTY

Catholic Church: 7,379

United Methodist Church: 2,298

Lutheran Church, Missouri Synod: 2,237

Wesleyan Church: 1,210

Presbyterian Church (USA): 1,141

County total: 84 congregations; 21,549 adherents

VAN BUREN COUNTY

Catholic Church: 9,537

United Methodist Church: 2,286

Lutheran Church, Missouri Synod: 1,328

Reformed Church in America: 1,080

Seventh-day Adventist Church: 814

County total: 91 congregations; 23,509 adherents

(Data on religious denominations are from: *"Religious Congregations and Membership in the United States 2000: An Enumeration by Region, State and County Based on Data Reported by 149 Religious Bodies,"* The Glenmary Research Center, Nashville, Tenn. The data were acquired from the *American Religion Data Archive* [www.thearda.com], and are used with permission.)

WEATHER & NATURAL DISASTERS

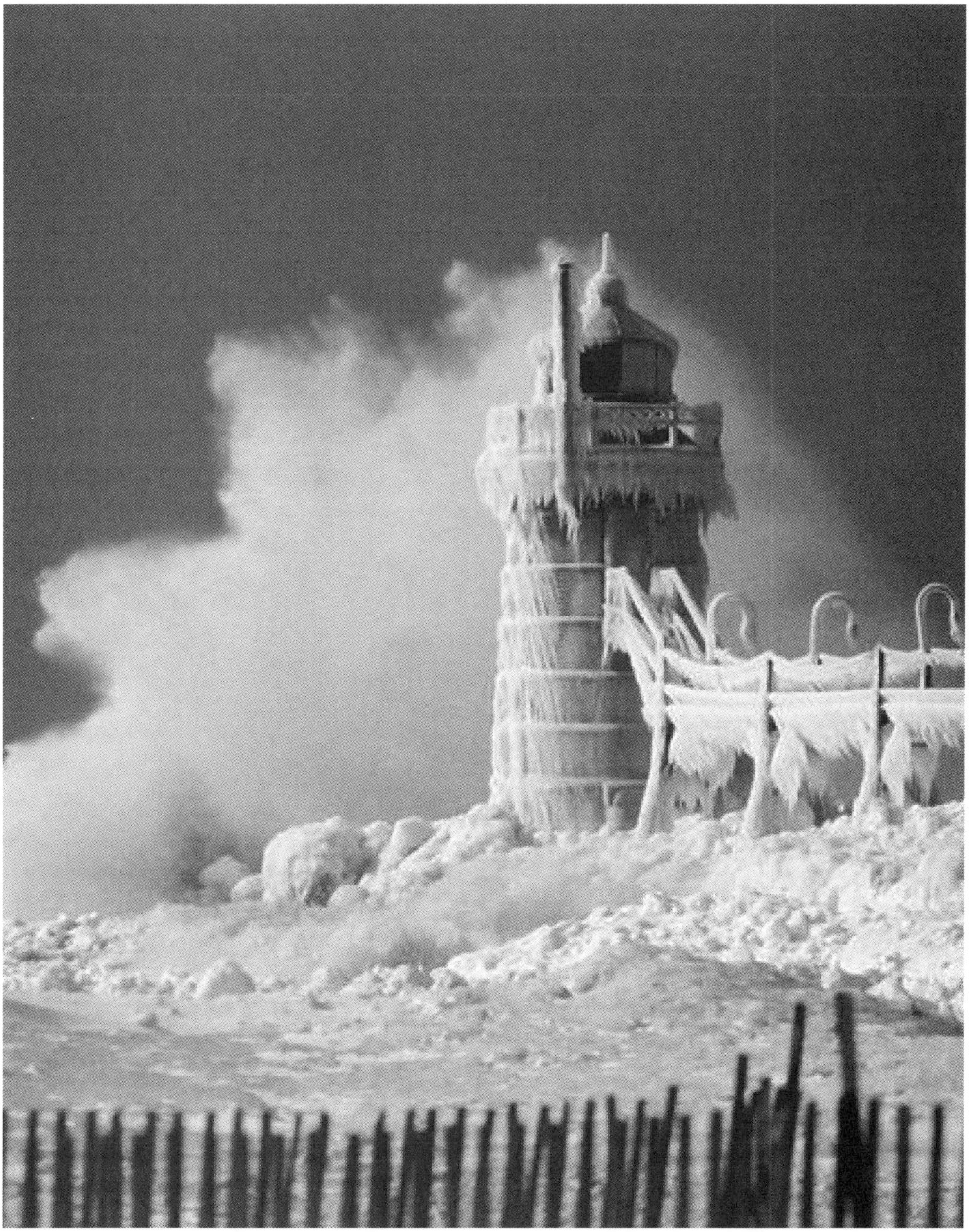

Previous page: Winter's fury batters the South Pier Light at South Haven (photo: Jennifer Giesey)

WEATHER AND NATURAL DISASTERS

Other regions of America can boast of having taller buildings, higher mountains, or better sports teams than West Michigan. But when it comes to weather, we've got them all beat. This is truly a four-season place, with summer days that can reach 100 degrees, winter nights that sometimes dip to 20-below, and spring and fall with everything in between.

We have rain, snow, ice, sleet, fog, ice-fog, black ice, Alberta clippers, lake-effect snow, tornadoes, thunderstorms (including thundersnow), and big cyclonic weather systems that pinwheel in from the southern plains.

We don't have hurricanes, thankfully, though we have felt an occasional earthquake. Weather systems from Oklahoma and from Canada show up here, after getting a special West Michigan personality on the trip across Lake Michigan.

(Michigan's official motto is "If you seek a pleasant peninsula, look around you." Our unofficial meteorological slogan is: "If you don't like the weather, wait a minute.")

The Earth Moved ...

West Michigan isn't known as a high-risk area for earthquakes, but quakes do occasionally happen close enough to be felt here.

Early settlers in Michigan felt the effects of a huge quake in 1811, centered near New Madrid, Mo. The Richter scale for measuring earthquake intensity hadn't been invented at the time, but scientists now estimate the New Madrid quake had a magnitude of 8.0 – which would make it the strongest ever reported in the United States.

The strongest quake ever reported to have occurred within Michigan was on Aug. 9, 1957, when an earthquake with a magnitude of 4.6 struck southeast of Kalamazoo.

The movement was felt as far north as Muskegon. Some homes in the area around Colon in St. Joseph County experienced broken windows, cracked plaster and chimney damage, according to the United States Geological Survey.

On occasion, West Michigan has also felt the effects of quakes that originated in nearby states or in Canada.

In 1925, a 6.7 magnitude quake centered near Quebec was felt by people in Grand Rapids. The shock waves from a 5.8 magnitude quake that hit upstate New York in September 1944 also made it here.

The most recent quake felt by a significant number of people in West Michigan was on Nov. 9, 1968, when a 5.5 magnitude seismic event was recorded in southern Illinois along the New Madrid Fault.

Proving that winter can be fun, a racer heads down the luge at Muskegon State Park (photo courtesy of David Kenyon, Michigan DNR)

SNOW

If earthquakes are a rarity, snow is an every-year occurrence in this part of the world. The average winter snowfall in West Michigan ranges from a high of about 100 inches at Muskegon to less than 50 in the area around Sturgis in St. Joseph County.

The difference is mostly due to the phenomenon of lake effect snow. Still, many of the heaviest snowfalls are associated with low-pressure systems that carry in moisture from the Great Plains or the Gulf of Mexico.

The Great Blizzard of Jan. 26, 1978 left 30 inches of snow in Muskegon and 19 inches in Grand Rapids.

That day's weather was the result of two storms that merged over the Great Lakes. The first storm, which originated over Texas and Louisiana, carried plenty of moisture. The second was a low pressure center and an arctic air mass that dropped from Canada into Northern Minnesota. When the jet stream pushed these two air masses into each other, they formed a blizzard that people still talk about nearly 30 years later.

The only comparable winter storm on record is the "White

Hurricane" of November 1913, when a similar combination of northern and southern storms created winds and snow that led to the sinking of more than a dozen ships on the Great Lakes.

Artist-enhanced radar image shows a typical West Michigan lake effect snow pattern

LAKE-EFFECT SNOW

Lake effect snow is a simple thing, really. Here's how it works:

A swatch of cold, clear air blows down from Canada, bringing starry nights and single-digit temperatures to Minnesota and Wisconsin. Prevailing westerly winds move that air out over Lake Michigan, where the surface temperature of the water may be 25 to 40 degrees warmer.

The five-degree air picks up warmth and moisture from the 35-degree water. Because warm air is lighter than cold air, it rises and, away from the warm surface of the lake, begins to cool off again. The moisture condenses as it cools and a cloud develops. Still moving east, the air mass crosses the shoreline into West Michigan. It rises and cools some more. And then it dumps eight inches of snow in your driveway.

Simple.

According to the National Oceanic and Atmospheric Administration (NOAA), a pretty specific set of circumstances are needed to create the lake effect. The cold air has to cross at least 50 miles of open water, the water should be at least 25 degrees warmer than the air, and the wind should be at least 10 miles per hour. Generally speaking, the greater the temperature difference between air and water, the more snow will result.

Occasionally, lake effect snow can blow as far inland as Ionia County, but it's usually much heavier in the counties closest to Lake Michigan. Winds from the west-northwest commonly drop their load of hexagonal crystals over Muskegon, Ottawa and Allegan counties. If the wind comes more from the north, it can direct the snow toward Benton Harbor and New Buffalo. Many a winter traveler on the way to Chicago has encountered white-out conditions on that section of I-94, even while the sun was shining five miles further inland.

Snow produced by the lake effect tends to be fluffier (less dense, in the words of meteorologists) than snow brought in by other storm systems. That's thought to be a result of the cold temperatures often associated with the lake effect.

Lake effect snow is most common in early winter, when the water in the Big Lake is still relatively warm. On those rare occasions when Lake Michigan freezes all the way across, the lake effect machine stops altogether.

Without the lake effect, West Michigan would likely get 40 to 50 inches of snow a winter, about the same as Milwaukee or Madison, Wis. Instead, Muskegon averages about 100 inches a year, Hart gets 90, Holland nearly 80 and Grand Rapids about 70.

TORNADOES

Michigan isn't part of "Tornado Alley" – that distinction applies to a broad band of the Great Plains extending from Texas to the Dakotas – but we do see enough twisters to keep the National Weather Service on guard.

Michigan has an average of 16 tornadoes per year. They usually occur in April, May, June or July, most commonly in late afternoon or early evening. Michigan's worst tornado, by far, was a 1953 storm that roared through the southeastern part of the state and killed more than 100 people in and around Flint.

West Michigan has experienced a number of devastating tornadoes over the years. Four storms stand out:

Hudsonville, April 3, 1956. The twister touched down near Saugatuck, then moved north into Ottawa and Kent counties. In all, there were 18 deaths and 340 injuries in Allegan, Ottawa, Kent and Montcalm counties. Most of the deaths were in Hudsonville, where the tornado rushed through as an F-5 monster. It is still considered the most powerful tornado ever to hit West Michigan.

Comstock Park, April 11, 1965.
A tornado that was part of what is remembered as the Palm Sunday storms killed five people in and around Comstock Park, just north of Grand Rapids, and injured a total of 142 people. Storms raged throughout the South and Midwest on that day, a week before Easter, killing 271 people and injuring 3,400 in several states.

Kalamazoo, May 18, 1980.
Five were killed and 79 injured as a tornado followed Main Street into downtown Kalamazoo, destroying part of Gilmore Brothers' Department Store. More than 1,000 homes were damaged by the storm.

Dowagiac, July 13, 1992.
A storm pushed through Cass County, injuring 25 people, including residents of a migrant farm worker camp near Dowagiac.

NUMBER OF TORNADOES, BY COUNTY, 1950-2004:

Allegan County:	24
Barry County:	17
Berrien County:	29
Cass County:	14
Ionia County:	16
Kalamazoo County:	21
Kent County:	30
Mecosta County:	9
Montcalm County:	10
Muskegon County:	7
Newaygo County:	11
Oceana County:	5
Ottawa County:	18
St. Joseph County:	9
Van Buren County:	16

TORNADO DEATHS AND INJURIES, 1950-2004

Allegan County:
34 injured, 2 killed

Barry County:
7 injured, none killed

Berrien County:
15 injured, none killed

Cass County:
25 injured, none killed

Ionia County:
7 injured, none killed

Kalamazoo County:
107 injured, 5 killed

Kent County:
310 injured, 9 killed

Mecosta County:
10 injured, none killed

Montcalm County:
6 injured, none killed

Muskegon County:
none injured, none killed

Newaygo County:
3 injured, 2 killed

Oceana County:
4 injured, none killed

Ottawa County:
201 injured, 14 killed

St. Joseph County:
none injured, none killed

Van Buren County:
26 injured, none killed

TORNADO CLASSIFICATIONS (THE FUJITA SCALE)

F-0: Winds up to 72 mph. May cause light damage such as broken tree branches or damaged chimneys.

F-1: 73-112 mph. Moderate damage. May peel shingles off roofs, overturn mobile homes or damage garages.

F-2: 113-157 mph. Significant damage. Large trees uprooted; mobile homes demolished, roofs blown off frame houses.

F-3: 158-206 mph. Severe damage. Roof and walls destroyed, cars overturned, sections of forest uprooted.

F-4: 207-260 mph. Devastating damage. Even well-constructed walls may be leveled. Houses blown off foundations.

F-5: 261 mph and more. Incredible damage. Homes may be lifted off foundations and carried considerable distances. Autos thrown as far as 100 meters.

About 90 percent of all tornadoes identified in Michigan have been of the F-0, F-1 or F-2 varieties, according to the National Oceanic and Atmospheric Administration. Since 1950, the state has seen seven F-5 tornadoes and 30 rated as F-4.

TEMPERATURE AND RAINFALL

West Michigan is only about 150 miles long, from north to south. But combine that distance with the influence of the Big Lake, and it's enough to make a huge difference in climate and growing seasons from one corner of the region to another.

The growing season in favored locations near Lake Michigan in the southern part of the region may be as much as six weeks longer than in inland counties farther north.

In Big Rapids, for example, National Weather Service records show an average of 128 days between the last

32-degree night in the spring, and the first 32-degree night in the fall.

South Haven, according to the same set of records, averages 183 days.

The records show a 50 percent probability in any given year that the last spring frost in South Haven will occur on or before April 24. For Big Rapids, the 50-percent-probability date is May 19.

Those are averages, of course. As every gardener knows, there are no guarantees when it comes to weather. To be safe, most gardeners wait several weeks past the "average" last frost to put their tender plants in the ground.

The traditional guideline of Memorial Day generally works for all but the coldest sites.

Here is a sampling of average temperature and precipitation figures for West Michigan weather stations. All are based on at least 30 years of records.

BIG RAPIDS

Median length of growing season: 128 days
Last spring frost: May 19
First autumn frost: Sept. 25

Month	Avg. High	Avg. Low	Precip.	Snowfall
January	28.9	11.4	2.17	20.6
February	32.6	12.7	1.56	13.3
March	42.4	21	2.38	9.3
April	55.8	32	2.95	2.5
May	69.3	43.1	3.2	0
June	77.7	52.1	3.23	0
July	82.1	56.8	2.68	0
August	79.3	55.1	4.24	0
September	70.9	46.3	3.88	0
October	58.6	36.3	2.96	0.4
November	44.3	27.7	2.99	6.7
December	33	17.6	2.36	17.5
Annual	56.2	34.4	34.58	70.3

GRAND RAPIDS

Median length of growing season: 156 days
Last spring frost: May 5
First autumn frost: Oct. 8

Month	Avg. High	Avg. Low	Precip.	Snowfall
January	29.4	15.6	2.03	21.2
February	32.6	17.3	1.53	11.6
March	43.2	25.6	2.59	8.2
April	56.6	35.6	3.48	2.9
May	69.7	46.3	3.35	0
June	78.6	55.7	3.67	0
July	82.6	60.5	3.56	0
August	80	59	3.78	0
September	72.1	50.9	4.28	0
October	59.9	40.1	2.8	0.5
November	45.8	31.2	3.35	7.3
December	33.9	21.4	2.7	18.9
Annual	57.1	38.2	37.12	70.7

GREENVILLE

Median length of growing season: 137 days
Last spring frost: May 15
First autumn frost: Sept. 29

Month	Avg. High	Avg. Low	Precip.	Snowfall
January	29	13.2	1.83	20
February	32.9	15.1	1.48	13.2
March	43.8	23.4	2.28	9.8
April	57.9	33.8	3	2.7
May	70.5	44.7	3.44	0
June	79.3	53.7	3.37	0
July	83.4	57.7	2.88	0
August	80.9	56.3	4.21	0
September	73	48.6	3.7	0
October	60.9	38.4	2.93	0.4
November	45.9	29.1	3.14	6.1
December	33.7	18.9	2.45	17.3
Annual	57.6	36.1	34.71	69.4

GULL LAKE (Kalamazoo County)

Median length of growing season: 160 days
Last spring frost: May 4
First autumn frost: Oct. 11

Month	Avg. High	Avg. Low	Precip.	Snowfall
January	31.3	15.8	2.15	18
February	35.4	17.4	1.77	11.2
March	46.5	26.1	2.66	5.5
April	59.5	36.4	3.82	1.4
May	72	47.3	3.49	0
June	80.8	56.7	3.86	0
July	84.5	61.3	3.69	0
August	82.2	60	3.93	0
September	74.9	52.5	4.25	0
October	62.8	41.9	3.1	0.4
November	48.2	32.4	3.37	5
December	35.8	21.9	2.98	17.1
Annual	59.5	39.1	39.05	59.7

HART

Median length of growing season: 148 days
Last spring frost: May 12
First autumn frost: Oct. 8

Month	Avg. High	Avg. Low	Precip.	Snowfall
January	28.9	15.4	2.57	31
February	31.9	16.3	1.73	18.7
March	41.3	23.8	2.4	8.5
April	54	34	2.86	2.1
May	67.1	43.9	3.04	0
June	75.6	53.5	3.29	0
July	80.2	58.2	2.85	0
August	77.8	57.5	4.09	0
September	70.2	49.9	3.86	0
October	58.2	39.9	3.56	0.2
November	44.9	30.8	3.29	6.3
December	33.6	21.4	2.65	24
Annual	55.3	37.1	36.19	90.9

HOLLAND

Median length of growing season: 154 days
Last spring frost: May 8
First autumn frost: Oct. 10

Month	Avg. High	Avg. Low	Precip.	Snowfall
January	31.5	17.6	2.27	27.5
February	35.1	19.1	1.48	15.5
March	45.2	26.6	2.07	6.1
April	57.2	36	3.17	1.7
May	69.6	46.2	3.43	0
June	78.8	55.1	3.57	0
July	82.8	60	3.58	0
August	81	59	3.75	0
September	73.4	51.7	4	0
October	61.1	41.5	2.94	0.3
November	47.8	32.6	3.36	5.6
December	36.2	22.9	2.87	21.3
Annual	58.3	39	36.49	78.1

MUSKEGON

Median length of growing season: 156 days
Last spring frost: May 6
First autumn frost: Oct. 9

Month	Avg. High	Avg. Low	Precip.	Snowfall
January	29.4	17.5	2.22	31.5
February	32.1	18.6	1.58	17.2
March	42.2	25.8	2.36	9.6
April	54.6	35.4	2.9	2.8
May	67	45.5	2.95	0
June	75.7	54.6	2.58	0
July	80.2	60.2	2.32	0
August	78.3	59.2	3.77	0
September	70.5	51.2	3.52	0
October	58.6	41.1	2.8	0.5
November	45.4	32.3	3.23	8.1
December	34.3	23.1	2.64	27.3
Annual	55.7	38.7	32.87	97

SOUTH HAVEN

Median length of growing season: 183 days
Last spring frost: April 24
First autumn frost: Oct. 24

Month	Avg. High	Avg. Low	Precip.	Snowfall
January	31.7	19	2.21	22.4
February	34.4	21.1	1.62	13.2
March	44.2	28.7	2.19	5.3
April	54.8	37.6	3.22	1.1
May	65.7	47.4	3.09	0
June	74.9	56.9	3.32	0
July	79.2	62.5	3.59	0
August	78.3	61.9	3.64	0
September	72.1	54.7	4.05	0
October	61.4	44.7	2.85	0.2
November	48.1	34.6	3.34	3.1
December	36.8	24.9	2.81	21.6
Annual	56.8	41.2	35.82	66.8

THREE RIVERS

Median length of growing season: 153 days
Last spring frost: May 4
First autumn frost: Oct. 5

Month	Avg. High	Avg. Low	Precip.	Snowfall
January	31.2	15.3	1.97	11.8
February	35.4	17.5	1.63	8.2
March	46.6	26.5	2.61	5.5
April	59.3	36.1	3.33	1.5
May	71.6	46.7	3.67	0
June	80.7	56.1	3.75	0
July	84.1	60	3.94	0
August	81.8	58.1	3.83	0
September	74.8	50.4	3.66	0
October	62.7	39.6	3	0.5
November	48.3	31	2.96	3.9
December	36	21	2.61	11.1
Annual	59.4	38.2	36.96	42.5

CULTURE

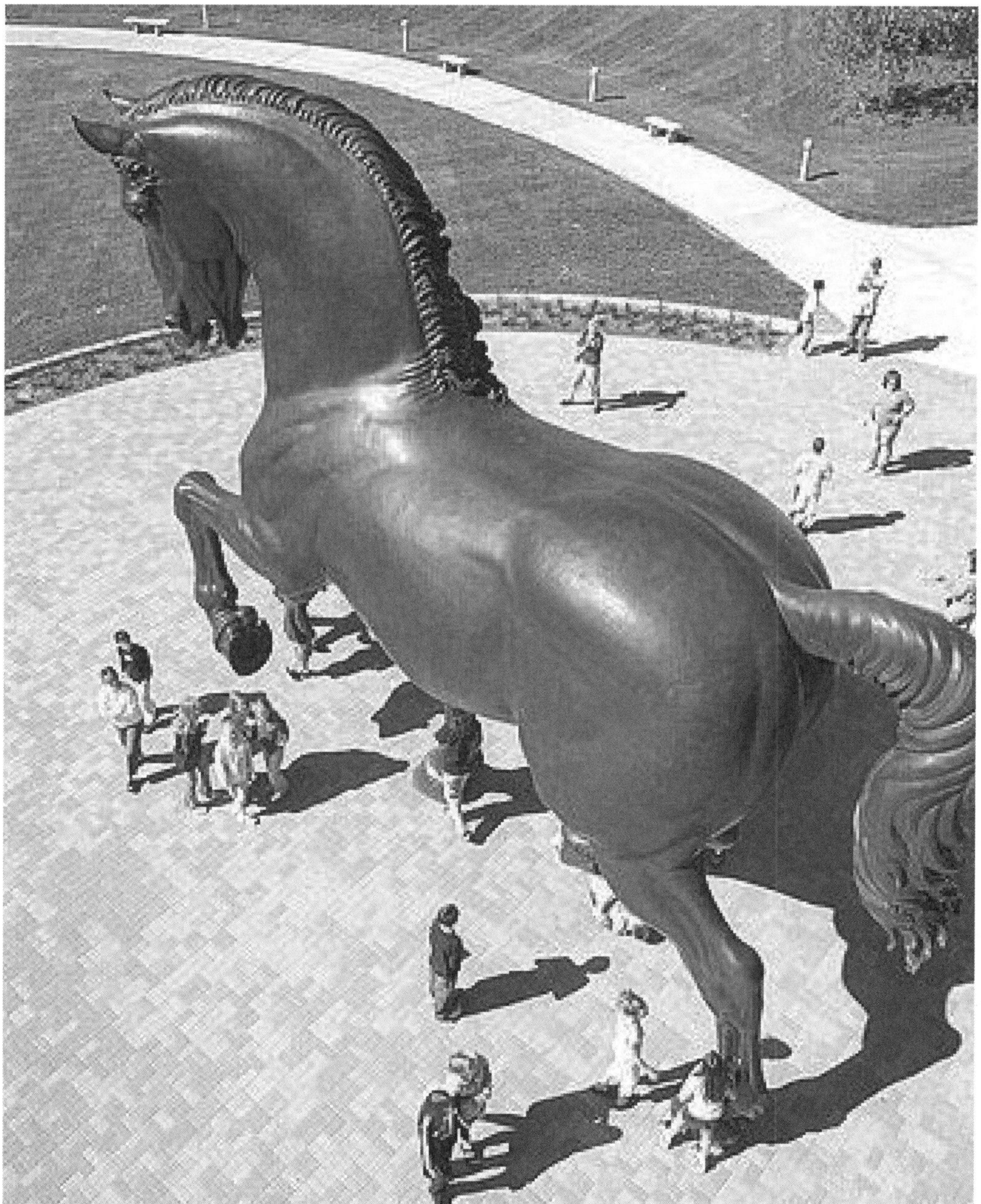

Previous page: The American Horse towers over visitors at Meijer Gardens in Grand Rapids (photo courtesy of Frederick Meijer Gardens)

CULTURE

Culture is that intangible something that unites – and sometimes divides – human populations. In that sense, it's probably stored deep within all of us. We can also gain a better understanding of our culture through local architecture, museums, art galleries, theaters and other institutions that reflect the lives and attitudes of the people who live here.

West Michigan has no shortage of these institutions. Some, like the spectacular Frederick Meijer Gardens and Sculpture Park in Grand Rapids, are easy to identify as "cultural experiences." Others, the Kalamazoo Nature Center, for example, may seem at first to be something else – perhaps recreation or nature study. But in a region only a few generations removed from the "natural" world that existed before logging and industrialization, the story of nature is an integral part of our culture.

Here is a look at some of the sites where West Michigan culture is recorded and shared.

GERALD R. FORD MUSEUM

The presidential museum opened in 1981 on the west bank of the Grand River, facing the Amway Grand Plaza Hotel and Grand Rapids' convention center. The museum's permanent

A sculpture and fountain grace the entry to the Gerald R. Ford Museum (photo courtesy of Gerald R. Ford Museum)

exhibits focus on the life and times of Gerald Ford, the Grand Rapids man who served in the nation's highest office from 1974-77. A full-size replica of the Oval Office is included, as well as such artifacts as Richard Nixon's letter of resignation. The galleries also have space for traveling exhibits from the National Archives. The Ford Museum is a triangular building with a wall of windows that look out over a fountain and reflecting pool, a riverfront park, and the Grand Rapids skyline. A fenced grotto on the museum grounds is reserved as a burial site for the former president and Mrs. Ford.

For more information, call (616) 254-0400, or visit www.fordlibrarymuseum.gov on the Internet.

THE GILMORE CAR MUSEUM

The Gilmore Car Museum has been a top attraction for automotive enthusiasts since it opened in 1966 on 90 acres of farmland near Hickory Corners in Barry County. Today, the site houses about 200 cars, in historic red barns clustered on the landscaped grounds. The museum has three miles of road, a 1930's service station, a train depot and cars dating from the 1899 Locomobile up through modern muscle cars. The Classic Car Club of America, the Pierce-Arrow Foundation and the Tucker Historical Collection are all housed on the site as partners with the Gilmore Museum.

The site is open from May through October. In addition to the permanent collection, the Gilmore hosts a number of car shows and other events through the summer.

For more information, call (269) 671-5089, or visit www.gilmorecarmuseum.org on the Internet.

KALAMAZOO NATURE CENTER

The Kalamazoo Nature Center, at 7000 N. Westnedge Avenue, is known to bird-lovers as one of the best nature-interpretive sites in the Midwest. The main site covers more than 1,100 acres of forest, fen and prairie.

The center includes an 11-acre arboretum, along with an interpretive center that encircles a tropical rainforest inside a three-story atrium. Also on the site is the 1858 DeLano homestead, which is open for special events.

The nature center also preserves natural features on nearly 3,000 acres at other sites, making it the largest nature center in the Midwest, in terms of land base. The center, founded in 1960, has an extensive education and outreach program that includes summer camps, classroom activities and a maple syrup festival.

For more information, call (269) 381-1574 or visit www.naturecenter.org on the Internet.

FREDERICK MEIJER GARDENS AND SCULPTURE PARK

Though it's among the youngest of West Michigan's cultural attractions, Meijer Gardens has quickly moved to the top of the list. The facility opened in 1995 through donations from the owner of the Meijer retail chain, in partnership with the Grand Rapids Horticultural Society. The 125-acre site includes wetlands, gardens, a concert venue, nature trails, the state's largest tropical conservatory, and a sculpture collection that has gained wide acclaim. The site was visited by 600,000 people in 2005. The park's major sponsor, Frederick Meijer, gained international attention in the 1990s with his support for a project to sculpt a 24-foot-tall bronze horse, based on the notes of Leonardo DaVinci. The American Horse in now among more than 160 pieces of sculpture permanently installed in indoor and outdoor settings. Included are works by Rodin, Oldenburg, Degas, DiSuvero and other prominent artists.

The Lena Meijer Conservatory at Meijer Gardens is the largest such facility in the state (photo courtesy of Frederick Meijer Gardens)

For more information, call (888) 957-1580 or visit www.meijergardens.org on the Internet.

Richard Hunt's sculpture, "And You Seas," stands near the mouth of the St. Joseph River (photo: Ed Hoogterp)

THE KRASL ART CENTER

The Krasl, on a bluff in St. Joseph, overlooking Lake Michigan, has a permanent sculpture collection that's exhibited at the gallery and other sites around Southwest Michigan. One of its best known pieces is "And You Seas," a monumental stainless steel sculpture by Richard Hunt, which is permanently installed near the mouth of the St. Joseph River in Silver Beach Park. In addition to its own sculpture collection, Krasl has four interior galleries that host a continuing series of traveling exhibitions. The temporary exhibitions include paintings, photography, folk arts and other media, often from such institutions as the Smithsonian and the Detroit Institute of Arts. The Krasl Art Fair on the Bluff, held each July, has been rated as one of America's top 100 fine art and craft fairs.

For more information, call (269) 983-0271 or visit www.krasl.org on the Internet.

DOWNTOWN MUSKEGON CULTURAL ATTRACTIONS

Muskegon's downtown has lost most of its retail business and is in the process of rebuilding, but it has retained a lively cultural center that includes museums, historic sites and performance spaces in the Frauenthal Center and L.C. Walker Arena. The main Muskegon County Museum features local history exhibits and a research archive with a huge collection of photography. The museum also operates a historic fire barn and the Hackley-Hume historic site, which includes two of the best preserved mansions from the late 19th century period when the city was awash in money from a lumber boom. The collection at the Muskegon Museum of Art, also downtown, includes works by such icons as Edward Hopper and Winslow Homer.

For more information on the art museum, call (231) 720-2570 or visit www.muskegonartmuseum.org on the Internet. For the County Museum, call (231) 722-0278 or visit www.muskegonmuseum.org on the Internet.

PUBLIC MUSEUM OF GRAND RAPIDS

The Grand Rapids museum dates its origin to 1854. Today it includes the VanAndel Museum Center downtown, the Norton Mounds historic landmark, and the Voight House, a well-preserved Victorian mansion in the Heritage Hill district.

The VanAndel Museum Center is a $42 million facility that opened in 1994 on the West Bank of the Grand River. It features a range of permanent exhibits on such themes as the city's furniture industry and the historic groups of people who have lived in the Grand River Valley. There's also a huge skeleton of a finback whale. The center also houses the Roger B. Chaffee Planetarium and a 1928 Spillman Carousel in a circular gallery that extends out over the river.

For more information call (616) 456-3977 or visit www.grmuseum.org on the Internet.

GRAND RAPIDS ART MUSEUM

Architect's rendering shows façade of Grand Rapid Art Museum, slated to open in 2007 (photo courtesy of Grand Rapids Art Museum)

After almost a century in buildings designed for other uses – including a former house and a former post office – the Grand Rapids Art Museum is getting a $55 million home of its own.

Construction began in 2005 on the 125,000 square foot museum on Monroe Center, adjacent to the downtown green space of Rosa Parks Circle. The new facility is expected to open in 2007. The art museum's permanent collection has more than 6,000 items including photography, prints, paintings, sculpture, crafts and furniture pieces.

For more information, call (616) 831-1000 or visit www.gramonline.org on the Internet.

DOWNTOWN KALAMAZOO CULTURAL ATTRACTIONS

Downtown Kalamazoo has a popular concert venue in the State Theater, a community theater organization in the Kalamazoo Civic Theater, an art museum and a historical museum, all within a few blocks.

The Kalamazoo Valley Museum is housed in a $20 million building that opened in 1996, following a public fund-raising campaign. The museum, at the head of the Kalamazoo Mall, is run as an arm of Kalamazoo Valley Community College. It includes historical exhibits, a planetarium and the Mary Jane Stryker Theater, which shows classic and independent films and also hosts musical performances and other public events. The museum also has a host of hands-on exhibits to help young people understand the Kalamazoo Valley region.

Kirk Newman's 1974 sculpture "People" welcomes visitors to the Kalamazoo Institute of Art (photo: Ed Hoogterp)

The Kalamazoo Institute of Arts, in an award-winning building across from Bronson Park, has a collection of 4,000 objects, including paintings, photos and sculpture.

For more information on the Kalamazoo Valley Museum, call (800) 772-3370 or visit www.kalamazoomuseum.org on the Internet. For the art institute, call (269) 349-7775 or visit www.kiarts.org on the Internet.

KALAMAZOO AIR ZOO

The Kalamazoo Air Zoo is an aviation and aerospace museum with more than 50 aircraft on display, including an F-14, F-18 and SR-71 Blackbird spy plane. The Air Zoo is on Portage Road in Kalamazoo, adjacent to the Kalamazoo - Battle Creek

International Airport. In addition to the aircraft displays, the Air Zoo offers visitors a chance to try out four separate full-motion flight simulators. Sometime in 2007 the Air Zoo hopes to open a new "Michigan Space and Science Center" which would display an 83-foot redstone rocket, moon rocks, and other items previously housed at the Michigan Space Center in Jackson.

For more information, call (866) 524-7966 or visit www.airzoo.org on the Internet.

OUR LONE AMUSEMENT PARK

Michigan's Adventure Amusement Park, near Muskegon, is the state's largest amusement and water park. It's also one of West Michigan's top tourist attractions.

The park opened in 1956 as Deer Park, and soon began adding small carnival-style rides. Today, it has more than 60 rides, including a popular wooden roller coaster named "Shivering Timbers," and a 1,500 foot water ride called "Grand Rapids" that was new in 2006.

Since 2001, the park has been owned by Cedar Fair L.P., the company that owns the Cedar Point amusement park in Ohio. Michigan's Adventure is open from Memorial Day through Labor Day weekend.

For information, call 231-766-3377 or visit www.michigansadventure.com on the Internet.

WEST MICHIGAN MUSEUMS AND HISTORICAL SOCIETIES:

Ada – The Averill Historical Museum, operated by the Ada Historical Society, includes photographs and local artifacts relating to the community and its first settler, Rix Robinson. In summer and fall, the museum grounds are the site of a farmers market. It is open on weekends. For more information, call (616) 676-9346.

Allegan – The Allegan County Historical Society operates two sites. The Old Jail Museum in Allegan features period rooms and other artifacts in a former Allegan County Jail building. It's open Fridays and Saturdays in summer, or by appointment. The Pioneer Village on the Allegan County Fairgrounds includes nine restored buildings and a large collection of 19th century farm and home memorabilia. It's open during the county fair, which begins the weekend following Labor Day. For more information, call (269) 673-8292.

Alto – The Bowne Township Historical Society maintains a local history collection in the Bowne Township Historical Museum in Alto and at the one-room Bowne Center School. The buildings are open from 2-4 p.m. on the first Sundays of June, July, August and September, or by appointment. For more information, write to P.O. Box 36, Alto, MI 49302, or visit www.bownehistory.org on the Internet.

South Haven – The Michigan Flywheelers Museum is an organization dedicated to the preservation of antique tractors, gasoline engines and steam engines. The group's 80-acre property near South Haven is open weekends in the summer. It hosts one of the state's largest antique tractor shows each September. For more information visit www.michiganflywheelers.org on the Internet.

Barryton – The Barryton Area Museum includes a one-room schoolhouse and attached museum. The collection includes photographs and items associated with local history. It's open Saturday afternoons in the summer only.

Belding – The Belding Museum collects historical materials from the Belding area. Much of the focus is on the period of the local silk industry, from 1880-1935. The museum is open on the first Sunday afternoon of each month. For more information, write to the museum at PO Box 45, Belding, MI 48809.

Benton Harbor – The Morton House Museum, in an 1849 home that is the city's oldest dwelling, includes rooms furnished as in the period when four generations of the pioneer Morton family lived there. The home is open for tours from April through

October at 1-4 p.m. on Thursdays and 2-4 p.m. on Sundays. For more information call the museum at (269) 925-7011.

Benton Harbor – One of the region's more interesting historical sites is Mary's City of David, a religious community dating to 1903. The site's museum is open 1-5 p.m. on Saturdays and Sundays from June through September. Tours of the site begin at 1:30 p.m. on those days. For more information call (269) 925-1601 or visit www.maryscityofdavid.org on the Internet.

Berrien Springs – The 1839 Berrien County Courthouse Museum is the oldest surviving county courthouse in Michigan. It stands with other historic buildings on a pubic square that is said to be the Midwest's best preserved mid-19th century governmental complex. The museum and grounds are open Tuesday through Friday most of the year and also on weekends in summer. For more information, call (269) 471-1202, or visit www.berrienhistory.org on the Internet.

Berrien Springs – The Horn Archeological Museum, at Andrews University has an extensive collection of artifacts from archeological expeditions in the Middle East. Included are thousands of clay tablets with cuneiform writing dating back as far as 4,000 years ago. The museum is normally open to the public, but was closed for renovation in 2005. For more information, call (269) 471-3273, or visit www.andrews.edu/ARCHEOLOGY on the Internet.

Big Rapids – The Jim Crow Museum of Racist Memorabilia at Ferris State University is designed to "Promote the examination of historical and contemporary expressions of racism." The one-room museum displays advertisements, cartoons, caricatures and other examples of racist attitudes. It is open by appointment only. For more information, visit www.ferris.edu/jimcrow on the Internet.

Big Rapids – The Mecosta County Historical Museum in Big Rapids displays a local history collection and archives. For more information, write to the museum at: 129 S. Stewart Ave, P.O. Box 613, Big Rapids, MI 49307.

Buchanan – Pears Flour and Grist Mill is a historic water-powered mill, built in 1857 and restored to working order. The mill building is the centerpiece of a gathering place and community green in downtown Buchanan. The mill is normally open on summer weekend afternoons. For more information, call (269) 695-2057.

Caledonia – The Caledonia Historical Society maintains a museum and history room in the Caledonia branch of the Kent County District Library. The historical collection may be seen during regular library hours. For more information, call (616) 891-1502.

Cannonsburg – The Cannon Township Historical Museum, in a storefront in Cannonsburg, includes a local history collection. It's open from 2-4 p.m. on Sundays from May through September. For more information, call (616) 874-6865.

White Pigeon – The 1831 Land Office Museum, in one of West Michigan's oldest surviving buildings, is maintained by the St. Joseph County Historical Society, which is based in Centreville. The building is open by appointment only.

Coloma – The North Berrien Historical Society Museum preserves the history of the Paw Paw Lakes area, including Coloma, Watervliet and surrounding townships. The five-building complex is open from May through October, 1-4 p.m., on Wednesdays, Saturdays and Sundays. For more information, call (269) 468-3330, or visit www.northberrienhistory.org on the Internet.

Comstock Park – The Alpine Historical Commission, appointed by the Alpine Township board, oversees a local history museum in the original township hall, constructed in 1860. The building is open the third Sunday of each month from 2-5 p.m.

Constantine – The Gov. John S. Barry Historical Society operates a local history museum in the historic home of John S. Barry, a Constantine store owner who, in 1842, became Michigan's fourth governor. The building is thought to be the oldest frame structure in Constantine. It is open to the public on special occasions, or by appointment. For more information, write to the John S. Barry Historical Society, P.O. Box 68, Constantine, MI 49042.

Coopersville – The Coopersville Farm Museum, near the city's downtown, is built around the John Deere collection of a local resident. The museum regularly changes its agriculture-related exhibits, showing both old and new equipment. The farm museum is open year-round, but hours vary by season. For more information, call (616) 997-8555 or visit www.coopersvillefarmmuseum.org on the Internet.

Coopersville – The Coopersville Historical Museum in downtown Coopersville features a wide range of local artifacts. One room focuses on Del Shannon, the Rock and Roll Hall of Fame inductee who grew up here as Charles Westover. For more information, call (616) 837-6978, or visit www.coopersville.com/museum on the Internet.

Delton – The Bernard Historical Museum consists of seven buildings – including one that served as a doctor's office and hospital for the museum's founder – on a scenic site overlooking Crooked Lake. The museum has a collection of some 25,000 artifacts. The Bernard Museum is open daily in July and August, and on Sundays only in June and September. For more information, call (269) 623-3565 or visit www.delton-mi.com/bernard on the Internet.

Douglas – The Saugatuck-Douglas Historical Society creates a new local history exhibit each year for its Pump House Museum. The displays usually live up to the community's reputation as one of the most creative places in Michigan. The facility is open daily, noon to 4 p.m., from Memorial Day through Labor Day, and on Sundays in September and October. For more information call (269) 857-7900.

Dowagiac –The Museum at Southwestern Michigan College exhibits such locally made products as Round Oak stoves, Heddon fishing lures and a 1908 Lindsley automobile as part of a collection of more than 17,000 artifacts. The museum is open Tuesday-Saturday, 10 a.m. to 5 p.m. For more information, call (800) 456-8675, or visit www.swmich.edu/museum on the Internet.

Dowagiac – The Heddon Museum, operated by Don and Joan Lyons as a labor of love, contains more than 1,000 fishing lures and other items. Most of the material is associated with the Heddon Company, a Dowagiac firm founded by James Heddon, who is credited with inventing the artificial fishing lure. The museum is in the original Heddon factory building, which now serves as headquarters for the Lyons' plumbing business. The museum is open Tuesday evenings, 6:30-8:30 p.m., and the last Sunday of each month from 1:30-4 p.m. or by appointment. For information, call (269) 782-4068.

Edmore – The Old Fence Rider's Historical Center is a project of local resident Carm Drain. It's a western-heritage museum with exhibits that include historical flags, Civil War memorabilia and antique barbed-wire fencing, along with other details of America's westward expansion. For information, call (989) 427-5222.

Edwardsburg – The Edwardsburg Museum is housed in two 1860-era buildings that were once part of a hotel. On exhibit are materials of significance to Edwardsburg and the surrounding area. An addition to the current space is under construction. The museum has been open Wednesday through Saturday from 10 a.m. to noon, and Sunday from 2-4 p.m. For more information, write to P.O. Box 694, Edwardsburg, MI 49112.

Grand Haven – The Tri-cities Historical Museum, in an 1870 train depot and 1871 storefront near downtown Grand Haven, tells the story of the history of Grand Haven, Spring Lake and Ferrysburg. On permanent exhibit is a 400-ton steam locomotive, the Pere Marquette 1223, that was on display at the Michigan State Fairgrounds in the 1960s and 70s. Additional displays focus on fur trading, lumbering, shipping and other aspects of local history. The museum is open year-round, from Tuesday through Sunday. For more information, call (616) 842-0700 or visit www.tricitiesmuseum.org on the Internet.

Grand Rapids – The Gaines Township Historical Society oversees a historical collection at the Township Library, and the restored 120-year-old DeTray schoolhouse, which contains school historical materials and other historical archives.

Grandville – The Grandville Historical Commission operates a small local history museum on the lower level of Grandville City Hall. The museum is open the first Thursday of each month, from 1-4 p.m. The commission also oversees a restored one-room schoolhouse in the city's Heritage Park. For more information, write to Grandville Historical Commission, 3195 Wilson Ave, Grandville, MI 49418.

Greenville – The Flat River Historical Museum is located on the site where Greenville founder John Green built a home, dam and sawmill on the Flat River in 1844. The two museum buildings have a large collection of lumber-era implements, industrial products, Native American artifacts and other items of local historical interest. A recent, somewhat bittersweet, addition is the last appliance made by Electrolux at Greenville's former Gibson refrigerator plant, which closed in 2006, putting some 2,700 people out of work. The museum is open Saturday and Sunday, 2-4:30 p.m. For more information, call (616) 754-5296, or visit www.flatriverhistoricalsociety.org on the Internet.

Hart –The Oceana County Historical and Genealogical Society has its headquarters in the historic Chadwick-Munger house, a cut-fieldstone dwelling in downtown Hart. The all-volunteer association also operates the Oceana County Historical Park in Mears, which includes the home of the late newspaper publisher Swift Lathers. The Historical Park is open on weekend afternoons in the summer. The headquarters building is staffed each Wednesday from 10 a.m. to 5 p.m. For more information, call (231) 873-2600, or visit www.oceanahistory.org on the Internet.

Hartford – The Van Buren County Museum on Red Arrow Highway is housed in an 1884 building that once served as the county poorhouse. In addition to the three floors of artifacts in the impressive brick building, the museum contains a replica of a log cabin. The museum is open Wednesday and Saturday from 10 a.m. to 4 p.m., and Sunday from 1-5 p.m. For more information, call (269) 621-2188.

Hastings – Historic Charlton Park, on the Thornapple River near Hastings, is among Michigan's most popular historical village museums. The village consists of 25 historic homes and other buildings moved here from throughout Barry County. The village, owned by Barry County, is open daily, 9 a.m. to 5 p.m., from Memorial Day through Labor Day. A beach and other portions of the park outside the historic village are open year round, weather permitting. For more information, call (269) 945-3775 or visit www.charltonpark.org on the Internet.

Holland – The Holland Museum encompasses three sites that tell the story of the town, and of the Dutch and other ethnic groups that call it home. The main museum includes displays on such topics as the arrival of the Dutch colonists in 1847 and the devastating fire that destroyed most of the town in 1871. The Cappon House, built in 1874, details the lives of a family that struggled before attaining considerable wealth. The nearby Settlers House provides an example of the simpler life led by working-class residents in the late 1800s. For more information, call (888) 200-9123 or visit www.hollandmuseum.org on the Internet.

Holland – Windmill Island, a 36-acre island where the Black River enters Lake Macatawa, is home to the 240-year-old DeZwaan windmill that was dismantled and brought here from the Netherlands in 1965. The working windmill is surrounded by parkland and flowers, along with a museum, gift shop and other structures. In summer, visitors can tour the 85-foot-tall windmill and – if there's enough wind – watch operators grind grain into flour. The windmill hasn't become a major tourist attraction, as town fathers hoped in the 1960s. But it has become a local landmark and, for those with the inclination to pay the admission fee to visit the island, it's an interesting stop. For more information, visit www.cityofholland.com on the Internet.

Ionia – The Ionia County Historical Society maintains a museum inside the historic John C. Blanchard house in Ionia. The house itself, built of locally fired brick and faced with Ionia sandstone, is well worth a look. The rooms include Victorian era furnishings. The Ionia Historical Museum, in the basement, has exhibits on local history. For more information: write to P.O. Box 1776, Ionia, MI 48846, or visit www.ioniahistory.org on the Internet.

Jenison – The Jenison Historical Association and Museum operates the Jenison Museum in a historic home in Ottawa County's Georgetown Township. The facility holds an open house the third Saturday of each month, March through October. The building features 1900-era furnishings and local history displays. For information, write to the historical society at PO Box 664, Jenison, MI 49428.

Lowell – The Lowell Area Historical Museum, in a historic 1873 home on Main Street has been described as one of America's best small-town museums. It includes exhibits on the community's history, agriculture and industry, as well as Victorian furnishings and gardens. There's also a gallery on the history of the Lowell Showboat. The building is open Tuesday, Thursday, Saturday and Sunday afternoons, year-round. For more information call (616) 897-7688 or visit www.lowellmuseum.org on the Internet.

Middleville – Historic Bowens Mills is a privately owned historical attraction in Barry County's Yankee Springs Township. The site has been used as a sawmill and grist mill since the 1830s. It's open Tuesday through Saturday afternoons, from Memorial Day through Christmas. For more information visit www.bowensmills.com on the Internet.

Sidney – Montcalm County Heritage Village was a project for the Michigan Sesquicentennial in 1987. The site, on the campus of Montcalm Community College, has a number of historic buildings moved from other locations in the county. Included are a log cabin, and a train depot, complete with a huge locomotive. An annual Heritage Village celebration is held in August. For more information, call (989) 328-2111 or visit www.montcalm.org on the Internet.

Niles – The Fort St. Joseph Museum houses local history and Native American artifacts in the former carriage house of the Chapin Mansion. The mansion itself now serves as Niles City Hall. The museum, located behind City Hall, has a much larger collection than those found in most small cities. That's not surprising, since the Niles area has a rich history dating back to the establishment of a mission and fort in the late 1600s. For more information, call (269) 683-4702.

Otsego – The Otsego Area Historical Society operates a local history museum, which opened in 1994 in a restored waterworks building. The building is open Saturday afternoons. For more information call (269) 692-3775 or visit www.otsegohistory.org on the Internet.

Portage – The Celery Flats Interpretive Center is part of the Portage city park system. It tells the story of farming in the Kalamazoo area – and much more. The center includes an 1856 one-room schoolhouse, a 1931 grain elevator, a historic home and the Hayloft Theatre, which is active in summer. For more information call (269) 329-4522.

St. Joseph – The Fort Miami Heritage Society of Michigan operates a museum and community center in a restored historic church building. A major exhibit on the region's fruit-growing industry opened in 2005, and other exhibits are also on display in the society's Priscilla U. Byrns Heritage Center. (Fort Miami was the name given by French explorer Robert de La Salle to a temporary garrison he established in 1679 at the present site of St. Joseph.) The exhibits are open Tuesday through Saturday year-round, and also on Sunday in summer months. For more information call (269) 983-1191 or visit www.fortmiami.org on the Internet.

South Haven – The Liberty Hyde Bailey Museum is in the 1857 farmhouse that was the birthplace of famed horticulturalist Liberty Hyde Bailey. The museum includes artifacts from the Bailey family as well as other items relating to local history. The home is the oldest in South Haven. The museum and gardens are open Thursday through Monday afternoons most of the year. It's open only on weekends in January and February. For more information call (269) 637-3251, or visit http//lhbm.south-haven.com on the Internet.

Vicksburg — The Vicksburg Historical Society operates a local history museum in the former Grand Trunk Railroad Depot. The building houses more than 10,000 artifacts. Also on the grounds are several historic buildings that were moved to the site. The museum hours vary during the year. For more information call (269) 649-1733.

Zeeland – The Dekker Huis Museum, operated by the Zeeland Historical Society, is in an adjoining house and storefront formerly owned by Dirk Dekker. The buildings, dating from 1876, house artifacts from the local community and from the province of Zeeland in the Netherlands. The building is open on Saturdays in the winter and Thursday and Saturday in spring and summer. For more information, call (616) 772-4079.

ARCHITECTURE

West Michigan is filled with architectural wonders. From our early history we have a few surviving log cabins and frame structures such as the White Pigeon Land Office, built about 1830, or the Calkins Law Office in Grand Rapids, which dates from about 1835.

A number of towns have churches and commercial blocks dating from the time of the Civil War or before. Then, there are the fabulous Queen Anne style homes built for the emerging upper class in the late 19th century. The 20th century brought new designs in steel and masonry.

Choosing the best from all those structures is a nearly impossible task that involves subjective judgments. Fortunately, the Michigan Society of Architects has already done most of the work. In 1980, the society compiled a list of the 50 most significant structures in the state. The list includes several West Michigan structures, along with such state-recognized icons as the Mackinac Bridge, the Grand Hotel on Mackinac Island and the Renaissance Center in Detroit.

Here are 10 West Michigan examples of great architecture, drawing on the expertise of the architectural society and the 1993 book *Buildings of Michigan,* by Kathryn Eckert.

Architect Frank Lloyd Wright and his wife, Olgivanna, visit the Meyer May house in 1949 (photo courtesy of Grand Rapids Public Library)

Meyer May House (1909) – This home in Grand Rapids' Heritage Hill district is one of several Frank Lloyd Wright designs in West Michigan. Others include the "Usonian" designs in Kalamazoo's Parkwyn Village. The May house stands out because of the impeccable restoration – right down to recreating the furniture specified by Wright – funded by Steelcase Corp. It's one of only two Prairie-style Wright homes in Michigan, according to architectural historian Kathryn Eckert. The house is open for public tours at specified times.

Grand River Fish Ladder (1975) – This functional concrete sculpture made the Michigan Society of Architects' list of the 50 most significant structures in the state. The functional part is a series of baffles that allow fish, especially migrating salmon and steelhead, to pass the Fourth Street Dam in downtown Grand Rapids. The design, by Joseph Kinnebrew, allows visitors to view the river, the migrating fish and the city's skyline.

The 1892 Niles train depot is still in use as an Amtrak station (photo: Ed Hoogterp)

Niles Train Depot (1892) – The Richardsonian Romanesque building, with its 65-foot-tall clock tower, was completed as a showpiece for passengers traveling on the Michigan Central Railroad to the Chicago World Columbian Exposition in 1893. The brown sandstone depot has been employed several times as a movie backdrop. It's still in use on the Amtrak line between Detroit and Chicago. In summer it's surrounded by gardens.

Amariah T. Prouty House (1852) – This wood-framed Kalamazoo dwelling is built in a gothic-revival style. Its unique scrollwork is one of the features that raise it "far above the typical house of the same general style" according to the Michigan Society of Architects. The architects group named it in 1980 as one of Michigan's 50 most significant buildings.

Michigan architects named the Prouty House in Kalamazoo as one of Michigan's most distinctive homes (photo: Ed Hoogterp)

Kalamazoo Institute of Arts (1961) – The art institute building, on the fringe of Bronson Park in downtown Kalamazoo, was on the list of the state's 50 most significant structures compiled by the Michigan Society of Architects. Kathryn Eckert referred to Bronson Park as "Michigan's finest civic square." The architectural society called the art institute "one of the finest facilities in the state," and said the building is "a symbol of a city which cares very much about its role as a city of art."

Kalamazoo State Hospital Water Tower (1895) – This 175-foot tall brick structure is a Kalamazoo landmark, appearing as a castle tower overlooking the grounds of the state psychiatric hospital. State officials planned to demolish the tower in 1974, along with some other structures on the aging psychiatric facility. But local residents objected and raised money to preserve the tower, which is visible from much of the city.

The state hospital water tower is visible from much of Kalamazoo (photo: Ed Hoogterp)

Richardson Silk Mill (1887) – This industrial building in Belding was the site of a mill where as many as 1,200 workers made silk thread in the late 19th and early 20th centuries. The four-story plant, with its square stair towers, represents a fine example of late 19th century industrial architecture, according to architectural historian Kathryn Eckert. The century-old factory was converted to apartments in 1986, making it one of the first industrial structures in West Michigan to be adapted for residential use.

St. Francis De Sales Catholic Church is a Muskegon-area landmark (photo: Ed Hoogterp)

St. Francis De Sales Church (1967) – This Norton Shores landmark, by world famous designer Marcel Breuer was on the Michigan Society of Architects' list of the 50 most significant buildings in Michigan. The design manages to express pleasantly curving lines, despite its construction of solid concrete. In *The Buildings of Michigan,* architectural historian Kathryn Eckert said the 75-foot tall banner-shaped concrete trapezoid represented a new approach to religious architecture.

Berrien County Courthouse (1839) – This wooden structure in Berrien Springs is the oldest surviving courthouse in West Michigan. It was built at a time when Berrien Springs was the seat of government for Berrien County. That function moved long ago to St. Joseph, and the old wooden courthouse is now a museum. Tall white columns on the front give it the look of a Greek temple.

Charles Hackley's mansion is now part of the Muskegon Historical Museum (photo: Ed Hoogterp)

Hackley House (1889) – This home of Muskegon lumber baron Charles Hackley is among the state's best examples of Queen Anne style architecture. It has been lovingly restored and is open as a unit of the Muskegon Museum. In *The Buildings of Michigan*, architectural historian Kathryn Eckert cited the house's "assorted gables, clustered chimneys, bays and porches, and an octagonal corner tower." The interior, she noted, "is even more lavishly ornamented."

COMMUNITY THEATERS

Live theater in West Michigan is definitely not dead. (Maybe that's why it's called live.)

From high school plays to professional touring company productions of Broadway hits, area residents can choose from literally hundreds of shows.

The Community Theatre Association of Michigan lists 19 West Michigan community groups as members. That figure doesn't include summer stock, university productions, or touring troupes that come into the area.

Here's a look at some of the larger groups:

Grand Rapids Civic Theatre is the largest community theater organization in Michigan, with more than 6,000 season ticket holders. The organization was founded in 1926, which places it among the oldest theater groups in the nation. It operates in the former Majestic Theater in downtown Grand Rapids.

(A spelling note: The official Associated Press Stylebook says the word is spelled T-H-E-A-T-E-R. But many of the organizations prefer the more elegant spelling that ends in R-E. We follow their wishes, whenever we can.)

Grand Rapids also has a popular summer theater group, **Community Circle Theatre,** which works from Aquinas College's Performing Arts Center.

Spectrum Theater in Grand Rapids is a building, rather than a drama troupe. The modern 250-seat space provides a venue for four groups: Actors Theatre, Grand Rapids Community College Players, Jewish Theatre of Grand Rapids and the Heritage Theatre Group.

The Kalamazoo Civic Theatre was founded in 1929. Since then it has produced more than 500 plays. Most of those performances have been in the 1929 Civic Auditorium, and the troupe has also taken productions as far away as Europe.

Other long-established companies include the **Twin Cities Players,** founded in St. Joseph in 1932, and the **Muskegon Civic Theatre,** which traces its roots to 1936.

Theaters operating out of historic venues include the **Tin Shop Theatre** in Buchanan (www.tinshoptheatre.org) founded in 1985 in a 150-year-old factory building, and the **Beckwith Theatre Company** (www.beckwiththeatre.org) in Dowagiac, active since 1990 in the old Beckwith Theatre.

The Barn Theatre in Augusta (www.barntheatre.com) is Michigan's oldest professional summer-stock theater. It's been active since 1946, under management of the Ragotzy family. The auditorium is a converted dairy barn just outside Augusta in Kalamazoo County. Such well-known performers as Tom Wopat, Marin Mazzie and Dana Delaney have appeared in The Barn.

Kalamazoo's **New Vic Theatre** (www.newvictheatre.org) performs in a cabaret-style atmosphere in a downtown setting. The non-profit theatre was founded in 1967.

College and university offerings include Hope College's popular summer repertory theater in Holland, and Grand Valley State's annual Shakespeare Festival in late summer.

CONCERT VENUES

Live music can happen just about anywhere: Around the campfire at Warren Dunes State Park; on summer city sidewalks; or at every tavern in every town.

But when it comes to top regional and national acts, they tend to choose more traditional auditoriums. Here is a rundown of West Michigan's popular entertainment venues.

Frauenthal Center for the Performing Arts. This restored, 1930 movie palace in downtown Muskegon seats 1,748 people. A $16 million renovation and modernization in 1998 was financed through a local bond issue. The theater is used for productions of the Muskegon Civic Theatre and the West Shore Symphony, as well as for traveling shows and other cultural and entertainment events. It's the home of the Miss Michigan Pageant. The smaller Beardsley Theater is part of the same complex. For more information, visit www.frauenthal.info on the Internet.

The Sturges-Young Community Center, in Sturgis, includes meeting rooms and a 969 seat auditorium that is used for high school plays, local theater productions and traveling shows. A recent series sponsored by the Sturgis Arts Council included comic impressionist Rich Little and a traveling off-Broadway musical revue. The city-owned center is named for two families who donated money to build the facility in the 1950s. The similarity between "Sturges," the name of one of the donors, and the city name "Sturgis" is just a coincidence, according to center administrators. For more information, call (269) 651-8541 or visit www.ci.sturgis.mi.us on the Internet.

DeVos Performance Hall, in downtown Grand Rapids, seats 2,400. It's home to the Grand Rapids Symphony, the Broadway Theatre Guild, Grand Rapids Ballet Company and Opera Grand Rapids. It has also hosted such entertainment acts as The Moody Blues, Jimmy Buffet, Jerry Seinfeld and Bill Cosby. The hall was updated in 2004 as part of the expansion of the city's downtown DeVos Place convention center. For more information, visit www.devoshall.com on the Internet.

VanAndel Arena is home to the Grand Rapids Griffins Hockey team and the Grand Rapids Rampage Arena Football League team. With seating for just over 12,000 for stage events, VanAndel is West Michigan's largest indoor venue. It's also one of the most successful arenas in America, having hosted such acts as Elton John, Kid Rock, WWE wrestling, Kenny Chesney and Disney's Stars on Ice. The arena is at the south end of downtown Grand Rapids. A popular nightclub district has grown up around it in the historic Heartside district. For more information visit www.vanandelarena.com on the Internet.

Miller Auditorium, at Western Michigan University, with a seating capacity of 3,497, is the largest theater setting in West Michigan, and the third largest in the state. It is perennially ranked among the top performing-arts centers in the nation. Miller opened in 1968, and was refurbished in 1998. Performances in 2005-06 included Michael Flatley's "Lord of the Dance," "The Phantom of the Opera," the Kalamazoo Symphony Orchestra, and country singer Vince Gill. For more information, visit www.millerauditorium.com on the Internet.

Audience members dance in the aisle during a concert at the Meijer Gardens Amphitheater (photo courtesy of Frederick Meijer Gardens)

Frederick Meijer Gardens in Grand Rapids opened its outdoor amphitheater in 2003. The 1,800 seat amphitheater hosts a popular summer concert series that has featured such musicians as Keb' Mo', Art Garfunkel, Branford Marsalis and Natalie MacMaster. For more information, visit www.meijergardens.org on the Internet.

Wings Stadium, in Kalamazoo, is home ice for the Kalamazoo Wings minor league hockey team. The stadium has arena-style seating for 5,100 for hockey. It can accommodate up to 8,023 for stage events with added floor seating. The facility, built in 1974, has hosted everything from the Harlem Globetrotters basketball show to the rock band Motley Crue. Elvis Presley played here twice in the 1970s, including a memorable performance on April 26, 1977, less than four months before his death. For more information, visit www.wingsstadium.com on the Internet.

L.C. Walker Arena, in Muskegon, is West Michigan's most venerable hockey stadium, and also is used for other entertainment and community events. The arena opened in 1960. It seats 5,100 for hockey, and up to 6,300 for other events, depending on the configuration. L.C. Walker Arena is home to the Muskegon Fury minor league hockey team. For more information, call (231) 726-2939 or visit www.lcwalkerarena.com on the Internet.

The State Theater in Kalamazoo bills itself as "West Michigan's Premier Live Concert Venue." And who can argue? The downtown Kalamazoo theater, built in 1927, has hosted "everything from vaudeville to Alice Cooper." The 1,500 seat auditorium is known for its interior décor, which reflects the atmosphere of the golden age of movie theaters. It has been the site of several popular cable television stand-up comedy shows, including performances by Tim Allen and Larry, the Cable Guy. For more information, call (269) 345-6500, or visit www.kazoostate.com on the Internet.

Mendel Center, at Lake Michigan College in Benton Harbor, includes the 1,500 seat Mainstage performing arts center. The 2005-06 season offered everything from comedian Paula Poundstone to a touring production of "The Mikado." For more information visit www.lmcmainstage.org on the Internet.

Williams Auditorium, at Ferris State University in Big Rapids, seats 1,644 people. It is home to the Ferris State Theater group, and hosts a regular schedule of entertainers and speakers. Recent performers included "Cherish the Ladies," a popular Irish-American musical ensemble. For more information visit www.ferris.edu/arts on the Internet.

MOVIES

West Michigan isn't Hollywood, but we do show up occasionally on the silver screen. Here, with assistance from the Michigan Film Office, is a partial list of recent movies that featured scenes from West Michigan.

The 1989 Christmas movie **"Prancer,"** starring Sam Elliott and Cloris Leachman, used exteriors from the town of Three Oaks.

Grand Haven's scenery apparently fits well in sequels. Some scenes from **"American Pie II"** were shot there, as was part of the 1971 movie **"Planet of the Apes II."**

Niles has shown up in several films, chiefly because of the look of its outstanding Amtrak Station. Films that used the station include **"Continental Divide"** (1981, starring John Belushi); **"Midnight Run,"** (1988, starring Robert DeNiro) and **"Only the Lonely,"** (1991, starring John Candy).

The 2002 underwater horror film **"Below"** was shot partially in Muskegon. Scenes include the submarine *USS Silversides* and the surface of Lake Michigan.

"Flirting With Disaster," a 1991 film with a cast that included Ben Stiller, Alan Alda, Mary Tyler Moore, Patricia Arquette and Tia Leoni, included scenes from Battle Creek and Kalamazoo.

Scenes from Kalamazoo also appear in 1978's **"Blue Collar,"** which starred Richard Pryor and Harvey Kietel. The show was directed by Grand Rapids native Paul Schrader.

Schrader shot much of his 1979 film **"Hardcore,"** in Grand Rapids. The movie starred George C. Scott and Peter Boyle.

The 2002 film, **"Road to Perdition,"** starring Tom Hanks and Paul Newman, featured a number of location shots along the Lake Michigan shoreline in Ottawa and Allegan counties.

CLASSICAL MUSIC

The Grand Rapids Symphony is a professional regional orchestra that plays in DeVos Performance Hall and also offers a summer series of outdoor pops concerts at Cannonsburg Ski Area. The orchestra was founded in 1930, and began employing full-time professional musicians in the 1970s. In 1986, Catherine Comet became music director and conductor, the first woman to lead a professional regional orchestra. The music director since 1998 has been David Lockington.

The Kalamazoo Symphony Orchestra has been cited as a model for orchestras in small cities. The group was formed in 1921, largely through the efforts of Leta G. Snow, a local woman who recruited musicians from other areas and found them jobs and housing in Kalamazoo.
A recent fund-raising drive brought in enough money to endow several full-time positions as artists-in-residence with the symphony. The orchestra performs at Western Michigan University's Miller Auditorium and other venues.

Muskegon's **West Shore Symphony Orchestra,** founded in 1938, is a professional orchestra that performs in the historic Frauenthal Theater. Music Director Scott Speck is co-author of three books that explain classical music to non-musicians: *Classical Music for Dummies, Opera for Dummies* and *Ballet for Dummies.*

MARITIME ATTRACTIONS

Shipping and other activities on Lake Michigan and the shoreline have played a huge part in the historical and cultural development of West Michigan. Here are some of the region's maritime attractions.

MUSKEGON

The Great Lakes Naval Memorial and Museum, in Muskegon, is home to the

World War II submarine *USS Silversides,* and the prohibition-era Coast Guard Cutter *McLane.* The 312-foot *Silversides* served in the Pacific, and was berthed in Chicago as an educational tourist attraction until she was brought to Muskegon in 1987.

Tours are offered daily May through September, and on weekends in April and October.

For more information, call (231) 755-1230, or visit www.silversides.org on the Internet.

The ***Milwaukee Clipper,*** a 361-foot vessel that carried automobiles and passengers between Muskegon and Milwaukee from 1941 to 1970, is open for tours while undergoing restoration. The ship was built in 1905 and christened *Juniata.* It was renamed *Milwaukee Clipper* in 1941, after being modernized and converted from coal to fuel oil. After being retired, the ship was docked as a floating museum at Chicago's Navy Pier. She was purchased by a local preservation group and moved back to Muskegon in 1997. For more information, write to SS Milwaukee Clipper Preservation, Inc, P.O. Box 1370, Muskegon, MI 49433, or visit www.milwaukeeclipper.com on the Internet.

The Lake Express *ferry travels between Muskegon and Milwaukee (photo courtesy of Lake Express LLC)*

The *Lake Express* high-speed ferry carries autos and passengers on a 2-½ hour trip across Lake Michigan between Muskegon and Milwaukee. The ferry runs from May through October, with two or three crossings a day, depending on the time of year. The 190-foot-long catamaran-style vessel carries up to 46 autos and 248 passengers. It can reach speeds up to 40 mph. For more information, call 866-914-1010, or visit www.lake-express.com on the Internet.

SAUGATUCK-DOUGLAS

The *SS Keewatin,* a retired 350-foot rail and passenger ferry, has been docked as a maritime museum at Saugatuck since the late 1960s. The boat served the Canadian Pacific Railroad on Lake Superior and Lake Huron from 1908 to 1965. The steamship, with it's elegant passenger accommodations and historic engine room, is open for tours from Memorial Day weekend through Labor Day. For more information, call (269) 857-2464 or visit www.keewatinmaritimemuseum.com on the Internet.

The tall ship Friends Good Will *is based in the harbor at South Haven (photo courtesy of Michigan Maritime Museum)*

SOUTH HAVEN

The Michigan Maritime Museum, on the waterfront in Black River Harbor, is one of the state's best sources of information on ships and shipping. It's also an interesting museum, with displays of vessels ranging from an ancient dugout canoe to a tall-masted sailing ship, the *Friends Good Will.* The museum is open daily from Memorial Day to Labor Day, and every day but Tuesday from Labor Day to Memorial Day. For more information call (800) 747-3810 or visit www.michiganmaritimemuseum.org in the Internet.

LIGHTHOUSES

Michigan, with its "inland coast" along the busy shipping lanes of four of the five Great Lakes, has the most lighthouses of any state. Here is a brief guide to the eight lights along the West Michigan lakefront.

St. Joseph North Pier Lights
The first lighthouse on Michigan's Lake Michigan shore was built here, near the mouth of the St. Joseph River. That first light is long gone, but two picturesque lights and a raised metal "catwalk" remain on the concrete pier on the north side of the river. The lighthouses are visible across the channel from St. Joseph's Silver Beach. The north pier is accessible from Tiscornia Park. The St. Joseph Light appeared on a U.S. Postage stamp in 1995

as part of a commemorative series on Great Lakes lights.

South Haven Light
The round, steel tower, painted red with a black top, sits at the end of a concrete pier that protects South Haven's harbor at the mouth of the Black River. The area is accessible from the city's South Beach park, which is in walking distance from downtown South Haven.

Holland Harbor Light: "Big Red"
The distinctive red structure with its gabled roof and square tower is known locally as "Big Red." It's on a short pier on the south side of the Macatawa channel, directly across from the popular beach at Holland State Park. There is only limited public access to the breakwall where the lighthouse stands, so the best way to view the building is from the state park, where visitors often see sailboats cruising past the lighthouse.

Grand Haven Lights
The Grand Haven Pier is home to two lights, linked by a metal catwalk. The inner light is a 51-foot cylindrical tower about halfway out the pier, while the outer light is a square, red building on a cement bulkhead at the end of the breakwall. The pier and lights are adjacent to Grand Haven State Park, and are linked to downtown Grand Haven by a popular walkway. A walk on the pier is almost a requirement of a visit to the state park. It's also a traditional spot for perch fishers.

Muskegon South Pier Light
The red cylindrical tower was built in 1903 on a stub pier between the breakwalls that protect Muskegon Harbor. The city's Pere Marquette Park and a U.S. Coast Guard Station are on shore adjacent to the harbor. Across the channel is Muskegon State Park, which extends several miles north along the lakeshore.

A sailboat passes Holland's "Big Red" lighthouse (photo: Ed Hoogterp)

White River Light
The White River Light, at the White Lake Harbor near Whitehall, has been converted into a nautical museum. It has the traditional "lighthouse" look, with a tower extending above the roof of the keeper's quarters. The brick building is open from Memorial Day through Labor Day. Visitors may climb the stairs to the top of the eight-sided tower for a view of the lake.

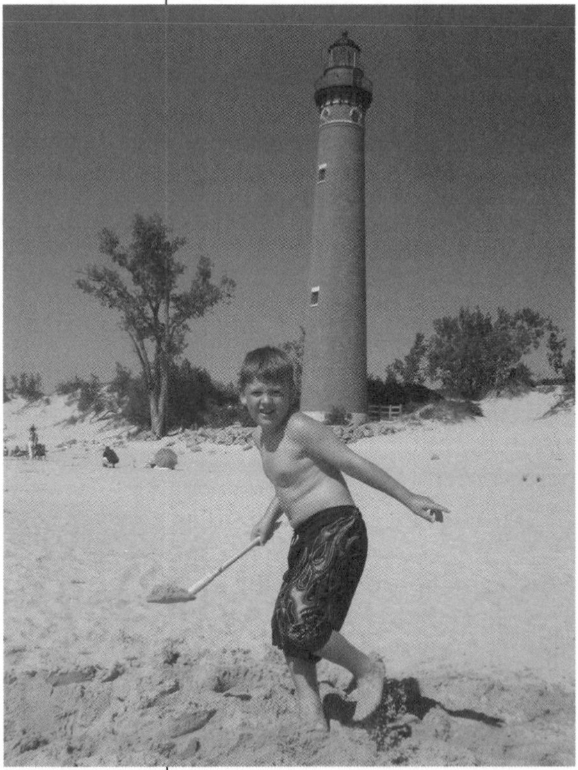

A young tourist enjoys the sand at Little Point Sable (photo: Ed Hoogterp)

Little Point Sable Light
There's no "house" here in the sand dunes of Silver Lake State Park. What's left is a tall, narrow brick tower and the barely visible foundation of a former light-keeper's house. The tower was once painted white to increase it's visibility from out on the lake. Today, it is a natural brick color standing just up from the waterline on a sandy beach that's popular with sunbathers and swimmers.

Pentwater Pier Lights
There's not much of a lighthouse here – just a 25-foot white steel tower on a blocky concrete pier. But the spot's worth visiting anyway. The pier protects Pentwater Lake, a popular recreational harbor. It sits alongside Charles Mears State Park, where sunbathers enjoy watching a steady stream of recreational boats cruise past the light.

FESTIVALS AND EVENTS

From the time the snow melts in spring, until the last autumn leaves have fallen from the trees, West Michigan has a festival or fair just about every week. Some of them celebrate local products; some commemorate early settlers or ethnic groups; others are held mainly to give residents a reason to get out and smell the flowers.

Whatever the reason, several West Michigan festivals are

recognized as being among the biggest and the best in the nation. Here are some of our top annual events.

Benton Harbor/St. Joseph Blossomtime Festival of Southwest Michigan
Early May (2006 dates, April 30-May 7)

The Blossomtime Festival traces its roots to 1906, when a local pastor urged his flock on a spring Sunday to look at the blossoming fruit trees and reflect on the symbols of renewed life.

Today, the annual event is called the oldest festival in the state. It draws on 25 communities in southwest Michigan. The colorful Blossomtime Parade, which crosses the St. Joseph River from St. Joseph to Benton Harbor, attracts as many as 250,000 spectators. For more information, call (269) 926-7397 or visit www.blossomtimefestival.org on the Internet.

St. Joseph Venetian Festival
Mid-July (2006 dates: July 13-16)

The Venetian Festival, held each July since 1979, is one of the state's premier festivals, with live entertainment including national and local acts. The four-day event draws about 200,000 spectators and participants each year. Signature events include the Blessing of the River, along with a lighted boat parade, and a classic boat parade. Also included in this celebration of life on the waterfront are day and evening concerts, dancing, sand sculpture, a car show, a craft show, fireworks, food booths, boat rides and a 5k/10k walk and run. For more information, call (269) 983-7917, or visit www.venetian.org on the Internet.

Grand Haven Coast Guard Festival
Mid-Summer (2006 dates, July 28-Aug. 6)

The annual Coast Guard Festival has been going on in Grand Haven since 1935. The mid-summer celebration includes ship tours, waterfront entertainment, fireworks, a boat parade and a street parade.

The Coast Guard often dispatches one or more cutters to the event. For more information, call (888) 207-2434 or visit www.ghcgfest.org.

South Haven National Blueberry Festival
Mid-August (2006 dates, August 10-13)

South Haven sets in the midst of America's prime blueberry region, so this festival is right at home. The Blueberry

Festival features main stage entertainment and blueberry-themed events including pie-eating contests and an arts and crafts fair in this Van Buren County beach town. If you need a reason to visit South Haven in August, this is as good as any. For more information, visit www.blueberryfestival.com on the Internet.

Former Gov. John Engler dons Dutch garb as part of a Tulip Time tradition (photo courtesy of Tulip Time, Inc.)

Holland Tulip Time
Early May (2006 dates: May 6-13)

The top entertainment at this festival seems a bit time-worn (the 2006 headliner was Frankie Avalon). But, the truth is, nobody really minds. Tulip Time is about flowers (obviously) and parades. The festival opens with a "Volksparade" that traditionally features Michigan's governor in Dutch garb carrying a broom to help sweep the street. The main event is the Meijer Muziekparade, which showcases about 40 marching bands, a like number of floats, and more people dancing in wooden shoes than you care to count. For more information, call (800) 822-2770 or visit www.tuliptime.com on the Internet.

Grand Rapids Festival of the Arts
First full weekend of June (2006 dates, June 2-4)

Festival of the Arts is America's largest all-volunteer arts event. The three day celebration is sometimes called the Calder Festival, perhaps because the main stage is in the shadow of Alexander Calder's massive downtown sculpture. Festival weekend draws as many as 500,000 visitors, even without headline entertainment. It offers hundreds of local acts on several downtown stages. There's also an art sale and show, activity areas, and dozens of popular food booths featuring ethnic treats. For more information, visit www.festivalofthearts.org.

Muskegon Summer Celebration
Early July (2006 dates, June 29 – July 9)

Summer Celebration is an 11-day, entertainment-driven festival that annually draws as many as half a million people to the port city. Nationally known acts play at Heritage Landing on the downtown Muskegon Lake shoreline. Other events include a craft market, sand sculpture contest and more. For more information, call (231) 722-6520 or visit www.summercelebration.com on the Internet.

BIG TIMES IN SMALL TOWNS

The major festivals and events get most of the attention, but the events in small towns and villages all have their own charm. It's in these intensely local celebrations that we can learn the history of the potato or the wonders of the mighty asparagus. Besides, they're just plain fun. Here are a few that have stood the test of time.

Carson City – Frontier Days. 2006 dates, June 1-4.

Shelby – National Asparagus Festival (alternates with Hart). 2006 dates, June 9-11.

Fremont – National Baby Food Festival. 2006 dates, July 18-22.

Greenville – Danish Festival. 2006 dates, July 17-20.

Big Rapids – Riverdays Festival. 2006 dates, Aug. 31-Sept 4.

Newaygo – Logging Festival. 2006 dates, Sept. 1-4.

Edmore – Potato Festival. 2006 dates, Sept. 7-10.

Zeeland – Pumpkin Festival. 2006 dates, Oct. 5-7.

Cedar Springs – Red Flannel Days. 2006 dates, Oct. 6-7.

COUNTY AND COMMUNITY FAIRS

A county fair means cows and sheep, bunnies and chickens, prize-winning pies and giant tomatoes. It also means a lighted midway, elephant ears, caramel corn and cheesy-but-fun games of chance. In West Michigan's top fairs, it also means a chance to see some of the nation's best-known entertainers, especially in the country-music genre. With all that, plus tractor pulls, harness racing and demolition derbies, who would want to be anywhere else? Here's some information on West Michigan's fairs.

The Allegan County Fair, in Allegan, is billed as the largest in Michigan. The eight-day event begins the Friday after Labor Day (2006 dates, Sept. 8-16). Headline entertainment runs strongly toward country music (Toby Keith and the Charlie Daniels

Band in 2005) and also includes Christian and rock music. There's also a local historical village, a rodeo, harness racing, a huge midway and all you'd expect at a fair. For more information, call (888) 673-5601 or visit www.allegancountyfair.org on the Internet.

The Ionia Free Fair, in late July (2006 dates, July 20-29) is rated as one the nation's 50 largest fairs, with 2005 attendance of more than 400,000. It calls itself the world's largest free fair. The local fair board tried charging admission in 2004 but gave up the idea after one year. While there's no charge to get into the fair, you do need to buy a ticket to see the headline entertainment. Over the years, the fair's grandstand has hosted such acts as Johnny Cash, Tim McGraw, Def Leppard and Nelly. For more information, call (616) 527-1310 or visit www.ioniafreefair.com on the Internet.

St. Joseph County Grange Fair, takes place in mid-September (2006 dates, Sept. 17-23) at the fairgrounds in Centreville. This fair, in an area of traditional small farms, features such events as harness racing, bull-riding and super motocross. The headline entertainer scheduled in both 2005 and 2006 was country singer Trace Adkins. For more information call (269) 467-7036 or visit www.centrevillefair.com on the Internet.

The Berlin Fair, in Marne, was first held in 1856 by the Ottawa Agricultural Society. The fair stresses agricultural events, and also includes a midway and such grandstand events as demolition derby. The Berlin Raceway is on the fairgrounds, just west of Grand Rapids. The Berlin Fair is held in mid-July (2006 dates: July 16-22) For more information, call (616) 677-1140 or visit www.berlinfair.org on the internet.

The Ottawa County Fair has the location and timing to make it a great event, even if the fairgrounds were empty (which they're not). The site is on the road to Holland State Park, which is the busiest unit in the state park system. The late July fair (2006 dates, July 24-29) comes at a time when the area is at its busiest. The fair features a large midway, a rodeo, harness racing, demolition derby, community stage and lots of kids with animals. A great mid-summer event.

Berrien County Youth Fair, Berrien Springs, mid-August. (2006 dates, Aug 14-19)

Barry County Fair, Hastings, mid-July. (2006 dates, July 17-22)

Cass County Fair, Cassopolis, first week in August. (2006 dates, July 31-Aug. 5)

Hudsonville Community Fair, late August. (2006 dates: Aug. 21-26)

Kalamazoo County Fair, Kalamazoo, early August. (2006 dates Aug. 6-12)

Kent County Youth Fair, Lowell, early August. (2006 dates, Aug. 6-12)

Lake Odessa Fair, Lake Odessa, late June. (2006 dates, June 26 – July 1)

Mecosta County Agricultural Fair, Big Rapids, early July. (2006 dates, July 9-15)

Montcalm County 4H Fair, Greenville, early July. (2006 dates, July 2-8)

Muskegon County 4-H Fair, Ravenna, late July. (2006 dates, July 25-30)

Newaygo County Agricultural Fair, Fremont, early August. (2006 dates, Aug. 6-12)

Oceana County Fair, Hart late August. (2006 dates, Aug. 23-26)

Sparta Area Fair, Sparta, mid-July. (2006 dates, July 12-16)

Van Buren Youth Fair, Hartford, mid-July. (2006 dates, July 17-22)

NATURE CENTERS

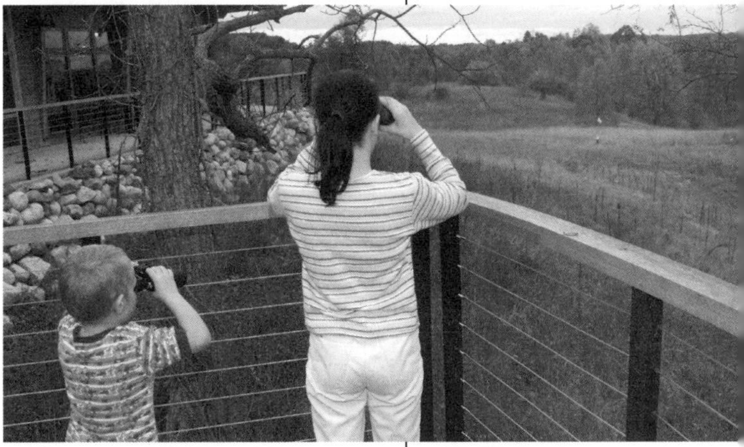

Visitors look for wildlife at the Pierce Cedar Creek Institute in Barry County (photo courtesy of Pierce Cedar Creek Institute)

Pierce Cedar Creek Institute
The Pierce Cedar Creek Institute, near Dowling in Barry County, is an ecological center and field station created by the Willard G. and Jessie M. Pierce Foundation. (Mr. Pierce was a founder of Flex-Fab Corp. in Hastings.) The 660-acre property opened to the public in 2001.

It includes an interpretive center and six miles of trails that skirt forests, prairies, wetlands and open-water ponds. The institute provides research opportunities for students at colleges in Michigan and Indiana, and is open to the public. For more information, visit www/cedarcreekinstitute.org on the Internet.

Fernwood Botanical Garden, Niles
Fernwood began in the 1940s as the home of Kay and Walter Boydston, who developed the first gardens there. Beginning in the 1960s, Niles philanthropists Lawrence and Mary Plym financed its conversion into a public botanical garden and nature center. Today, the 100-acre center includes a nature center, visitor center, 40-acre arboretum and restored tallgrass prairie, in addition to the popular gardens. For more information, visit www.fernwoodbotanical.org on the Internet.

Sarrett Nature Center
Sarrett Nature Center, along the Paw Paw River north of Benton Harbor, is an 800 acre natural area affiliated with the Audubon Society of Michigan. It includes both upland forest and wetlands, including a rare fen ecosystem. There are more than five miles of trails, and an interpretive center. Sarrett is engaged in a $1.5 million fund-raising effort to renovate existing facilities and add a 70-foot tower to let visitors observe the natural area from tree-top level. For more information, call (269) 927-4832.

Gillette Nature Center
The Gillette Nature Center, in Hoffmaster State Park, tells the story of the Lake Michigan Sand Dunes. The park is on the Lake Michigan shoreline between Grand Haven and Muskegon. Its miles of shoreline dunes provide the perfect setting for the indoor interpretive center. For more information call (231) 798-3573.

Kalamazoo Nature Center
The Kalamazoo Nature Center, north of Kalamazoo, is known as one of the best nature-interpretive sites in the Midwest. The site covers more than 1,100 acres of forest, fen and prairie.

The center includes an 11-acre arboretum, along with an interpretive center that encircles a tropical rainforest inside a three-story atrium. Also on the site is the 1858 DeLano homestead, which is open for special events. For more information, call (269) 381-1574 or visit www.naturecenter.org on the Internet.

WINE IN WEST MICHIGAN

Michigan's thriving wine-making industry died in 1920, when the 18th Amendment to the United States Constitution banned the manufacture and sale of "intoxicating liquors."

West Michigan's grape growers were fortunate, however. A Welch's Grape Juice plant had opened in 1919 in Lawton, so they still had a market for their Concord and Niagara grapes.

When America's experiment with prohibition ended in 1933, most of the area's grapes continued to go for juice. A few wineries – including St. Julian, which was founded in Canada in 1921 and moved to Paw Paw in 1936 – used the local grapes to make the sweet wines that were common in those years.

St. Julian is the state's largest and oldest winery. Warner Vineyards, founded in 1938 in Paw Paw, is the second oldest.

When America's tastes turned from the sweet Concord wines to dryer European-style vintages in the 1960s and 70s, Michigan was largely left out. But in the 1980s and 90s, the state gradually began to adapt. Growers near the Lake Michigan shore began to experiment with French-American hybrid grapes and with the famous "vinifera" grape varieties such as Johannisberg Riesling, chardonnay and pinot noir.

They discovered those grapes could survive and provide the raw material for decent wines. And as Michigan winemakers continued to work with the new vineyards they found ways to make the Michigan wines better than just decent. Today, the Michigan wine business remains small. Michigan's 43 commercial wineries produce more than 200,000 cases of wine annually, making the state 13th in wine production.

The majority of the state's wineries and vineyards are in either of two regions: the Traverse City area of Northwest Michigan, and the Lake Michigan Shore area in the southwest. Both regions, sell much of their production through tasting rooms at the winery site.

Despite the relatively small production, Michigan's product gains more respect with each passing year. St. Julian was named in 1998 as the Taster's Guild International "Winery of the Year." That's the only time the award has gone to a winery outside California or France.

Other wineries in the two main regions have become important links in the local tourism economies. Wine tours from one tasting room to the next are a popular summer and fall activity.

Here is a list of West Michigan wineries with public tasting rooms

Contessa Wine Cellars
3235 Friday Road
Coloma, MI 49038
(269) 468-5534
On the Internet:
www.contessawinecellars.com

Domaine Berrien Cellars
398 East Lemon Creek Road
Berrien Springs, MI 49103
(269) 473-WINE (9463)
On the Internet:
www.domaineberrien.com

Fenn Valley Vineyards
6130 122nd Avenue
Fennville, MI 49408
(269) 561-2396
On the Internet:
www.fennvalley.com

Karma Vista Vineyards
6991 Ryno Road
Coloma, MI 49038
(269) 468-WINE (9463)
On the Internet:
www.karmavista.com

Lemon Creek Winery
533 East Lemon Creek Road
Berrien Springs, MI 49103
(269) 471-1321
On the Internet:
www.lemoncreekwinery.com

Round Barn Winery
10981 Hills Road
Baroda, MI 49101
(800) 716-9463
On the Internet:
www.roundbarnwinery.com

St. Julian Wine Company
716 South Kalamazoo Street
Paw Paw, MI 49079
(269) 657- 5568 or
(800) 732-6002
On the Internet:
www.stjulian.com

Tabor Hill Winery & Restaurant
185 Mt. Tabor Road
Buchanan, MI 49107
(800) 283-3363
On the Internet:
www.taborhill.com

Warner Vineyards
706 South Kalamazoo Street
Paw Paw, MI 49079
(269) 657-3165 or
(800) 756-5357
On the Internet:
www.warnerwines.com

Peterson & Sons Winery
9375 East P Avenue
Kalamazoo, MI 49001-9762
(269) 626-9755
On the Internet:
www.naturalwine.net

Tartan Hill Winery
4937 South 52nd Avenue
New Era, MI 49446
(231) 861-4657

Jomagrha Winery
7365 South Pere Marquette Hwy., Pentwater, MI 49449
(231) 869-4236
On the Internet:
www.jomagrha.com

FIRST & BEST

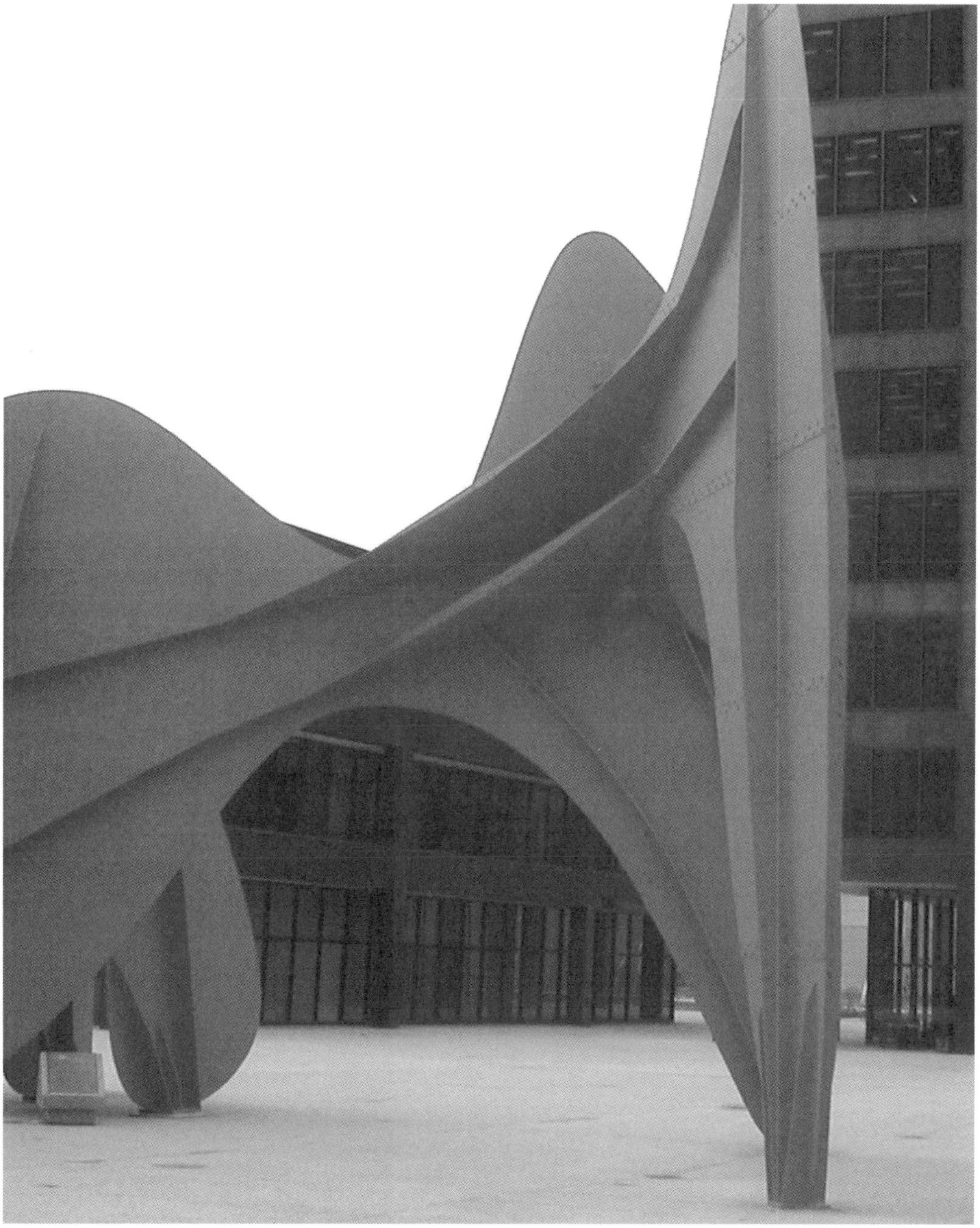

Photo on previous page: Ed Hoogterp

THE FIRST, THE BIGGEST AND THE MOST

Over the years, West Michigan has been home to pioneers in such diverse activities as fishing, flying, fluoridation and furniture. As the 21st century begins, the region remains a leader in the things we do best. Here a few of the ways that West Michigan has distinguished itself.

A lot of pickles

Holland is home to the world's largest pickle factory. The H.J. Heinz Co. plant there can process a million pounds of cucumbers each day during its busy season. West Michigan farms are among the nation's leaders in production of cucumbers for processing.

Electrifying the Rapids

Grand Rapids was the site of one of America's first hydroelectric generating plants, and possibly the first commercial electric lighting service, according to historian Z.Z. Lydens. An early industrialist named William Powers, who had interests in everything from factories to gypsum mines, organized the Grand Rapids Electric Light and Power Co. in 1880. On July 22 of that year, he used water from a canal along the Grand River to power a dynamo that supplied power to outdoor lighting near downtown stores. Powers' company eventually became part of what is now Consumers Energy.

Into the Blue

West Michigan is definitely blueberry central. More of the marble-sized blue fruit is produced here than anywhere else in the country. In fact, Van Buren and Ottawa counties together produce more blueberries than any other state.

The first artificial fishing lure.

James Heddon was a Dowagiac beekeeper who was among America's largest honey producers in the 1880s. But he's most famous for what started out as a hobby. According to the legend, Heddon was sitting beside the Dowagiac Mill Pond one summer day, whittling a piece of wood. When he casually tossed his work into the pond, a big bass rose to the surface and attacked it. A great idea was born. Heddon whittled a crude frog and discovered he could cast it into the pond and catch fish. After a few refinements, he opened a factory making the first artificial fishing lures. Many of the Heddon company's early products are on display in a small museum in his original factory building in Dowagiac.

The Peppermint King

Albert May Todd of Kalamazoo was known as "The Peppermint King." Around 1900, the A.M. Todd Co., produced as much as 90 percent of the nation's peppermint. Todd, a chemist who was born in St. Joseph County, established the huge Mentha plantation in Van Buren County and built a factory in Kalamazoo to extract the mint oil. The company is still in business, as the oldest and largest American producer of peppermint oil.

The airplane "Miss Grand Rapids" prepares to fly a furniture delivery to Detroit in 1928 (photo courtesy of Grand Rapids Public Library)

First scheduled air passenger service

On July 31, 1926, the nation's first scheduled air passenger service began from Kent County Airport on a plane named Miss Grand Rapids. The flights linked Grand Rapids and Detroit. Two years later, the same airline made the first air delivery of furniture. (Just why anyone needed a piece of furniture delivered by airplane in 1928 remains a mystery.)

Fluoridation

In 1944, the Grand Rapids City Commmission voted to add a small amount of fluoride to the city water system, as part of a test to show whether the substance would reduce tooth decay. School children born after fluoridation began were monitored for 15 years. The study showed a decline of about 60 percent in tooth decay. Since then, fluoride has been added to the water systems in a number of cities. It continues to have opponents, who regard it as either a colossal mistake or a Communist plot. The U.S. Centers for Disease Control says fluoridation is a cost effective public health measure.

First in Flight

By some reckonings, Silver Beach in St. Joseph was the site of the world's first powered airplane flight, by a man named Augustus Moore Herring. The date was Oct. 11, 1899, more than three years before the Wright Brothers' famous flight at Kitty Hawk, N.C.

Herring claimed to have flown his flying machine about 50 feet along the Lake Michigan shore. Eleven days later, he managed another brief flight, this time witnessed by a newspaper reporter who said the craft barely skimmed above the sand for 8 to 10 seconds.

Herring's flying machine was a double-winged glider with an engine that ran on compressed air. The air was capable of powering the engine only for about 30 seconds. Apparently because of that limitation, he was never widely recognized as the pioneer of flight.

Another record-breaking flight from the same location did receive recognition. In July of 1913, Logan A. "Jack" Vilas made a 60-mile hop to Chicago in a Curtiss bi-plane flying boat. It was by far the longest over-water flight at the time, eclipsing the record of about 20 miles that had been set on a flight across the English Channel.

Food for baby

The year was 1927, and Dorothy Gerber was tired of straining peas for her infant daughter. So, as the story goes, she persuaded her husband to try making strained baby foods at his canning company in Fremont. The rest is history. By 1928, the company was marketing baby-ready peas, prunes, carrots and spinach. The sketch of the Gerber Baby began appearing about the same time. And, urban myths aside, the baby is NOT a young Humphrey Bogart. The charcoal sketch is by artist Dorothy Hope Smith. The subject was Ann Turner Cook, who grew up to become an English teacher.

Kitty Litter

Today, it's hard to imagine owning a cat without Kitty Litter or some other brand of commercial cat box filler. But before Ed Lowe, cat owners provided a box of sand or, more likely, sent Kitty outside to do her business in the neighbors' rhododendrons.

Back in 1947, Lowe was fresh out of the Navy and working for his father, selling sawdust and clay as industrial absorbants. A neighbor in Cassopolis came over one day asking for some sawdust to put in her cat box, and Ed persuaded her to try a bit of an absorbant clay product. When she came back for more a few days later, Lowe saw the possibilities. He wrote the words "Kitty Litter" on a few bags of the stuff and brought it to a very skeptical pet store owner. The store owner gave those first bags away, no charge. His patrons liked it so much they were willing to pay Lowe's asking price – 65 cents for 10 pounds – for their next bags.

Lowe spent years hawking Kitty Litter from the trunk of his car at pet stores and cat shows around the country. It paid off. By the time he sold his business, in 1985, he was bringing in more than $200 million a year. Lowe, who died in 1995, used much of his fortune to create the Edward Lowe Foundation, in Cassopolis, which provides training for entrepreneurs.

"I got my Hush Puppies on..."

The Wolverine Shoe and Tanning Co., owned by the Krause family in Rockford, was known in the first half of the 20th century for its indestructable workboots, made from the hides of workhorses. But by the end of World War II, as tractors replaced horses, the hides (known as "horse butts" in the tannery trade) became less available. Instead of giving in, Wolverine concentrated on an underused resource: Pigskin.

Pig physiology had always presented challenges for tanners. The skins have more fat than horsehide or cowhide, and pores left by pig-hair create a surface that won't hold a shine.

Wolverine developed a technological solution to remove the fat, and a marketing plan to sidestep the shine problem.

Instead of trying to polish the new leather, they sanded it to a soft suede. In 1959, they introduced the world to Hush Puppies, the casual shoes made of "breathin' brushed pigskin," so comfortable they felt like slippers, and so uncool they were hip. Sort of.

Today, Wolverine World Wide markets athletic and work footwear and dress shoes under a number of brands. But the company is still identified with Hush Puppies.

Public Art

Alexander Calder's La Grande Vitesse, installed in 1969 on a public square in downtown Grand Rapids, was the first

"La Grande Vitesse" dominates Calder Plaza in Grand Rapids (photo: Ed Hoogterp)

work of sculpture purchased through a grant from the National Endowment for the Arts. The square where the red steel sculpture stands is now known as Calder Plaza. The scuplture was once controversial – some Grand Rapids residents would have preferred a fountain – but is now part of a city logo that appears on everything from street signs to garbage trucks.

The Paper City

The Kalamazoo Paper Company began operations in 1867, and by the end of the 19th century paper mills were distributed along the Kalamazoo River from Kalamazoo to Allegan.

By the time of World War II, the area around Kalamazoo boasted the world's largest concentration of papermaking companies. The companies accounted for as much as half the area's employement. They also succeeded in making the Kalamazoo River one of the most polluted streams in the nation. By about 1970, the industry was in decline, and by 2005 it had nearly disappeared, except for the empty mills in towns along the river.

The Celery City

Kalamazoo introduced America to celery – literally. In the 1870s, salespeople actually hawked celery to travelers on trains passing through town. The vegetable, which was unknown to most Americans at the time, grew well in mucky soils around Kalamazoo. Dutch immigrant farmers, who knew how to work the wet, heavy soil, planted hundreds of acres of the stuff and Kalamazoo became "The Celery City." Most of the crop is gone now, replaced by housing developments or greenhouses for bedding plants. The Celery Flats Interpretive Center in Portage tells the story of the vegetable that was once synonymous with the region. Today, Hudsonville, in Ottawa County, is the center of West Michigan's celery production.

The Bedding Plant City

When Kalamazoo County got out of the celery business, much of the land was converted to greenhouses for producing the potted flowers and bedding plants that are sold in garden centers throughout America. Michigan leads the nation in producing those plants, and Kalamazoo is by far Michigan's leading county.

The world's largest weather vane towers over Montague (photo: Ed Hoogterp)

The toughest sub on the Great Lakes

The *USS Silversides,* now docked at Muskegon as a Naval museum, was active in the Pacific for most of World War II. The sub's crew was credited with sinking 23 ships, most of them cargo vessels bound for Japan. That was the third highest total for any submarine in the war. And since most of the others have long since been recycled into tin cans and automobiles, *Silversides* is the champion among surviving World War II subs. The 312-foot ship came to Chicago as a training vessel, and was towed to Muskegon in 1987. It's the star attraction of the Great Lakes Naval Memorial and Museum.

The best peaches

The redhaven peach, which may be the finest-tasting fresh fruit on earth, was developed in South Haven by horticulturists at the Michigan State University experiment station. Since its release in 1940, redhaven has become the most widely planted freestone peach variety in the world.

The world's largest weather vane

The world's largest weather vane sits along the main road in Montague, twisting slowly, slowly in the wind. The vane, made by Whitehall Products, is a copper image of a sailing ship named the *Elle Ellenwood.* The entire thing, including the tower and the directional arrow, stands 48 feet tall and 26 feet long. It weighs in at just over two tons, and it really does move with the breeze.

The world's smallest newspaper

Every Friday from 1914 to 1970, Swift Lathers' opinions were "Ripe in the Land of Mears."

Lathers, a schoolteacher and landowner, was founder, owner and editor of the Mears Newz, published in the crossroads community of Mears, midway between Hart and Silver Lake in Oceana County. He proudly billed his four-page, postcard-size publication as the smallest newspaper in the world.

For 56 years, the price stayed the same: 50 cents a year (or $1 for six months). By the time Lathers died of a heart attack in 1970, his blend of anti-tax ranting, down-home wisdom and libertarian philosophy had earned him subscribers in 38 states.

"People should walk more and ride less," he wrote in 1954. "They should work harder at finding contentment than at making money."

The sheet, published on a hand-operated press, always looked pretty much the same.

There was a main headline stating that Autumn Leaves (or cherries, or freezing temperatures or whatever) "are ripe in the Land of Mears."

Then came an essay on the news of the day, heavily leavened with Swift's opinions, and finally a rundown of the comings and goings of his Oceana County subscribers. Advertisments ("Barber Dick can make you look slick. The barber shop, Mears") were slipped in pretty much wherever they fit, usually in the same typeface as the news.

Around 1940, Lathers set about building a miniature village three miles back in the sand dunes. He spent considerable time there, dreaming of a simple life among what one contemporary described as "a collection of shacks."

"When the world rejoices, I rejoice with it," Lathers once wrote. "When the world goes wrong, I go to the hills."

Hiram's harvester

Hiram Moore of Climax developed the first mechanical combine (a machine that harvests, threshes and cleans field grain all in one process) in the early 1830s and demonstrated it on the Climax Prairie in Kalamazoo County. Several others, including Cyrus McCormick, of Virginia, were developing mechanical harvesters at the same time, and it was McCormick's famous reaper that made it to the history books. Moore's harvester – which was pulled by 16 horses – could handle up to 20 acres a day. It was the only one of the early machines that could both cut and thresh the grain. Moore's investors included Lucius Lyon, one of Michigan's first U.S. senators. But his big, unwieldy machine couldn't compete with McCormick's simpler design. After years of working on his machine, Moore finally gave up. It would be nearly 100 years before someone else's mechanical combine became a standard farm machine.

Anna's carpet cleaner

Back in the 1870s, Melville and Anna Bissell were running a small crockery shop in Grand Rapids, when Melville invented a nifty little gadget to help his wife clean the dust off the store's carpet. His device had two rotary brushes inside a sort of metal dustpan. When you pushed it across the floor, the brushes would spin, sweeping dust and dirt into the pan. He patented it as the Bissell Carpet Sweeper, and soon the family was in a whole new business. Melville died in 1889, just six years after the first Bissell factory was built. But the company didn't falter. Anna Bissell took the reins, as America's first female corporate CEO, and guided the firm into the 20th century. While carpet sweepers are no longer considered state-of-the art in the dirt-collection business, Bissell is still thriving as an international cleaning-products company, based in Grand Rapids.

City of millionaires

At the time of the American Civil War, Muskegon was a small town clustered around a harbor with a few sawmills. But in the years after the war, Muskegon was in the perfect spot to provide lumber for Chicago and other cities in the Midwest. The demand grew rapidly, especially after the Great Chicago Fire in 1871. By the late 1880s, Muskegon was known as the Lumber Queen of the World. It had 47 sawmills, one of the busiest harbors on the Great Lakes, and, supposedly, more millionaires per capita than any other commnity in America. There are no official statistics to support the millionaire claim, but it's definitely true that such lumber barons as Martin Ryerson and Charles Hackley played a major part in West Michigan's history.

The Gibson Guitar

Orville Gibson was a native New Yorker who came to Kalamazoo about 1880, and gradually got into the business of hand-crafting mandolins from old furniture wood. In 1904, he and several investors established the Gibson Mandolin-Guitar Co. Gibson himself grew tired of the big-business aspect of the new company and went back to New York. But his company thrived. In 1952, Gibson introduced the famous Les Paul electric guitar. In the 1960s, the company had 1,000 employees and turned out as many as 1,000 instruments a day. Guitar sales slacked off considerably after the 60s, and the company eventually abandoned Kalamazoo in favor of Nashville, Tenn. Several former Gibson employees created a new company, Heritage Guitars, which continues to make instruments in a small portion of the former Gibson factory.

BUSINESS

Photo on previous page courtesy of Grand Rapids Public Library

BUSINESS

First, there was fur.

In the centuries after Marquette and LaSalle set foot in West Michigan, the economy would draw value from farms and furniture, drugs and dishwashers, cars and guitars.

But first, there would be fur.

Postcard view shows Stickley Brothers furniture factory in the early 1900s (photo courtesy of Grand Rapids Public Library)

A casual reader of Michigan history might think the fur trade was limited to the Straits of Mackinac, where America's first millionaire, John Jacob Astor, built the Great Lakes headquarters for his American Fur Co. in the early 1800s.

But many of the furs that made it to Mackinac came from animals trapped along the rivers that flow into Lake Michigan. Astor employed traders up and down the lake to barter with Indian and French trappers for the skins of beaver, muskrat and assorted members of the weasel family.

West Michigan pioneers like Rix Robinson, Joseph Bertrand and Louis Campau were heavily involved in the fur business.

(In case anyone thinks globalization and conspicuous consumption are modern inventions, the skins of animals trapped in the 18th century along little West Michigan streams eventually found their way to Europe, where the fur was used in the manufacture of fancy hats.)

The appetite for fur was so intense that most of the animals had been trapped out from rivers around the Great Lakes by the 1820s. As the business moved farther west, Michigan's Indians, who had relied for generations on the fur trade, were left with empty forests and no way to buy the muskets, iron cookware and other goods that had become part of their lifestyle.

With the furs gone, the farmers and woodcutters were not far behind. The natives were soon persuaded to sign away their rights to the land, in exchange for money, whiskey, and other considerations.

By the middle 1820s, white settlers from New York and Ohio were making their way to the attractive prairies in Kalamazoo, St. Joseph and Cass counties. By the 1830s, free-flowing streams that once supported the fur industry were being dammed for water power.

The lure of cheap farmland – $1.25 an acre at the government land office in White Pigeon – brought settlers into Michigan. And the very nature of the place brought industry along with the budding agriculture.

Trees felled while clearing the land had to be cut into lumber; grain needed to be ground into flour and meal. Wagons, boats and (a few decades later) railroads were needed to bring produce down to Lake Michigan where it could be shipped off to market. That required energy, and the technology of the day was to use the weight of falling water to turn grindstones and saw blades.

Water-powered mills were established in St. Joseph County before 1830 at Mottville and Meek's Mill (now Constantine). William Powers and Lucius Lyon were building a water-power canal around the rapids of the Grand River within 10 years of the founding of Grand Rapids. Water power available along the Kalamazoo River helped make Kalamazoo a leading paper manufacturer in the 1860s, a position it held well into the 20th century.

As the state's population doubled and redoubled in the 1800s, Michigan produced an astonishing variety of manufactured goods.

There was furniture making in Grand Rapids. Silk in Belding. Wagons, windmills, woodstoves and paper in Kalamazoo. Sawmills crowded around Muskegon Lake (and to a lesser extent just about everywhere else). Grist mills appeared in every town with wheat or corn to grind and a creek big enough to turn the stones.

Dowagiac was home of the Round Oak Stove Co, making pot-bellied woodstoves that heated thousands of homes. In Three Oaks, hundreds of employees worked at Warren

Featherbone Co., which took feathers from the area's turkey farms and converted them to corset stays. Needless to say, both companies are long gone. But the multi-story buildings still stand at the center of the towns.

If corsets and woodstoves failed to make the leap into modern lifestyles, other Michigan companies were able to adapt.

The Upjohn Co. has been absorbed twice since W.E. Upjohn invented his "friable pill" in the 1880s. The company is now part of Pfizer Corp., and workers are still making medicine in Kalamazoo.

Grand Rapids' makers of traditional wooden household furniture are pretty much gone, but now the region is the national center of office furniture design and manufacturing.

Manufacturing employment in Michigan has been falling since about 1960.

West Michigan remains a manufacturing center. But changing times have taken a toll on many of the venerable names of the 20th century. In 1908, Frank Gibson went into business in Greenville making wooden ice-boxes. The Gibson Refrigerator Co. grew to become the largest refrigerator manufacturer in the nation. In the 1930s, Gibson began making electric models, which included an ultra-modern option: A light that (supposedly) went off when the door was closed.

Gibson eventually became part of the multi-national Electrolux, which continued making refrigerators in Greenville until 2006, when it transferred the last of the local production to Mexico to take advantage of cheaper labor. The move cost 2,700 jobs in West Michigan.

Gibson Guitars (originally made in Kalamazoo), Brunswick bowling balls

Vintage Checker Cab is on display at the Kalamazoo Valley Museum (photo: Ed Hoogterp)

(Muskegon) and Heddon fishing lures (Dowagiac) are now made elsewhere. Checker Cabs and R.C. Allen mechanical adding machines aren't made at all. But, you can still buy Simplicity dress patterns, Heinz pickles, Whirlpool stoves and Gerber baby foods made in West Michigan.

And let's not forget flypaper. There was a time when the glue-covered paper, made by Tanglefoot Co. in Grand

Rapids, was a standard product in homes everywhere. Homeowners would set the product on a table or hang it from a lamp. Insects would land on it and get stuck. When the paper was full of bug carcasses, the homeowner would toss it out and put up a new sheet.

The development of insecticides for home use cut into the flypaper market, but Tanglefoot managed to stick around. Today, it's a popular product among organic farmers, who use it as a non-chemical means of controlling insects in orchards and garden plots.

Which just goes to show that sometimes an old idea can be the newest thing.

EMPLOYMENT TRENDS

West Michigan saw large increases in employment during the boom years from 1995-2000. But since 2000, the number of jobs has actually decreased in most of the region's labor market areas. The largest losses have been in manufacturing. Those have been partially offset by an increase in employment in the health care area.

The patterns vary considerably from one metro area to another.

The Grand Rapids, Holland and Grand Haven areas saw major increases in manufacturing from 1995-2000, largely as a result of growth in office furniture and auto parts manufacturing. Those areas lost thousands of jobs when the economy softened.

Kalamazoo began losing manufacturing jobs earlier, largely as a result of downsizing in the paper industry and mergers that affected the metro area's pharmaceutical manufacturers.

Benton Harbor continued a decades-long trend of manufacturing losses tied to appliance manufacturers and auto suppliers.

And Muskegon, with a more diverse core of manufacturing businesses, has weathered the 21st century downturn much better than its neighbors in Kent and Ottawa counties.

The following employment statistics are provided by the Michigan Department of Labor and Economic Growth. The numbers on employment by industry sector are compiled for metropolitan areas, and are not available for all individual counties. The government has changed the definitions of some sectors during the 10-year period covered by these statistics. The numbers should be seen as estimates and used only to illustrate the larger trends involved.

Grand Rapids-Wyoming Labor Market Area (Kent, Barry, Ionia and Newaygo counties)

Employment category	1995	2000	2005
Total employment	351,800	405,200	385,600
Manufacturing	85,500	90,200	73,500
Retail trade	40,400	46,600	42,900
Prof. and Business services	39,000	55,700	52,800
Educ. and Health services	38,500	44,500	52,700
Gov't (including schools)	34,500	37,300	37,900

Holland-Grand Haven Labor Market Area (Ottawa County)

Employment category	1995	2000	2005
Total employment	101,500	120,400	112,500
Manufacturing	39,200	44,400	35,300
Retail trade	10,100	12,300	10,200
Prof. and Business services	8,700	11,100	12,100
Educ. and Health services	7,100	8,900	9,800
Gov't (including schools)	11,800	13,700	15,000

Kalamazoo-Portage Labor Market Area (Kalamazoo and Van Buren counties)

Employment category	1995	2000	2005
Total employment	139,700	150,000	144,900
Manufacturing	32,100	30,800	24,400
Retail trade	16,000	17,100	17,600
Prof. and Business services	12,100	14,500	14,300
Educ. and Health services	16,800	17,500	20,000
Gov't (including schools)	26,600	27,000	23,400

Muskegon – Norton Shores Labor Market Area (Muskegon County)

Employment category	1995	2000	2005
Total employment	58,400	65,100	66,100
Manufacturing	14,000	15,100	13,600
Retail trade	9,000	9,800	10,800
Prof. and Business services	2,700	3,700	4,100
Educ. and Health services	7,600	8,100	10,500
Gov't (including schools)	8,900	9,400	9,500

Benton Harbor – Niles Labor Market Area (Berrien County)

Employment category	1995	2000	2005
Total employment	71,100	73,300	63,600
Manufacturing	20,900	19,900	14,400
Retail trade	N/A	N/A	7,800
Prof. and Business services	6,000	6,500	4,800
Educ. and Health services	7,500	8,700	9,600
Gov't (including schools)	8,800	9,000	8,000

UNEMPLOYMENT

The number of people out of work in West Michigan has been above the national average in the years since the mild recession of 2001. Figures from the United States Bureau of Labor Statistics show that unemployment dropped significantly in the region from 1995 to 2000, and has risen in every county since then. Labor experts say the unemployment increase is largely due to troubles in Michigan's manufacturing economy.

Unemployment in West Michigan (Annual percentage by county)

County	1995	2000	2004
Allegan County	3.7	2.9	7.2
Barry County	4.1	3.3	5.9
Berrien County	5.4	3.7	7.8
Cass County	4.7	3.2	4.7
Ionia County	6.1	3.7	8.1
Kalamazoo County	3.4	3.0	5.8
Kent County	3.7	3.1	6.9
Mecosta County	5.3	4.3	7.2
Montcalm County	7.5	4.1	8.1
Muskegon County	6.4	4.1	7.9
Newaygo County	9.9	4.6	8.1
Oceana County	11.3	5.8	8.9
Ottawa County	3.2	2.7	5.6
St. Joseph County	4.2	3.4	6.8
Van Buren County	6.5	4.0	7.4

MAJOR EMPLOYERS

Counting the precise number of employees at any large company is a tricky business. For one thing, large employers are constantly gaining and losing people. For another, some firms use temps or contract workers to fill gaps in their regular staff. And then there are the questions of part-time workers, interns, and people on family leave or temporary lay-off.

All of this means that the numbers in the list that follows are, by necessity, estimates. And no one is suggesting that the 2,500 jobs at McDonald's are the equivalent of about the same number of jobs at General Motors.

Still, a job is a job. The kids who work evenings at Mickey D's (and the moms who work the lunch hour) are all part of the same economy as the folks on the line at GM.

Here is a list of major employers in West Michigan. Some of the data comes from the Right Place, Inc; Southwest Michigan First, and West Michigan Business Review. It is used here with permission.

Meijer, Grand Rapids

Locations throughout West Michigan

Retail stores and distribution, 14,000 employees

Spectrum Health, Grand Rapids

Locations throughout West Michigan

Hospital and health services, 12,000 employees

U.S. Postal Service

Mail and package delivery

Locations throughout West Michigan, 5,400 employees

Spartan Stores – Grand Rapids (merged with D&W stores)

Locations throughout West Michigan

Grocery wholesale and retail, 5,000 employees

Pfizer Inc., Kalamazoo, Holland

Pharmaceutical manufacturing and research, 5,000 employees

Steelcase Inc., Grand Rapids

Office Furniture, 5,000 employees

Johnson Controls Inc., Automotive Group, Holland

Automotive Services, 4,500 employees

Herman Miller, Inc., Zeeland-Holland

Office furniture systems, 4,500 employees

Wal-Mart Stores, Inc.

Locations throughout West Michigan

Retail stores, 4,400 employees

Borgess Health Alliance Inc., Kalamazoo-Dowagiac

Hospital and health services, 4,300 employees

Bronson Healthcare Group, Inc., Kalamazoo, Oshtemo, Plainwell, Portage

Hospital and health services, 4,100 employees

Alticor Inc. (Amway), Ada

Consumer products, 4,000 employees

Western Michigan University, Kalamazoo

Locations throughout West Michigan

Higher education, 3,800 employees

Grand Rapids Public Schools, Grand Rapids

Public school system, 3,400 employees

Lakeland Regional Health System, St. Joseph

Locations throughout West Michigan

Hospital and health services, 3,100 employees

Target Corp.

Distribution center, stores throughout West Michigan

General merchandise retail, 3,000 employees

Whirlpool Corp., Benton Harbor-St. Joseph

Manufacturer of appliances, 3,000 employees

Haworth Corp., Holland

Office furniture, 2,800 employees

St. Mary's Health Care, Grand Rapids

Hospital and health services, 2,500 employees

Fifth Third Bank, Grand Rapids

Locations throughout West Michigan

Banking and financial services, 2,500 employees

McDonald's Corp.

Locations throughout West Michigan

Fast food restaurants, 2,500 employees

Perrigo Co., Allegan-Holland-Montague

Generic and over-the-counter pharmaceuticals, 2,400 employees

General Motors Corp., Metal Fabricating Div., Grand Rapids

Automotive parts manufacturer, 2,300 employees

Metropolitan Health Corp., Grand Rapids

Locations throughout West Michigan

Hospital and health services, 2,200 employees

Magna Donnelly Corp. Holland, Alto, Grand Haven, Kentwood, Norton Shores

Automotive mirrors, electronics and glass systems, 2,200 employees

Kalamazoo Public Schools, Kalamazoo

Public school system, 2,100 employees

Lacks Enterprises Inc., Grand Rapids, Kentwood

Automotive and electronics parts manufacturers, 2,100 employees

Howmet Corp. (Alcoa), Whitehall

Manufacturer for aerospace and industrial markets, 2,000 employees

Wolverine World Wide Inc., Rockford, Cedar Springs, Big Rapids

Footwear and leather products, 2,000 employees

Gentex Corp., Zeeland

Automatic mirrors and fire protection equipment, 2,000 employees

County of Kent

County government, 2,000 employees

National City Bank, Northwest

Locations throughout West Michigan

Banking and financial services, 2,000 employees

Mercy General Health Partners, Muskegon

Hospital and health services, 2,000 employees

Ferris State University, Big Rapids, Grand Rapids

Higher education, 1,950 employees

United Parcel Service Inc.

Locations throughout
West Michigan

Package delivery and specialized transportation and logistics services, 1,900 employees

Quality Dining Inc.,

Locations throughout
West Michigan

Operates 175 restaurants, 1,900 employees

Grand Valley State University, Allendale

Locations throughout
West Michigan

Higher education, 1,850 employees

Gordon Food Service Inc., Grand Rapids

Locations throughout
West Michigan

Wholesale and retail food distributor, 1,800 employees

City of Grand Rapids

City Government, 1,700 employees

Hope Network, Grand Rapids

Locations throughout
West Michigan

Rehabilitation, training, and housing for people with disabilities, 1,700 employees

JSJ Corp. (Including GHSP) Grand Haven

Diversified manufacturing, 1,700 employees

Benteler Automotive Corp., Grand Rapids, Galesburg, Wyoming

Automotive chassis, exhaust systems and structural products, 1,700 employees

Siemens Logistics and Assembly Systems (Dematic), Grand Rapids

Conveyors, storage retrieval systems and guided vehicles, 1,600 employees

Lear Corp., Mendon, Grand Rapids, Walker

Interior systems and components for auto industry, 1,500 employees

Home Depot U.S.A. Inc.

Locations throughout
West Michigan

Home improvement and building supply retailer, 1,500 employees

Holland Community Hospital, Holland, Douglas, Hamilton

Hospital and health services, 1,500 employees

Meridian Automotive Systems, Grand Rapids, Ionia

Manufactures molded and stamped auto components, 1,500 employees

Stryker Corp., Kalamazoo

Manufactures orthopedic implants and medical equipment, 1,450 employees

Indiana Michigan Power Co. (Cook Nuclear Plant), Bridgman

Electric utility and nuclear power generation, 1,415 employees

Advance Publications Inc., Grand Rapids, Kalamazoo, Muskegon

Publisher of Grand Rapids Press, Kalamazoo Gazette, Muskegon Chronicle. 1,400 employees

Delphi Corp., Grand Rapids, Coopersville

Automotive engine component manufacturer, 1,400 employees

Foremost Corp. of America, Caledonia

Insurance, 1,400 employees

Metron Integrated Health Systems, Grand Rapids

Locations throughout West Michigan

Nursing homes and health care services. 1,400 employees

Forest Hills Public Schools, Grand Rapids

Public school system, 1,350 employees

County of Muskegon

County Government, 1,300 employees

Robert Bosch Corp., Kentwood, St. Joseph

Manufactures automotive equipment, home appliances and more, 1,300 employees

SBC Communications Inc. (AT&T)

Locations throughout West Michigan

Telecommunications services, 1,300 employees

Summit Polymers Inc., Portage, Sturgis, Vicksburg

Injection-molded plastics for auto industry, 1,250 employees

Smiths Aerospace Inc., Grand Rapids

Military and commercial avionics systems, 1,200 employees

Packerland-Plainwell Inc. (formerly Murco Foods), Plainwell

Beef packing plant, 1,200 employees

Hackley Hospital, Muskegon

Hospital and health services, 1,200 employees

Parker-Hannifin Corp., Otsego, Kalamazoo, Martin, Richland

Diverse manufacturer for aerospace and industrial applications, 1,150 employees

County of Ottawa

County government, 1,100 employees

Grand Rapids Community College, Grand Rapids

Higher Education, 1,100 employees

Bradford-White Corp., Middleville, Niles

Manufactures water heaters, 1,100 employees

Portage Public Schools, Portage

Public school system, 1,100 employees

Shape Corp., Grand Haven

Custom Roll-forming, ultra-high-strength steel, 1,100 employees

Kentwood Public Schools, Kentwood

Public school system, 1,100 employees

Pine Rest Christian Mental Health Services, Grand Rapids

Locations throughout West Michigan

Mental health services, 1,100 employees

Kalamazoo Valley Community College, Kalamazoo

Higher education, 1,050 employees

County of Kalamazoo

County government, 1,050 employees

American Axle & Manufacturing Inc., Three Rivers

Manufactures drive shafts and axles for auto industry, 1,050 employees

Huntington Bank, Columbus, Ohio

Locations throughout West Michigan

Banking and financial services, 1,000 employees

Michigan Medical, MMPC, Grand Rapids

Locations throughout West Michigan

Physicians and health services, 1,000 employees

ADAC Plastics, Inc, Grand Rapids

Auto parts, injection moldings, 1,000 employees

HEALTH CARE

If other sectors of the West Michigan economy have faltered in recent years, health care has remained strong. A dozen health care organizations are listed among the top regional employers, with 1,000 or more employees.

Of course, health care is more than just a business. Especially if you're the one who's sick. Nearly all medical services are available in West Michigan, from emergency care to open-heart surgery.

In 2005, four West Michigan facilities were named among the top 100 hospitals by Solucient, an Illinois company that tracks outcomes and performance. Bronson Methodist in Kalamazoo made the list among teaching hospitals, Holland Hospital among medium-sized community hospitals, and both Mecosta General, in Big Rapids and Gerber Memorial, in Fremont were named among the top small community hospitals.

The health care system has grown increasingly complex, with outpatient surgery centers, long-term acute care hospitals, free-standing emergency med-centers and other facilities blurring the lines between doctors' offices, hospitals and nursing homes.

The region's largest health care organization is Spectrum Health in Grand Rapids, which includes the former Blodgett and Butterworth hospitals and several outlying facilities, as well as DeVos Children's Hospital and Meijer Heart Center at the Butterworth site.

The best hospital name is also in Grand Rapids: The Mary Free Bed Rehabilitation Hospital. The Mary Free Bed name dates from 1891, when a group of women started a fund drive to endow a "free" bed in a local hospital for use by the poor.

Their fund-raising gimmick was to ask for a donation from anyone named Mary – or anyone who knew someone named Mary. Their "Mary Free Bed" eventually grew into a hospital of its own. Today it has a national reputation as a rehabilitation and physical therapy center.

Here are the hospitals of West Michigan

Forest View Hospital

62 bed, psychiatric facility
(No emergency room or intensive care unit)
1055 Medical Park Drive, SE
Grand Rapids MI 49546
(616) 942-9610
www.forestviewhospital.com

Holland Community Hospital

167 bed acute care facility
(Includes emergency department and intensive care unit)
602 Michigan Ave.
Holland, MI 49423
(616) 392-5141
www.hoho.org

Ionia County Memorial Hospital

60 bed acute care hospital
(Includes emergency department and coronary intensive care unit)
479 Lafayette St.
Ionia, MI 48846
(616) 527-4200
www.ioniahospital.org

Kalamazoo Psychiatric Hospital

210 bed state-owned psychiatric facility
(No emergency or intensive care)
1312 Oakland Dr.
Kalamazoo, MI 49008
(269) 337-3000

Mary Free Bed Rehabilitation Hospital

80 bed rehabilitation facility
(No emergency or intensive care)
235 Wealthy St. SE
Grand Rapids, MI 49503
(616) 242-0300
www.mfbrc.com

Metropolitan Hospital

169 bed acute care facility
(Includes emergency department and intensive care unit)
1919 Boston SE
Grand Rapids, MI 49506
(616) 252-7200
www.metrohealth.net

North Ottawa Community Hospital

81 bed acute care facility
(Includes emergency department and intensive care unit)
1309 Sheldon Road
Grand Haven, MI 49417
(616) 842-3600
www.noch.org

Pine Rest Christian Mental Health Services

56 bed psychiatric facility
(No emergency or intensive care unit)
300 68th Street SE
Grand Rapids, MI 49501
(616) 455-5000
www.pinerest.org

Saint Mary's Health Care

230 bed acute care facility
(Includes emergency department and intensive care unit)
200 Jefferson Street, SE
Grand Rapids, MI 49503
(616) 752-6090
www.smmmc.org

Spectrum Health – Blodgett Campus

291 bed acute care facility
(Includes emergency department and intensive care unit)
1840 Wealthy Street SE
Grand Rapids, MI 49506
(616) 774-7444
www.spectrum-health.org

Spectrum Health – Butterworth Campus

924 bed acute care facility
(Includes emergency department and intensive care unit)
The site includes DeVos Children's Hospital and the Meijer Heart Center
100 Michigan Street NE
Grand Rapids, MI 49503
(616) 391-1774
www.spectrum-health.org

Spectrum Health – Kent Community Campus

76 bed long term care facility
(No emergency care department or intensive care unit)
750 Fuller NE
Grand Rapids, MI 49503
(616) 486-3000
www.spectrum-health.org

Spectrum Health – Greenville United Memorial Health Center

55 bed acute care facility
(Includes emergency department and intensive care unit)
615 South Bower Street
Greenville, MI 48838
(616) 754-4691
www.um.spectrum-health.org

Zeeland Community Hospital

60 bed acute care facility
(Includes emergency department and intensive care unit)
100 Pine Street
Zeeland, MI 49464-1619
(616) 772-4644

Allegan General Hospital

54 bed acute care facility
(Includes emergency department and intensive care unit)
555 Linn Street
Allegan MI 49010
(269) 673-8424
www.aghosp.org

Borgess Medical Center

286 acute care facility
(Includes intensive care unit and emergency department)
1521 Gull Road
Kalamazoo, MI 49048
(269) 226-7000
www.borgess.com

Borgess-Lee Memorial Hospital

15 bed critical access hospital
(Includes emergency department and special care unit)
420 West High Street
Dowagiac, MI 49047
(269) 782-8681
www.borgess.com

Borgess-Pipp Hospital

43 bed acute care facility
(Includes emergency department)
411 Naomi Street
Plainwell, MI 49080
(269) 685-0700
www.borgess.com

Bronson Methodist Hospital

323 bed acute care facility
(Includes emergency department and intensive care unit)
601 John Street
Kalamazoo, MI 49007
(269) 341-7654
www.bronsonhealth.com

Bronson Vicksburg Hospital

18 bed acute care facility
(Includes emergency department)
13326 North Boulevard Street
Vicksburg, MI 49097
(269) 649-2321
www.bronsonhealth.com

Community Hospital Watervliet

42 bed acute care facility
(Includes emergency department and intensive care unit)
400 Medical Park Drive
Watervliet, MI 49098
(269) 463-3111
www.communityhospital-watervliet.com

Lakeland Hospital – Niles

89 bed acute care facility
(Includes emergency department and intensive care unit)
31 North Saint Joseph Avenue
Niles, MI 49120
(269) 683-5510
www.lakelandhealth.org

Lakeland Hospital – St Joseph

254 bed acute care facility
(Includes emergency department and intensive care unit)
1234 Napier Avenue
Saint Joseph, MI 49085-2112
(269) 983-8300
www.lakelandhealth.org

LakeView Community Hospital

33 bed acute care facility
(Includes emergency department and intensive care unit)
408 Hazen Street
Paw Paw, MI 49079-3141
(269) 657-3141
www.lakeviewcares.com

Pennock Hospital

89 bed acute care facility
(Includes emergency department and intensive care unit)
1009 West Green Street
Hastings, MI 49058-1709
(269) 945-3451
www.pennockhealth.com

South Haven Community Hospital

29 bed acute care facility
(Includes emergency department and intensive care unit)
955 South Bailey Avenue
South Haven, MI 49090
(269) 637-5271
www.shch.org

Sturgis Hospital

49 bed acute care facility
(Includes emergency department and intensive care unit)
916 Myrtle Avenue
Sturgis, MI 49091
(269) 651-7824
www.sturgishospital.com

Three Rivers Health

40 bed acute care facility
(Includes emergency department and intensive care unit)
701 South Health Parkway
Three Rivers, MI 49093
(269) 278-1145
www.threeriversheath.org

Gerber Memorial Health Services

83 bed acute care facility
(Includes emergency department and intensive care unit)
212 South Sullivan Street
Fremont, MI 49412
(231) 924-3300
www.gerberhospital.org

Hackley Hospital

152 bed acute care facility
(Includes emergency department and intensive care unit)
1700 Clinton Street
Muskegon, MI 49442
(231) 726-3511
www.hackley.org

Hackley Lakeshore Hospital

24 bed acute care facility
(Includes emergency department)
72 South State Street
Shelby, MI 49455
(231) 861-2156
www.hackley.org

Mecosta County General Hospital

27 bed acute care facility
(Includes emergency department and intensive care unit)
405 Winter Avenue
Big Rapids, MI 49307
(231) 796-8691
www.mcghhospital.com

Mercy General Health Partners – Mercy Campus

175 bed acute care facility
(Includes emergency department and intensive care unit)
1500 East Sherman Boulevard
Muskegon, MI 49444
(231) 739-9341
www.mghp.com

Mercy General Health Partners – Muskegon General Campus

112 bed acute care facility
1700 Oak Avenue
Muskegon, MI 49444
(231) 739-9341
www.mghp.com

Sheridan Community Hospital

25-bed acute care hospital
(Includes emergency department)
301 N. Main St.
PO Box 279
Sheridan, MI 48884
(989) 291-3261
www.sheridanhospital.com

Carson City Hospital

77-bed acute care hospital
(Includes emergency and intensive care units)
406 E. Elm St.
PO Box 879
Carson City, MI 48881
(989) 584-3131
www.carsoncityhospital.com

Kelsey Campus, Spectrum Health, United Mem.

25-bed critical access hospital
(Includes emergency department)
418 Washington Ave.
Lakeview, MI 48850
(989) 352-7211
www.um.spectrum-health.org

THE NEWS MEDIA

The news media in West Michigan and all of America has changed dramatically in recent decades, with the advent of wireless communication, cable television, satellite broadcasting, the Internet and digital photography.

But for all those changes, residents still get much of their news and advertising information the same place they got it in the 1970s: Local television and newspapers. Here is a list of news outlets in West Michigan:

Allegan

Allegan County News

Weekly newspaper, circulation 5,500

231 Trowbridge
PO Box 189

Allegan, MI 49010

(269) 673-5534

Berrien Springs

The Journal Era

Weekly newspaper, circulation 2,000

PO Box 98
Berrien Springs, MI 49103

(269) 473-5421

Big Rapids

The Pioneer

Daily newspaper, circulation 5,859

502.N State
Big Rapids, MI 49307

(231) 796-4831

Carson City

Carson City Gazette

Weekly newspaper, circulation 10,000 (free + paid)

211 W. Main
Carson City, MI 48811

(989) 584-3967

Climax

The Climax Crescent

Weekly newspaper, circulation 850

150 N Main St.
Climax, MI 49034

(269) 746-4331
www.climaxcrescent.com

Decatur

Decatur Republican

Weekly newspaper, circulation 1,600

PO Box 36
120 South Phelps St.
Decatur, MI 49045

(269) 423-2411

Dowagiac

Dowagiac Daily News

Daily newspaper,
circulation 1,850

205 Spaulding St.
PO Box 30
Dowagiac, MI 49047

(269) 782-2101

Edwardsburg

The Argus

Weekly newspaper,
circulation 1,800

217 N. 4th St.
Niles, MI 49120

(888) 725-0108
www.edwardsburgargus.com

Freeport

Freeport News

Weekly newspaper,
circulation 600

129 Division St.
Freeport, MI 49325

(616) 765-8511

Fremont

Times-Indicator

Weekly newspaper,
circulation 7,500

TI Publications

44 W. Main St.
Fremont, MI 49412

(231) 924-4400
www.timesindicator.com

Grand Haven

Grand Haven Tribune

Daily newspaper,
circulation 9,850

101 North Third St.
Grand Haven, MI 49417

(616) 842-6400
www.grandhaventribune.com

Grand Rapids

Grand Rapids Magazine

Regional magazine,
monthly circulation 17,000

Gemini Publications

549 Ottawa Ave. NE, Suite 201,
Grand Rapids, MI 49503

The Grand Rapids Press

Daily newspaper, circulation:
136,000 daily; 186,000 Sunday

155 Michigan St. NE
Grand Rapids, MI 49503

(616) 222-5400
www.mlive.com

The Grand Rapids Times

Weekly newspaper;
African-American interest

PO Box 7258
2106 Eastern Ave. SE
Grand Rapids, MI 49503

(616) 245-8737

WGVU/WGVK Television
Channel 35 (Grand Rapids) and 52 (Kalamazoo)
Public Television from Grand Valley State University

301 W. Fulton St.
Grand Rapids, MI 49504

www.wgvu.org

WOOD-TV 8

Commercial television, Channel 8, NBC

120 College Ave. SE,
Grand Rapids, MI 49503

(616) 456-8888
www.woodtv.com

WXMI-TV 17

Commercial television, Channel 17, Fox

3117 Plaza Drive NE
Grand Rapids, MI 49525

(616) 364-8722
www.wxmi.com

WZZM - TV 13

Commercial television, Channel 13, ABC

PO Box Z
Grand Rapids, MI 49501

(616) 785-1313
www.wzzm.com

Grand Rapids and suburbs

Advance Newspapers

Weekly free-circulation newspapers

Circulation 225,000 total for 14 editions including *East Grand Rapids Cadence* and *Wayland Penasee Globe*

PO Box 9
Jenison, MI 49429

(616) 669-2700
www.advancenewspapers.com

Greenville

Greenville Daily News

Daily newspaper, circulation 8,500

1091 N. Lafayette
Greenville, MI 48838

(616) 754-9301

Hart

Oceana's Herald-Journal

Weekly newspaper, circulation 7,500

123 State St.
Hart, MI 49420

(231) 861-2126

Hastings

The Hastings Banner

Weekly newspaper, circulation 7,000

J-Ad Corp

PO Box B
Hastings, MI 49058

Holland

Holland Sentinel

Daily newspaper, circulation: daily 18,600; Sunday 20,300

54 W. 8th Street
Holland, MI 49423

(616) 392-2311

Ionia

Ionia Sentinel-Standard

Daily newspaper, circulation 3,100

114 N. Depot St.
Ionia, MI 48846

(616) 527-2100
www.sentinel-standard.com

Kalamazoo

Kalamazoo Gazette

Daily newspaper: circulation: daily 53,600; Sunday 71,800

401 S. Burdick St.
Kalamazoo, MI 49007

(269) 345-3511
www.mlive.com

WWMT-TV 3

Commercial television, channel 3, CBS

590 W. Maple St.
Kalamazoo, MI 49008

(269) 342-2737
www.wwmt.com

Kalamazoo-Battle Creek

WOTV-41

Commercial television, channel 41, ABC

5200 W. Dickman Road
Battle Creek, MI 49016

www.wotv-com

Lowell

Lowell Ledger

Weekly newspaper, circulation 2,200

PO Box 128
105 North Broadway
Lowell, MI 49331

(616) 897-9621
www.Lowellbuyersguide.com

Marcellus

Marcellus News

Weekly newspaper, circulation 1,400

PO Box 227
Marcellus, MI 49067

(269) 646-2101
www.marcellusnews.com

Muskegon

The Muskegon Chronicle

Daily newspaper, circulation: daily 44,000; Sunday 49,000

981 3rd St.
PO Box 59
Muskegon, MI 49443

(231) 722-3161
www.mlive.com

New Buffalo

New Buffalo Times

Weekly newspaper, circulation 5,000

PO Box 369
102 S. Whittaker
New Buffalo, MI 49117

(269) 469-1000

Niles

Niles Daily Star

Daily newspaper, circulation 2,650

217 N. 4th Street
Niles, MI 49120

(888) 725-0108
www.nilesstar.com

St. Joseph

The Herald-Palladium

Daily newspaper, circulation: daily 28,000; Sunday 30.000

3450 Hollywood Road
PO Box 128
St. Joseph, MI 49085

(269) 429-2400
www.heraldpalladium.com

Saugatuck

The Commercial Record

Weekly newspaper, circulation 2,000

3217 Blue Star Hwy
PO Box 246
Saugatuck, MI 49453

(269) 857-2570
www.allegannews.com

Sturgis

Sturgis Journal

Daily newspaper, circulation 7,500

Hometown Communications, Inc.

209 John St.
PO Box 660
Sturgis, MI 49091

(269) 651-2296
www.sturgisjournal.com

Three Rivers

Three Rivers Commercial-News

Daily newspaper, circulation 3,500

124 N. Main St.
PO Box 130
Three Rivers, MI 49093

(269) 279-7488

Watervliet

Tri-City Record

Weekly newspaper, circulation 2,500

138 N. Main St.
PO Box 7
Watervliet, MI 49098

(269) 463-6397
www.tricityrecord.com

Whitehall

White Lake Beacon

Weekly newspaper,
circulation10,000

432 Spring St., PO Box 98
Whitehall, MI 49461

(231) 894-5356
www.whitelakebeacon.com

Zeeland

Zeeland Record

Weekly newspaper,
circulation 1,200

1622 Elm St.
Zeeland, MI 49464

(616) 772-2131

SPORTS & RECREATION

Previous page: Former major-league pitcher Phil Regan, who managed the West Michigan Whitecaps in 2002-03, explains the rules to an umpire (photo courtesy of West Michigan Whitecaps)

SPORTS and RECREATION

West Michigan doesn't get much national exposure in the world of sports. We look to Detroit or Chicago for major professional sports teams. And many West Michigan residents identify with collegiate athletics outside our region, especially at the University of Michigan, Michigan State University and the University of Notre Dame.

But don't take that to mean that the region lacks activities in sports and recreation. Western Michigan University has a full compliment of Division 1 intercollegiate sports, and Ferris State plays hockey at the top collegiate level. Grand Valley State operates one of the nation's top Division II sports programs, while Calvin, Hope and Kalamazoo colleges are forces in the small-college Division III.

West Michigan natives have played in all the major sports leagues, and the region has supported teams on the minor league level. In addition, such local events as auto racetracks and high school sports rivalries attract hundreds of thousands of fans each year. Here's a look at sports and recreation in West Michigan.

MAJOR LOCAL EVENTS

The Fifth-Third River Bank Run
This 25-kilometer (15-mile) event, which begins and ends in downtown Grand Rapids, is regarded as the top footrace in Michigan, and one of the top in the nation. The race, held each May, annually draws thousands of athletes, including local recreational joggers and international elite runners. Since the race's inception in 1978, winners have included Olympic marathon medalists Joan Benoit Samuelson and Bill Rodgers.

Gus Macker 3-on-3 Basketball.
The Gus Macker "empire" began in 1974 as a neighborhood game in Lowell. Scott McNeal (alias Gus Macker) and a group of friends held a tournament for three-person teams in McNeal's parents' driveway. The annual tournament became a neighborhood event and ultimately outgrew its hometown. In 1987, the main tournament moved to Belding, and McNeal's Gus Macker organization began sponsoring tournaments in other cities. In 2006, more than 50 Gus Macker tournaments were scheduled in North America.

Tennis in Kalamazoo
The United States Tennis Association's Boys Tennis Championship, at Kalamazoo College's Stowe Stadium, is considered to be the nation's top tournament for male tennis

players age 18 and under. Such future stars as Michael Chang, Arthur Ashe, Pete Sampras and Jimmy Connors have played in the annual event. The 10-day competition, held each August, draws nearly 400 top players. Kalamazoo has been the site of the championships since 1943.

ALL AMERICAN GIRLS PROFESSIONAL BASEBALL LEAGUE

This association of women's baseball teams was established during World War II by Chicago Cubs owner Philip K. Wrigley,

Grand Rapids Chicks catcher turns a double play in a 1948 victory over the Kenosha Comets at South Field (photo courtesy of Grand Rapids Public Library)

who was concerned that major league baseball might disappear as many players joined the war effort. A fictionalized version of the women's baseball story was told in the 1992 film "A League of Their Own," starring Tom Hanks, Madonna, and Geena Davis. During parts of its 11-year existence, the league had West Michigan franchises in Grand Rapids, Kalamazoo and Muskegon.

The Grand Rapids Chicks began their history as a 1944 expansion team in Milwaukee. The franchise moved to Grand Rapids in 1945, and played there until the league went out of business, after the 1954 season. The Chicks won the league championship three times while in Grand Rapids.

The Muskegon Lassies were born in 1946 as an expansion team. They moved a few counties to the south in 1950, becoming the **Kalamazoo Lassies**. The Kalamazoo team won the last AAGPBL championship in 1954.

The Muskegon Belles played in the league in 1953, and folded before the 1954 season. The team was created in 1943 as the Racine Belles, one of four original AAGPBL teams. The Belles moved to Battle Creek in 1950 and to Muskegon in 1953.

MINOR LEAGUES

BASEBALL

The West Michigan Whitecaps began play in 1994 at Old Kent Park, just north of Grand Rapids. The Class A Midwest League franchise was moved from Wisconsin, where it had been known as the Madison Muskies. The Whitecaps were initially affiliated with the Oakland A's, but joined the Detroit Tigers minor league system in 1997.

The Whitecaps broke Class A attendance records their first three years of existence, drawing 547,401 fans in 1996. In recent seasons, attendance has hovered between 350,000 and 400,000 a year.

Old Kent Bank, which bought the naming rights to the privately financed stadium, was purchased by Fifth Third Bank in 2002, and the stadium's name was changed to Fifth Third Ballpark. Seating capacity is just over 10,000.

The Kalamazoo Kings baseball team has played in the independent Frontier League since 2001. The team drew more than 130,000 fans to Homer Stryker Field in Mayor's Riverfront Park in 2005 while winning the league championship. The Frontier League was founded in 1993. It is an independent league, which means it is not part of the major league farm system.

A sunset crowd watches minor league baseball at Fifth Third Ballpark in Comstock Park (photo courtesy of West Michigan Whitecaps)

BASKETBALL

The Grand Rapids Tackers played from 1962-73 in the Midwest Professional Basketball League, the North American Basketball League, and the Continental Basketball Association. The team's home games were generally at the Godwin High School Fieldhouse or the old Grand Rapids Civic Auditorium. Tacker alumni included Dr. M.C. Burton and Herschell Turner, who became community leaders in Grand Rapids. (The CBA in which the Tackers played was not the same organization as the present Continental Basketball Association.)

The Grand Rapids Hoops were formed as a Continental Basketball Association expansion team in 1989. The team was purchased by the founders of the Gus Macker organization in 1994, and the name was changed to the **Grand Rapids Mackers.** Another sale restored the name to the Hoops before the 1996 season. The Hoops/Mackers played in the Welsh Civic Auditorium until 1996, when they moved to the new VanAndel Arena. The CBA folded during the 2000-2001 season. The Hoops finished that season at the Deltaplex as a member of the International Basketball League.

The Michigan Mayhem began play in Muskegon's L.C. Walker Arena as a Continental Basketball Association expansion team in 2004. (The league re-formed in 2001 as a merger of the CBA, the International Basketball League and the International Basketball Association.)

The Grand Rapids Flight and **Holland Blast** are members of a new league, the International Basketball League, which plays a 20-game schedule from March through June.

HOCKEY

The International Hockey League came to Muskegon in 1960, the year the L.C. Walker Arena was dedicated. The Arena was home ice to the IHL franchise known as the **Zephyrs** (1960-65), **Mohawks** (1965-84) and **Lumberjacks** (1984-92). The Lumberjacks moved to Cleveland in 1992, a time when the IHL was expanding into larger markets.

The following year, the **Muskegon Fury** was established as a member of the Colonial Hockey League. The Fury has been the home team at L.C. Walker Arena since 1993. The club has been highly successful on the ice, winning the Colonial Cup in 1999, 2002, 2004 and 2005. The Colonial League changed its name to the United Hockey League (UHL) in 1997.

The Kalamazoo Wings joined the International Hockey League in 1974, playing in the new Wings Stadium. The team changed its name to the **Michigan K-Wings** in 1995. Kalamazoo ended its affiliation with the IHL in 2000.

The league folded the following year. The Madison Kodiaks franchise of the United Hockey League was relocated to Wings Stadium for the 2000 season and renamed the Kalamazoo Wings. That version of the team continues to play at Wings Stadium.

The Grand Rapids Rockets (1950-56) and **Owls** (1977-80) were IHL teams that played in a 1940s era building known first as The Stadium and later as Stadium Arena. The building has since been redeveloped as the Deltaplex and continues in use as a concert venue and exhibition hall.

The Grand Rapids Griffins were founded in 1996 as an IHL franchise to play in the new VanAndel Arena. The Griffins stayed with the IHL until the league's demise in 2001, and switched to the American Hockey League, where they still play. The Griffins are affiliated with the Detroit Red Wings.

ARENA FOOTBALL

The Grand Rapids Rampage Arena Football League team has played in VanAndel Arena since 1998. Arena football is an indoor version of football, with fewer players on the field and rules that emphasize passing and scoring. The Rampage franchise began its history as the Washington Commandos in 1987, the year the AFL was founded. It later became the Detroit Drive (1988-94) and the Massachusetts Marauders (1994). The franchise was inactive at the time it was purchased by D.P. Fox Inc. and brought to Grand Rapids as the Rampage. The team hosted and won the league championship game, ArenaBowl XV, in 2001.

SPORTS PROFESSIONALS FROM WEST MICHIGAN

BASEBALL

Here's a sports trivia quiz:

In the 1999 World Series, a New York Yankees player who grew up in West Michigan stroked a crucial home run in game three, and then caught the last out in the next game to preserve the Yankees' four-game sweep over Atlanta. Can you name the player?

If you said Derek Jeter, well, nice try.

Jeter, the Yankees' shortstop since 1995 and a graduate of Kalamazoo Central High School, is certainly Major

League baseball's best-known West Michigan connection.

But in 1999, another local player also had a key role in the Yankees' World Series triumph.

It was Chad Curtis, a centerfielder from Middleville, who hit the deciding homer in the 10th inning of game three, and then caught a fly ball for the final out in the Yankees' four-game sweep.

The following year, the Yankees won again. And this time Jeter was named World Series MVP.

Curtis, a former Detroit Tiger, played three more years before retiring to his West Michigan home.

Baseball has a proud tradition in West Michigan, with more than 60 players from the region making it to the big leagues at some time over the past century or so.

Here are a few of the highlights:

Howard Bailey, of Grand Haven and Grand Valley State, pitched six games with Detroit from 1981-83.

Cornelius "Neil" Berry, an infielder from Kalamazoo and Western Michigan University, played from 1948 to 1954 for Detroit, Chicago, the St. Louis Browns and Baltimore.

Anthony "Bunny" Brief, born Anthony Grzeszkowski in Remus, played outfield and first base from 1912-1917 with the St. Louis Browns and two other teams.

Chris Burkam of Benton Harbor had one at-bat for the Browns in 1915. He struck out.

Jerry Byrne of Parnell pitched three games for the White Sox in 1929.

Greg Cadaret of Detroit and GVSU pitched in the big leagues for 10 years. In 1991 he appeared in 68 games as a relief pitcher with the Yankees. He also pitched in the 1988 World Series for Oakland.

Jim Command, of Moline got into 14 games with the Philadelphia Phillies in 1954 and 55. Command was for years a popular force in amateur baseball in Grand Rapids.

Mark Dewey of Jenison and GVSU appeared in more than 200 games as a relief pitcher for San Francisco, Pittsburgh and the New York Mets from 1990-96.

John "Lefty" Dobb of Muskegon pitched two innings for the White Sox in 1924, with no wins or losses.

Rob Ellis of Grand Rapids played in the outfield for Milwaukee from 1971-75.

Horace "Hod" Fenner of Martin and Kalamazoo College pitched two games for the White Sox in 1921.

Ira Flagstead of Montague was an outfielder for several teams, including Detroit, in a 14-year career from 1917-30. He finished with a very respectable .290 batting average.

Brent Gates of Grandville attended the University of Minnesota, and had a seven-year major league career, 1993-99, after being drafted by the Oakland A's. He later served as manager of the West Michigan Whitecaps.

Bobby Grich, born in Muskegon, was a six-time all-star during a 17-year major league career with the Orioles and Angels.

Dave Gumpert, of South Haven and Aquinas College, appeared in more than 80 games during a five-year career with the Tigers, Cubs and Royals.

Mike Hart of Kalamazoo played five games in the outfield for Texas in 1980.

Ed Hemingway of Sheridan played the infield for three different teams from 1914 to 1918.

Charlie Hemphill of Greenville compiled a .271 average as an outfielder for six teams in a career that spanned from 1899 to 1911. **Frank Hemphill**, also of Greenville, played in just a few games, for Chicago in 1906 and Washington in 09.

Ed Hendricks of Zeeland pitched four games for the New York Giants in 1910, recording one loss and no wins.

Clint Hurdle, a Big Rapids native, played from 1977-87, serving on four teams and finishing with a batting average of .259. Hurdle came up big in the 1980 World Series, hitting .417 for the Kansas City Royals. Hurdle has been manager of the Colorado Rockies since 2002.

Ron Jacobson of Kalamazoo and Western Michigan University played infield for the White Sox and Red Sox from 1954-60.

Jim Johnson of Muskegon and WMU pitched three games – winning one – for San Francisco in 1970.

Jim Kaat, of Zeeland, pitched for 25 years, from 1959-83, and recorded 283 victories, mostly with the Minnesota Twins. The lefty was a 20-game winner three times, and also pitched in three all-star games. Kaat was a member of the Washington Senators when that team moved to Minnesota and became the Twins in 1961.

Bill Killefer of Bloomingdale played from 1909-21 as a catcher for St. Louis, Philadelphia, and the Chicago Cubs. "Reindeer Bill" batted .238 for his 13 year career. He also managed the Cubs from 1921-25 and the St. Louis Browns from 1930-33.

Wade "Red" Killefer of Bloomingdale was a utility player with several teams from 1907-16. He played with Ty Cobb in Detroit at the beginning of his career.

Frank Kitson of Hopkins compiled a 128-117 record as a pitcher for five teams from 1898-1907.

Rick Kreuger of Grand Rapids and Michigan State pitched for Boston and Cleveland from 1975-78. He compiled a 2-2 won-lost record.

Bob Kuhn of Vicksburg pitched one game for the Cleveland Indians – and lost – in 1924.

Dave Machmer of St. Joseph and Central Michigan University played infield for California and Detroit in a two-year career from 1978-79.

Edmund "Stubby" Magner of Kalamazoo was a 5 foot, 3 inch shortstop for 13 major league games in 1911. Stubby also played at Cornell University before turning pro.

Matt Mantei of Stevensville was drafted by Seattle in 1991, the year he graduated from River Valley High School. He recorded 93 saves in a 10-year pitching career interrupted by injuries.

Charlie Maxwell, born in Lawton, near Paw Paw, is among the all-time most popular Detroit Tigers. Maxwell attended WMU before his 14 year Major League career that included stops at Boston, Detroit and Cleveland. As a Tiger in 1956, "Ol' Paw Paw" had a .326 batting average, 28 home runs and 95 runs batted in. He was an all-star in 1956 and 57.

Rick Miller of Grand Rapids and MSU, played outfield from 1971-1985 in Boston and Cleveland. He had more than 1,000 hits in his 15-year career, and was awarded a 1978 Gold Glove for his defensive prowess in center field.

Bill Morley of Holland took the field with the Washington Senators for two games in 1913. The second-baseman batted three times and had no hits.

Harry Niles of Buchanan played for five years, from 1906-1910. He was an outfielder, and finished with a .247 batting average.

Kirt Ojala of Kalamazoo and the University of Michigan pitched for the Florida Marlins from 1997-99. He appeared in 41 games in 1998.

Frank "Stubby" Overmire of Moline and Western Michigan University pitched in the big leagues from 1943-52, mostly with Detroit. After his retirement, Overmire was a long- time employee of the Tigers. He died in 1977 in Lakeland, Fla.

Pat Paige, of Paw Paw, pitched a pair of games for Cleveland in 1911.

Alfred Platte of Grand Rapids made it to the majors in 1913. The outfielder appeared in nine games, batted .111 and made two errors.

Ross Powell of Grand Rapids and U-M appeared in 48 games as a relief pitcher for several National League teams from 1993-95.

Phil Regan, born in Otsego, had a long career as a pitcher and later as a coach and manager. He played from 1960 to 1972, first as a starting pitcher for Detroit and later for the Dodgers, Cubs and White Sox as one of baseball's top relief pitchers. He managed the Baltimore Orioles in 1995, and also has served as baseball coach at Grand Valley and manager of the West Michigan Whitecaps.

Leon Roberts, of Vicksburg and the University of Michigan, played in the majors from 1974-84. He played outfield for six teams, including Detroit (1974-75). His best year was 1978, when he batted .301 and hit 22 home runs for Seattle.

Dave Rozema of Grand Rapids played from 1977-86 for Detroit and Texas. He had an impressive 15-7 record as a Tiger rookie in 1977.

Dave Schmidt, born in Niles, compiled a 54-55 record with 50 saves while pitching for five different teams from 1981-92.

Mike Squires of Kalamazoo and Western Michigan University played infield for the White Sox from 1975-85. He was a 1981 Gold Glove winner.

Mickey Stanley of Grand Rapids played for the Tigers from 1964-78. He was a decent hitter (.248 career batting average) but a great defensive center fielder who won four Gold Glove awards. In the 1968 World Series, he switched to shortstop to make room for aging star Al Kaline to play in the outfield.

Dick Terwilliger of Sand Lake pitched three scoreless innings in his one game with St. Louis in 1932.

Matt Thornton of Three Rivers and GVSU pitched 19 games with Seattle in 2004.

Andy Van Hekken of Holland came up with the Tigers in 2002 and looked good while posting a 1-3 record and 3.00 earned run average. His career was hampered by injuries and as of 2005 he hadn't made it back to the majors.

John VanderWal of Grand Rapids and Western Michigan University has played first base or outfield with eight major league teams since 1991. His best year was 2000 when he batted .299 with 24 home runs for Pittsburgh.

Clyde "Buzzy" Wares of Vandalia batted .220 as an infielder with the St. Louis Browns in 1913-14.

George Zuverink of Holland pitched eight years in the big leagues, from 1951-59. He was with Detroit for part of 1954 and 1955. His best year was 1957, when he won 10 games and had a 2.48 earned run average with Baltimore.

BOXING

The region also has a storied history in the sweet science of boxing.

The Greatest of All Time, **Muhammad Ali,** moved to Southwest Michigan in the middle of his career, and trained on his farm near Berrien Springs for several fights. He lives there now, but suffers from a form of Parkinson's Disease related to his boxing career.

Kenny Lane, born in Big Rapids in 1932, fought out of Muskegon and was among the world's best lightweights in the 50's and 60s. He fought for the world championship three times, including two memorable losses to hall of famer Carlos Ortiz. After his career, Lane continued to train young fighters in Muskegon.

Buster Mathis (1943-1995), a huge (some said fat – but not to his face) heavyweight from Grand Rapids, was a national Golden Gloves champ who beat Joe Frazier for the right to represent the United States in the 1964 Olympics. Unfortunately, Mathis suffered a broken hand, and Frazier went to Tokyo in his place, winning the gold medal. As a pro, Mathis had a 30-4 record, including losses to Frazier and Muhammad Ali. His son, **Buster Mathis, Jr.,** also was a professional boxer who came close to the top of the heavyweight division before losing to Mike Tyson in 1995.

Another Grand Rapids heavyweight, **Tony Tucker,** briefly held one version in the heavyweight crown in 1987, when he defeated James "Buster" Douglas for the International Boxing Federation title. He lost the title to Mike Tyson in his next fight.

The Mayweather clan from Grand Rapids has been among the most successful boxing families ever. **Floyd Mayweather Sr.** was a top welterweight in the 70s and 80s who later served as trainer for Oscar de la Hoya.

Roger Mayweather, Floyd Sr's brother, held two world titles, in the junior lightweight and junior welterweight divisions, in the 1980s.

Floyd Mayweather Jr., born in 1977, won a bronze medal in the 1996 Olympics and has since held world pro titles in the super featherweight, light weight and super lightweight divisions.

Stanley Ketchel (1886-1910) of Grand Rapids was known as "The Michigan Assassin," and is regarded as one of the best middleweight fighters in history. In 1909, Ketchel fought heavyweight champion Jack Johnson. Johnson, who outweighed Ketchel by about 40 pounds, won in 12 rounds. Ketchel was shot to death in 1910, apparently in a dispute over a woman.

BASKETBALL

Chet Walker, of Benton Harbor, may have been West Michigan's best basketball player – so far. Walker attended Bradley University after graduating from Benton Harbor. He began his NBA career in 1962. In a 13-year career, mostly with Philadelphia and Chicago, Walker averaged 18 points a game and was named as an all-star seven times.

Don Nelson, cited as one of the NBA's top 10 coaches, was born in Muskegon in 1940. He graduated from high school in Illinois and played college basketball at Iowa. In the NBA, he spent 14 years as a player, and more than 20 as a coach for four teams.

Loy Vaught of Kentwood helped the University of Michigan to the NCAA title in 1989, and was drafted in the first round by the L.A. Clippers. At the height of his career, in the 96 and 97 seasons, he averaged double figures in both points and rebounds. Vaught moved to the Detroit Pistons in 1999, but by then his game was hampered by injuries.

Chris Kaman, of Wyoming's Tri-Unity Christian High School and Central Michigan University, was a first round pick in 2003 by the Los Angeles Clippers. He averaged better than 9 points and six rebounds a game in 2005.

Chris Crawford of Comstock played at Marquette and was

drafted in 1997 by the Atlanta Hawks. In 2004, he averaged better than 10 points a game for the Hawks. He was on the injured list when he was waived the following season.

Dillard Crocker, a 6-4 swingman from Niles, went from Western Michigan University to a four-year career in the NBA, where he averaged 13.6 points a game in 1950.

Paul Griffin of Shelby also attended Western before playing in the NBA from 1977-83 as a forward for the New Orleans Jazz and San Antonio Spurs. In his best year, 1981, Griffin averaged 6.1 rebounds and 6.1 points a game.

Ben Handlogten, a 6-10 power forward from Allendale and WMU, spent nearly 10 years playing overseas before catching on with the Utah jazz for parts of 2004 and 2005.

Kevin Loder of Ross Beatty High School in Cassopolis went to Alabama State to play college ball in the late 1970s. He was drafted by the Kansas City Kings in 1981, and played from 82-84 for the Kings and the San Diego Clippers.

Anthony Miller of Benton Harbor was the state's Mr. Basketball in 1990. He played at Michigan State, and was drafted by the Golden State Warriors in 1994. He played parts of eight seasons in the NBA, with four different teams.

Steven Scheffler graduated from Grand Rapids Forest Hills Northern High School and went on to be named Big Ten player of the year at Purdue. He played parts of seven seasons in the NBA with four teams.

Tom Scheffler, of St. Joseph, also played at Purdue. He was drafted in 1977 by the Indiana Pacers, and played in the NBA in 1985 with the Portland Trail Blazers.

Matt Steigenga of Grand Rapids South Christian was Michigan's Mr. Basketball in 1988 before playing four years at Michigan State. He was drafted by the Chicago Bulls in 1992. His NBA career lasted for two games in 1997.

FOOTBALL

West Michigan football players in NFL (grouped by home town)

Robert Jackson played at Allendale High School and Central Michigan University before beginning his seven-year career (1981-88) as a defensive back for the Cincinnati Bengals.

Pete Gent of Bangor and Michigan State, played five years, 1964-68, as a wide

receiver for the Dallas Cowboys, catching four touchdown passes during his career.
Dave Behrman, of Dowagiac, played at Michigan State and then had a career as an offensive lineman with the Buffalo Bills and Denver Broncos from 1963-67.

Mike Teeter, of Fruitport, played at Michigan, and was a defensive lineman at Miami and Houston from 1991-94.

George Andrie, a 1958 graduate of Grand Rapids Catholic Central, played at Notre Dame and went on to an 11-year career with the Dallas Cowboys. The defensive lineman played in five consecutive Pro Bowls, from 1965-69.

Mike Kadish, of Grand Rapids Catholic Central and Notre Dame, played on the defensive line for the Buffalo Bills from 1973-81.

Mike Keller, a 1967 graduate of Grand Rapids Catholic Central, went to Michigan and was a linebacker with Dallas in the NFL in 1972.

Terry Barr, a wide receiver from Grand Rapids Central, played for the Detroit Lions from 1957-65. His best years were 1963 and 64. He caught passes for more than 1,000 yards in each of those years, scored 22 touchdowns, and played in two Pro Bowls.

Clarence Ellis, of Grand Rapids Central, played defensive back at Notre Dame and then for the Atlanta Falcons from 1972-74. Ellis had eight interceptions in his three-year career.

Rocky Rosema, a Grand Rapids Central grad, was a linebacker at Michigan and then at St. Louis in the NFL from 1968-71.

Mitch Lyons, a wide receiver from Forest Hills Northern, played from 1993 to 1999 with Atlanta and Pittsburgh, after a collegiate career at Michigan State.

Gary Hogeboom, of Grand Rapids Northview, played quarterback in the NFL from 1980 to 1989. In a career spent with three teams, he threw 49 touchdown passes. Hogeboom briefly became a celebrity in 2005 when he appeared as a contestant on the television reality show "Survivor."

Bob Lurtsema graduated from Grand Rapids Ottawa Hills in 1960, attended three colleges, and had an illustrious 11-year career as a defensive lineman with New York, Minnesota and Seattle.

Mike Prindle, of Grand Rapids Union, played in college at Western Michigan and served as the Detroit Lions' kicker for three games in 1987.

Kelly Butler, an offensive lineman from Grand Rapids Union High School and Purdue University, went from the Detroit Lions practice squad in 2004 to a starting tackle's job in 2005.

Mike Franckowiak, played quarterback at Grand Rapids West Catholic and led Central Michigan to the Division II national championship in 1974. He played in 1975-78 with Denver and Buffalo.

Ty Hallock, a running back from Greenville, played at Michigan State and then was a member of three NFL teams, including Detroit, from 1993-99.

Matt Vanderbeek, of Holland West Ottawa, played at Michigan State from 1986-89, and as a defensive lineman and linebacker with Indianapolis, Dallas and Washington from 1990-96.

Ray Bentley, of Hudsonville, was a defensive leader at Central Michigan, and played linebacker in the NFL with Buffalo and Cincinnati from 1986-92.

Joel Smeenge, of Hudsonville, was a defensive end and linebacker who recorded 35 sacks while playing with New Orleans and Jacksonville in the NFL from 1990-2000.

Paul Grasmanis graduated from Jenison in 1992 and went to Notre Dame. He was drafted by Chicago in 1996 and played with the Bears, Rams, Broncos and Eagles in the NFL.

Scott Rehberg, of Kalamazoo Central High School, played on the offensive line at Central Michigan, and then with New England, Cleveland and Cincinnati in the NFL.

Duane Young, of Kalamazoo Central, played at Michigan State and then had a six-year pro career (1991-98) with San Diego and Buffalo.

T.J. Duckett, of Kalamazoo Loy Norrix, was an All-American high school player as both running back and linebacker. He retained his All-American status as a running back at Michigan State. Duckett was drafted in the first round by the Atlanta Falcons in 2002. In his first four years with the Falcons he scored 31 touchdowns.

Mike Dumas, a Lowell grad, played at Indiana and went on to an eight-year pro career as a safety for Houston, Buffalo, Jacksonville, and San Diego.

Noah Herron, of Mattawan, played with the Green Bay Packers and Pittsburgh Steelers in 2005 as a running back.

Jerald Collins, a 1965 Muskegon High School graduate, played linebacker at Western Michigan and, from 1969-71, with the Buffalo Bills.

Earl Morrall, a 1952 Muskegon High School graduate, played quarterback in the NFL for six different teams from 1956-76. Morrall was a two-time Pro-Bowler who passed for more than 20,000 years in his career.

Bobby Morse, a 1983 graduate of Muskegon Catholic Central, went to Michigan State and then to the NFL, where he was a running back and kick returner with Philadelphia and New Orleans from 1987-91.

Carl Russ graduated from Muskegon Heights in 1971. He played linebacker at Michigan and was in the NFL with Atlanta and the New York Jets from 1975-77.

Mark Konecny, a 1981 Mona Shores graduate, attended Alma College and played in the NFL as a running back and kick returner in 1987 with Miami and `88 with Philadelphia.

Curtis Adams graduated from Muskegon Orchard View in 1980, went to college at Central Michigan and played from 1985-89 in the NFL with San Diego. The running back scored seven touchdowns during his pro career.

John Williams, of Muskegon Reeths-Puffer, graduated from high school in 1979, went to Wisconsin, and played in the NFL with Dallas, Seattle, New Orleans and Indianapolis from 1985-97.

Joe Berger, a 2000 graduate of Newaygo, played on the offensive line at Michigan Tech, and was a rookie in 2005 with the Miami Dolphins.

Al Brenner, of Niles, played for Michigan State and was a defensive back on the New York Giants in 1969 and 70.

Jason Babin, of Paw Paw, played linebacker at Western Michigan and joined the Houston Texans in 2004 and 2005.

Todd Herremans, of Ravenna, played college football at Saginaw Valley State and went to Philadelphia in the NFL in 2005 as a rookie. He's a 320-pound tackle.

Dave Whitsell, a defensive back from Shelby, played from 1958-69 with the Lions, Bears and Saints. He made it to the Pro Bowl in 1967.

Rob Fredrickson, of St. Joseph, graduated from Michigan State in 1993 and was the top draft choice of the L.A. Raiders in 1994. He had a nine-year career as an NFL linebacker with the Raiders, Lions and Cardinals.

Ron Stehouwer, a 1955 Wayland High School graduate, played in college at Colorado State and was an offensive lineman with Pittsburgh in the NFL from 1960-64.

Ron Essink graduated from Zeeland High School in 1976 and starred as an offensive lineman at Grand Valley, where he also was an All-American wrestler. He played with the Seattle Seahawks from 1980-86.

Jay Riemersma graduated from Zeeland in 1991, played tight end at Michigan, and had an eight-year NFL career with Buffalo and Pittsburgh from 1997-2004. He caught 23 touchdown passes in his pro career.

TRACK

Jackson Volney Scholz, of Buchanan, won Olympic gold as a member of the American 400-meter relay team in 1920, and again as an individual in the 200-meter sprint in 1924. He's best known for his second-place finish at 100 meters in 1924. That race, won by Britain's Harold Abrahams, was the subject of the 1981 movie "Chariots of Fire."

Greg Meyer, of Grand Rapids, won the Boston Marathon in 1983, and at one time held a number of distance running records. He's a member of the national Distance Running Hall of Fame and a seven-time winner of the Riverbank Run in Grand Rapids.

Brian Diemer of Grand Rapids won the bronze medal in the steeplechase at the 1984 Olympics. He qualified again for the Olympics in 1988 and 1992, when he was a captain of the American Team. He is cross country coach at Calvin College.

Marion Ladewig dominated women's professional bowling in the 1950s (photo courtesy of Grand Rapids Public Library)

BOWLING

Marion Ladewig, born in 1914 in Grand Rapids, won the All-Star tournament eight times from 1949 to 1963, and was named woman bowler of the year nine times during the same period. In her 1951 All-Star tournament victory, her average score was 247 – which would have won the men's tournament that year.

HORSE RACING

Julie Krone, of Eau Claire, is considered by many to be the world's finest female jockey – and among the best regardless of gender. Krone, who dropped out of high school at age 15 to start riding professionally, was the first woman to win one of racing's triple-crown events (the 1993 Belmont Stakes, aboard Colonial Affair). She was also the first female to win a Breeder's Cup race, and the first to be inducted into the horse racing Hall of Fame. She retired in 1998, after a series of injuries, but later resumed racing. She has won more than 3,500 races in her career.

West Michigan's lone pari-mutuel horse track is Great Lakes Downs, a thoroughbred track in Muskegon. In addition to live racing, the track offers a simulcasting service that lets race fans place bets on races at other tracks around the country. Harness racing – but not pari-mutuel betting – is an annual feature of several county fairs in West Michigan. The prestigious Wolverine Futurity harness races takes place each July at the Ottawa County Fair in Holland.

AUTO RACING

Johnny Benson, Jr., of Grand Rapids, has been a fixture since 1996 on the NASCAR and Craftsman Truck racing circuits. His one NASCAR win came in the 2002 Pop Secret Microwave Popcorn 400 at North Carolina Speedway. His NASCAR winnings over a 10-year period totaled over $15 million.

Gordon Johncock, of Hastings, came up through sprint cars and Midwest Modifieds to become a star of the USAC circuit in the 60s, 70s and 80s.

He twice won the Indianapolis 500 – 1973 and 1982 – and was the USAC points champion in 1976. Johncock is a member of the International Motor Sports Hall of Fame.

WESTERN MICHIGAN AUTO RACETRACKS

When the national media speak or write of auto racing, the subjects tend to be the mega-races such as the 500-mile classics at Indianapolis and Daytona.

But racing at another level – just as intense but not quite so expensive – is thriving in West Michigan.

Short track races featuring stock cars, sprint cars, motorcycles and even go-karts draw hundreds of thousands of fans each summer at West Michigan speedways. Drag-races on high-tech paved strips or on sand straightaways have their own following. Several tracks have been in business on the same sites for more than 50 years.

West Michigan racing facilities range from some of the best short-track operations in the nation, to low-key operations where just about anyone with a lot of nerve and a bit of mechanical knowledge can become a racer.

Here's a list of the area's tracks:

PAVED OVALS:

Berlin Raceway
2060 Berlin Fair Drive
Marne, MI 49435
(616) 677-0122
www.berlinraceway.com

This 7/16 mile paved oval on the Berlin Fairgrounds is one of the America's top short tracks, with racing every Saturday night from April through September. The track has been in business since 1950. It's owned by the West Michigan Whitecaps. NASCAR driver Johnny Benson Jr. is a partner in the operation.

Galesburg Speedway
573 S. 38th St.
Galesburg, MI 49053
(269) 665-4600
www.galesburgspeedway.com

The Galesburg speedway has an unbanked quarter-mile paved oval, with a figure-eight for special races. Stock-car racing is every Saturday night, in season, with special events on Sundays. The facility has been on the same site since a dirt-track opened here in 1947.

Kalamazoo Speedway
7656 Ravine Rd.
Kalamazoo, MI 49009
(269) 692-2423
www.kalamazoospeedway.com

Saturday night racing from April to October features several classes of stock cars on this NASCAR-sanctioned 3/8 mile track. The site has hosted auto racing since 1950. The modern, high-banked oval has seating for some 6,500 fans.

Mottville Speedway
US-12, Mottville, MI 49042
(574) 215-4288
www.mottvillespeedway.com

This track, along US-12 in St. Joseph County, has been in

operation since 1950. Racing is held every Friday and Saturday from March to November on the quarter-mile low-banked asphalt track.

Thunder Valley Motorsports
58671 M-40 Highway
Jones, MI 49061
(269) 244-5321

With a 3/8 mile oval and seating for more than 7,000 spectators, this popular Cass County track, a few miles north of the Indiana border, attracts more than 125,000 fans each year.

DIRT-TRACK OVALS

Bob's Family Raceway
9575 Mick Road
Clarksville, MI 48815
(616) 693-2744
www.bobsfamilyraceway.com

This facility in Ionia County features a summer schedule of sand drag races and scrambles on a 3/10-mile dirt track.

Crystal Motor Speedway
8315 Sidney Rd
Sidney, MI 48818
(989) 235-5200
www.crystalmotorspeedway.com

This popular mid-Michigan track has stock-car racing every Saturday night. Included are late models, pro stocks and more.

Hartford Speedway Park
301 Bowie Street
Hartford, MI 49057
(269) 621-4482
www.hartfordspeedwaypark.com

This speedway, just off I-94 midway between Kalamazoo and Benton Harbor, features Friday night stock-car racing throughout the summer on a banked, half-mile clay oval.

I-96 Speedway
3823 W. Portland Rd.
Lake Odessa, MI 48849
(616) 642-0555
www.i96speedway.com

This Ionia County track, near the Lake Odessa exit from I-96, features a summer-long schedule of dirt-track racing on half-mile, quarter-mile and eighth-mile ovals. A new track for quads and dirt bikes was to open in the summer of 2006.

Mid-Michigan Raceway Park
7573 Hayes Rd.
Fenwick, MI 48834
(989) 637-4353
www.mmracewaypark.tripod.com

This park, north of Muir in Ionia County, features stock cars and Michigan Modifieds on Saturdays. The racetrack is a third-of-a-mile dirt oval.

Orleans Raceway (Belding)
7940 Canfield Road
Belding MI 48809
(616) 794-2810
www.orleansraceway.us

Stock car racing is scheduled on Friday nights on this banked, 3/8-mile dirt oval in Ionia County. The track has also sponsored mud bogs and a "snow derby."

Thunderbird Race Park
350 W. Riley-Thompson Road
Muskegon, MI 49456
(231) 766-3300
www.thunderbirdracepark.com

This facility in Muskegon County's Dalton Township has been in operation since the early 1950s. It features a 3/8 mile banked clay track as well as a quarter-mile paved drag strip. Dirt-track races are on Saturdays, with the drag strip active Sunday afternoons. New in 2005 is a motocross track with racing Saturday mornings and afternoons.

Winston Motor Speedway
7834 S. 72nd Ave.
P.O. Box 306
Rothbury, MI 49461
(231) 893-3023
www.winstonmotorspeedway.com

The 3/8 mile clay track, just off US-31 in Oceana County, hosts stock car racing each Friday evening from April to September. Saturday events, one night a month, include powder-puff races, demolition derbies and other events.

DRAG STRIPS

Mid-Michigan Motorplex
2589 N. Wyman Rd.
P.O. Box 667
Stanton, MI 48888
(989) 762-5043
www.midmichmotorplex.com

This Montcalm County strip, formerly known as Central Michigan Dragway, is open from April through October and annually hosts national championship events.

Silver Lake Sand Dragway
(West Michigan Sand Dragway)
7186 West Deer Road
Mears, MI 49436
(231) 873-2778

This unique Oceana County strip, near the Silver Lake sand dunes, features specially built dragsters and custom-made dune buggies, racing on sand. Races are held weekly from May to October.

Thunderbird Race Park
350 W. Riley-Thompson Road
Muskegon, MI 49456
(231) 766-3300
www.thunderbirdracepark.com

This facility in Muskegon County's Dalton Township has been in operation since the early 1950s. It features a 3/8 mile banked clay track as well as a quarter-mile paved drag strip. Dirt-track races are on Saturdays, with the drag strip active Sunday afternoons. New in 2005 is a motocross track with racing Saturday mornings and afternoons.

US-131 Motorsports Park
1249 12th St.
Martin, MI 49070
(269) 672-7800
www.us131motor-sportspark.com

Events are held weekly from April to October on this world-class drag-racing facility. It features elite racers from all classes of drag-racing vehicles. The track, once known as the Martin Dragway, is visible alongside US-131, midway between Grand Rapids and Kalamazoo.

ROAD COURSES

Grattan Raceway Park
7201 Lessiter Road
Belding, MI 48809
(616) 691-7221
www.grattanraceway.com

Though the address is Belding, the track is actually located in Kent County's Grattan Township. The 2.2 mile road course is used every weekend from May through October for sports car, motorcycle and motocross events.

Gingerman Raceway
61414 Phoenix Road
South Haven, MI 49090
(269) 253-4445
www.gingermanraceway.com

This 1.9 mile road course opened in 1996. It was developed by Chicagoan Dan Schnitta, who also owns the Gingerman Tavern, near Wrigley Field. The course is often used on weekends for sports car club events that are open to the public. Weekday usage is mainly for driving schools and other private activities.

HIGH SCHOOL SPORTS CHAMPIONS

High school sports, of course, are part of an educational program that builds healthy minds, strong bodies, and good citizens. By participating in athletics, teenagers learn about teamwork, discipline, preparation and sportsmanship.

Just incidentally, they also provide a source of community pride.

So, just in case anyone's keeping score, here's a list of state championships won by West Michigan schools since 1950. The information comes from the Michigan High School Athletic Association. It's part of a master list maintained by Bill Khan of the *Flint Journal* newspaper, and it is used with permission.

(The football and basketball championships are statewide. In most other sports, MHSAA has separate state championship events for the Upper and Lower peninsulas.)

Allegan High School

1991-92 Wrestling, Class B

Allendale High School

1976-77 Softball, Class D
1988-89 Softball, Class D
1999-00 Boys cross country, Class C

Bangor High School

1959-60 Boys basketball, Class C

Belding High School

1994-95 Football, Class B
1997-98 Football, Class C

Benton Harbor High School

1963-64 Boys basketball, Class A
1964-65 Boys basketball, Class A
1969-70 Boys track, Class A
1983-84 Girls track, Class A

Benton Harbor St. John H.S.

1949-50 Boys track, Class D

Berrien Springs High School

1978-79 Volleyball, Class C
1979-80 Softball, Class C
1979-80 Volleyball, Class C
1981-82 Volleyball, Class C
1983-84 Baseball, Class C
1983-84 Volleyball, Class C
1984-85 Volleyball, Class C
1985-86 Volleyball, Class C
1988-89 Baseball, Class C

Big Rapids High School

1990-91 Boys cross country, Class B
1992-93 Girls cross country, Class B
2000-01 Boys cross country, Div. 2
2001-02 Boys cross country, Div. 2

Big Rapids Crossroads High School

2004-05 Girls cross country, Div. 4

Bridgman High School

1986-87 Baseball, Class D
1987-88 Boys golf, Class D

Buchanan High School

1975-76 Boys basketball, Class C
1977-78 Boys basketball, Class C
1984-85 Baseball, Class C
1990-91 Girls basketball, Class C
1998-99 Boys track, Class C
2002-03 Boys tennis, Div. 4

Burr Oak High School

1996-97 Softball, Class D
1997-98 Softball, Div. 4

Caledonia High School

1993-94 Girls cross country, Class B
1994-95 Girls cross country, Class B
1994-95 Girls track, Class B
1995-96 Girls cross country, Class B
1996-97 Boys cross country, Class B
1996-97 Girls cross country, Class B
2001-02 Girls golf, Div. 2

Carson City – Crystal High School

1973-74 Boys cross country, Class C
1982-83 Girls track, Class C
1994-95 Boys cross country, Class C
1995-96 Girls cross country, Class C
1996-97 Girls cross country, Class C

Cassopolis High School

1970-71 Boys golf, Class C
1972-73 Boys golf, Class C
1990-91 Boys track, Class C

Cedar Springs High School

1994-95 Wrestling, Class B

Centreville High School

1997-98 Boys track, Class D

Climax-Scotts High School

1974-75 Baseball, Class D
1975-76 Baseball, Class D
1983-84 Baseball, Class D
2004-05 Football, Div. 8

Colon High School

1988-89 Baseball, Class D

Comstock High School

1985-86 Volleyball, Class B
1986-87 Volleyball, Class B
1988-89 Volleyball, Class B
1989-90 Volleyball, Class B
1990-91 Volleyball, Class B
1992-93 Volleyball, Class B
1993-94 Boys track, Class B
1994-95 Boys track, Class B
1995-96 Volleyball, Class B

Comstock Park High School

1951-52 Boys golf, Class C
1973-74 Wrestling, Class C
1987-88 Boys golf, Class C
1988-89 Boys golf, Class C

Constantine High School

1992-93 Wrestling, Class C
2004-05 Football, Div. 6

Covert High School

1955-56 Boys track, Class D
1956-57 Boys track, Class D
1959-60 Boys track, Class D
1963-64 Boys track, Class D
1964-65 Boys basketball, Class D
1964-65 Boys track, Class D
1965-66 Boys basketball, Class D
1965-66 Boys track, Class D
1969-70 Boys track, Class D
1970-71 Boys basketball, Class D
1981-82 Boys basketball, Class D
2000-01 Boys basketball, Class D

Decatur High School

1998-99 Baseball, Div. 4
2001-02 Baseball, Div. 4
2002-03 Baseball, Div. 4

Dowagiac High School

1951-52 Boys tennis, Class B
1961-62 Boys track, Class B
1990-91 Football, Class BB

East Grand Rapids High School

1949-50 Boys basketball, Class C
1949-50 Boys golf, Class C
1949-50 Boys swimming, Class B
1949-50 Boys track, Class C
1950-51 Boys golf, Class B
1950-51 Boys swimming, Class B
1951-52 Boys swimming, Class B
1952-53 Boys swimming, Class B
1953-54 Boys swimming, Class B
1954-55 Boys swimming, Class B
1954-55 Boys tennis, Class B
1955-56 Boys swimming, Class B
1955-56 Boys tennis, Class B
1956-57 Boys swimming, Class B
1957-58 Boys swimming, Class B
1957-58 Boys track, Class B
1958-59 Boys swimming, Class B
1959-60 Boys swimming, Class B
1959-60 Boys tennis, Class B
1960-61 Boys swimming, Class B
1961-62 Boys swimming, Class B
1964-65 Boys tennis, Class A
1969-70 Boys tennis, Class A
1970-71 Boys tennis, Class A
1971-72 Boys tennis, Class A
1972-73 Boys tennis, Class A
1974-75 Boys tennis, Class B
1975-76 Boys swimming, Class B
1976-77 Football, Class B
1976-77 Boys swimming, Class B
1976-77 Boys tennis, Class B
1977-78 Boys swimming, Class B

1977-78 Boys tennis, Class B
1978-79 Girls golf, Open
1978-79 Boys swimming, Class B
1978-79 Girls swimming, Class B
1978-79 Boys tennis, Class B
1979-80 Boys swimming, Class B
1979-80 Girls swimming, Class B
1979-80 Girls tennis, Class B
1980-81 Boys swimming, Class B
1981-82 Boys swimming, Class B
1981-82 Girls swimming, Class B
1982-83 Girls swimming, Class B
1983-84 Football, Class B
1983-84 Girls swimming, Class B
1984-85 Girls swimming, Class B
1984-85 Girls tennis, Class B
1985-86 Girls swimming, Class B
1985-86 Girls tennis, Class B
1986-87 Girls swimming, Class B
1986-87 Girls tennis, Class B
1987-88 Girls tennis, Class B
1988-89 Girls swimming, Class B
1992-93 Girls swimming, Class B
1992-93 Girls tennis, Class B
1993-94 Football, Class BB
1993-94 Girls swimming, Class B
1994-95 Girls tennis, Class B
1995-96 Football, Class BB
1995-96 Girls tennis Class B
1996-97 Boys skiing, Class B
1996-97 Girls tennis, Class B
1997-98 Girls tennis, Div. 3
1998-99 Girls golf, Div. 3
1998-99 Boys skiing, Class B
1998-99 Girls swimming, Class B
1998-99 Girls tennis, Div. 3
1999-00 Girls soccer, Div. 3
1999-00 Girls swimming, Class B

2000-01 Girls soccer, Div. 3
2000-01 Girls swimming, Class B
2000-01 Boys tennis, Div. 3
2000-01 Girls tennis, Div. 3
2001-02 Girls soccer, Div. 2
2001-02 Girls swimming, Class B
2001-02 Girls tennis, Div. 3
2002-03 Football, Div. 3
2002-03 Boys tennis, Div. 3
2002-03 Girls tennis, Div. 3
2003-04 Girls cross country, Div. 2
2003-04 Football, Div. 3
2003-04 Girls tennis, Div. 3
2004-05 Girls cross country, Div. 2

East Kentwood High School

1979-80 Girls gymnastics, Open
1981-82 Girls gymnastics, Open
1982-83 Boys swimming, Class A
1988-89 Boys swimming, Class A
1989-90 Hockey, Class A
1989-90 Volleyball, Class A
1999-00 Girls gymnastics, Open
1999-00 Volleyball, Class A
2001-02 Boys golf, Div. 1

Eau Claire High School

1992-93 Boys track, Class C

Edwardsburg High School

1976-77 Volleyball, Class C

Fremont High School

1976-77 Boys cross country, Class B
1983-84 Boys cross country, Class B
1985-86 Boys cross country, Class B
1989-90 Boys cross country, Class B
1991-92 Boys cross country, Class B

1993-94 Boys cross country, Class B
1997-98 Girls cross country, Class B

Fruitport High School

2004-05 Volleyball, Class C

Fulton-Middleton High School

1989-90 Boys track, Class C
1998-99 Football, Class DD

Galesburg High School

1950-51 Boys tennis, Class C
1953-54 Boys tennis, Class C

Galesburg-Augusta High School

1961-62 Boys tennis, Class C
1962-63 Boys tennis, Class C
1964-65 Boys tennis, Class C
1968-69 Boys tennis, Class C
1969-70 Boys tennis, Class C
1970-71 Boys tennis, Class C

Gobles High School

1953-54 Boys basketball, Class D
1984-85 Football, Class D

Grand Rapids Baptist High School

1993-94 Boys golf, Class D
1996-97 Boys golf, Class D

Grand Rapids Catholic Central High School

1982-83 Boys cross country, Class B
1984-85 Baseball, Class B
1984-85 Boys cross country, Class B
1987-88 Girls cross country, Class B
1987-88 Football, Class B
1998-99 Competitive cheer, Class B

Grand Rapids Christian High School

1979-80 Girls cross country, Class B
1979-80 Girls track, Class B
1997-98 Girls basketball, Class A
1998-99 Boys soccer, Div. 2
2001-02 Boys soccer, Div. 2

Grand Rapids Covenant Christian High School

1972-73 Boys basketball, Class D
1992-93 Boys basketball, Class D
1993-94 Boys basketball, Class D

Grand Rapids Creston High School

1979-80 Volleyball, Class A

Grand Rapids East Christian High School

1965-66 Boys basketball, Class B
1966-67 Boys cross country, Class B

Grand Rapids Forest Hills Central High School

1993-94 Girls swimming, Class A
1994-95 Girls swimming, Class A
1995-96 Boys skiing, Class A
1997-98 Boys tennis, Div. 2
2002-03 Boys tennis, Div. 2
2004-05 Girls soccer, Div. 2
2004-05 Boys soccer, Div. 2

Grand Rapids Forest Hills Northern High School

1977-78 Volleyball, Class C
1978-79 Football, Class C
1981-82 Girls golf, Open
1983-84 Boys golf, Class C
1994-95 Boys tennis, Class B
1997-98 Boys tennis, Div. 3
2001-02 Volleyball, Class A
2002-03 Girls tennis, Div. 2
2003-04 Girls tennis, Div. 2

Grand Rapids Lee High School (also see Wyoming Lee)

1952-53 Boys tennis, Class C
1953-54 Boys tennis, Class C

Grand Rapids Northview High School

1967-68 Boys cross country, Class B
1988-89 Boys track, Class B
1990-91 Softball, Class B

Grand Rapids Ottawa Hills High School

1950-51 Boys track, Class A
1951-52 Boys golf, Class A
1967-68 Boys basketball, Class A
1968-69 Boys basketball, Class A
1989-90 Girls basketball, Class A
1996-97 Boys basketball, Class A

Grand Rapids South Christian High School

1964-65 Boys cross country, Class B
1987-88 Boys basketball, Class B
1988-89 Girls basketball, Class B
2002-03 Boys basketball, Class B
2002-03 Football, Div. 4
2004-05 Boys basketball, Class B

Grand Rapids Union High School

1952-53 Boys cross country, Class A
1953-54 Boys cross country, Class A

Grand Rapids West Catholic High School

1970-71 Boys cross country, Class B
1979-80 Girls basketball, Class B
1983-84 Girls gymnastics, Open
1990-91 Girls basketball, Class B
2003-04 Boys cross country, Div. 3

Grandville High School

1961-62 Wrestling, Class B
1976-77 Boys golf, Class A
1988-89 Boys golf, Class A
1992-93 Wrestling, Class A
1996-97 Competitive cheer, Class A
1996-97 Football, Class A
1996-97 Girls golf, Class A
1997-98 Competitive cheer, Class A
1997-98 Girls golf, Class A
2003-04 Competitive cheer, Class A

Grandville Calvin Christian High School

1987-88 Softball, Class C
1989-90 Boys golf, Class C
1992-93 Softball, Class C
1993-94 Baseball, Class C
1993-94 Boys basketball, Class C
1995-96 Baseball, Class B

Hamilton High School

1983-84 Boys Basketball, Class C

Hartford High School

1987-88 Baseball, Class C
1993-94 Football, Class CC

Hastings High School

1965-66 Boys golf, Class B
1973-74 Girls golf, Open

Hesperia High School

2004-05 Boys cross country, Div. 4

Holland High School

1970-71 Boys tennis, Class A
1971-72 Boys tennis, Class A
1985-86 Girls gymnastics, Open

1993-94 Girls gymnastics, Open
1994-95 Girls gymnastics, Open
1995-96 Girls gymnastics, Open
1996-97 Girls gymnastics, Open
2003-04 Boys swimming, Class A

Holland Christian High School

1952-53 Boys tennis, Class B
1953-54 Boys tennis, Class B
1962-63 Boys tennis, Class B
1964-65 Boys tennis, Class B
1975-76 Softball, Class B
1986-87 Boys soccer, Class B
1987-88 Boys swimming, Class B
1988-89 Boys swimming, Class B
1993-94 Girls tennis, Class B
1996-97 Girls swimming, Class B
2003-04 Boys soccer, Div. 2

Holland West Ottawa High School

1964-65 Boys swimming, Class B
1968-69 Boys swimming, Class B
1969-70 Boys swimming, Class B
1970-71 Boys swimming, Class B
2002-03 Baseball, Div. 1

Holton High School

1993-94 Volleyball, Class C

Hudsonville High School

2003-04 Boys bowling, Class A

Hudsonville Freedom Baptist High School

2002-03 Boys soccer, Div. 4

Hudsonville Unity Christian High School

1973-74 Girls basketball, Class B
1991-92 Softball, Class B
2003-04 Boys bowling, Class B
2004-05 Girls soccer, Div. 3

Ionia High School

1963-64 Boys gymnastics, Open
1974-75 Girls track, Class B

Jenison High School

1986-87 Softball, Class A
1987-88 Softball, Class A
1989-90 Softball, Class A
1991-92 Softball, Class A
1993-94 Softball, Class A
1994-95 Softball, Class A

Kalamazoo Central High School

1949-50 Boys basketball, Class A
1950-51 Boys basketball, Class A
1950-51 Boys cross country, Class A
1954-55 Boys cross country, Class A
1964-65 Boys track, Class A
1970-71 Boys tennis, Class A
1972-73 Girls tennis, Open
1993-94 Girls golf, Class A
1994-95 Girls golf, Class A
1995-96 Girls golf, Class A
1995-96 Volleyball, Class A

Kalamazoo Christian High School

1958-59 Boys basketball, Class C
1972-73 Boys tennis, Class C
1981-82 Boys cross country, Class C
1982-83 Boys basketball, Class C
1995-96 Softball, Class C
1996-97 Softball, Class C

1997-98 Softball, Div. 3
1998-99 Softball, Div. 3
1999-00 Softball, Div. 3
2000-01 Boys basketball, Class C
2001-02 Softball, Div. 3
2002-03 Girls soccer, Div. 4
2003-04 Girls soccer, Div. 4

Kalamazoo Hackett High School

1974-75 Boys tennis, Class C
1976-77 Boys golf, Class C
1984-85 Boys tennis, Class C
1991-92 Boys soccer, Class C
1992-93 Boys soccer, Class C
1994-95 Boys soccer, Class C
1995-96 Boys soccer, Class C
1997-98 Girls cross country, Class C
1999-00 Girls cross country, Class C
2001-02 Girls soccer, Div. 4

Kalamazoo Loy Norrix High School

1974-75 Girls tennis, Class A
1975-76 Boys golf, Class A
1975-76 Boys tennis, Class A
1976-77 Boys tennis, Class A
1978-79 Boys tennis, Class A
1981-82 Boys tennis, Class A
1991-92 Girls tennis, Class A

Kalamazoo St. Augustine High School

1949-50 Boys tennis, Class C
1953-54 Boys tennis, Class C
1963-64 Boys tennis, Class C

Kalamazoo State High School

1949-50 Boys tennis, Class B
1954-55 Boys golf, Class B
1955-56 Boys golf, Class B
1956-57 Boys tennis, Class B

Kalamazoo University High School

1957-58 Boys tennis, Class B
1958-59 Boys tennis, Class B
1959-60 Boys tennis, Class A
1961-62 Boys tennis, Class B
1962-63 Boys golf, Class B
1963-64 Boys golf, Class B
1963-64 Boys tennis, Class B
1964-65 Boys golf, Class B
1965-66 Boys tennis, Class B

Lakeview High School

1956-57 Boys basketball, Class C

Lawrence High School

1997-98 Football, Class DD

Lawton High School

1966-67 Boys cross country, Class C
1967-68 Boys cross country, Class C
1984-85 Wrestling, Class D
1985-86 Wrestling, Class D
1986-87 Wrestling, Class D
1989-90 Wrestling, Class D
2001-02 Boys cross country, Div. 4

Lowell High School

2001-02 Wrestling, Div. 2
2002-03 Football, Div. 2
2003-04 Wrestling, Div. 2
2004-05 Football, Div. 3

Marcellus High School

1985-86 Softball, Class D

Martin High School

1987-88 Football, Class D
1987-88 Wrestling, Class D

Mendon High School

1972-73 Boys track, Class D
1973-74 Boys track, Class D
1982-83 Football, Class C
1989-90 Football, Class D
1990-91 Wrestling, Class D
1991-92 Football, Class DD
1993-94 Football, Class DD
1995-96 Football, Class DD
1996-97 Girls track, Class D
1997-98 Girls cross country, Class D
1997-98 Volleyball, Class D
1998-99 Girls cross country, Class D
1998-99 Volleyball, Class D
1999-00 Football, Div. 8
2000-01 Volleyball, Class D
2001-02 Football, Div. 8
2002-03 Football, Div. 7

Middleville Thornapple-Kellogg High School

1995-96 Wrestling, Div. 3
1999-00 Girls cross country, Class B
2000-01 Girls cross country, Div. 2
2001-02 Girls cross country, Div. 2

Muskegon High School

1986-87 Football, Class A
1989-90 Football, Class A
2004-05 Football, Div. 2

Muskegon Catholic Central High School

1971-72 Boys cross country, Class B
1974-75 Boys golf, Class B
1974-75 Girls track, Class B
1976-77 Girls track, Class B
1977-78 Girls track, Class C
1978-79 Boys golf, Class C

1980-81 Football, Class B
1982-83 Football, Class B
1990-91 Football, Class C
1990-91 Boys golf, Class C
1991-92 Football, Class C
1995-96 Football, Class C
2000-01 Football, Div. 8
2001-02 Boys tennis, Div. 4

Muskegon Christian High School

1957-58 Boys basketball, Class C
1957-58 Boys tennis, Class C
1961-62 Boys basketball, Class C
1964-65 Boys basketball, Class C
1969-70 Boys basketball, Class C

Muskegon Heights High School

1953-54 Boys basketball, Class A
1955-56 Boys basketball, Class A
1956-57 Boys basketball, Class A
1961-62 Boys track, Class A
1973-74 Boys basketball, Class B
1977-78 Boys basketball, Class B
1977-78 Boys track, Class B
1978-79 Boys basketball, Class B
1983-84 Girls track, Class B

Muskegon Mona Shores High School

1989-90 Boys golf, Class A
1990-91 Girls gymnastics, Open
1991-92 Boys golf, Class A
1991-92 Girls gymnastics, Open
1999-00 Hockey, Div. 2
2000-01 Boys golf, Div. 1

Muskegon Oakridge High School

1997-98 Football, Class CC

Muskegon Orchard View High School

2004-05 Football, Div. 4

Muskegon Reeths-Puffer High School

1972-73 Boys golf, Class B
1992-93 Football, Class A

Muskegon St. Joseph High School

1952-53 Boys basketball, Class D

Muskegon Western Michigan Christian H.S.

1974-75 Boys cross country, Class C
1984-85 Baseball, Class D
1988-89 Boys soccer, Class C
1991-92 Boys basketball, Class D
1995-96 Boys soccer, Class D
1998-99 Boys basketball, Class D
2003-04 Boys soccer, Div. 4
2004-05 Boys soccer, Div. 4

New Buffalo High School

1962-63 Boys basketball, Class D
1982-83 Baseball, Class D
1994-95 Baseball, Class D
1999-00 Boys cross country, Class D
2004-05 Baseball, Div. 4

Newaygo High School

1984-85 Girls basketball, Class C
1985-86 Girls basketball, Class C

Niles High School

1949-50 Boys cross country, Class B
1949-50 Boys track, Class B
1963-64 Boys golf, Class A

Niles Brandywine High School

1986-87 Baseball, Class C
2000-01 Softball, Div. 3

North Muskegon High School

1976-77 Girls track, Class C
1978-79 Girls track, Class C
1979-80 Girls track, Class C
1991-92 Boys golf, Class D
1995-96 Boys golf, Class D
1996-97 Competitive cheer, Class D
1997-98 Boys golf, Class C
1998-99 Girls track, Class D

Otsego High School

2000-01 Wrestling, Div. 3

Parchment High School

1975-76 Volleyball, Class B
1985-86 Boys soccer, Class B
1999-00 Volleyball, Class C

Paw Paw High School

1998-99 Boys soccer, Div. 3

Pewamo High School

1959-60 Boys cross country, Class C

Pewamo-Westphalia High School

1984-85 Boys golf, Class C
1985-86 Boys golf, Class C
1993-94 Competitive cheer, Class C
1994-95 Competitive cheer, Class C
1995-96 Competitive cheer, Class C
1996-97 Competitive cheer, Class C
1998-99 Competitive cheer, Class C-D
2002-03 Competitive cheer, Class C-D

Plainwell High School

1955-56 Boys tennis, Class C
1988-89 Boys golf, Class B
1997-98 Boys swimming, Class B
1998-99 Competitive cheer, Class B
2000-01 Boys soccer, Div. 3

Portage High School

1956-57 Boys cross country, Class B

Portage Central High School

1976-77 Softball, Class A
1999-00 Girls soccer, Div. 2
2000-01 Boys tennis, Div. 2
2001-02 Baseball, Div. 1

Portage Northern High School

1976-77 Girls tennis, Class A
1977-78 Girls tennis, Class A
1981-82 Volleyball, Class A
1984-85 Volleyball, Class A
1985-86 Volleyball, Class A
1986-87 Volleyball, Class A
1991-92 Volleyball, Class A
1992-93 Volleyball, Class A
1993-94 Volleyball, Class A
1994-95 Volleyball, Class A
1996-97 Softball, Class A
1996-97 Volleyball, Class A
1998-99 Volleyball, Class A
1999-00 Softball, Div. 1
1999-00 Boys track, Div. 1
2000-01 Boys soccer, Div. 2
2000-01 Softball, Div. 1
2001-02 Softball, Div. 1

Portland St. Patrick High School

1980-81 Softball, Class D
1992-93 Football, Class D
1992-93 Boys golf, Class D
1994-95 Girls basketball, Class D
1995-96 Girls basketball, Class D
1996-97 Girls basketball, Class D
1999-00 Girls basketball, Class D
2000-01 Girls basketball, Class D
2002-03 Girls basketball, Class D

Ravenna High School

1994-95 Football, Class C
1996-97 Football, Class C
1997-98 Football, Class C
2003-04 Football, Div. 6

Remus High School

1961-62 Boys cross country, Class C
1962-63 Boys cross country, Class C

Remus Chippewa Hills High School

1982-83 Baseball, Class B

Richland Gull Lake High School

1988-89 Boys soccer, Class B
1991-92 Girls soccer, Class B
1993-94 Boys soccer, Class B
1993-94 Volleyball, Class B
1998-99 Boys cross country, Class B

Rockford High School

1988-89 Girls gymnastics, Open
1998-99 Girls cross country, Class A
1999-00 Girls cross country, Class A
1999-00 Girls track, Div. 1
2000-01 Boys cross country, Div. 1

2000-01 Girls cross country, Div. 1
2000-01 Boys swimming, Class A
2001-02 Girls cross country, Div. 1
2002-03 Boys basketball, Class A
2002-03 Boys cross country, Div. 1
2002-03 Girls cross country, Div. 1
2002-03 Girls track, Div. 1
2004-05 Football, Div. 1

Saranac High School

1977-78 Baseball, Class D
1980-81 Volleyball, Class D
1989-90 Volleyball, Class C

Schoolcraft High School

1958-59 Boys track, Class D
1988-89 Football, Class D
1989-90 Football, Class C
1992-93 Girls cross country, Class D
1996-97 Boys golf, Class C
1998-99 Boys golf, Div. 4
2001-02 Football, Div. 6
2002-03 Boys golf, Div. 4

Shelby High School

1968-69 Wrestling, Class C
1970-71 Boys basketball, Class C
1971-72 Boys basketball, Class C
1971-72 Wrestling, Class C

South Haven High School

1969-70 Wrestling, Class B
1984-85 Volleyball, Class B
1992-93 Boys cross country, Class B
2003-04 Boys soccer, Div. 3

Sparta High School

1962-63 Boys cross country, Class B

Spring Lake High School

2001-02 Girls cross country, Div. 3

St. Joseph High School

1950-51 Boys basketball, Class B
1952-53 Boys basketball, Class B
1956-57 Boys track, Class B
1971-72 Boys cross country, Class A
1978-79 Girls track, Class B
1988-89 Boys cross country, Class B
1996-97 Boys track, Class B

St. Joseph Lake Michigan Catholic High School

1978-79 Softball, Class C
1988-89 Girls basketball, Class C
1994-95 Competitive cheer, Class D
1995-96 Competitive cheer, Class D

Stanton Central Montcalm High School

1980-81 Boys golf, Class C

Stevensville Lakeshore High School

1980-81 Volleyball, Class B
1989-90 Baseball, Class B
1990-91 Boys soccer, Class B
1994-95 Softball, Class B
1994-95 Volleyball, Class B
1996-97 Softball, Class B
1997-98 Softball, Div. 2
2003-04 Softball, Div. 2

Sturgis High School

1960-61 Boys tennis, Class B
1966-67 Boys tennis, Class B

1967-68 Boys tennis, Class B
1968-69 Boys tennis, Class B
1969-70 Boys tennis, Class B
1970-71 Boys tennis, Class B
1975-76 Boys cross country, Class B
1976-77 Volleyball, Class B
1979-80 Girls golf, Open
1987-88 Volleyball, Class B
1998-99 Baseball, Div. 2

Three Oaks River Valley High School

1978-79 Boys basketball, Class C
1994-95 Baseball, Class C
1996-97 Baseball, Class C

Three Rivers High School

2003-04 Football, Div. 4

Vicksburg High School

1963-64 Boys cross country, Class B
1973-74 Boys tennis, Class B

Walkerville High School

1987-88 Girls basketball, Class D
1988-89 Girls basketball, Class D

White Pigeon High School

2003-04 Boys golf, Div. 4

Whitehall High School

1958-59 Boys golf, Class B
1963-64 Boys golf, Class B
1967-68 Boys golf, Class B
1995-96 Boys track, Class B
1998-99 Girls cross country, Class B
2000-01 Boys tennis, Div. 4

Wyoming High School

1961-62 Boys cross country, Class B

Wyoming Godwin Heights High School

1958-59 Boys cross country, Class B

Wyoming Kelloggsville High School

2000-01 Girls cross country, Div. 3

Wyoming Lee High School

1971-72 Boys cross country, Class C
1972-73 Boys cross country, Class C
1978-79 Boys cross country, Class C
1981-82 Girls cross country, Class D

Wyoming Park High School

1951-52 Boys tennis, Class C
1975-76 Baseball, Class B
1984-85 Football, Class B
1995-96 Softball, Class B

Wyoming Rogers High School

1998-99 Softball, Div. 2
2000-01 Softball, Div. 2
2004-05 Softball, Div. 2

Wyoming Tri-Unity Christian High School

1995-96 Boys basketball, Class D
2001-02 Boys basketball, Class B

Zeeland High School

1987-88 Girls swimming, Class B
1989-90 Boys swimming, Class B
1989-90 Girls swimming, Class B
1990-91 Boys swimming, Class B
1990-91 Girls swimming, Class B
1991-92 Girls swimming, Class B
1992-93 Girls swimming, Class B
1994-95 Girls swimming, Class B

CRIME

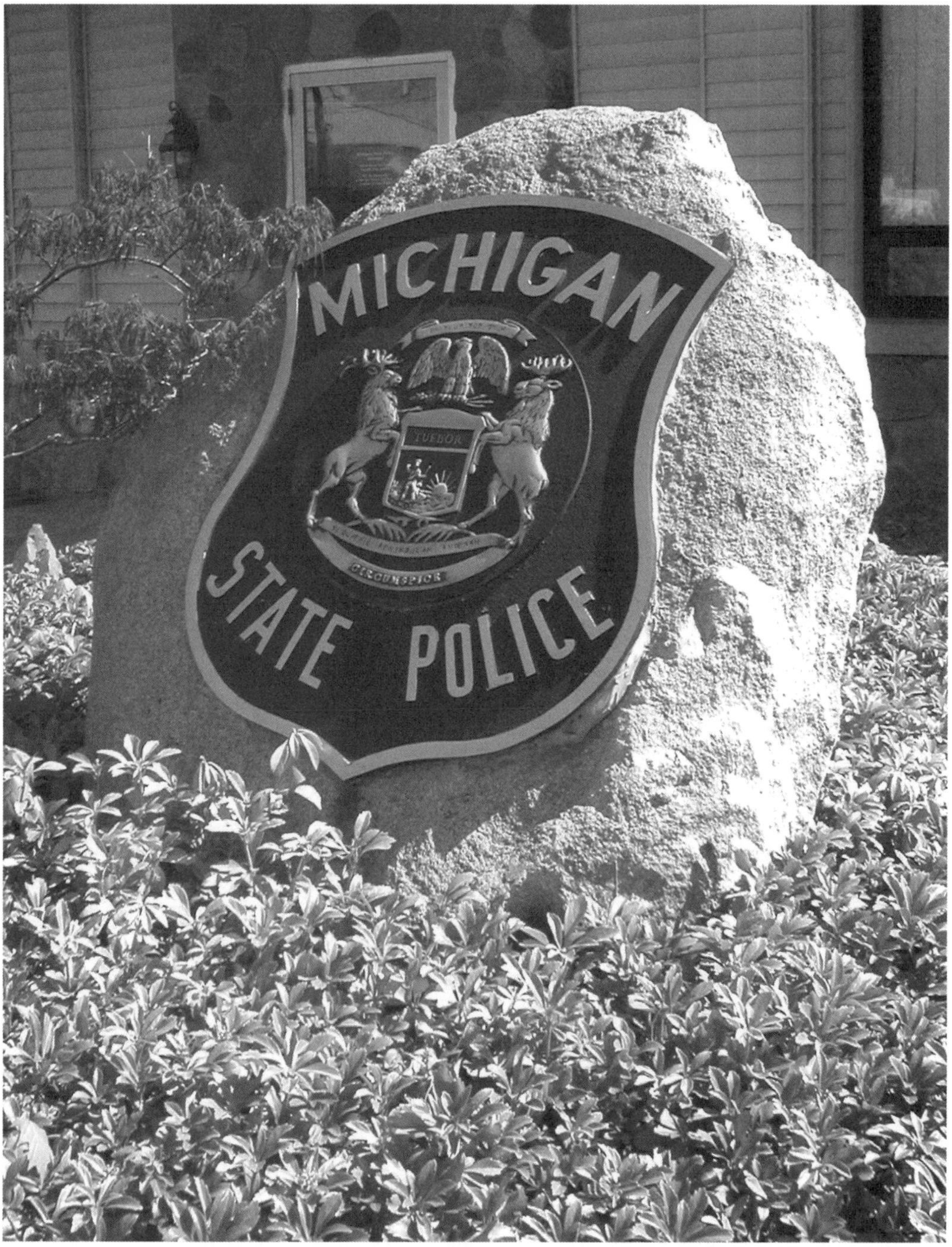

Previous page: A stone monument graces the entrance to the Michigan State Police post at Newaygo (photo: Ed Hoogterp)

CRIME

Here are a few true-crime stories from West Michigan's past.

Muskegon Shoot-out

Muskegon made the national newsreels in 1925 when a notorious bandit named George "Dutch" Anderson engaged in a downtown shoot-out with a local police officer, leaving both dead.

Anderson and his former partner, Gerald Chapman, were famous criminals of the day. They had been convicted of a multi-million-dollar mail-truck robbery in 1922, and later escaped from the federal penitentiary and murdered a policeman.

After Chapman was apprehended, Anderson apparently wandered through the towns of the Midwest and committed two more murders. Then, on Halloween night in 1925 he tried to pass a counterfeit $20 bill in a Muskegon café.

A suspicious manager notified the police. Detective Charles DeWitt Hammond came out to make the arrest, still unaware of the suspect's identity.

As described in *Michigan History Magazine*, Anderson grabbed a hostage, pulled out a gun and fired a volley of shots, hitting the detective and sending passers-by running for cover. But Detective Hammond wasn't finished. Despite his wounds, he chased the criminal down, wrestled away the gun, and shot Anderson to death.

Hammond was taken to Hackley Hospital, where he died of his wounds.

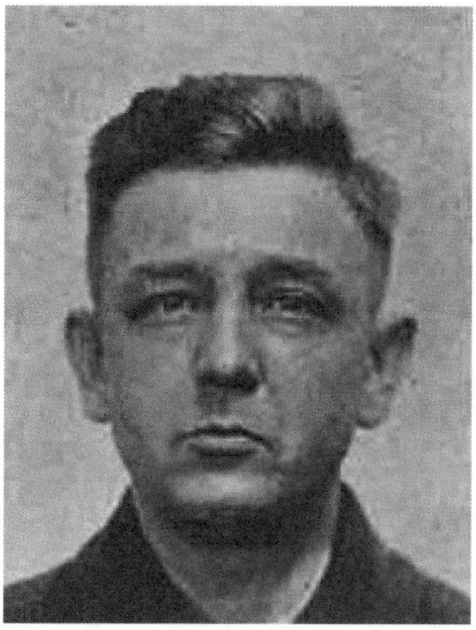

"Dutch" Anderson

The St. Valentine's Day Massacre: A Berrien County Connection

In December of 1929, a St. Joseph city police officer named Charles Skelly was questioning a man at a routine traffic accident, when the man shot and killed him.

The murderer escaped, but was quickly identified as a Chicago mob enforcer named Fred "The Killer" Burke. The investigation of officer Skelly's death took police to a home in nearby Stevensville, where Burke had been living. In his bedroom, they found an assortment of weaponry, including a pair of Thompson submachine guns.

Ballistics tests showed the two "tommy guns" had fired at least 70 bullets in a blood-spattered Chicago garage on Feb. 14, 1929. That was the St. Valentine's Day Massacre, when seven members of George "Bugs" Moran's crime family were killed, most likely at the hands of Fred Burke and three other thugs working for Al Capone.

Burke was eventually apprehended in Missouri and brought back to Michigan. He died in prison, while serving a life sentence for the murder of Officer Skelly.

As for the St. Valentine's Day massacre, it's still officially an unsolved crime. And the submachine guns are still being held as evidence in Berrien County.

The Allendale Horror

One of the region's most horrific crimes occurred March 13, 1982, when five members of an Allendale family were found dead in their home. For months, police traced every possible lead in an attempt to identify the killer of Robert and Mary Jane Paulson, and their three daughters, Cynthia, Carla and Casey.

Finally, four months after the Paulson slayings, Grand Rapids police made an arrest in what seemed to be an unrelated incident: a man named Maris Karklins had killed his own mother, after terrorizing neighbors by marching around in Nazi regalia.

In custody, Karklins admitted killing the Paulson family as well. The reason for the six killings apparently existed only in Karklins' own tortured mind. At his arraignment he told the judge that he had many aliases, including Adolf Hitler and Sun Yat-Sen. At one point he referred to Robert Paulson as a devil. Karklins was convicted and sentenced to life in prison, without parole.

Methamphetamine

In the movies or on TV, crime can seem exciting, interesting, almost glamorous. In real life, it's more often desperate, foolish and violent.

Crime in West Michigan doesn't generally approach the levels found in the nation's biggest cities, but there's still enough of it here to cause concern. In 2004, law enforcement agencies in the 15 counties reported a total of 49 cases of murder or manslaughter, and more than 1,200 sexual assaults.

The most common crimes are larceny and burglary, and police say much of that activity is associated with illegal drug use.

In the past few years, police have become increasingly worried about methamphetamine, an addictive drug that can be manufactured in makeshift laboratories. In 2002, police seized more than 50 "meth" labs in Allegan County, the most of any county in the state. Meth use goes against the major stereotypes of crime and drug use. It is often associated with rural areas, perhaps because some common farm chemicals can be used in the manufacturing process. And state statistics indicate that more than 90 percent of methamphetamine users are white.

Here are the numbers of meth labs seized by police from 2000 to 2004.

Allegan County:	151
Barry County:	38
Berrien County:	12
Cass County:	19
Ionia County:	8
Kalamazoo County:	73
Kent County:	15
Mecosta County:	1
Montcalm County:	4
Muskegon County:	8
Newaygo County:	3
Oceana County:	1
Ottawa County:	4
St. Joseph County:	46
Van Buren County:	82

CRIME RATES

Crime reports submitted to the Federal Bureau of Investigation are used to calculate the "crime rate" for individual communities. The rate reflects the number of crimes per 100,000 residents. The federal Uniform Crime Reporting system lists seven major categories of crime: Murder and non-negligent manslaughter, rape, robbery, aggravated assault, larceny, burglary, arson and motor vehicle theft. To figure out a community's crime rate, statisticians add the number of those crimes together, and do the math to calculate the number of crimes per 100,000 residents. The rate reflects all crimes reported in a given community, not just those committed by residents.

2004 crime rate for West Michigan Counties	Homicide	Sexual Assault	Aggrav. Assault	Larceny	Crime Rate
Allegan	2	47	163	1,006	**1,523**
Barry	3	30	74	598	**1,758**
Berrien	5	132	619	3,582	**3,593**
Cass	1	31	58	825	**2,597**
Ionia	1	56	117	1,015	**2,482**
Kalamazoo	5	110	557	7,287	**4,420**
Kent	19	267	2,018	14,136	**3,952**
Mecosta	1	31	61	911	**3,154**
Montcalm	0	61	74	959	**2,603**
Muskegon	4	143	688	6,287	**5,461**
Newaygo	2	51	116	790	**2,848**
Oceana	2	16	42	328	**1,932**
Ottawa	3	185	285	3,993	**2,304**
St. Joseph	0	68	161	1,332	**3,278**
Van Buren	1	47	200	1,500	**3,332**
West Michigan	**49**	**1,275**	**5,233**	**44,549**	**3,466**
Michigan	**638**	**5,516**	**31,792**	**190,489**	**3,531**

2004 Crime rates for West Michigan
Cities with population of 10,000 or more

	Homicide	Sexual Assault	Aggrav. Assault	Larceny	Crime Rate
Grand Rapids	12	83	1,377	6,531	5,928
Kalamazoo	1	45	319	2,989	6,298
Wyoming	1	59	205	1,286	3,488
Kentwood	2	24	82	1,100	3,537
Portage	0	17	46	1,752	4,758
Muskegon	1	64	317	2,116	8,412
Holland	0	35	91	1,024	3,973
Norton Shores	1	9	34	989	5,256
Walker	0	11	30	801	4,422
Grandville	1	12	17	840	7,080
Niles	0	21	56	478	5,970
Muskegon Hts.	2	17	183	744	12,975
Sturgis	0	18	30	298	3,912
Benton Harbor	3	20	272	411	10,478
Grand Haven	0	11	9	310	3,932
East Grand Rapids	0	0	4	124	1,755
Ionia	0	18	19	221	2,484
Big Rapids	0	10	19	237	3,059
Cities Total	**24**	**474**	**3,110**	**22,251**	**5,417**

STATE POLICE

When you're speeding down the freeway at 81 miles an hour, the last thing you want to see is a blue State Police cruiser parked along the roadside. But then, when you find yourself stuck on the roadside, that cruiser may be the first thing you want to see,

Here are the Michigan State Police posts in West Michigan:

Paw Paw: 5th District Headquarters

108 W. Michigan Ave.
Paw Paw, MI 49079
Telephone: (269) 657-6081

Paw Paw, Michigan State Police Post No. 51

43255 60th Ave.
Paw Paw, MI 49079
Telephone: (269) 657-5551

White Pigeon, Michigan State Police Post No. 52

101 US-131 North
White Pigeon, MI 49099
Telephone: (269) 483-7612

Niles, Michigan State Police Post No. 53

1600 Silverbrook Ave.
Niles, MI 49120
Telephone: (269) 683-4411

Bridgman, Michigan State Police Post No. 54

9301 Red Arrow Hwy.
Bridgman, MI 49106
Telephone: (269) 465-3111

South Haven, Michigan State Police Post No. 55

720 LaGrange St.
South Haven, MI 49090
Telephone: (269) 637-2126

Wayland, Michigan State Police Post No. 56

544 N. Main St.
Wayland, MI 49348
Telephone: (269) 792-2213

Hastings, Michigan State Police Post No. 58

1127 W. State St.
Hastings, MI 49058
Telephone: (269) 948-8283

Grand Rapids: 6th District Headquarters

588 Three Mile Rd.
Grand Rapids, MI 49544
Telephone: (616) 647-0800

Rockford, Michigan State Police Post No. 61

345 Northland Dr., NE
Rockford, MI 49341
Telephone: (616) 866-4411

Grand Haven, Michigan State Police Post No. 64

1622 S. Beacon Blvd.
Grand Haven, MI 49417
Telephone: (616) 842-2100

Newaygo, Michigan State Police Post No. 65

360 Adams
Newaygo, MI 49337
Telephone: (231) 652-1661

Hart, Michigan State Police Post No. 66

3793 W. Polk Rd.
Hart, MI 49420
Telephone: (231) 873-2171

Lakeview, Michigan State Police Post No. 67

10300 Howard City-Edmore Rd.
Lakeview, MI 48850
Telephone: (989)352-8444

Ionia, Michigan State Police Post No. 68

3140 S. State Rd.
Ionia, MI 48846
Telephone: (616) 527-3600

TRANSPORTATION

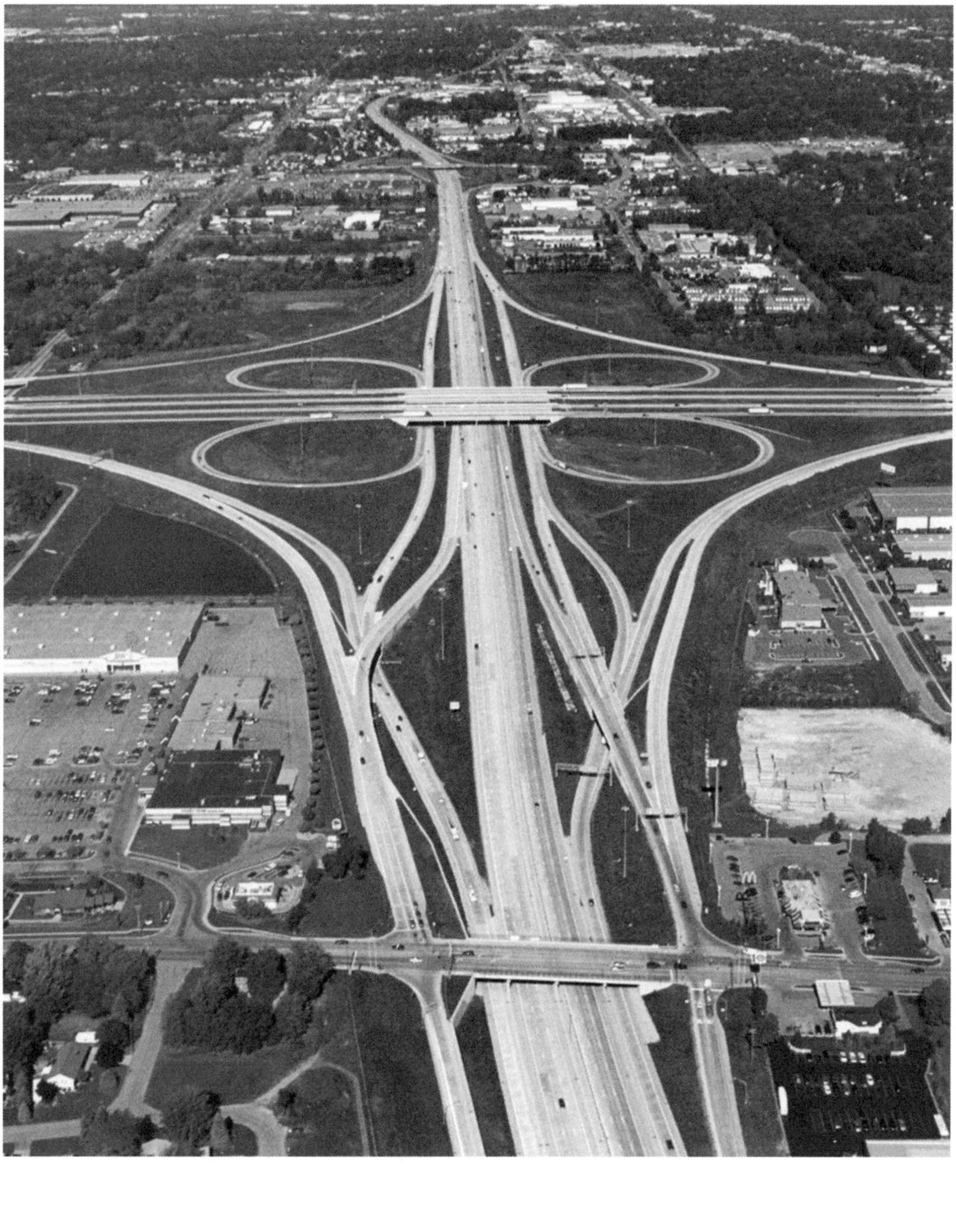

Previous page: Aerial view of intersection of US-131 and M-6, looking north. (photo courtesy of Michigan Department of Transportation)

TRANSPORTATION

Get your kicks, on M-66...

It's no surprise to anyone that cars and highways are a part of everyday life in West Michigan – and pretty much everywhere else in North America. But when you put the numbers together they can seem a bit over the top.

For example, we have almost one car for every man, woman and baby in West Michigan. And do we drive them!

According to the state Transportation Department, vehicles were driven a total of 21 BILLION miles on West Michigan roads in 2003. That's enough to get to the sun and back more than 100 times.

Here's another great statistic: More than half those miles (54 percent, actually) were driven on state trunklines that make up only about 7.5 percent of the total road miles in the region.

(The state trunkline system includes Interstate highways such as I-94, US-designated roads such as US-12, and state-numbered highways such as M-66. Other roads are classed as either county or local. They're all supported mainly by the money you pay in gasoline taxes.)

While the number of cars and the number of miles driven go up each year, the miles of road stay just about the same. Which just means that the roads keep getting more crowded.

The end of the US-131 expressway dumps heavy truck traffic into downtown Schoolcraft (photo: Ed Hoogterp)

Building new roads is at best a limited option. The most recent major road added in Michigan was M-6, the 20-mile expressway that runs south of Grand Rapids, connecting I-196 near Hudsonville to I-96 in Cascade Township. Cost of the new highway, which opened in 2004, was more than $30 million a mile.

A few new roads are proposed for the coming years. One is a US-31 expressway bypass of Grand Haven and Holland, which would run through farmland in western Ottawa County. Another is an extension of the US-131 expressway in Kalamazoo and St. Joseph counties, to replace about 30 miles of two-and four-lane surface road that runs from the Indiana Toll Road to just north of Schoolcraft.

One thing that's going down year-by-year (though it's still

far too high) is the number of people who die as a result of traffic accidents. Today's cars are much safer than those of past decades, thanks to such improvements as air bags, anti-lock brakes and child safety seats.

Of course, cars aren't quite the only way to get around West Michigan. Amtrak passenger trains travel on two routes through the region, buses travel the expressways, airports in Muskegon, Kalamazoo and Grand Rapids offer scheduled passenger service and dozens of general aviation airports cater to private and corporate planes.

If that's not enough modes of travel, consider the region's growing network of bicycle trails, built mainly along the rights-of-way of abandoned railroads.

Vehicle Registrations	2005	1995
Allegan	107,239	89,221
Barry	60,390	48,451
Berrien	153,883	142,037
Cass	49,894	44,233
Ionia	58,130	48,156
Kalamazoo	208,308	191,538
Kent	546,530	461,633
Mecosta	36,410	30,448
Montcalm	61,781	51,180
Muskegon	158,174	140,635
Newaygo	50,002	40,117
Oceana	27,997	23,093
Ottawa	235,828	185,508
St. Joseph	63,185	55,130
Van Buren	74,701	61,578

Total vehicle miles driven in each county (In millions of miles)

County	Total mileage	On state trunklines	On county/ local roads	Pct. on trunklines
Allegan	1,202	796	406	66.23%
Barry	435	228	207	52.36%
Berrien	2,098	1,207	891	57.54%
Cass	452	250	202	55.36%
Ionia	687	504	183	73.32%
Kalamazoo	2,577	1,107	1,470	42.97%
Kent	5,502	2,611	2,891	47.46%
Mecosta	414	311	103	75.19%
Montcalm	596	381	215	63.89%
Muskegon	1,402	670	732	47.82%
Newaygo	367	207	159	56.57%
Oceana	242	153	89	63.04%
Ottawa	1,969	987	982	50.13%
St. Joseph	580	335	244	57.84%
Van Buren	981	595	386	60.65%
W. Mich. total	**21,700**	**11,758**	**9,942**	**54.18%**
Michigan total	**100,192**	**53,408**	**46,784**	**53.31%**

Miles of state and local roads in each county

County	Total Road Miles	State trunkline miles	County/ local miles	Percent in state trunklines
Allegan	2,080	138	1,942	6.62%
Barry	1,263	119	1,144	9.40%
Berrien	2,000	208	1,792	10.42%
Cass	1,200	125	1,076	10.37%
Ionia	1,308	103	1,205	7.85%
Kalamazoo	1,873	121	1,751	6.48%
Kent	3,406	227	3,179	6.65%
Mecosta	1,289	108	1,181	8.37%
Montcalm	1,748	119	1,629	6.81%
Muskegon	1,746	96	1,650	5.51%
Newaygo	1,678	99	1,578	5.92%
Oceana	1,306	72	1,234	5.50%
Ottawa	2,037	114	1,923	5.59%
St. Joseph	1,303	124	1,179	9.51%
Van Buren	1,601	124	1,477	7.75%
W. Mich. total	**28,974**	**2,170**	**26,804**	**7.49%**
Michigan total	**120,440**	**9,722**	**110,718**	**8.07%**

Traffic Fatalities, 2000 – 2004						
County	2004	2003	2002	2001	2000	5-year total
Allegan	22	22	24	19	16	103
Barry	15	10	13	18	14	70
Berrien	19	25	28	29	27	128
Cass	15	12	17	7	14	65
Ionia	10	9	17	18	8	62
Kalamazoo	25	28	23	33	36	145
Kent	60	76	81	58	66	341
Mecosta	5	9	9	11	17	51
Montcalm	13	13	18	17	25	86
Muskegon	18	21	29	30	24	122
Newaygo	13	7	7	10	20	57
Oceana	6	10	14	7	10	47
Ottawa	22	31	27	33	39	152
St. Joseph	16	8	17	9	22	72
Van Buren	16	15	10	24	21	86
W. Mich. total	**275**	**296**	**334**	**323**	**359**	**1,587**
Michigan total	**1,159**	**1,283**	**1,279**	**1,328**	**1,382**	**6,431**

Average Daily Traffic Counts 2004

The Michigan Department of Transportation measures traffic volume at hundreds of locations around the state to determine future transportation needs. The results are used to calculate the average daily traffic at each site. Here are the counts for a few notable highways in West Michigan:

I-94

State Line: 40,500

Benton Harbor: 61,800

Portage, east of US 131: 86,900

I-96

Muskegon, at US-31: 26,400

Coopersville: 37,100

Walker, near Alpine Ave: 54,500

Grand Rapids, at East Belt Line: 101,000

Ionia, near M-66: 36,500

US-12

West of Niles: 17,800

Near Sturgis: 5,800

US-131

State Line: 9,700

Three Rivers: 18,600

South of Schoolcraft: 19,000

Kalamazoo, north of I-94: 44,000

Grand Rapids, S-Curve: 97,600

Grand Rapids, north of I-196: 116,000

Big Rapids: 17,800

M-51

South of Dowagiac: 14,700

Niles: 27,000

US-31

State Line: 16,500
Holland: 40,200
Grand Haven: 45,500
Grand River Bridge: 65,500
Muskegon, at Sherman Blvd: 56,400
Pentwater: 9,000

M-66

Sturgis: 18,400
South of Ionia: 17,700
South of Stanton: 9,700
North of Barryton: 3,700

M-37

Near Hastings: 15,900
Walker (Alpine Avenue): 57,300
Newaygo: 14,300
Lilley: 3,300

M-40

Allegan: 15,500

I-196

North of Saugatuck: 27,000
Holland: 9,400
Jenison: 40,100
Grand Rapids, east of US 131: 84,500

S. Westnedge Ave

Portage, north of I-94: 31,000

M-43

Kalamazoo, east of US 131: 32,500

28th Street

Cascade Township, west of I-96: 44,000
Wyoming, east of US 131: 49,500

AUTO AND PASSENGER FERRY

The *Lake Express* Ferry, inaugurated in 2004, restored Lake Michigan Ferry Service that had disappeared with the demise of the *Milwaukee Clipper* in the 1970s. (Cross lake service continued in Northern Michigan on the Great Lakes Carferry Service, based in Ludington.)

The Lake Express *reaches speeds of 40 mph on Lake Michigan (photo courtesy of Lake Express, LLC)*

Lake Express is a 192-foot catamaran that reaches speeds of 40 mph while crossing between Muskegon and Milwaukee in just over two hours. The vessel runs from late April through late October, making three daily crossings in each direction at the height of the summer season. It has space for 46 cars and 250 passengers.

One-way fares for 2006 were $65 for each vehicle, $55 for each adult passenger, and $30 for each child, age 5-17.

For more information, call (866) 914-1010, or visit www.lake-express.com on the Internet.

BICYCLE RAIL-TRAILS

As West Michigan railroads went out of business and the tracks were removed, a number of old rail corridors have been converted to non-motorized trails for use on foot or bicycle. The following list shows some trails that are open to the public. More are likely to open in the future, and local governments are working on plans to link some of the trails together.

Fred Meijer Heartland Trail, 30 miles, Montcalm County. Towns include Greenville, Sidney, Stanton, McBride, Edmore, Cedar Lake and Vestaburg.

Grand Haven-Holland Trail, 20 miles, Ottawa County. Towns include Grand Haven and Holland.

Hart-Montague Trail, 22 miles, Muskegon and Oceana counties. Towns include Hart, Mears, Shelby, Rothbury, Montague and Whitehall.

Kal-Haven Trail, 34 miles, Kalamazoo and Van Buren counties. Towns include Kalamazoo, Gobles, Bloomingdale, Lacota and South Haven.

Musketawa Trail, 24 miles, Muskegon and Ottawa counties. Towns include Muskegon, Ravenna, Conklin and Marne.

Paul Henry –Thornapple Trail, 42 miles, Kent, Barry and Eaton counties. Portions are still under development. Will include Kentwood, Middleville, Hastings, Nashville and Vermontville.

White Pine Trail, 94 miles, Kent, Montcalm, Mecosta, Osceola and Wexford counties. Towns include Grand Rapids, Rockford, Cedar Springs, Howard City, Big Rapids, Reed City, LeRoy and Cadillac.

AMTRAK passenger train service

Amtrak operates two passenger train routes through Western Michigan.

The Pere Marquette line runs once daily in each direction from Grand Rapids to Chicago. The route includes stops at Grand Rapids, Holland, Bangor, Benton Harbor-St. Joseph, and New Buffalo. The train trip from Grand Rapids to Chicago takes about four hours.

The Blue Water and Wolverine lines stop at Niles, Dowagiac and Kalamazoo en route between Chicago and eastern Michigan. Four trains a day traverse the state on those lines, with some express trains passing through Dowagiac and Niles without stopping.

The Blue Water and Pere Marquette routes receive a subsidy of some $7 million a year from the Michigan Department of Transportation. Continuation of those lines has seemed tenuous at times in recent years, as some state lawmakers questioned the size of the subsidy.

TAKING THE BUS

Inter-city bus lines, operated by Greyhound and Indian Trails, run through West Michigan on Interstate 94, 96 and 196, as well as the US-131 expressway. Riders can make connections to the north (Traverse City and Mackinac) or to Lansing, Detroit or Chicago.

West Michigan cities with bus terminals include: Benton Harbor, Big Rapids, Grand Rapids, Kalamazoo, Muskegon, Paw Paw and South Haven. Limited service bus stops are listed in Cedar Springs, Howard City, Morley, New Buffalo, Plainwell, Rockford and Stanwood.

For schedule and fare information, call (800) 231-2222, or visit www.greyhound.com on the Internet.

AIRPORTS

While schedules and services often change, West Michigan has three airports that offer scheduled passenger service: Muskegon County Airport; Kalamazoo-Battle Creek International Airport, and Gerald R. Ford International Airport at Grand Rapids.

Here are 2005 total passenger counts at the three sites:

Muskegon: 71,514

Kalamazoo-Battle Creek: 468,335

Grand Rapids: 2,090,505

The statistics make Grand Rapids the state's second busiest airport (after Detroit Metro). Kalamazoo-Battle Creek is No. 5, and Muskegon is No. 10 among Michigan's 18 licensed air carrier airports.

Overall, Michigan has a total of 250 airports licensed for air carrier service or general aviation. Here is a list of the West Michigan facilities, arranged by city.

Allegan, Padgham Field (35D)

Elevation: 708 feet

Main runway: 3,500 feet, paved

Benton Harbor, SW Michigan Regional Airport (BEH)

Elevation: 643 feet

Main runway: 5,109 feet, paved

Berrien Springs, Andrews University Airport, (C20)

Elevation: 668 feet

Main runway: 4,100 feet, paved

Big Rapids, Roben-Hood Airport (RQB)

Elevation: 990 feet

Main runway: 4,300 feet, paved

Carson City, Mayes Airport (47G)

Elevation: 790 feet

Main runway: 2,100 feet, turf

Dowagiac Municipal Airport (C91)

Elevation: 748 feet

Main runway: 4,700 feet, paved

Fremont Municipal Airport (3FM)

Elevation: 772 feet

Main runway: 6,500 feet, paved

Fruitport, Flying A Ranch (39Z)

Elevation: 630 feet

Main runway: 1,900 feet, turf

Grand Haven Memorial Airpark

Elevation: 604 feet

Main runway: 3,750 feet, paved

Grand Rapids, Gerald R. Ford Intl. Airport (GRR)

Elevation: 794 feet

Main runway: 10,000 feet, paved

Grant Airport (01C)

Elevation: 815 feet

Main runway: 2,130 feet, turf

Greenville Municipal Airport (6D6)
Elevation: 855 feet
Main runway: 4,200 feet, paved

Hart-Shelby, Oceana County Airport (C04)
Elevation: 910 feet
Main runway: 3,500 feet, paved

Hastings Airport (9D9)
Elevation: 801 feet
Main runway: 3,900 feet, paved

Holland, Park Township Airport (HLM)
Elevation: 603 feet
Main runway: 2,274 feet, paved

Holland, Tulip City Airport (BIV)
Elevation: 698 feet
Main runway: 6,263 feet, paved

Ionia, Ionia County Airport (Y70)
Elevation: 818 feet
Main runway: 4,300 feet, paved

Jenison, Riverview Airport (08C)
Elevation: 603 feet
Main runway: 3,920 feet, paved

Kalamazoo, Kalamazoo/Battle Creek Intl. Airport (AZO)
Elevation: 874 feet
Main runway: 6,500 feet, paved

Kalamazoo, Newman's Airport (4N0)
Elevation: 840 feet
Main runway: 2,506 feet, turf

Kent City, Wilderness Airpark (24M)
Elevation: 785 feet
Main runway: 2,208 feet, turf

Lakeview, Griffith Field (13C)
Elevation: 969 feet
Main runway: 3,500 feet, paved

Lowell City Airport (24C)
Elevation: 681
Main runway: 2,700 feet, paved

Mecosta, Canadian Lakes Airport (0C5)
Elevation: 960 feet
Main runway: 3,800 feet, turf

Mecosta-Morton Airport (27C)
Elevation: 1,022 feet
Main runway: 2,000 feet, turf

Muskegon, Muskegon County Airport (MKG)
Elevation: 628 feet
Main runway: 6,501 feet, paved

Niles, Jerry Taylor Memorial Airport (3TR)
Elevation: 750 feet
Main runway: 4,100 feet, paved

Nunica, Hat Field Airport (5N7)
Elevation: 630 feet
Main runway: 3,200 feet, turf

Nunica, Jablonski Airport (33C)
Elevation: 634 feet
Main runway: 2,199 feet, turf

Parchment, Triple-H Airport (2H4)
Elevation: 785 feet
Main runway: 2,600 feet, turf

Paw Paw, Almena Airport (2C5)
Elevation: 740 feet
Main runway: 3,300 feet, turf

Plainwell Municipal Airport (61D)
Elevation: 722 feet
Main runway: 2,650 feet, paved

Pullman, Walle Field (M86)
Elevation: 635 feet
Main runway: 1,750 feet, turf

Rockford, Wells Airport (35C)
Elevation: 890 feet
Main runway: 2,200 feet, turf

Rothbury, Double JJ Resort Airport (42N)
Elevation: 689 feet
Main runway: 3,600 feet, turf

Schoolcraft, Prairie Ronde Airport (P97)
Elevation: 890 feet
Main runway: 2,450 feet, turf

South Haven Area Regional Airport (LWA)
Elevation: 666 feet
Main runway: 4,800 feet, paved

Sparta, Paul C. Miller Airport (8D4)
Elevation: 761 feet
Main runway: 2,925 feet, paved

Stanwood, Cain Field (38C)
Elevation: 889 feet
Main runway: 3,450 feet, turf

Sturgis, Kirsch Municipal Airport (IRS)
Elevation: 925 feet
Main runway: 5,200 feet, paved

Three Rivers, Dr. Haines Airport (HAI)
Elevation: 824 feet
Main runway: 4,000 feet, paved

Watervliet Municipal Airport (40C)
Elevation: 656 feet
Main runway: 2,600 feet, turf

Wayland, Calkins Field (41C)
Elevation: 740 feet
Main runway: 2,200 feet, turf

White Cloud Airport (42C)
Elevation: 914 feet
Main runway: 2,900 feet, paved

Zeeland, Ottawa Executive Airport (Z98)
Elevation: 740 feet
Main runway: 3,800 feet, paved

POLITICS

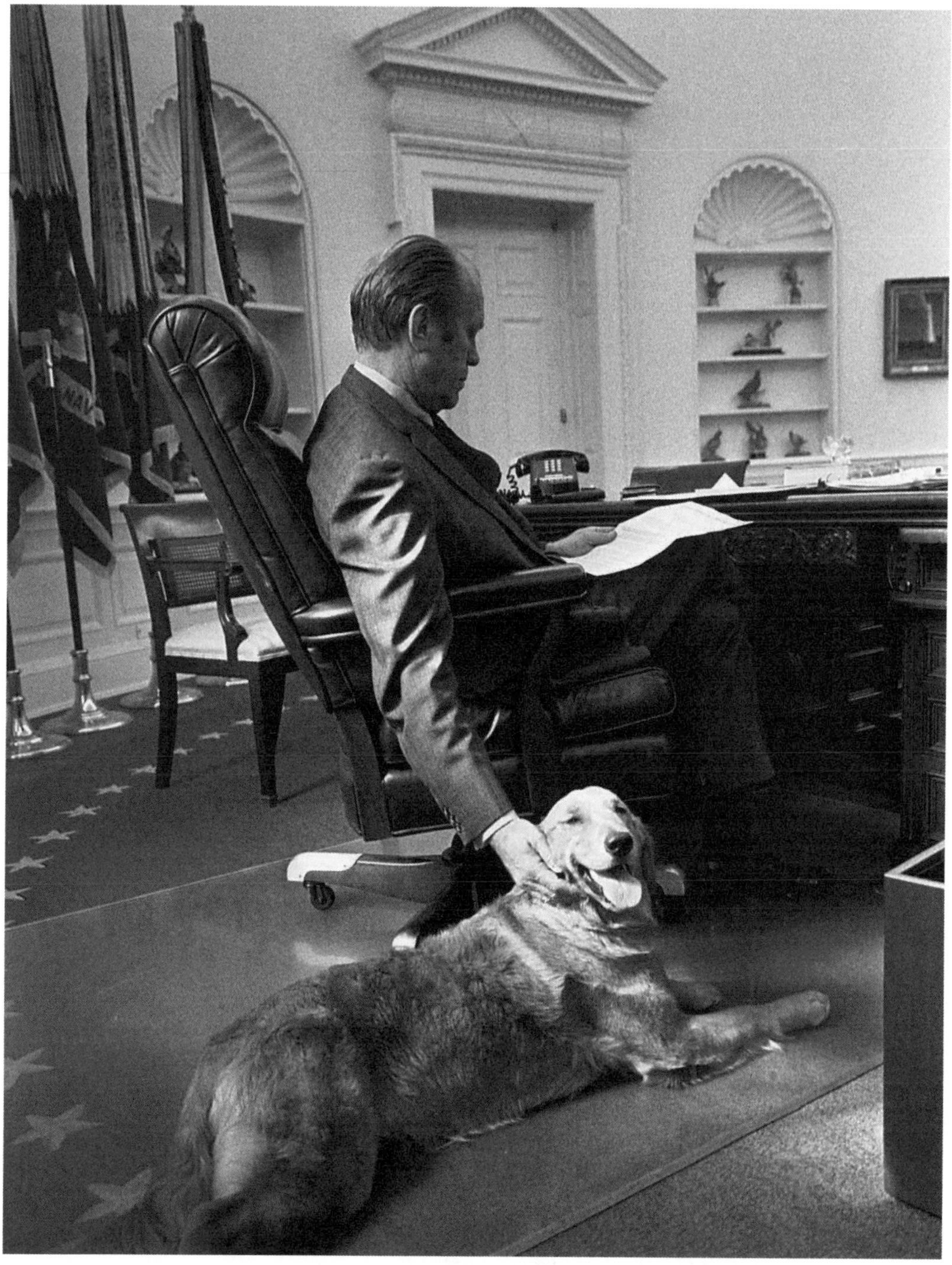

Previous page: President Ford, in a quiet moment in the Oval Office (photo courtesy of Gerald R. Ford Library)

POLITICS AND GOVERNMENT

Gerald R. Ford, Michigan's one and only president

West Michigan's best-known politician is Gerald R. Ford, the 38th president of the United States. Ford wasn't actually a West Michiganian when he was born. For that matter, he wasn't even a Ford when he was born.

The future president was born to Leslie and Dorothy King in Omaha, Neb., on July 14, 1913. He was christened Leslie Lynch King, Jr.

The Kings were divorced soon afterward, and Dorothy returned to her hometown of Grand Rapids. There, in 1916, she married Gerald Rudolf Ford. Her new husband took her son as his own, and the youngster became known as Gerald R. Ford Jr., called Junior by the family.

Ford was a football star at Grand Rapids South High School and the University of Michigan. He worked his way into Yale Law School, and came home with a law degree in 1941, the year America entered World War II.

When he returned from the Navy in 1946, the local political scene was changing. Ford was among a group of young men, mostly military veterans, who challenged Republican incumbents in the 1948 primaries. He won, and served in Congress from 1949 until 1973. He was House Republican leader for the last eight years of his Congressional service.

Jerry Ford meets with Kent County farmers after winning his first election in 1948 (photo courtesy of Gerald R. Ford Library)

On Oct. 10, 1973, Vice President Spiro Agnew resigned and took a "no-contest" plea to charges that he had accepted bribes in his previous job as governor of Maryland. On Oct. 12 of that year, President Richard Nixon announced that his choice to replace Agnew as vice president

Jerry and Betty Ford, at home in the 1950s (photo courtesy of Gerald R. Ford Library)

was U.S. Rep. Gerald R. Ford of Michigan.

Less than a year later, the Watergate scandal forced Nixon himself out of the White House. When Nixon resigned, effective Aug. 9, 1974, Ford became president of the United States.

Ford's 31 months in the presidency were marked by battles with the Democratic majority in Congress, and continuing public anger over the Watergate scandals. Ford became a lightning rod for some of that anger when he pardoned former President Nixon for any crimes that might have been committed while in office.

Also during Ford's term, America celebrated its bicentennial, and the long war in Vietnam finally came to a close.

The First Lady, Betty Ford, became a much-loved national figure for the candor and grace with which she handled her breast cancer.

In 1976, Ford lost his re-election bid to Jimmy Carter.

The Fords retired to a home on a golf course near Palm Springs, Cal. Two years later, Mrs. Ford revealed that she was being treated for alcoholism and an addiction to prescription pain-killers. Her experience led her to establish the Betty Ford Center in Palm Springs. The center is still one of America's best known institutions for treating substance abuse.

NOTABLE LEADERS FROM WEST MICHIGAN

West Michigan has been home to a number of prominent political leaders over the years. Here are a few of them:

Lucius Lyon (1800-1851), a surveyor and developer who had a hand in founding several towns – including Grand Rapids, Lyons and Schoolcraft – was one of two U.S. senators sent to Washington when Michigan became a state in 1837.

John M. Barry (1802-1870), of Constantine, was Michigan's fourth governor, serving from 1842-46, and again from 1851-52. His home in Constantine is on the National Register of Historic Places and is used as a museum.

Epaphroditus Ransom (1787-1859), one of Kalamazoo's most prominent early residents, was chief justice of the Michigan Supreme Court from 1843-48, and governor from 1948-50.

Woodbridge N. Ferris (1852-1928), the founder of Ferris State University and Muskegon Business College, served as governor from 1913-16 and later as U.S. senator from Michigan until his death in 1928.

Fred W. Green (1871-1936), of Ionia, a Republican and a veteran of the Spanish-American War, served two terms as governor, from 1927-30.

Kim Sigler (1894-1953), a Republican from Hastings, was the most recent governor from West Michigan. He served one term, from 1947-48. He died with three others in a 1953 accident when his small plane hit a television tower near Augusta in Kalamazoo County.

William Alden Smith (1859-1932) was born in Dowagiac and lived most of his life in Grand Rapids. He served in the U.S. House of Representatives from 1895-1907, and in the U.S. Senate from 1907-1919. He was an unsuccessful candidate for the Republican presidential nomination in 1916.

Arthur H. Vandenberg (1884-1951), a newspaper editor from Grand Rapids, was appointed to fill a U.S. Senate seat after Woodbridge Ferris's death in 1928. Vandenberg, a Republican, was regarded as a conservative and an isolationist early in his career. But at the close of World War II he gave his support to the Marshall Plan and the formation of the United Nations, helping bring members of his party into a bipartisan foreign policy that endured for most of the next two decades.

Richard F. VanderVeen (1922-2006), of East Grand Rapids, was the only Democrat in memory to represent the Grand Rapids area in Congress. VanderVeen won a 1974 special election to replace Gerald Ford, after Ford was appointed to the vice presidency. VanderVeen was re-elected to one full term, and then was defeated by Republican Harold S. Sawyer in 1976.

David Stockman grew up in St. Joseph and was elected to Congress from Southwest Michigan in 1977. He gained national attention in 1981, when he accepted the job of budget director for newly elected President Ronald Reagan. Stockman engaged in a largely unsuccessful effort to cut the federal budget. He famously told the news media that he had been taken "to the woodshed" after making disparaging remarks about the supply-side economics that were the centerpiece of Reagan's economic policy.

Dennis W. Archer was born in Detroit in 1942 and was raised in Cassopolis. He graduated from Western Michigan University. Archer served on the Michigan Supreme Court from 1985-90, and was mayor of Detroit from 1994-2000.

Howard E. Wolpe, III, born in California in 1939, was a Kalamazoo city commissioner and a professor at Western Michigan University before he became a state legislator and then a U.S. congressman. Wolpe represented the Kalamazoo area from 1979-93. He was Democratic nominee for governor in 1994, losing the general election to incumbent Gov. John Engler. Wolpe later served in the Clinton Administration as a special envoy to the Great Lakes region of Africa.

Russell Kirk (1918-1994), was an early intellectual force behind the conservative movement that spawned such national figures as Barry Goldwater and Ronald Reagan. Kirk, who lived in the small town of Mecosta, near Big Rapids, was an author, scholar and syndicated columnist. His 1953 book, *The Conservative Mind,* is considered a classic of the genre. President Reagan once referred to him as "The prophet of American conservatism."

The Russell Kirk Center, in Mecosta, continues to sponsor educational activities in the Kirk tradition.

PARTY POLITICS

Political experts in Michigan sometimes calculate a party's "base" strength in a given area by looking at races for state educational boards. It's assumed that voters know little about candidates for those posts, so the vote generally reflects a preference for the party, rather than the candidate. Adding together the totals for multiple candidates in each party tends to smooth out the variations that can result when one party fields a candidate who's either local or particularly well-known.

The chart on the next page shows party strength in West Michigan counties based on the 2004 vote for state Board of Education positions. The percentages consider only the vote for Democratic and Republican candidates. They do not reflect the minor parties that took about 6 percent of the vote in the 2004 state board races.

County	Republican Strength	Democratic Strength
Allegan	66.2%	33.8%
Barry	62.7%	37.3%
Berrien	57.0%	43.0%
Cass	58.8%	41.2%
Ionia	61.4%	38.6%
Kalamazoo	50.5%	49.5%
Kent	61.5%	38.5%
Mecosta	57.3%	42.7%
Montcalm	58.2%	41.8%
Muskegon	44.2%	55.8%
Newaygo	61.6%	38.4%
Oceana	57.3%	42.7%
Ottawa	75.1%	24.9%
St. Joseph	63.6%	36.4%
Van Buren	54.5%	45.5%
West Michigan	**60.1%**	**39.9%**
Statewide	**48.1%**	**51.9%**

2004 Presidential Election Results

County	Total votes	George W. Bush		John Kerry	
Allegan	53,907	34,022	63.1%	19,355	35.9%
Barry	30,272	18,634	61.6%	11,312	37.4%
Berrien	74,671	41,076	55.0%	32,846	44.0%
Cass	22,697	12,964	57.1%	9,537	42.0%
Ionia	27,618	16,621	60.2%	10,647	38.6%
Kalamazoo	119,783	57,147	47.7%	61,462	51.3%
Kent	290,891	171,201	58.9%	116,909	40.2%
Mecosta	17,581	9,710	55.2%	7,730	44.0%
Montcalm	26,734	14,968	56.0%	11,471	42.9%
Muskegon	80,313	35,302	44.0%	44,282	55.1%
Newaygo	22,873	13,608	59.5%	9,057	39.6%
Oceana	12,297	6,677	54.3%	5,441	44.2%
Ottawa	128,643	92,048	71.6%	35,552	27.6%
St. Joseph	25,239	15,340	60.8%	9,648	38.2%
Van Buren	34,174	17,634	51.6%	16,151	47.3%
West Michigan	**967,693**	**556,952**	**57.6%**	**401,400**	**41.5%**
Michigan	**4,839,252**	**2,313,746**	**47.8%**	**2,479,183**	**51.2%**

CONGRESS AND THE LEGISLATURE

The Michigan Legislature is made up of two chambers, the 110-member House of Representatives and the 38-member Senate.

Under districts that were drawn up after the 2000 census, West Michigan has all or part of 23 House districts and 10 Senate districts. Of those 33 seats in the Legislature, 30 were held by Republicans in 2006, compared to only three held by Democrats.

Democrats held one house seat in each of the three main urban areas – Grand Rapids, Kalamazoo and Muskegon. Republicans had everything else, including the region's four seats in the United States Congress.

For mathematicians in the audience, that means 92 percent of the state and national legislative seats from West Michigan were occupied by Republicans. It DOESN'T mean that 92 percent of West Michigan residents are Republican of course. As the previous charts show, the breakdown is closer to 60-40 in favor of the Republican Party.

Members of the state House of Representatives serve two-year terms, and state senators serve for four years. A term-limit amendment, added to the Michigan Constitution by voters in 1992, limits house members to six years and senators to eight years of service.

All seats in both chambers are up for election in 2006, with new members taking office in January 2007.

Here's a rundown of West Michigan's state and national legislative districts, with the occupants as of 2006 and the results of the most recent election prior to 2006.

U.S. CONGRESSIONAL DISTRICTS:

District 2: Peter Hoekstra, Holland Republican.

The district includes all of Benzie, Lake, Manistee, Mason, Muskegon, Newaygo, Oceana, Ottawa and Wexford counties; plus, in Kent County, the townships of Alpine, Sparta and Tyrone and part of Solon Township; and in Allegan County the cities of Fennville, Holland and Saugatuck, the townships of Fillmore, Heath, Laketown, Manilus, Monterey, Overisel, Salem and Saugatuck, and part of Dorr Township.

2004 election results:
Peter Hoekstra (R), 225,343
Kimon Kotos (D), 94,040

District 3: Vernon Ehlers, Grand Rapids Republican

The district includes Barry and Ionia counties, and all of Kent County with the exception of the townships of Alpine, Sparta and Tyrone and part of Solon Township.

2004 election results:
Vernon Ehlers (R), 214,465
Peter Hickey (D), 101,395

District 4: Dave Camp, Midland Republican

The district includes Mecosta and Montcalm counties in West Michigan, plus Clare, Grand Traverse, Gratiot, Isabella, Kalkaska, Leelanau, Midland, Missaukee, Osceola, Roscommon and parts of Saginaw and Shiawassee counties.

2004 election results:
Dave Camp (R), 205,274
Mike Huckleberry (D), 110,885

District 6: Fred Upton, St. Joseph Republican

The district includes Berrien, Cass, Kalamazoo, St. Joseph and Van Buren counties; plus, in Allegan County, the cities of Allegan, Otsego, Plainwell and Wayland, and the townships of Allegan, Casco, Cheshire, Clyde, Ganges, Gunplain, Hopkins, Lee, Leighton, Martin, Otsego, Trowbridge, Valley, Watson, Wayland, and part of Dorr Township; and in Calhoun County, Leroy Township and part of Athens Township.

2004 election results:
Fred Upton (R), 197,425
Scott Elliott (D), 97,978

STATE HOUSE OF REPRESENTATIVE DISTRICTS:

District 59: Rick Shaffer, Three Rivers Republican

The district includes St. Joseph County, plus the following townships in Cass County: Calvin, Jefferson, LaGrange, Marcellus, Mason, Milton, Newberg, Ontwa, Penn, Pokagon, Porter and Volinia.

2004 election results:
Rick Shaffer (R), 27,044
Ed Pawlowski (D), 11,211

District 60: Alexander Lipsey, Kalamazoo Democrat

The district includes the City of Kalamazoo, plus Cooper Township and part of Kalamazoo Township.

2004 election results:
Alexander Lipsey (D), 24,473
Nick Fedesna, (R) 11,266

District 61: Jack Hoogendyk, Texas Township Republican

The district includes the cities of Portage and Parchment; townships of Alamo, Oshtemo, Prairie Ronde, and Texas; and part of Kalamazoo Township.

2004 election results:
Jack Hoogendyk (R), 28,167
James Houston (D), 23,150

District 63: Lorence Wenke, Richland Republican

The district includes, in Kalamazoo County, the city of Galesburg, plus the townships of Brady, Charleston, Climax, Comstock, Pavilion, Richland, Ross, Schoolcraft and Wakeshma. Also, part of Calhoun County.

2004 election results:
Lorence Wenke (R), 28,181
James Geary (D), 19,723

District 70: Judy Emmons, Sheridan Republican

The district includes all of Montcalm County; plus, in Ionia County, the cities of Belding and Ionia and the townships of Berlin, Easton, Keene, Orleans and Otisco.

2004 election results:
Judy Emmons (R), 22,744
Henry Sanchez (D), 11,732

District 72: Glenn Steil, Jr., Cascade Republican

The district includes, in Kent County, the city of Kentwood and the townships of Caledonia, Cascade and Gaines.

2004 election results:
Glenn Steil, Jr. (R), 33,283
Thomas Burke (D), 14,594

District 73: Tom Pearce, Rockford Republican

The district includes, in Kent County, the cities of Rockford and Cedar Springs, and the townships of Algoma, Cannon, Courtland, Nelson, Oakfield, Plainfield, Solon, Sparta, Spencer and Tyrone.

2004 election results:
Tom Pearce (R), 35,035
Frederick Clowney (D), 15,277

District 74: William VanRegenmorter, Georgetown Township Republican

The district includes, in Ottawa County, the city of Coopersville and the townships of Crockery, Georgetown, Polkton, Tallmadge and Wright; and in Kent County, the city of Grandville and the township of Alpine.

2004 election results: William VanRegenmorter (R), 38,380
Dawn Sloboda (D), 12,009

District 75: Jerry Kooiman, Grand Rapids Republican

The district includes part of the city of Grand Rapids, generally east of Fuller and Eastern avenues.

2004 election results:
Jerry Kooiman (R), 21,273
Christopher Vogt (D), 19,465

District 76: Michael Sak, Grand Rapids Democrat

The district includes part of the city of Grand Rapids, generally west of Fuller and Eastern avenues.

2004 election results:
Michael Sak (D), 21,109
Holly Zuidema (R), 9,591

District 77: Kevin Green, Wyoming Republican

The district includes, in Kent County, the city of Wyoming and the township of Byron.

2004 election results:
Kevin Green (R), 26,158
Albert Abbasse (D), 11,459

District 78: Neal Nitz, Baroda Republican

The district includes, in Berrien and Cass Counties: The cities of Buchanan, New Buffalo, Niles and Dowagiac, plus the townships of Baroda, Berrien, Bertrand, Chikaming, Galien, New Buffalo, Niles, Oronoko, Pipestone, Three Oaks, Weesaw, Howard, Silver Creek and Wayne.

2004 election results:
Neal Nitz (R), 21,884
Michael Gordon (D), 15,434

District 79: John Proos, IV, St. Joseph Republican

The district includes, in Berrien County, the cities of Benton Harbor, Bridgman, Coloma, St. Joseph and Watervliet, plus the townships of Bainbridge, Benton, Coloma, Hagar, Lake, Lincoln, Royalton, Sodus, St. Joseph and Watervliet.

2004 election results:
John Proos, IV (R), 26,377
Princella Tobias (D), 15,703

District 80: Tonya Schuitmaker, Lawton Republican

The district includes all of Van Buren County, plus the city of Otsego and the townships of Otsego and Watson in Allegan County.

2004 election results:
Tonya Schuitmaker (R), 21,610
Art Toy (D), 15,459

District 86: Dave Hildenbrand, Lowell Republican

The district includes, in Kent County, the cities of Walker, Lowell and East Grand Rapids, and the townships of Ada, Bowne, Grand Rapids, Grattan, Lowell, and Vergennes, plus a portion of the north end of the city of Grand Rapids.

2004 election results:
Dave Hildenbrand (R), 34,664
James Turner (D), 15,994

District 87: Gary Newell, Saranac Republican

The district includes all of Barry County, plus, in Ionia County, the city of Portland and the townships of Berlin, Boston, Campbell, Danby, Ionia, Lyons, North Plains, Odessa, Orange, Portland, Ronald, and Sebewa.

2004 election results:
Gary Newell (R), 28,482
David Brinkert (D), 15,689

District 88: Fulton Sheen, Plainwell Republican

The district includes all of Allegan County, with the exception of the city of Otsego and the townships of Otsego and Watson.

2004 election results:
Fulton Sheen (R), 31,300
Marty Fleser (D), 15,282

District 89: Barbara Vander Veen, Allendale Republican

The district includes, in Ottawa County, the cities of Ferrysburg and Grand Haven, plus the townships of Allendale, Grand Haven, Olive, Park, Port Sheldon, Robinson and Spring Lake.

2004 election results: Barbara Vander Veen (R), 32,769
Rebecca Arenas (D), 12,884

District 90: Bill Huizenga, Zeeland Republican

The district includes, in Ottawa County, the portion of the city of Holland within Ottawa County, plus the cities of Hudsonville and Zeeland and the townships of Blendon, Holland, Jamestown and Zeeland.

2004 election results:
Bill Huizenga (R), 32,383
Jo Bartlett (D), 7,607

District 91; David Farhat, Fruitport Republican

The district includes, in Muskegon County, the cities of Montague, Norton Shores, Roosevelt Park and Whitehall, and the townships of Blue Lake, Casnovia, Cedar Creek, Dalton, Egelston, Fruitport, Holton, Montague, Moorland, Ravenna, Sullivan, White River and Whitehall, plus, in Ottawa County, the township of Chester.

2004 election results:
David Farhat (R), 22,327
Nancy Frye (D), 20,578

District 92: Doug Bennett, Muskegon Township Democrat

The district includes, in Muskegon County, the cities of Muskegon, Muskegon Heights and North Muskegon, plus the townships of Fruitland, Laketon, and Muskegon.

2004 election results:
Doug Bennett (D), 22,498
Bob Cutler (R), 11,804

District 100: Geoff Hansen, Hart Republican

The district includes Oceana, Newaygo and Lake counties.

2004 election results:
Geoff Hansen (R), 23,270
Ronald Griffin (D), 14,863

District 102: Darwin Booher, Evart Republican

The district includes Mecosta, Osceola and Wexford counties.

2004 election results:
Darwin Booher (R), 26,000
Paul Challender (D), 14,761

STATE SENATE DISTRICTS:

District 16: Cameron Brown, Fawn River Township Republican

The district includes St. Joseph, Branch, Hillsdale and Lenawee counties.

2002 election results:
Cameron Brown (R), 39,894
Dudley Spade (D), 25,604

District 20: Tom George, Texas Township Republican

The district includes all of Kalamazoo County, plus the townships of Paw Paw and Antwerp in Van Buren County.

2002 election results:
Tom George (R), 44,642
Ed LaForge (D), 34,327

District 21: Ron Jelinek, Three Oaks Republican

The district includes Berrien and Cass counties, plus all of Van Buren County with the exception of the townships of Paw Paw and Antwerp.

2002 election results:
Ron Jelinek (R), 43,239
Art Toy (D), 23,473

District 24: Patricia Birkholz, Saugatuck Township Republican

The district includes Allegan, Barry and Eaton Counties.

2002 election results:
Patricia Birkholz (R), 57,906
Tami Bridson (D), 32,170

District 28: Ken Sikkema, Wyoming Republican

The district includes, in Kent County, the cities of Cedar Springs, East Grand Rapids, Rockford, Walker and Wyoming, and the townships of Ada, Algoma, Alpine, Bowne, Byron, Caledonia, Cannon, Courtland, Gaines, Grand Rapids, Nelson, Oakfield, Plainfield, Solon, Spencer and Tyrone.

2002 election results:
Ken Sikkema (R), 72,993
Michelle Berry (D), 25,425

District 29: Bill Hardiman, Kentwood Republican

The district includes, in Kent County, the cities of Grand Rapids, Kentwood and Lowell, plus the townships of Cascade, Grattan, Lowell and Vergennes.

2002 election results:
Bill Hardiman (R), 44,202
Steve Pestka (D), 36,746

District 30: Wayne Kuipers, Holland Republican

The district includes Ottawa County, plus, in Kent County, the city of Grandville and the township of Sparta.

2002 election results:
Wayne Kuipers (R), 71,160
John O'Brien (D), 21,701

District 33: Alan Cropsey, DeWitt Republican

The district includes Ionia, Montcalm, Isabella and Clinton counties.

2002 election results:
Alan Cropsey (R), 45,487
Mark Munsell (D), 26,800

District 34: Gerald Van Woerkam, Norton Shores Republican

The district includes Muskegon, Newaygo, Oceana and Mason counties.

2002 election results:
Gerald VanWoerkam (R), 42,180
Bob Shrauger (D), 41,233

District 35: Michelle McManus, Lake Leelanau Republican

The district includes Mecosta, Osceola, Lake, Clare, Manistee, Wexford, Missaukee, Roscommon, Benzie, Leelanau and Kalkaska counties.

2002 election results:
Michelle McManus (R), 51,405
Carl Dahlberg (D), 30,942